D1732713

Pushing the Margins:
Native and Northern Studies

Edited by
Jill Oakes, Rick Riewe, Marlyn Bennett and Brenda Chisholm

A publication of the
Departments of Native Studies and Zoology, and the
Faculty of Graduate Studies
University of Manitoba

Celebrating 25 Years of Excellence,
1975-2000

Pushing the Margins: Native and Northern Studies is a refereed publication.

Native Studies Press
535 Fletcher Argue Building
Winnipeg, Manitoba
Canada
R3T 5V5
Phone (204) 474-9266
Fax (204) 474-7657

For information on past (pre-1999) publications contact Elaine Maloney at the Canadian Circumpolar Institute (780) 492-4512.

All profits from the sale of this group are used to support the refereed publication of Aboriginal scholarship at the University of Manitoba.

Cover Design by Shout Visual Communications and Karen Armstrong
Cover Photographs by Rick Riewe
Printed in Canada by Hignell Book Printing

Canadian Cataloguing in Publication Data

Main entry under title:
Pushing the Margins: Native and Northern Studies

"A publicationn of the Departments of Native Studies and Zoology, and the Faculty of Graduate Studies, University of Manitoba."
Includes bibliographical references.
ISBN 0-9686138-1-0

1. Native peoples--Canada.* 2. Native peoples--Canada--Study and teaching (Higher).* 3. Canada, Northern--Social conditions. 4. Canada, Northern--Study and teaching (Higher). 5. University of Manitoba. Dept. of Native Studies. I. Oakes, Jill E. (Jillian Elizabeth), 1952-II. University of Manitoba. Dept. of Native Studies. III. University of Manitoba. Dept. of Zoology. IV. University of Manitoba. Faculty of Graduate Studies.
E78.C2 P87 2000   971.9'00497   C00-920207-2

Celebrating 25 Years of Excellence 1975-2000

Table of Contents

II. Culture and Colonization

V. Environment and Traditional Ecological Knowledge

Preface

Most of these papers were presented at the **Northern and Aboriginal Issues** lecture series held during the fall and winter of 1999-2000 at the University of Manitoba. Issues facing the daily lives of Northerners and Aboriginal peoples were explored in this series organized and co-chaired by Jill Oakes (Native Studies), Rick Riewe (Zoology), and William (Skip) Koolage (Anthropology). Papers were written by Aboriginal practitioners, junior and senior academics, and community leaders in the fields of history, nursing, social work, recreation, education, management, geography, resources management, zoology, theatre, women's studies, political studies, law, psychology, education, anthropology, architecture and native studies. The authors have diverse backgrounds, world views, and philosophies; they share a sincere respect for the issues facing Northerners and Aboriginal peoples.

The following papers are divided into five sections: education, culture and colonization, health and self-government, oral traditions, and environment and traditional ecological knowledge. The first section explores the evolution of native studies at the University of Manitoba from the perspectives of students and staff. The second section discuss escolonization through drama, poetry, recreation, and communication. The third section explores health and self-government issues pertinent to child and family welfare, violence, and healing. The fourth section presents oral histories from an Elder, a woman who drank during her pregnancy, and a homeless woman. The final section explores environmental issues and management using western science and traditional ecological knowledge, such as climate change, contaminants, population, and blueberry management.

Acknowledgements

Financial support from the following departments, faculties, institutes and offices at the University of Manitoba is gratefully acknowledged: Departments of Anthropology, Community Health Sciences, Economics, Educational Administration, Foundations and Psychology, French, Spanish and Italian, History, Native Studies, Women's Studies and Zoology; the Faculties of Architecture, Arts, Graduate Studies, Human Ecology, I. H. Asper School of Business, Medicine, Nursing, Physical Education and Recreation Studies, Science, and Social Work; Natural Resources Institute, Institute for the Humanities, and the Office of the President. As well, experts from Canada, from a wide range of backgrounds, are gratefully acknowledged for their role as referees. Their feedback is sincerely appreciated in this refereed publication celebrating Aboriginal scholarship.

The Beginning of Native Studies at the University of Manitoba

William Koolage[1]

Abstract

The Province of Manitoba is proud of its multi-cultural heritage and vitality. It recognizes and promotes the maintenance of this vitality in its ethnic and multi-ethnic festivals and the study of its diverse cultural traditions and languages in university departments and programs. However, the cultural heritage of the Native Peoples of Manitoba and Canada in general were not similarly and equally represented in the University context in the early 1970s. In 1971, members of the Indian, Métis, Eskimo Student Association began to seek advice on the establishment of a Chair of Native Studies at the University of Manitoba to rectify this situation. This paper is an informal account of the attempts to implement first a 'Program' and later a 'Department' of Native Studies at the University of Manitoba.

Introduction

In the early 1970s, there were six Native Canadian 'ethnic' groups living in Manitoba: Métis [40,000 (Canadian Welfare Council Map) to 80,000 (Manitoba Métis Federation 1973:3)], Cree (19,000), Anishinaabe [Ojibwa or Saulteaux (14,500)], Sayisi Dené [Chipewyan (800)], Sioux (1500) (Indian Affairs Branch 1970:14-15), and Inuit (100). Although there were 3 universities and 3 community colleges in Manitoba at the time, none had a Department of Native Studies. The University of Manitoba was the largest with 18 faculties teaching 13,377 students, 10 percent of whom were graduate students. In addition to Arts and Science faculties, the

University has most of the province's professional and graduate schools including medicine, law, architecture, agriculture, engineering, commerce, social work, education, and others. The University of Winnipeg (2353 students) and Brandon University (1196 students) were primarily involved in undergraduate teaching (Task Force 1973). The enrolments of students with Native ancestry were approximately 65, 20 and 200 respectively in the above mentioned universities. While there was a healthy rivalry between the universities, there was increasing concern over the higher costs per student at Winnipeg and Brandon as well as a non-intellectual, financial concern over 'overlap' or course duplication at the various universities.

The multi-cultural or 'multi-ethnic' composition of the community was reflected in some specialized departments in the Faculty of Arts at the University of Manitoba and some more general and traditional departments at all three universities. These departments taught not only language and literature, but also 'about' the culture and society of the respective 'ethnic' groups represented. The more specialized departments included Icelandic, Slavic Studies, and Near Eastern and Judaic Studies. The more traditional departments were Romance Languages (French, Spanish, and Italian), German, English, and Classics. Interestingly, most of these departments were grossly overstaffed but supported by the provincial government and most of the instructors were members of the ethnic groups about whom they taught. It was in this context that the Indian, Métis, and Eskimo Student Association requested attention to their cultural heritage.

The Development of Native Studies

During the 1970-71 academic year, there was a growing awareness at the University of Manitoba that only a very small proportion of Aboriginal students entered post-secondary institutions and even fewer completed their studies. On June 15, 1971 the Senate of the University of Manitoba struck an Ad Hoc Committee chaired by S. Standil (and later chaired by Bruce Sealey) "to consider and recommend to Senate on ways and means that might be employed by the University of Manitoba to facilitate the university education of Native Persons" (Senate 1972:1). Native students and representatives of the Manitoba Indian Brotherhood (MIB) and the Manitoba Métis Federation (MMF) were represented on this committee, notably Ovide Mercredi and Moses Okimow from the Indian, Métis, Eskimo Students Association (IMESA), Verna Kirkness (MIB), and John Chartrand (MMF) as well as the heads of various departments or their delegates. The original investigations of this committee centered upon admissions requirements, available bursaries and scholarships, and obtaining peer counsellors for Native students (Senate 1972:1).

At this time the only course in the university dealing specifically with the Native Peoples of Canada was an undergraduate level cross-cultural education course taught by Bruce Sealey. Anthropology had a meagre six course undergraduate program which did not include area courses, History had no specific course on the history of the Canadian Indian and Métis, and there were no courses in other departments with any degree of attention given to Aboriginal persons.

During the fall of 1971, Ovide Mercredi and Moses Okimow approached myself and other staff members about possible models at the university for the establishment of a Chair of Native Studies. I suggested that other 'ethnic studies' departments such as Slavic Studies, Near Eastern and Judaic Studies, and Icelandic Studies might be used as a model. On February 9, 1972 the Indian, Métis, and Eskimo Student Association presented a brief to President Ernest Sirluck, to the Senate Ad Hoc Committee, and subsequently to the Hon. Saul Miller, Minister of Youth and Education for the province on March 14, 1972. The IMESA proposal called for: a Chair of Native Studies at the University of Manitoba; hiring of one or two professors, "preferably of Native ancestry", to develop and teach interdisciplinary courses on "history, culture, and contemporary problems of native peoples in Canada"; an advisory committee of Native persons to suggest long range plans; overseeing research projects concerning Native peoples; the cross-cultural education courses to be available to students in Arts and Sciences; and that the Native Studies courses be open to all students (IMESA 1972:1-2). A petition circulated by IMESA obtained 1200 names supporting the proposal. The rationale for this program was best stated by students:

> It is true that most Native students in attendance at the university are here to learn a set of skills, knowledge, and understandings which will allow them to enter into the dominant white society as productive and competing members of that society. Though we may be seeking to become teachers, lawyers, social workers, doctors, etc. we seek, in addition to the skills of these vocations, to acquire an insight into all aspects of life. We wish to study our history and our culture, its clashes with the European invaders and subsequent accommodations and changes. This knowledge we seek in order to

better understand ourselves, our people and our present predicament. We hope that knowledge gained in this area will allow us to see present problems in a perspective through which we may determine possible solutions. (IMESA 1972:1)

The Senate Ad Hoc Committee debated the proposal and stated "while this committee supports the eventual development of a Department of Native Studies" Senate should approve "in principle the establishment of a Chair of Native Studies" in the Faculty of Arts which would monitor an inter-departmental program leading to a 'Minor' (18 hours) in Native Studies, develop specific courses in Native Studies, and have an advisory committee which included representatives of Native organizations (Senate 1972:4). This committee also recommended that a research component be built into the program, be sensitive to the concerns of Native Peoples, and be related to a specific research centre on campus. This committee discussed whether to recommend a 'Department' of Native Studies or simply a Chair of Native Studies to develop a 'Program'. We opted for the 'Chair' and 'Program' which we felt would meet the least resistance within the many different levels of university committees, faculty councils, the Senate, Board of Governors, and the Universities Grants Commission; however, there was resistance.

Ten days prior to the submission of the Senate Ad Hoc Committee report (June 30, 1972), this committee struck a Curriculum Sub-Committee consisting of Bruce Sealey, Verna Kirkness, Moses Okimow, and myself as chairman. Working under a July 5th deadline, I met with two of the committee members individually (the other member was unavailable at that time) and we designed a tentative curriculum for an interdisciplinary Major and Minor in Native Studies with 4 new half-courses (semester) to be taught by a person hired as Head of the program. The proposed half-course titles were modeled after the Dartmouth College Native American Studies Program. The course titled "Introduction to Native Studies" was designed to focus upon Native Peoples viewpoints as illustrated by Indian, Métis, and Inuit authors, journalists, and artists. "Native Studies: The Contemporary Society" was designed to explore topics including: the reserve, educational, legal, political, and economic systems, as well as contemporary communities. The other two half-courses were "Independent Reading and Research" and "Seminar in Native Studies: Selected Topics". The 'Program' was designed to be handled by one person, limiting the 'core courses' to twelve credit hours in Native Studies yet thirty credit hours were needed for a 'Major'. Additional courses in anthropology, economics, geography, history, political studies, psychology, sociology, and education were cross-listed for completion of the major and minor in Native Studies. The utilization of guest speakers was also to be an intrinsic part of the program.

Events Effecting the Development of Native Studies

The report of the Curriculum Sub-Committee was presented to the Chairman of the Senate Ad Hoc Committee for inclusion in the presentation to the Senate Executive meeting in July. Due to time limitations and the lack of further formal meetings of the Senate Committee, this report was not ratified by the Senate Committee. During the next three months, the report was 'misplaced' twice.

Several events during the spring of 1972 effected the development of Native Studies at the University of Manitoba. One of these was a meeting of researchers involved in research among Native Peoples in the province. The meeting was stimulated in part by a statement by the Manitoba Indian Brotherhood calling for research sensitive to the needs of Native Peoples as viewed by Native Peoples themselves and in part by a memorandum from the Curator of Northern Ethnology of the Manitoba Museum of Man and Nature seeking to compel researchers to submit all research plans to established Native Organizations. At a meeting on February 21, 1972 Tom Shay, John Matthiasson, and I met with representatives from the Manitoba Indian Brotherhood, the Manitoba Métis Federation, the Indian and Métis Friendship Centre, one anthropologist from the University of Winnipeg (none of the social/ cultural anthropologists from either Winnipeg or Brandon would attend), and Museum personnel to discuss research ethics and feedback of information to communities in the province. Professors Shay, Matthiasson, and I submitted a "Statement on Community Research" which subscribed to the ethical codes of the American Anthropological Association and the Society for Applied Anthropology as well as calling for feedback of research findings to communities, communities' prior consent and participation in research, and the organization of a research information centre similar to that adopted in British Columbia. Except for a statement of "Correlative Mandates for Research" submitted by the Manitoba Indian Brotherhood calling for 'relevant' research, there were no positive steps taken by any of the other groups represented. Subsequently, a Native People's Research Coordinating Committee was formed with a representative of each organization and each university with the exception of Brandon University. The "Statement on Community Research" was adopted as a code of ethics and a means of disseminating information was set up through the Museum of Man and Nature, but the committee soon lapsed due primarily to a lack of response from other researchers and the departure of the committee chairman from the province. While the "Statement on Community Research" was distributed widely both within and outside of the province, the 'selective' ignorance of this statement at the University of Winnipeg was to cause further problems.

During April, 1972 the Donner Canadian Foundation wrote to President Sirluck (and presumably other Western Canadian university presidents) soliciting proposals for Native Studies Programs. President Sirluck passed this letter on to the Senate Ad Hoc Committee. (The Donner Canadian Foundation was at that time supporting part of the program of the Trent University Department of Native Studies and had also requested proposals from a research centre at the University of Manitoba.) Some of the discussions in the Senate Committee revolved around the research component of the Donner request and discussions were held between the Chairman of the Senate Committee and the Chairman of the research centre about the possibility of the research centre's taking over the research and training component of a proposal to the Donner Foundation. As an associate member of the research centre's Policy Committee, I should have known better than to permit such an involvement without an active attempt to find an alternative. I had previously proposed to the research centre that some extra funds be made available for the training of students of Native ancestry in interdisciplinary research techniques through current research projects and that new projects sensitive to the needs of the province's Native Peoples be developed. This proposal was turned down in favour of supporting the writing of several research reports which had already been supported by the research centre. In essence, Native students lost out on an opportunity to learn research skills through the very research centre which was to be related to the Native Studies Program.

From June to mid-August of 1972, I worked with the research centre on a research proposal which was to be combined with the Senate proposal for a Native Studies Program for submission to the Donner Canadian Foundation. My emphasis was that research be sensitive to the needs of Native Peoples as they viewed their needs, the training and financial support of Native students in learning research and analysis skills, and the development of *new* courses in an interdisciplinary (inter-departmental) major and minor in Native Studies. While I was in the field during late August, the proposal was rewritten and submitted, omitting the proposed curriculum component except for possible cross-listed courses in existing departments and de-emphasizing the training and support of students of Native ancestry. Actually, the final submission looked like a glorification of the research centre's past exploits. The Donner Foundation, to the best of my knowledge, never responded to that proposal.

The Revised Proposal

During the fall of 1972, the Universities Grants Commission returned the Senate Committee's proposal for a Native Studies Program to the Faculty of Arts for further clarification with respect to curriculum, asking specifically what new courses were to be developed and would the program include the teaching of Native languages? Evidently, the Curriculum Sub-Committee's report had never been forwarded to the Universities Grants Commission.

In January, 1973, Don McCarthy (Dean, Faculty of Arts) convened an Ad Hoc Sub-Committee on Native Studies under the chairmanship of Fred Stambrook (Professor, Department of History). The committee included Edwin Jebb, President of IMESA, Ovide Mercredi, Moses Okimow, and five members of various Arts departments with research experience with Native Peoples. This committee met five times between January 16 and March 2, 1973 and had the excellent advice of Walter Currie (Head, Native Studies, Trent University), Joseph Handley, Arthur Blue, Chris Wolfart (Professors), and Don McCarthy.   The committee also benefited from discussions with and presentations by Roger Buffalohead and D'Arcy McNickle at the Trent University Forum on Native Studies, February 8 - 10.

The Arts Ad Hoc Sub-Committee on Native Studies had the specific tasks of preparing "a proposal for a program in Native Studies" and preparing "a response to certain questions posed by the Universities Grants Commission" (Arts 1973:1). The committee's discussions concerning curriculum, the structure of the 'Program' and then the proposed 'Department', library resources, and possible enrolments led to a set of recommendations and a lengthy report being presented to various levels of the University's governing bodies and ultimately to the Universities Grants Commission. This Sub-Committee endorsed the principle that "In multicultural Canada, a study of the Native heritage has validity for all students" (Arts 1973:1; Senate 1972:2), and that the best organizational system to provide Native Studies would be a 'Department', not a 'Program'. The Arts Ad Hoc Sub-Committee on Native Studies recommended:

1. That there be established within the Faculty of Arts a

Department of Native Studies.

2. That the Department of Native Studies shall offer the following programs: a. a Major in Native Studies; b. a Minor in Native Studies; and c. a Minor in Native Languages.

3. That there be introduced for the 1973-74 session the course xx:120 The Native People of Canada (6 credit hours). A survey of the political, social and economic situations of the contemporary Indian, Métis, and Eskimo people of Canada. . . .

4. That further courses be developed and designed by the Department of Native Studies. . . .

5. That (certain) . . . existing courses (in anthropology, history, sociology, geography, and economics) be placed on the list of courses approved for the Major and Minor programs in Native Studies.

6. That the Major in Native Studies conform to the following pattern - (30 credit hours of course work of which 18 must be from 'core courses').

7. That a Minor in Native Studies conform to the following pattern - (18 credit hours of which 12 must be from 'core courses').

8. That the Minor in Native Languages, to begin in the 1974-75 session, conform to one of the following patterns - (18 credit hours).

9. That students be permitted to take both a Major in Native Studies and a Minor in Native Languages.

10. That the Ad Hoc Senate Committee give attention to the provision of scholarships and extension type courses; developing new courses in existing faculties, including the professional schools; and the securing of external funding for the community involvement programs. (Arts 1973: 5-8)

The following courses were designed by the committee as 'possible' offerings within a Department of Native Studies. The final course development was to be done by the new Head of the Department:

xx:120 The Native Peoples of Canada (6); xx:090 Introductory Cree (6); xx:130 Intermediate Cree (6); xx:220 Native Societies and Political Process 6; xx:230

Cree Literature (3); xx:231 Cree Creative Writing(3); xx:232 The Structure of the Cree Language (3); xx:320 Modernization and Native Peoples (6); xx:321 The Native Identity; xx:322 Methodological Approaches to Native Studies (3); xx:329 Independent Research (3)(Arts 1973:Annex III:1-2)

The 'possible' course outlines, details for the Major and Minors, and library search scrupulously followed the university pattern for the introduction of any new program of studies. Compromises were made within the committee on the wording of course descriptions, whether to have full year or half year courses, and other details in order to minimize any 'nit-picking' criticisms which might delay approval for a Department of Native Studies. The committee was also careful to ensure that the new courses did not duplicate already existing courses - a matter of great concern to a cost-counting Universities Grants Commission as well as existing departments jealous of their own 'intellectual domains'.

The report of the Arts Sub-Committee was approved by the Arts Program and Approvals Committee on March 15 and submitted to the Arts Faculty on April 10, 1973. At the Arts Faculty meeting, there was a great deal of resistance to the establishment of a new department primarily from members of departments which were currently over-staffed and especially fearful of losing students to a new department (and possibly losing staff due to decreased enrolment). The skilful and astute handling of the Arts debate over a 'program' versus a 'department' by Fred Stambrook was instrumental in the proposal for a Department of Native Studies being approved by that council. The proposal was ultimately approved by Senate on May 15 and by the Board of Governors on June 7, 1973. The report was then submitted to the Universities Grants Commission for approval and funding.

During March 16 - 18, 1973 IMESA at the University of Manitoba and IMESA at Brandon University hosted a Native Studies Conference in Winnipeg and invited members of the three universities, the local Native organizations, the Minister of Youth and Education, and Walter Currie. The purpose of the meeting was to discuss the best location in Manitoba for Native Studies and to compare notes on what various universities were proposing or doing with respect to Native Studies. While the participation of staff and administrative personnel from Brandon and Winnipeg was less than enthusiastic, the participation by Indian and Métis students and representatives of the local Native community was so enthusiastic as to extract a statement from the Minister of Youth and Education that Native Studies belonged in all universities. Such an endorsement apparently had little effect on the government when it came to granting the funds for such a Department. During the summer of 1973, the first course (xx:120 The Native Peoples of Canada) in the proposed Department of Native Studies was placed in the university calendar and scheduled in a one-hour time slot on Tuesday, Thursday, and Friday. On July 5, Don McCarthy asked me to teach the course since we had not received final approval from the Universities Grants Commission and a Department Head could not be hired at this late date. I agreed to teach the course for one year only and on the condition that a person of 'Native cultural heritage' with intense and prolonged experience as a member of an Indian, Métis or Inuit culture be hired as Head of the Department and teach this course in the future. On August 1, 1973 I was informed that the Universities Grants Commission had not yet approved the University of Manitoba's proposal. They had 'delayed' any decision pending further meetings among the three universities.

At this time, I had no explanations for the Universities Grants Commissions' actions, since their deliberations and decisions were not open to the public. It seems likely that the Commission received several other proposals from various Brandon University groups, received criticisms privately similar to those delivered publicly by the University of Winnipeg, and wanted to 'economize' on any such programs by involving all three universities in a program spanning all three universities. The criticisms levelled publicly against the proposed Department of Native Studies were exceedingly uninformed. The University of Winnipeg's critique and my various replies are summarized below as an example of the 'problems' facing the introduction of Native Studies into university curricula. The criticisms centred upon four main points: 1) Winnipeg could see no apparent reason for favouring a departmental structure over an inter-departmental program, 2) there was concern that the proposed courses duplicated courses already taught in the university, 3) without knowledge of who was to teach these courses there was little reason to alter the above views, and 4) there was a concern that 'field experience' as mentioned "was lacking in any understanding of the complexities involved in such an undertaking" (Winnipeg 1973: 1-2).

My various replies to these criticisms noted that, within the University of Manitoba context and in light of 'program' experience elsewhere, programs do not have equal stature with departments with respect to control of their own curriculum and funds, representation on faculty councils and committees, attractiveness to staff, solid financial commitments by universities, funds for library acquisitions and guest speakers, and released time for staff to meet the many community requests for assistance. Programs also tend to have too many persons involved administratively in decision making, such as administrative assistants who have no knowledge of the needs and requirements of such academic programs, for example, special class scheduling to accommodate guest speakers. The proposed courses did not duplicate any courses then taught at the University of Manitoba and the Department of Anthropology even dropped a 'proposed' course so that there would be no 'semblance' of duplication. The proposed courses were to be taught by new staff of Native cultural heritage, unhindered by existing departmental structures and concerns, who would be able to provide fresh perspectives, expertise, and extensive experience in presenting this important aspect of Canada's multi-cultural heritage. The concern over 'field experience' was known by members of the Arts Ad Hoc Sub-Committee and it was expected that only advanced students would be working with local communities and Native organizations with their prior consent and knowledge. While public criticisms are easily countered, they are time-consuming to answer and often indicative of private criticisms which are more influential in delaying decisions.

During late August and early September, 1973 Ovide Mercredi and I attempted to design a course outline for xx:120 which would accommodate the Native students' and organizations' desires for increased emphasis on the views of Native Peoples themselves as well as the social science emphasis contained in the actual course description in the university calendar. The texts selected included volumes authored or edited by persons of Native cultural heritage as well as other social scientists. *Indians Without Tipis*, edited by Bruce Sealey and Verna Kirkness, is a collection of articles written by persons of Native ancestry in Manitoba and dealing with education, history, politics, and prejudice in the province. *The Only Good Indian*, edited by Waubageshig (Professor Harvey McCue), is a collection of essays by Canadian Indians. *The Unjust Society*, by Harold Cardinal is a scathing critique of the Canadian Government's 'termination' policy of 1969 as well as other aspects of the larger society which control the lives of Indian people in Canada. Vine Deloria's *Custer Died For Your Sins* added a comparative note on the American situation in caustically witty fashion. The two social science texts were Nagler's edited volume, *Perspectives on the North American Indians*, containing mostly articles from sociology with a few from anthropology, and Dosman's *Indians: The Urban Dilemma*, a political science polemic.

The course readings, lectures, and guest speakers (who were also donating their time) treated topics such as treaties and Aboriginal rights, identity, Indian Affairs and government policies and practices, pluralism, education, religion, economics, urbanism, relocation (removal) policies, community organization, micro- and macro-politics, and a series of community studies emphasizing but not limited to the Province of Manitoba. The course had 60 students, of whom 25% were Indian or Métis. From an evaluative point of view, it had been of only moderate success. Both Ovide Mercredi and I had overly heavy full time commitments in our regular positions which meant that papers and examinations were not returned promptly to the students. A two month delay in the principal text (Sealey and Kirkness 1973) caused some problems at the beginning of the course. The students responded most enthusiastically to the guest speakers of Native cultural heritage who were articulate and knowledgeable. These speakers presented many different viewpoints on many topics with a sensitivity respected by both Native and non-Native students. They were able to illustrate their generalizations on education, politics, identity, and other topics with examples drawn from a lifetime of experience as an Indian or Métis in Canadian society. The one-hour time slot was a chronic problem for myself and the guest speakers who preferred a two or three hour time period so that students could have a chance for meaningful questions and discussions.

During October and November, 1973, preliminary plans were made for a meeting of the presidents of the three universities and members of the Native student groups and local organizations. The Indian, Métis, Eskimo Student Association, Ovide Mercredi, and I decided during this time to delay the numerous requests from local television and radio stations, as well as the press, for interviews about the proposed Department and the delay in its establishment. It was felt that if solid recommendations came from a meeting of the various groups and resulted in the Universities Grants Commission's approval for the Department, then many aspects of the delays involved were better left unsaid at that time. If the Universities Grants Commission delayed its decision for yet another year, then the media might be useful for pushing the government into action.

The meeting of the presidents of the universities and members of IMESA (Manitoba), Brandon University Native Students and IMPACTE, the Manitoba Indian Brotherhood, and the Manitoba Métis Federation was held on January 4, 1974. Two significant recommendations to the Universities Grants Commission came forth from this meeting based on *unanimous* approval of motions by Ovide Mercredi and Dave Courchene, President of the Manitoba Indian Brotherhood. Mr. Mercredi proposed

"That the Universities Grants Commission be advised to approve the establishment of a Department of Native Studies in each of the three Universities of this Province when any such proposal comes under their active consideration for approval." Dr. Courchene proposed "That this conference recommend that the Universities Grants Commission immediately approve the establishment of a Department of Native Studies at the University of Manitoba and that the Universities Grants Commission consider favourably the development of departments of Native Studies at the other two universities."

Conclusion

As of February 3, 1974 we had no word on whether the Universities Grants Commission had met and whether or not they had approved the proposal for a Department of Native Studies. It was already late in the year for hiring a Head for a department should approval be given. Finally, in 1975, the Universities Grants Commission approved a Department of Native Studies. This was the third department established in Canada, after the universities of Lethbridge and Trent.

References

Arts. 1973. *Report of the Arts Ad Hoc Sub-Committee on Native Studies*. Winnipeg: University of Manitoba Memo.

Canada. 1972. *Canada Year Book*. Ottawa: Information Canada.

Canada. 1968. *Canadian Welfare Planning Council Map of Manitoba Showing Areas Populated by Indians and Métis*. Winnipeg.

Cardinal, H. 1969. *The Unjust Society: The Tragedy of Canada's Indians*. Edmonton: M.G. Hurtig.

Curriculum.1972. *Curriculum Sub-Committee Interim Report, Senate Ad Hoc Committee on Native Peoples' Program*. Winnipeg: University of Manitoba. Memo.

Deloria, V. 1969. *Custer Died for Your Sins: An Indian Manifesto*. New York: Avon Books.

Dosman, E. 1972. *Indians: The Urban Dilemma*. Toronto: McClelland and Stewart.

Frisch, J. 1971. 'Action' anthropology, 'scientific' anthropology, and American Indians, In Anthropologist: In *Service or Disservice to the American Indian*. Detroit: New University Thought Publishing Co.

Indian Affairs Branch. 1970. *Linguistic and Cultural Affiliations of Canadian Indian Bands*. Ottawa: Queen's Printer.

IMESA. 1972. *A Proposal Concerning the Establishment of a Chair of Native*

14

Studies at the University of Manitoba. Winnipeg. Memo.

Manitoba Métis Federation. 1973. *Questions and Answers Concerning the Métis.* Winnipeg: Manitoba Métis Federation Press.

Maquet, J. 1964. Objectivity in anthropology. *Current Anthropology* 5:47-55.

Miller, F. 1971. Involvement in an urban university. In J. Waddell and O. Watson (Eds.) *The American Indian in Urban Society.* Boston: Little, Brown and Company.

Nagler, M. 1972. *Perspectives on the North American Indians.* Toronto: McClelland and Stewart.

Sealey, B. and Kirkness, V. 1973. *Indians Without Tipis: A Resource Book by Indians and Métis.* Winnipeg: William Clare (Manitoba) Ltd.

Senate. 1972. *Interim Report of the Senate Ad Hoc Committee on Native Peoples's Program.* Winnipeg: University of Manitoba. Memo.

Shay, T., Matthiasson, J., and Koolage, W. 1972. *Statement on Community Research.* Winnipeg: Department of Anthropology, University of Manitoba. Memo.

Task Force. 1973. *Task Force on Post-Secondary Education in Manitoba (Report).* Winnipeg: Government of Manitoba.

Waubageshig (Ed.). 1970. *The Only Good Indian: Essays by Canadian Indians.* Toronto: New Press.

Weir, T. 1960. *Economic Atlas of Manitoba.* Winnipeg: Department of Industry and Commerce.

Winnipeg. 1973. *Arts and Science Studies Sub-Committee Report on Proposed Department of Native Studies, University of Manitoba.* Winnipeg: University of Winnipeg: Typescript.

---

1   William (Skip) Koolage (PhD) is a professor in Anthropology at the University of Manitoba. This paper is an updated version of Koolage, W. 1974. Native Studies at the University of Manitoba, Symposium: North American Native Studies: Their Programs and Contributions. XLI International Congress of Americanists, Mexico, D.F.. *University of Manitoba Anthropology Papers, No.8: North American Native Studies: Their Programs and Contributions, V.1.*

Native Students Role in Establishing the Department of Native Studies

Kathi Kinew[1]

Abstract

In the early 1970s, Aboriginal students played an essential role in the establishment of the Department of Native Studies at the University of Manitoba, bridging the divide between faculty, administration and the wider Native community outside the university. This paper includes reflections from the student leaders, 25 years later!

Introduction

University students at the turn of the millennium have the opportunity for Aboriginal studies at almost every university in Canada; several universities and colleges have Departments of Native Studies. In the early 1970s, Trent University took the lead in Canada, following the University of Minnesota in the U.S.A., to establish a Department of Native Studies. Unbeknownst to many in the 1970s, institutions of higher education across North America were built on prime land belonging to Aboriginal peoples. Ivy League universities in the United States, including Harvard, Princeton, and the Colleges of Dartmouth and of William and Mary, used Indian land on the condition that Indian students be a significant part of their student body (Garrod and Larimore 1997). Following the foundational years in higher education of the 18th and 19th centuries, fewer and fewer Native students were welcomed. Eleazar Wheelock, the founder of Dartmouth College made promises for "the education and instruction of youth of the Indian tribes in reading, writing and all parts of learning which shall appear necessary and expedient for civilizing and Christianizing children of pagans as well as English youth and others"; however, by 1829, his original commitment was completely forgotten (Garrod and Larimore, 1997:8). It was not until 1970 that a president of Dartmouth reaffirmed a commitment to Native American education and pledged to recruit and enroll a significant number of Native students.

During the 19th and 20th centuries, particularly in the United States, university murals portrayed Indians as savages and university rituals defiled Aboriginal ceremonies, reflecting, and likely fostering, many of the perspectives held by mainstream society about Aboriginal people (Garrod and Larimore 1997). For example, it was not until 1992 that "the seniors of Dartmouth College dropped the 121-year-old Class Day tradition of smashing peace pipes on the Old Pine Stump after hearing complaints that the practice [was] offensive to Comanches, Sioux and other Native Americans who regard pipe-smoking ceremonies as sacred" (Lest the Old Traditions Fail 2000).

In 1877, the University of Manitoba was the first university established in western Canada, "joining St. Boniface College, St. John's College, and Manitoba College to confer degrees on their graduates" (University of Manitoba 1999-2000). These individual colleges were established decades before, for the purpose of educating the children of the fur trade, notably the Métis sons of the Red River settlement. The University of Manitoba remains situated today on the banks of the Red River, on lands likely considered part of the 1.4 million acres owed to the children of the Métis under the Manitoba Act, 1870, and part of the original lands of the Anishinaabeg who negotiated Treaty #1 in 1871 (Sprague 1984).

In Canada, Native students were lost within the confines of the residential school system, and so few individuals attended, that the issue of higher education for Aboriginal people was ignored in public debate (RCAP 1996, Miller 1996, Milloy 1999, Aboriginal Healing Foundation 1991). Although Aboriginal peoples had long argued that their treaty and Aboriginal rights included the right to education to the highest levels, it was not until the late twentieth century that these protests and petitions were heard. By the mid twentieth century, many people were calling the institutions of higher education to account and proposals were presented to bring the place of Aboriginal peoples into present and future perspective.

This is a story of how a group of First Nations, Métis and Inuit students at the University of Manitoba decided to make a difference: they pursued the establishment of the Department of Native Studies, which became a reality in 1975. They were, for the most part, undergraduate students who registered in the faculties of Arts or Education for the 1970-74 years. They were in their early or mid twenties, and had lived a life, some with family obligations, some not. They met together, formed their own students association, and then made their presence known on campus. The purpose of this paper is to provide reflections from the Aboriginal student leaders involved 25 years ago. In their telling, the students honored the professors and the Aboriginal leaders who worked with such dedication to ensure that a Department would be established. This is also a chapter in the history of Aboriginal organizations in Manitoba, as the students clearly said without the leadership of Dave Courchene, President of the Manitoba Indian Brotherhood, in particular, and Angus Spence of the Manitoba Métis Federation, George Munroe of the Indian Métis Friendship Centre and Marion Ironquill Meadmore, the first female Aboriginal lawyer in Manitoba, none of their on-campus efforts would have been enough.

"We were trying to make a difference", recalls Yvonne Monkman Black (2000), as she sits in the welcome room of Ma Mawi Chi Itata Family Services in downtown Winnipeg. "You know in the early 1970s, we thought we'd be in our 20s forever. So we (Aboriginal students) just did what was necessary for people to recognize us and to respect our people". The seventies were "a hangover of the mystique from the sixties", according to Stan Harper (2000). "You know flower children and all that. The students were very friendly. They believed in civil rights, equality. In some ways, it was easier then, I think." Monkman echoed those sentiments, "The profs didn't know what to do with us, the visible Indians, the outspoken ones. They wanted to be so enlightened and would try so hard to understand our situation."

Aboriginal news witnessed an historic time of change. In June 1970, the Alberta Indian Association (AIA) of Chiefs led by Harold Cardinal called for recognition of special 'Citizens Plus' status. The AIA 'Red Paper' was presented in opposition to the federal White Paper of 1969, which had stated its case for an end to the Indian Act and any semblance of special rights. Before a year had elapsed, Canadians witnessed the Prime Minister reverse his policy and "acknowledge that his government had been naive in some of its proposals" (Winnipeg Free Press, Jan.8, 1971). And, in 1971, Helen Betty Osborne, a young Cree student attending high school in The Pas was brutally murdered. It took sixteen years to break what became known as the "conspiracy of silence" for two of the four men present to stand trial which lead to the Aboriginal Justice Inquiry.

In the fall of 1970, 11 Native students registered in Arts or

Education courses had more immediate concerns: getting an education and having fun. (Aside from the people interviewed for this article, founding members of IMESA included Judy Courchene, Marlene Courchene, Ken Linklater, George Shingoose, John Alooloo, Sharon Thibeault, Richard Linklater, and Shirley Olson.) Just getting registered was a challenge. Monkman was glad to have had help to register or believes she likely would have quit before even starting; Harper laughs at the wild goose chase he was sent on, by senior students enjoying his predicament and sending him to wrong lineups and rooms; he ended up taking three days to register. These eleven were part of an estimated 50 Aboriginal students of the 13,377 students enrolled full time (Koolage 1974).

"We were so insignificant (in numbers). I wondered how I'd survive. I'd look all over for someone who looked like me", said Yvonne Monkman. "I don't know how the students who came before us made it." She had attended school regularly at her home in Manigotaagan and Hecla Island, and then went to the Cranberry Portage residential school to complete grade 12. The strict regime and boredom of the new school led her to rebel. She didn't last the semester and went to Winnipeg where she worked in every assembly line she could find, counting screws for packaging, preparing home wine-making kits, making TV antennae. Monkman began to get involved at the Indian Métis Friendship Centre, where there was always something to do. "We started a program for little kids. It was actually the first Aboriginal Headstart in Canada, for Cree and Ojibway children, ages 4-6 years old." After working for a couple of years with the program, the first female Aboriginal lawyer in Manitoba, Marion Meadmore, was encouraging her that the Centre could do so much more with the program if there were accredited staff. Yvonne Monkman decided to go to university to obtain a two year teaching certificate.

Ovide Mercredi had been a field worker with the Manitoba Métis Federation for a few years. Due to the inequities of the Indian Act and its arbitrary administration, at this time, Ovide Mercredi was classified as being a non-status Indian. Mercredi regained his rightful status as a Treaty Indian in 1985, and was able to continue his work for treaty and Aboriginal rights. Mercredi served as National Chief of the Assembly of First Nations, the organization representing status Indians, from 1991-1997. In the early 1970s, Mercredi was married with young children when he attended the University of Winnipeg to finish his grade 12. He was one of the people who congregated at the Indian Métis Friendship Centre. There Ovide Mercredi, Yvonne Monkman and friends organized 'dry' dances and socials at Club 376. It was a fun place to get together without alcohol. And the young people would always be talking about social issues, things that mattered to them as Aboriginal people.

"Everything we talked about, George Munroe (Indian Métis Friendship Centre organizer) would take a step further. He would organize us to make presentations, march to the offices of politicians, do whatever was needed to act on the things we talked about", says Yvonne Monkman. "Although it was really important to us, we never realized how much impact our actions would have for the future." In response to a question for this article, Monkman said, "There was no issue of male or female taking the lead. Sometimes I would make the presentations, sometimes Ovide or someone else would. We didn't think that way. We were all in it together."

Moses Okemow, a Cree student from God's Lake reserve in northern Manitoba, and Stan Harper, an OjiCree student from Island Lake reserve, became actively involved in Aboriginal student life. Harper remembers Ovide Mercredi speaking to him in the cafeteria, about getting together with other Native students. Mercredi said he spoke to several people in the registration lineup. "We found out there were about 11 of us, and two Inuit students. In those days, we didn't know any better so we called ourselves the Indian Métis Eskimo [instead of Inuit] Students Association (IMESA)." Stan Harper remembers the excitement when the cool character from Couchiching reserve, Ken Linklater, half dragged this guy into our office, saying "'Look who I found, Look who I found!' It was an Eskimo (as we said in those days) - Johnny Alooloo from Pond Inlet". Monkman said, "We couldn't leave anyone out. There were two Eskimo students, so we had to be the Indian-Metis-Eskimo Students Association".

"We had a rule in IMESA", said Mercredi. "There would be no written constitution. Our business would all be according to the oral tradition. The President could only be one term so that we could develop leadership. Everybody got a chance." Mercredi became the first president, 1970-71; Moses Okemow followed in 1971-72, and Edwin Jebb, 1972-73. Mercredi said the International Students' Association had an office, so after we organized ourselves into IMESA, we negotiated to have an office. It was "the size of a broom closet", just inside the Students Union building (UMSU). Stan Harper and Moses Okemow remember there was just enough room for a desk and three chairs so they had to 'hang out' in series, handing the key to the next group getting together between classes. That next year, we got a bigger office, Monkman recalls. We joked about our place in university society because we got the room that the Gay Students moved out of. They moved upstairs to the room with windows. At least we were out of the broom closet. Usually, the students would meet at the cafeteria or at one of their home places.

Ovide began the fall of 1970 by contributing Jules Feiffer-like cartoons, under the title "The White Problem", for The Manitoban. (The Manitoban Oct. 30, 1970). Mercredi's cartoons were to appear regularly providing insights into the lives of Native peoples and their struggles with various forms of white oppression. Most of the incidents portrayed in these cartoons are based on actual experiences (The Manitoban Oct.2, 1970).

It was another student paper on campus that brought IMESA together on a definite mission. The engineering students had an annual event called a 'pub crawl', which they would then document for posterity in their newspaper, The Cursor. In January 1971, however, the students wrote a racist tract with photos of their pub crawl on Main Street, Winnipeg, "Where Winos Meet and Prairie Dogs Crawl" (The Manitoban Feb.2, 1971). With mean and biased comments about tomahawks, firewater, and war whoops, the article provoked an angry protest from many within and without the university. Lloyd Lenton of the Community Welfare Planning Council expressed dismay at the attitudes displayed toward Indian people, that "the University community was apparently not exempt (from) . . . the widespread ignorance and lack of respect for the Indians unusual predicament in our society" (The Manitoban Feb.19, 1971).

Monkman and Harper remember everyone, including non-Native students at the university, being very upset about the article. Okemow said that while people expected engineering students to be outrageous, this article was senseless, stupid and ignorant, in Mercredi's words. "Our initial reaction toward the article was one of anger, disgust, shock and disbelief" (The Manitoban Feb.2, 1971). Ovide Mercredi, president of IMESA, called a meeting with the Faculty of Engineering, the editor of The Cursor, and the writer of the article. IMESA warned of possible legal and other action and consulted with the Manitoba Indian Brotherhood, the Manitoba Métis Federation and the Indian Métis Friendship Centre. Monkman said IMESA did not ever meet the author (he hid), although she says she will never forget his name. IMESA did speak with the editor and other University spokespeople. The Cursor pulled all the newspapers and issued an apology, of sorts, stating that "there was no discrimination intended . . . it was a mistake on our part" (The Manitoban Feb.2, 1971). IMESA responded to wider student body through The Manitoban, which printed two full page stories about Native people and issues from Native perspectives. "We (IMESA) helped and worked with them. We reviewed every article," said Okemow.

The January 29th issue, which was printed after the controversial Cursor story, but before The Manitoban reported on it, had two articles by Clive Linklater ("Overcoming the white-man's myth", "Development requires that the true story of history be taught") from The Native People, "an Alberta paper published by Indians and Métis" (a predecessor to today's Windspeaker). There was also an excerpt of a speech to the Canadian Education Association by Douglas Cardinal, then a 36 year old Red Deer architect and spokesman for the Indian Association of Alberta (The Manitoban Jan. 29, 1971). The March 12, 1971, issue reprinted a speech of Chief Dan George, "Sad words and a savage reality":

> Let no one forget it . . . we are a people with special rights guaranteed to us by promises and treaties. We do not beg for these rights, nor do we thank you . . . we do not thank you . . . because we paid for them . . . and God help us the price we paid was exorbitant. (The Manitoban Jan. 29, 1971, said this was "swiped from The Meliorist").

Such words were being increasingly reported in the media since the consultative sessions to amend the Indian Act of 1968-69, and the united opposition of Aboriginal leaders to the federal government's 1969 White Paper. However, it was a time when university students, and Canadians as a whole, were largely unaware of what the Royal Commission on Aboriginal Peoples (1991-1996) would later call the 'abuse of power' and 'false assumptions' of the federal government policies of assimilation: the Indian Act, residential schools, relocations, and the treatment of Aboriginal veterans (RCAP 1996).

Aboriginal people did not give themselves time to heal from such trauma. It would take another generation to peel away the multi-layers of oppression, in what has been called the "inter-generational fallout from residential schools" or "the residential school syndrome" (Aboriginal Healing Foundation 1999). Rather, leaders of all ages and both sexes were driven to pursue their goals from the raw energy of anger, from their personal knowledge of the discriminatory treatment of their people and denial of their rights. The resilience of Aboriginal leadership was supported by their pride in being who they were, the First Peoples of Canada, and by their ever present humour, no matter what the situation.

"The Cursor article brought racism to the surface. A lot of people were upset" said Harper, "and it motivated people to act." IMESA did not let the pressure down but marched to the Mayor's office to press their demands for change. "It helped to get things moving and solidified the group." At the beginning of April, IMESA invited Mohawk political activist, Kahn Tineta Horn, representative of the Indians Free Legal Aid organization, to the university to speak on 'Indian Problems' (The Manitoban April 2, 1971). Monkman laughs, "Many older people (in the Aboriginal community) were afraid that we were going to be very radical or that we were just young and foolish." Instead, the students parleyed their new found public status into impressive steps toward respect and recognition for their people.

Over the next two years, "we gained a lot of respect", said Mercredi. "We (IMESA) lobbied for a (Native) students' lounge and a Native Students' advisor (Bette Spence, wife of Dr. Ahab Spence of the Manitoba Indian Brotherhood). We held the first PowWow at the university." IMESA began to press for the establishment of the Department of Native Studies. During 1971-72 and 1972-73 IMESA members were active in many fronts, and especially Moses Okemow (President 71-72) and Ovide Mercredi. In the fall of 1971, Ovide Mercredi 'and the Native Studies Group' (that is, 'native students and members of native community groups') offered a 'Native Views' course at 'UM Free You', (The Manitoban Sept. 21, 1971). A brainchild of the 1960s, free universities, like teach-ins, offered counter-culture views of many issues, to create free thinking and questioning among students and citizenry. Free of cost and "open to anyone who wants to come", Free You was based on "co-operative learning" and "people will be able to get out of any course what they want to with no pressure of tests, exams or assignments". Courses in existential philosophy, Women's Studies, creative motorcycling, advanced guitar, the penal code of Manitoba, and a sociology course taught by a professor who had been "fired for her ideas" teaching the same course the year before, were among those offered. Free You was pleased to offer a course in Native Views, "to provide a forum for the study of Indian and Métis history and problems, a field that the regular university pointedly ignores".

"Native Views" was designed to "cover a wide range of topics from native history (what really went on) to contemporary activities and problems", to "take a clear look at the problems and attempt to reach people, to forge links between the native peoples and white people. In some ways, it will be an experimental course, i.e. a prototype course for the Department of Native Studies to be established in the University" (The Manitoban Sept. 21, 1971). It was such a success that 20-60 students attended weekly. William Koolage (Professor in Anthropology) was a student in the Free You Native Views course and was able to use his positive experience to recommend Ovide Mercredi assist him in teaching the first Native Studies course approved by the University for the fall of 1973. In their second year of university, 1971-72, Mercredi and Okemow volunteered many hours to the Senate appointed committee. They remember particularly the dedication and hard work of Bruce Sealey, a Métis scholar, William (Skip) Koolage, and Fred Stambrook, who later became Dean of Arts and Vice-President of the university. Fred Stambrook's skillful strategizing is credited by many for the establishment of a Department instead of a Chair, together with work by Shirley Smith (Dean of Women) and Don McCarthy (Dean of Arts).

Committee work was not easy, the students found. "We worked on this committee all one winter, trying to keep up with our studies and doing other stuff with the Friendship Centre, the MIB and MMF. Dave Courchene got us involved in meetings with the (Manitoba) Museum as well. We wanted to sensitize and take back our research; we wanted research on us by us, from our own perspective. And we wanted to patriate artifacts." Some of these initiatives have progressed with the sensitive cooperation of museum curators Katherine Pettipas and Leigh Syms in the 1980s and a Cree graduate, consultant, author, and curator, Kevin Brownlee, in the late 1990s. Kevin Brownlee has produced major educational exhibits and programs in his home community of Nelson House and now works for the Government of Manitoba, organizing the patriation of human remains and sacred objects.

The university committee work was draining for the IMESA delegates. "I was surprised at the amount of opposition from the university," said Okemow. "You know the university is supposed to be open and knowledgeable but the administration said it wasn't good idea to have one department for one group. And yet there was Icelandic Studies, Slavic Studies. It was just so craven - they didn't want to give recognition to our people. They would sit there and tell us that other studies were fine but not us Aboriginal peoples, meaning that the oral tradition is not academic." At one point, Moses Okemow quit going to meetings because they seemed to be going nowhere. Professors Stambrook and Sealey urged Okemow to return. "They said, if you're genuinely interested in trying to set up a department, then go back and work at it. I did."

The IMESA students presented their proposal for a Chair in Native Studies to President Sirluck in February 1972. In words that were later chosen as the purpose of Native Studies in its first offering of courses in the fall of 1974, the students said:

Though we may be seeking to become teachers, lawyers,

social workers, doctors, etc., we seek, in addition to the skills of these vocations, to acquire an insight into all aspects of life. We wish to study our history and our culture; its clashes with the European invaders and subsequent accommodations and changes. . . . We hope that knowledge gained in this area will allow us to see present problems in a perspective through which we may determine possible solutions. . . . Many of the white students (1200 of whom had signed the year before as being interested in taking courses concerning native peoples of Canada) felt that somehow they too, like the Native students, were being denied an important aspect of the Canadian heritage by not having access to courses dealing with native peoples. (IMESA brief to President Sirluck, Feb. 9, 1972)

The Departmental goals included the above recommendations plus: "In addition, Native Studies seeks to extend to non-native students a knowledge of a non-Western cultural system that will promote understanding and respect". As a description of the road from the 1972 student brief to the establishment of the Department, Mercredi said, "the article Koolage wrote for the 1974 Native Studies symposium was dead on. He asked us to review it first." This is the participatory action research approach, practiced by Koolage years before Participatory Action Research was espoused by Anthropology and Native Studies as the most effective and culturally appropriate model.

IMESA organized two Native university student conferences, in March 1972 and 1973, which debated Native issues and promoted the establishment of the Department of Native Studies. The February 1st, 1972, issue of The Manitoban featured a two page spread, highlighting the IMESA students conference, with a review of Indian education in Manitoba and proposals by Bruce Sealey and students for reforms, including the establishment of a Department of Native Studies (The Manitoban Feb.1, 1972). The Manitoban excerpted the conference speech by the President of the MIB, urging the students to "step-by-step, issue by issue action that insists on results". The issue included a poem and graphics by renowned artist and poet Sarain Stump, and a biography about a 22 year old Cree student from Red Sucker Lake, Elijah Harper, which concluded "When Elijah completes his schooling he will go back to help others."

The 1973 conference reflected the progress the students and supportive faculty and Aboriginal organizations had made in their deliberations. This conference directed participants to "discuss Native Studies, its most suitable location, and other concerns of native university students". The universities of Brandon, Manitoba, and Winnipeg were competing for provincial government funding of this new department. Walter Currie, an Ojibway from Trent University, Rodney Soonias, a Cree from the Federation of Saskatchewan Indians Federated College, and Paul Voorhis, a linguist from Brandon University spoke the first day, with a panel of students from each of the three universities commenting and asking questions. On the second day, students heard from the Aboriginal politicians, Dave Courchene (PhD), President of the MIB, Angus Spence, President of the MMF, and Bill Thomas, Regional Director of Indian Affairs. Moderators of the panels included Verna Kirkness of the MIB, who became one of the most revered Aboriginal educators in Canada, and Sam Corrigan (Ph.D. formerly of University of Manitoba) and Don Robertson, both professors at Brandon University, the institution with the longest standing Native teaching training program in the province. While the President and Dean of Arts were busy elsewhere, the Dean of Students, Brian Ash, and Fred Stambrook, attended as members of the Senate Ad Hoc committee pursuing the establishment of the Department of Native Studies. The student commentators included Ovide Mercredi and Edwin Jebb of IMESA (U of M), with Maria Ross, Allan Ross, Stella Dysart and Sydney Muskego of IMESA (Brandon U).

These conferences were not highlights in the memory of the students interviewed, but part of the blur of activities they were organizing while attending to their studies, family and community responsibilities. However, the records that do exist document that representation of all three universities and the major Aboriginal organizations in Manitoba were involved in pressing for the establishment of Native Studies in institutions of higher education, and that students, particularly IMESA, faculty and organizational leaders all contributed ideas about the direction and design of the programs.

"We had a powerful ally in Dave Courchene, the President of the Manitoba Indian Brotherhood." Courchene had been awarded an honorary doctorate by the University of Manitoba in 1970, for his inspired leadership in promoting recognition and respect for Aboriginal peoples and socio-economic development in Manitoba reserves. The University powers were bound to listen to him. After the Ad Hoc committee reported back to Senate recommending a Department be established in March 1973, rather than a Chair or a program, the University seemed unable to act on the recommendation. Then Courchene spoke to the Senate of the University of Manitoba. They were so shaken that, according to an anonymous source, the President said he feared "flaming arrows would fly through (his) window".

Likely the source of some of Dave Courchene's fire was a UM memo "Additional Tips on Hiring Native People", about which he wrote a scathing letter to UM President Sirluck, July 5, 1973. Courchene dissected the 3 1/2 page memo in his 7 page letter, railing against its assumptions, that "non-Indians need to help Indian people to adjust to 20th century environment . . . to train Indian people to take 'their' role in the work force", or that "any special motivational training, other than strictly technical, is required". Courchene continued:

> If we had followed the assumptions implicit in this paper, we would certainly not have been able to accomplish any at all of the major developments that have taken place through band Council staffs, the Manitoba Indian Brotherhood staff, the Bi-Neh-Se and Me-Ke-Si workers. In the MIB alone, I have some 80 staff members, only 3 of whom are of no known Indian ancestry, and those are not anywhere near the policy making level.

Dave Courchene took umbrage at the memo's analysis of reasons given for not hiring 'disadvantaged' workers and the rationale as to why these reasons were not acceptable. One favorite of Courchene's seemed to be Point #8: "Lack of vitality; shuffles; slow-moving, lazy" with the rationale given in the UM memo that "someone who looks lazy on the job may be very productive - he may never waste time." To this, Courchene replied:

> As my staff shuffles and slow-moves and lazes its way into doing the job that literally hundreds of non-Indian academically highly qualified bureaucrats could not do for a hundred years; . . . as I shuffle and slow-move and laze my way around on a 20 hour day, 7 day a week schedule, I must say that we all do find it comforting that someone amongst your people at least feels that this shuffling may be appearances only! . . . [signing off] But, honestly, Ernest, can't you DO something about some of your Faculties? . . . Yours, Shuffling! in Brotherhood. (University of Manitoba, Department of Archives and Special Collections, file UA-29).

Within months, the Senate and Board of Governors had approved the establishment of a Department of Native Studies, much beyond the initial 1972 proposal of what some IMESA students, faculty and staff representatives from the MIB and MMF had at first thought possible. Courchene and the IMESA students also had an effect on the provincial Universities Grants Commission, who approved the UM proposal immediately, and later supported a Department of Native Studies at Brandon University, just as the MIB President had recommended.

The student leaders also remember the lighter side of their UM years. "It wasn't all work", said Okemow, "There was partying too but Ovide was straight because he was married and started a family. So he always took the initiative." Mercredi remembers a trip to Brandon University to meet with the Aboriginal students there for a weekend conference. "Dave Courchene - our biggest ally - arranged to rent two cars and we all piled in and drove through a blizzard. Brandon University had their BUNTEP and PENT teacher training programs for a while already and the students were organized but it was a good excuse to get us there. We slept (if at all) in two hotel rooms." Among those involved in Brandon University student politics were a future Chief of Norway House and future law graduand, Allan Ross, his wife Maria, a teacher, and Stella Cook Ness, a Cree linguist.

Harper recalls traveling with fellow student Elijah Harper during the 1972-74 years to visit cousins from Island Lake who were attending the University of North Dakota. They would meet Aboriginal students from North and South Dakota and Minnesota, attend their PowWow, and invite them back to Winnipeg. One memorable weekend in Winnipeg, the students attended the play, "The Ecstasy of Rita Joe", with the live performers joined by Chief Dan George as a character via video screen. These were heady days of pride in being Aboriginal, proud of what Indians and Métis and Eskimos has survived, and proud of what the students would ensure would be a better future.

These students of the early 1970s were surprised that it was twenty five years ago that the Department of Native Studies was established. At the time, they didn't know where their efforts would lead. For some, it seemed more effort was needed every time they went to the next level. "Later when I went to University of Manitoba law school," Okemow remembers, "it was the same experience. Lionel Chartrand (a Métis from St. Laurent) and Lloyd Stevenson (of Peguis First Nation), and I saw there was only a 3 credit seminar course on law and Aboriginal issues offered (by a non-Aboriginal professor). I didn't take it." (In the year 2000, the UM Law School now has one Native faculty member, Wendy Whitecloud, who teaches two 3 credit seminar courses (Aboriginal Peoples and the Law; Aboriginal Land Claims) and acts as the Native student advisor.

Student leaders from the 1970s heeded the words of Dave Courchene at their 1972 Native Students Conference:

> The nature of our struggle is Indian nationalism. . . Upon graduating, don't join those bureaucracies and those offices - our oppressors. Don't be (pulled) in by those white liberals who love us to death. Get that education and get out of here and go where the action is . . . to your people. . . . These 'past injustices' have almost brought us to cultural genocide. Our responsibility is not to provide leadership to white society but to create a revolution, to create a renewed respect for our heroes, our ancestors, our brothers, and ourselves. (The Manitoban Feb.1, 1972)

Yvonne Monkman Black returned to the early childhood education program at the Indian Métis Friendship, bringing her credentials to establish the program as a satellite of the Winnipeg #1 School Division. She worked for ten years overseeing the program for children ages 4-8 years, Cree in the morning and Ojibway in the afternoon, taking in children the schools could not manage - kids who were being expelled from kindergarten and grade 1. "We were preparing our children for mainstream education while keeping our culture and language strong". Eventually, the program was adopted into a regular Division School. Monkman went on to work for many Native organizations and is now financial officer for Ma Mawi Chi Itata Family Services, the first urban Aboriginal child welfare organization in Manitoba. Moses Okemow graduated from law and returned to his community to be Chief of God's Lake, 1977-81, 1985-88. He later worked at the Assembly of First Nations with Ovide Mercredi during his six year term in Ottawa, and is now working on special projects to do with Lands & Trusts at the Assembly of Manitoba Chiefs in Winnipeg. Stan Harper left university after his first two years but returned to finish his last year and graduate in 1984. Stan Harper honoured his grandfather who raised him by adding his name as Harper's legal name, and is proud to be known as Stan Harper Manoakeesick. He is the assistant director of Island Lake Tribal Council, in charge of all programs. Ovide Mercredi also graduated from law and continued his activism in many roles. As Regional Chief for Manitoba on the Assembly of First

Nations Executive, Mercredi was part of the Assembly of Manitoba Chiefs team in 1990 who supported and strategized with another University of Manitoba graduand, Member of the Manitoba Legislative Assembly Elijah Harper, to stop the Meech Lake amendment. Mercredi was elected National Chief of the Assembly of First Nations (1991-1997), and is widely respected for his outspoken, visionary leadership in which he ensured that Canadians understand and take into account treaties and Aboriginal rights. Due to Mercredi, Native Veterans will be visibly represented and honoured during national remembrances, national monuments will pay appropriate respect to the Aboriginal guides who took the 'explorers' on what University of Toronto historian Michael Bliss has called no more than 'conducted tours' of Canada. And, most importantly, the benchmark for constitutional recognition of Aboriginal self government has been raised to the level of the 1992 Charlottetown Accord, in which the right of self governance of Aboriginal peoples would be recognized as one of three orders of government in Canada. Quebec politicians in particular were chagrined at Mercredi's leadership and achievements. Mercredi presently resides in Ottawa, advising First Nations, lectures at Laurentian University in Sudbury, among other places, and has been working to develop a Centre for Indigenous Knowledge and Governance.

The University of Manitoba celebrates the anniversaries of the Department of Native Studies, and of Access and Engineering Access programs in the year 2000. There are now a full-time Aboriginal Students' Coordinator, an assistant advisor, and a resident elder, situated at the University Centre building, as well as staff complement for the Access programs. Aboriginal Focus Programs have a major presence in the Department of Continuing Education, with several off campus programs, including Social Work and Education at Sagkeeng First Nation, Roseau River First Nation, and Children of the Earth school in downtown Winnipeg. An accredited Nursing program is offered at Norway House First Nation. In partnership with the Aboriginal Focus Programs, the Centre for Indigenous Environmental Resources (CIER), established and operated by a Board of First Nations Chiefs from across Canada, offers an environmental education program to Native students. CIER graduates work in the field or transfer their credits to the equivalent of second year in Environmental Science or Native Studies. In 1998-99, Native Studies courses were being favoured by an increasing number of Arts students each year. The Department of Native Studies now offers graduate degrees in Native Studies, with a permanent faculty of six, half of whom are Aboriginal. [Editor's Note: The Faculties of Arts, Law,

Medicine, Education, Social Work, Engineering, Management, Continuing Education, Science, Schools of Fine Art and Music, Natural Resources Institute, Nursing are some of those faculties and schools which have developed programs, lecture series, faculty members, research and courses with Native Studies content. For example, the Faculty of Social Work program revisions have changed the profile of Social Workers from almost 100% non-Aboriginal 10 years ago to over 50% Aboriginal Social Workers today. The Faculty of Graduate Studies now supports scholarship in Native Studies with a $10,000 award for doctoral students. Professors in the Faculty of Medicine have developed internship and research programs with Aboriginal peoples in northern Manitoba and throughout the circumpolar region. This is only a beginning. Faculties are demanding support needed for the continued expansion of Native Studies scholarship across all disciplines in order to meet the needs of Aboriginal and non-Aboriginal students and staff. See Oakes 1999a, 1999b].

During the past twenty-five years, Aboriginal people have accomplished far more in so many fields than any outside observer could have predicted. The political, legal and constitutional, cultural, economic and social initiatives, achievements and innovations that First Nations, Inuit and Métis peoples have given to their own people and to Canada is laudable. Institutions of higher education may do well to consider whether they have kept apace.

Universities such as the University of British Columbia and University of Toronto who came later to the field of Native Studies now have First Nations Houses to welcome, orient and be a home away from home for their Aboriginal students. Yet, despite an action plan in 1998-99 for the University of Manitoba to be "the university of first choice by Aboriginal students" (University of Manitoba 1999), over 1000 full and part-time Aboriginal students make do with simply a larger lounge and offices than in 1972.

Despite the endangered state of over fifty Aboriginal languages in Canada, the University of Manitoba does not require Native Studies majors to take even one course in Aboriginal languages, and the course in language planning for communities is available only through the Department of Linguistics. Cree and Ojibway language programs are taught with sessional instructors instead of full time staff, even though Native languages were an integral part of the first proposal for the Department, and Elders caution that the key to personal and national identity, culture, science lie within the language. North America is the only homeland for Aboriginal languages.

Conclusions

To establish the Department of Native Studies at the University, it took dedicated efforts from within and without the institution. The students' role was multi varied, providing leadership and a constant presence and persistence with the faculty, the administration, and importantly with other students. They sought to make a difference, and they did, through organizing their own Indian Métis Eskimo Students Association and making it a visible presence on campus, contributing to The Manitoban, organizing and participating in Aboriginal student conferences, briefing Aboriginal organizational leaders and strategizing together, writing briefs and making presentations, attending meetings with faculty and strategizing, organizing protest marches - and participating in their classes and academic work. These skills were honed by the students during their early years on campus, and they have been used to impressive gains for their own communities years after graduation.

Student leaders listened to their mentors in the Aboriginal organizations who told them to study at institutions of higher education. The student leaders knew they had to ensure these institutions recognized the First peoples of Canada as leaders and contributors today and tomorrow, not as "living museum pieces of a century ago" (MIB President, Dave Courchene, upon being awarded an honorary doctorate by the University of Manitoba, Winnipeg Tribune, May 23, 1970). IMESA (Manitoba) worked to translate that recognition into continuing respect in the form of a Department of Native Studies and a place for Aboriginal students to feel welcome and encouraged. Students formed discussion groups at the Free You, called writers of racist tracts to account, and documented and lobbied for their ideas while pursuing their studies, enjoying their camaraderie, caring for their families, and staying connected to their communities. It is hoped that future generations of Aboriginal student leaders will benefit from generous mentoring and support of Aboriginal organizational leaders and university faculty to promote further changes. Aboriginal students are the natural links between their own communities, their organizations, and the academic institutions, as they inhabit all three at once. Along the banks of the Red River, in the land of Treaty #1 and the Red River Métis, there is a long path yet to travel for the recognition and respect that the Aboriginal student leaders of the early 1970s sought.

References

Aboriginal Healing Foundation. 1991. *Guide to Applicants*. Ottawa.

32

Aboriginal Justice Inquiry of Manitoba. 1991. Final Report Vol. 1:2. Ottawa.

Central City could Fail-Schreyer. 1971. Winnipeg Free Press, January 25.

Garrod, A. and Larimore, C. 1997. *First Person, First Peoples: Native American College Graduates tell their Life Stories.* Ithaca: Cornell U. Press.

Harper, S. 2000. Interview conducted in spring of 2000. Winnipeg, MB.

Koolage, W. 2000. Beginning of Native Studies. In J. Oakes, R. Riewe, M. Bennett, B. Chisholm (Eds.) *Pushing the Margins: Native and Northern Research.* Winnipeg: Native Studies Press. Adapted from paper in Symposium: North American Native Studies: Their Programs and Contributions. XLI International Congress of Americanists, Mexico, D.F. *U of M Anthropology Papers, No.8: North American Native Studies: Their Programs and Contributions, V.1.*

Lest the Old Tradition Fail. 2000. Dartmouth Alumni Magazine. June.

Miller, J.1996. *Shingwauk Vision: A History of Native Residential Schools.* Toronto: University of Toronto Press.

Milloy, J.1999. A national crime: The Canadian government and the residential school system, 1879-1986. *Manitoba Studies in Native History XI.* University of Manitoba Press.

Monkman Black, Y. (2000). Interview conduced in spring. Wpg., MB.

Oakes, J. 1999a. Northern and Native Research at the University of Manitoba. Winnipeg: Faculty of Graduate Studies and Dept of Native Studies.

Oakes, J. 1999b. Northern and Native Courses, Programs, and Research at the University of Manitoba. Winnipeg: Faculty of Graduate Studies and Department of Native Studies.

Royal Commission on Aboriginal Peoples (RCAP). 1996. *Final Report, Looking Forward, Looking Back, Gathering Strength.* 1-3.

Sprague, D. 1984. A serene atmosphere? Treaty #1 revisited. *Canadian Journal of Native Studies IV*(2):321-358.

The Manitoban, University of Manitoba Students Union, Winnipeg. v.57, n.15, October 30, 1970; v.57, n.8, October 2, 1970; v.57,n.34, Feb.2, 1971; v.57, n.39, Feb.19, 1971; v.57, n.33, January 29, 1971; v.57, n.47, April 2, 1971; v.58, n.8, September 21, 1971; v. 58, n.37, February 1, 1972.

The Winnipeg Tribune. May 23, 1970.

University of Manitoba. 1999. Action Plan

University of Manitoba. 1999-2000. *General Calendar.*

University of Manitoba, Department of Archives and Special Collections, Elizabeth Dafoe Library, Department of Native Studies files; Minutes of the Senate.

Weetamah, Winnipeg, Manitoba. v.10, issue 18, April 15th-May 1, 2000 Province says Yes to AJIC Recommendations (MB Gov't News Release)

Winnipeg Free Press. Jan.8, 1971; Jan.25, 1971; January 26, 1971.

---

[1] Kathi Avery Kinew (PhD) is a consultant to First Nations and also a sessional instructor at the University of Manitoba in the Department of Native Studies.

The Interdisciplinary Graduate Program in Native Studies

Jill Oakes[1]

Abstract

An interdisciplinary Masters in Native Studies proposal was approved, after hundreds of hours of meetings and pages of reports. Although the program has received tremendous support throughout all phases of development and implementation, limited resources remain a key concern.

Introduction

A graduate program based in holistic, interdisciplinary, Native Studies world views provides educational, cultural and economic benefits to Aboriginal and non-Aboriginal students, organizations, governments and institutions. Yet few Canadian universities offer graduate programs in Native Studies. In 1994, I was a new staff member in the Department of Native Studies with a passion for research and a vision for: Native Studies graduate students working in a variety of areas; staff and graduate students from all disciplines sharing their in sights on research at Native Studies seminars; conferences attracting scholars from other regions and other disciplines; refereed publications celebrating Aboriginal scholarship; a full component of staff; a meeting space for Native Studies staff and students; funds for scholarships; and much more. In other words, a fully operating department celebrating academic excellence in all forums.

At the time, the department offered a three-year degree. My first hurdle was to convince my colleagues that indeed it could be done; they were already swamped with teaching up to 24 credit hours of course work a year, working on their own doctoral degrees, and meeting community and family commitments. They were committed to the concept and enthusiastically made time to discuss and critique draft program proposals. In addition, staff from other departments lent their support. The university community was experiencing financial cut backs, staff retirements, program closures, potential mergers and other shrinking rather than expanding measures. The issue of insufficient resources has remained only partially resolved throughout the developing and maintaining processes.

The Process

Across Canada the number of Aboriginal students in post-secondary programs grew from 2500 in 1975 to 15,572 in 1988 (Frideres 1993). At the University of Manitoba (U of M), "The first exams set by the University of Manitoba were written on May 27, 1878. There were seven candidates and two [28%] of them were Aboriginal people" (Blanchard 1996:1). In 1970 there were 500 Aboriginal students and by 1985, 1800 had received university degrees at the U of M (HRD 1995). Although the percentage of Aboriginal graduates has dropped significantly, the demand for graduates with advanced degrees in Native Studies continues to expand. On February 19, 1986, Paul Chartrand organized a Native Studies Meeting inviting representatives from Aboriginal organizations, government, institutions and business to discuss the future goals and objectives of Native Studies at the U of M. One of the outcomes of the meeting were recommendations to establish a four-year Advanced Major and a Graduate Program open to students from all disciplines. It is unknown why proposals for an Advanced Major and Graduate Program in Native Studies were left undeveloped at that time.

In 1994, to identify continued community support and demand for an Advanced Major and Graduate Program, the Native Studies Advisory Council (over 60 representatives from university departments and Aboriginal organizations) was established. The Native Studies Program Planning Committee (a sub-committee of the Department of Native Studies Council with flexible membership of 'core' staff: Emma LaRocque, John Nichols, Fred Shore, Wanda Wuttunee, and I; and students: Belinda Vandenbroek, Kathi Kinew, Angela Busch, Bret Nickels, and others from the Aboriginal Student Association) was established to critique draft proposals. The draft program proposal reflected recommendations and approval received from the Native Studies Advisory Council, Native Studies Program Planning Committee, and Department of Native Studies Council 1994-1995. In 1995, we formed a Faculty of Graduate Studies

Steering Committee: Native Studies (FGSSC:NS) with Wendy Dahlgren (Associate Dean, Faculty of Graduate Studies) as the Chair. This committee included Senior Administrators and representatives from the Faculties of Arts, Sciences, professional faculties and Aboriginal scholars involved in Native Studies (e.g. Robert O'Kell, Associate Dean, Faculty of Arts, Laara Fitznor, professor, Faculty of Education, Stan Straw, Dick Johnson). Its mandate was to ensure all factors were considered and to confirm the appropriate approval process. At the inaugural meeting Jim Gardner (Vice-President) stated "Native Studies cannot be anything but interdisciplinary" and strongly supported the concept as outlined. Dick Johnson (Provost) recommended "treating this as a new program" (Minutes FGSSC:NS June 6, 1995). Tasks were assigned to further develop the concept: Stan Straw (Associate Dean, Faculty of Graduate Studies) drafted the supplemental regulations and I prepared the program proposal, course proposal and supporting documentation approved by the Department of Native Studies. The three proposed core courses were then submitted and approved at the June meeting of the Faculty of Graduate Studies Graduate Course and Regulation Approvals Committee; once approved by the Board of Graduate Studies Committee and Faculty Council the courses were offered January, 1996. In addition a Statement of Intent was submitted to "the University Grants Commission and we are awaiting a letter of permission . . . to further develop the proposal" (Minutes July 12, 1995:2). By January 1996 the supplementary regulations and program proposal (including a demand survey; letters of support from Aboriginal organizations, students, librarians, staff from all faculties, and staff at other universities; course outlines and course approval from other faculties; a brochure for incoming students; ethical guidelines; application procedures; and numerous other items) were unanimously approved by the Steering Committee. FGSSC:NS dissolved after appointing members to the newly formed Native Studies Graduate Program Committee (NSGPC) designed to administer the program (Chair, Stan Straw). With letters of support from the Department of Native Studies Council, Faculty of Arts, and many other individuals and organizations, the proposal was submitted to the Faculty of Graduate Studies, where it was observed as the most extensive proposal members recalled ever receiving. In the summer of 1996, Louise Forsyth (University of Saskatchewan) and Peter Kulchyski (Trent University) served as external reviewers. With their supporting reviews the proposal was submitted to the Senate Planning and Priorities Committee (SPPC).

On November 19th, 1996, John McIntyre (Chair, SPPC) submitted the committee's report stating "once this program is approved by the Senate and Board of Governors, [it] will not have to receive approval by the Universities Grants Commission as a new 'program' in light of the ruling recently received . . ." To this day, senior administrators have stated their surprise when they hear it has not ever been approved by the current equivalency to the Universities Grants Commission, as a result secure, long term provincial educational funds have never been assigned to this program. The SPPC report summarized the key components of the proposal and required a letter confirming agreement from the Deans of Arts and Graduate Studies on several items prior to approving it for submission to Senate, including (McIntyre 1996):

a) The Program Development Fund baseline funding for a Coordinator was "essential if the proposal is approved.";
b) "the Dean of Graduate Studies bears a special responsibility to ensure that appropriate advisory committees are in place prior to acceptance of students into the program.";
c) "a plan of course offerings (including undergraduate courses) and graduate student advisor assignments . . . confirmed as feasible by the Deans of the Faculties of Graduate Studies and Arts"; and
d) Criteria used to distinguish an MA degree and MSc degree was needed.

Raymond Currie (Dean, Faculty of Arts) and Ken Hughes (Dean, Faculty of Graduate Studies)(January 7, 1997) letter of confirmation stated:

a) The plan for course offerings was feasible;
b) The criteria for what constitutes an MA degree and a MSc degree depends on: "the nature of the thesis proposal, course work, and disciplines represented by the Thesis Advisory Committee";
c) The "Dean of Graduate Studies is committed to finding the resources required to offer the core courses in this program in the event that it is impossible for the Department of Native Studies or another Department to offer these courses" and these courses will be offered once a year;
d) "The Faculty of Graduate Studies will supply funds for teaching release for the program coordinator and for secretarial support" which will "normally be housed in the Department of Native Studies".

Later that year Senate approved the program, the first graduate students, Randall Brown, Bret Nickels and Barbara Pritchard, had almost completed their course work. Since then graduate students have included Yale Belanger, Marlyn Bennett, Ann Callahan, Shawn Charlebois, Donna Delaronde, Alison Dubois, Alison Edmunds, Jonathon Ellerby, Nahanni Fontaine, Catherine Glass, Chris Loewen, Lori Nordlund, Rishona

Slutchuk, Myrle Traverse, and Jennie Wastesicoot. The first three courses offered were: *Selected Topics in Native Studies, Seminar in Native Studies* and *Methods and Issues in Native Studies Research. Native Studies Colloquium* was added in 1999. Aboriginal instructors have included Paul Chartrand (Native Studies), Yvonne Pompana (Social Work), Laara Fitznor (Education), and Margaret and Jules LaVallee (Red Willow Lodge). Over 50 professors from different departments and over 15 Aboriginal experts from the community have served as Advisors or Committee Members for students in our program. This has enabled students interested in a wide range of research topics to obtain the academic support required to complete their degree. Without the ongoing support of these committed individuals, it would be impossible to provide such a diverse program. The educational opportunities of this program benefit all of us at a personal, regional, national, and international level.

Celebrating the Past, Present and Future

There are now over 400 researchers working in the fields of Native or Northern Studies at the University of Manitoba (Oakes 1999a, 1999b). Each year new certificate or certified programs with a Native Studies focus are approved in faculties across campus. Now that all the 'core staff' have completed doctoral degrees, our department has the largest number of professors in Native Studies with a PhD in Canada. Since 1994, the Department of Native Studies has produced a refereed publication each year, at first in cooperation with the Canadian Circumpolar Institute and now with our own Native Studies Press. Several student conferences have been organized which attracted participants from across Canada. One theme conference with international participants (over 300) was organized, papers were published in refereed format (Oakes *et al.* 1997). The interdisciplinary Masters in Native Studies Program is five years old and the administrative structure is under revision for more autonomy. Native Studies graduate students have presented at regional, national, and international conferences; served on committees and boards of national and international organizations; published in journals from a wide variety of disciplines; worked in regional, national and international Aboriginal organizations; and obtained funds in recognition for their excellence in Native Studies scholarship.

In addition to ensuring that students in the graduate program have an excellent range of academic opportunities, energies are now directed to developing a doctoral program in Native Studies. Fernando deToro (Dean, Faculty of Graduate Studies) established a doctoral scholarship in 1999 for students in any discipline whose research delves into issues facing

38

Aboriginal Peoples. Ongoing support for Native Studies scholarship and programs has been extremely strong from all sectors. Increased, secure long term financial support is required to ensure the success of this graduate program. It is critical to provide the resources needed to support Aboriginal and non-Aboriginal students and staff from all disciplines working in the interdisciplinary field of Native Studies.

Acknowledgements

Contributions from all members of the Program Planning Committee, Department Council, Steering Committee, Faculty Councils, Senate Committees and Sub-Committees; staff and students; thesis Advisors and Committee Members; and government departments, Aboriginal organizations and cultural institutions are gratefully acknowledged and sincerely appreciated. These contributions were critical to obtain University approval for the proposed program, as well as implementing and maintaining the Native Studies Graduate Program.

References Cited

Aboriginal Peoples Survey. 1991. *University Education and Economic Well-Being: Indian Achievement.* Hull:Statistics Canada

Blanchard, J. 1996. Memo to Department of Native Studies 'core' staff. April 30.

Currie, R. and Hughes, K. 1997. Letter submitted to the President, Jan. 7.

Frideres, J. 1993. *Native Peoples in Canada.* Scarborough, ON: Prentice Hall.

Human Resources Development Canada. 1995. *National Guide to College and University Programs.* Hull, Quebec.

McIntyre, J. 1996. Report from Senate Planning and Priorities Committee, November 19th, 1996.

Minutes, Faculty of Graduate Studies Steering Committee: Native Studies 1995-1996. University of Manitoba.

Oakes, J. 1999a. *Northern & Aboriginal Content in University of Manitoba Scholarship, Programs & Courses.* Report prepared for Department of Native Studies and Faculty of Graduate Studies.

Oakes, J. 1999b. *Northern & Aboriginal Studies Research at the University of Manitoba.* Report prepared for Department of Native Studies and Faculty of Graduate Studies.

Oakes, J., Riewe, R., Kinew, K., Koolage, W. 1997. *Sacred Lands.* Winnipeg, Edmonton: Native Studies, CCI.

[1] Jill Oakes (Ph.D.) is a Professor in the Department of Native Studies and currently coordinates the Native Studies graduate program at the University of Manitoba.

Canon Fodder:
Examining the Future of Native Studies

Joyce Green[1]

Abstract

This article considers the origins, nature and future of departments of Native Studies in Canadian academe. It argues that Native Studies is historically contingent on resistance to colonial relations. While Native Studies is multi disciplinary, it is also characterised by critical pedagogy and methodology. In a society where the population of Aboriginal people is increasing dramatically, it is especially important that institutions of higher learning provide all students with the information and analysis to better understand the history and the future of our common community. Therefore, universities must provide increased support for departments of Native Studies, and must better understand the sometimes conflicting demands made on Native Studies faculty members.

Introduction

Within academic disciplines, including Native Studies, that core of material which is viewed as foundational to the discipline and the base on which newer knowledge is based, whether critically or not, is called 'The Canon'. In terms of its centrality to academic work and its social significance, it is beyond critique. 'Canon fodder' refers to the material that disciplines bring forward for inclusion in the canon, broadening and deepening the canon, thereby providing tools for more complex and sophisticated treatment of old canon and new problems (Vickers 1997). Native Studies provides fodder that is, food for more, and different, and better scholarship

(LaRocque 1996). In this article, I review the reason for the emergence of Native Studies departments and consider Native Studies' location in the academic community, including Native Studies curriculum and faculty, and the relationship between departments and universities.

The Raison d'Etre of Native Studies

Critical scholarship has not often achieved the stature of canon, Karl Marx's critique of liberalism and capitalism being a notable exception. For the most part, knowledge, theory, analysis, and prescription that takes a radically different approach than the canon is burdened with a much heavier onus of validation. By this I mean that radical, critical, or marginal intellectual work is treated as *a priori* suspect, and those who engage in such scholarship must struggle against institutionalised biases against the significance or legitimacy of their work. So it is with Native Studies, which is occasionally alleged by its critics to be ideological or not academically sound.

Native Studies exists because of relations of oppression (LaRocque 1999). It exists because of the historical colonial relationship, in which the oppressor constructed knowledge as first, its own cultural and intellectual production; and second, as that which legitimated the colonial enterprise (Blaut 1993, Memmi 1965, Said 1993). The canon, constructed primarily by western European intellectuals, was imbued with and propagated the dominant philosophies, ideologies, and analytical forms of the dominators (Green 1995). Just as racism served an instrumental purpose in legitimating imperialism, so it justified obviating any indigenous knowledge, and dismissing critical analysis that questioned the hegemonic academy.

Native Studies' Location in the Academic Community

Native Studies is now a distinct discipline in most Canadian universities. It remains, for the most part, marginal in that it deals with material and context ignored by other departments. It continues to bear a very heavy burden of demonstrating its academic excellence and its rightful claim on university resources. It is doubly burdened because while it is an academic endeavour, it exists because of colonial political relations resulting in its erstwhile exclusion, and it is expected by coloniser and colonised to attend to very many needs which are not primarily, or in any way, academic.

The communities that form the bulk of its subject matter (Aboriginal communities) expect departments of Native Studies to perform several, sometimes conflicting, functions. Native Studies is expected to be an indigenous and anti-colonial intellectual space within what has generally been understood to be a racist institution. In Native Studies, materials about indigenous peoples are taken up, and indigenous people themselves can study and work. That is, it is on one level indigenous territory, taken from the colonial institution. As such, it is imbued with the political ethos of resistance and with the necessity of critical intellectual work. It also has a social function, constructed as the recruitment and retention of Aboriginal students (for example, see Recommendations 18 and 37 in Task Force 1998) who may find the colonial institution to be fairly hostile territory in several respects. Further, universities and Aboriginal communities both expect Native Studies to serve a liaison function in the following, sometimes contradictory ways. Including the support of Aboriginal students financially, academically (including with remedial work in certain cases) and culturally; doing community relevant research; articulating specific communities' political and other visions; and representing Aboriginal peoples within the academy and dominant community.

These kinds of expectations are not imposed on most other academics, and can lead to role conflict, personal overload, and criticism of Native Studies academics on arguably illegitimate grounds (for example, on their political stances, their research interests, their choice of residence, their historical antecedents, and so on). Committing time to these multiple expectations may place Aboriginal academics in positions where they are unable to meet the standard academic performance criteria that are based on the 'holy trinity' of teaching, research and community contribution. Simultaneously, the discipline, and those who practice it, are accountable to the academy and to the principles which govern public intellectuals; that is, to be measurably productive and meritorious. The academic expectations on faculty (and I agree with this expectation) are to teach, to research, and to do community work in order to obtain our professional and remunerative advancement. We are expected to teach in a way which will not be antagonistic of non-Native students, who are often the majority of our students. That is, in addition to teaching the curriculum, we are charged with doing anti-racist education in what is implicitly a racist environment. This means that we are vulnerable to charges such as bias and racism as we seek to interrogate history, politics and cultural materials in a critical fashion, the same topics which most of our students initially learned from the dominant perspective and are challenged to re-think.

The consequence is "the politics in our classrooms when students do not or will not understand the political nature of western epistemology . . ." (LaRocque 1999:60). Our teaching calls into question many foundational myths of the Canadian state. This pedagogy is sometimes uncomfortable for those who have absorbed these myths.

Curriculum of Native Studies

Native Studies curriculum is multi disciplinary; bound together with the theme of Aboriginality in experience, history, art, cultures, languages, politics, sociological and economic practices. Aboriginality itself is located in a history of oppression and dispossession. For example, the United Nations Draft Declaration on the Rights of Indigenous People[s] defines indigeniety (or Aboriginality) as characterised by anteriority (that is, occupation of the land prior to the current dominant society) and non-dominance in the contemporary government. This implies several methodological and pedagogical approaches, co-existing within one department, as well as faculty members' affinities for other departments. Native Studies exists precisely because the other disciplines were not doing this material, or not doing it well. The diversity of the curriculum imposes its own challenges for administration, and sometimes, for legitimacy in times of financial cutbacks. However, Native Studies is not solely responsible for all things Aboriginal. Some departments do and many should incorporate Native Studies canon into their material. Their canon is incomplete or wrong without, in Political Science for example, attending to the ways in which the Canadian state has been built on Aboriginal lands and resources, through state policy and without benefit to or agreement by Aboriginal nations. This has further implications for the study of the constitution, of public policy, and of citizenship.

Native Studies Faculty

Native Studies is a vibrant intellectual community promoting love of learning and providing rich, complex, original material for engagement. Native Studies stands the principles of academic rigour and excellence: there should be no puffball courses, and no easy passes for particular categories of students. Technical excellence is part of scholarly competence, and all students should be expected to read, and to write, at a level appropriate to their university level. Native Studies faculty generally are and must be active scholars: they teach, but they also research, write and publish. They participate in the wider university community. They are active in 'the community', whichever construction of community best suits them individually. Some work with Aboriginal communities; some within the academic world. Some are active in social movements. Some work with the media to promote scholarly and socially relevant analyses of such things as budgets and government policy, literature, and sociological phenomena, as they affect Aboriginal peoples.

Over the short and medium term, universities must allocate more teaching positions to Native Studies. I also envision institutional and faculty support for funds for Native Studies faculty research projects. I anticipate university administrators noting the changing demography, especially of the prairie provinces, with a significant rise in young Aboriginal populations potentially swelling student cohorts. This observation should motivate institutional support for departments of Native Studies, so that institutions of higher learning can adequately educate all students for a world in which Aboriginal people are a significant part of academic, political, corporate and social life. This point needs to be stressed: a major task of Native Studies is to educate non-Aboriginal students about the realities of their communities, grounded in colonial relations, the institutions of which perpetuate racist cultural assumptions, policy, and practices. In doing this, Native Studies is (Said 1994) an agent of change and of the search for equity and justice.

Many Aboriginal students study topics other than Native Studies, other departments must also include Native Studies in their curriculum and support the influx of Aboriginal students with services including increased budgetary allocations to scholarships, libraries and computer labs. It is important to promote Native Studies: academic credibility and collegiality; and also to promote interdisciplinary linkages. Virtually all departments should consider Aboriginal issues as part of their canon. Faculties must review cross-listing courses, thereby encouraging more students to take Native Studies material at a minimal institutional cost. Additionally, because of its multidisciplinary nature, many Native Studies faculty are well qualified to teach in other departments. Where this is of mutual interest and where sufficient replacement resources allow, such exchanges would be beneficial for all parties. Aboriginal researchers and researchers focussed on Aboriginal perspectives must be hired in all departments. Native Studies graduate programs need support from all faculties. As more students emerge with undergraduate degrees in Native Studies, there is a larger contingent looking for graduate opportunities in this field. Graduate courses and students lend to the credibility and profile of departments. They attract more funding. They are especially rewarding to faculty; indeed, the opportunity to work with graduates is an inducement in faculty recruitment.

Conclusion

We intellectuals who labour in the ivory towers are privileged by virtue of our education, profession, and our economic class. We who are located in disciplines that are a response to oppression also bear the burden of responsibility in ways that other academics may not. That is, we are called upon to use our measure of success in service of the continuing struggle for legitimacy and justice. "One task of the intellectual is the effort to break down the stereotypes and reductive categories that are so limiting to human thought and communication" (Said 1994:xi).

The impulse that brought many of us into the ivory towers is grounded in an analysis of political, social and economic injustice, as much as it is grounded in our love of intellectual life. That is, we are inherently political.

Yet, we are also academics. We are fiercely protective of our autonomy and our obligation to be critical thinkers at all times. We cannot become propagandists for any movement. We cannot be owned by organisations or constituencies. We have a role to play in resisting oppression; in theorizing its origins and demonstrating its effects; and in constructing alternatives. However, we must always be reflective and internally critical:

> Loyalty to the group's fight for survival cannot draw in the intellectual so far as to narcotize the critical sense, or reduce its imperatives, which are always to go beyond survival to questions of political liberation, to critiques of the leadership, to presenting alternatives that are too often marginalized or pushed aside as irrelevant to the main battle at hand. (Said 1994:41)

It is important for us to build relationships with the media, with social movements, with high schools, with Aboriginal organizations, and with scholarly communities. In doing so we raise the profile of our departments and increase the legitimacy of the discipline of Native Studies. We provide information to many communities. We counter the disinformation that has been propagated about Aboriginal people. We create the conditions for mutual recognition and respect among the different elements of Canadian society. We strengthen our discipline, other disciplines, and ultimately, we will become part of that foundation of knowledge that we know as the canon.

References

Green, J. 1995. Towards a detente with history: Confronting Canada's colonial legacy. *International Journal of Canadian Studies 12*(Fall):85-105.

LaRocque, E. 1996. The colonization of a Native woman scholar. In C. Miller and P. Chuchryk (Eds.) *Women of the First Nations: Power, Wisdom and Strength* pp. 11-18. Winnipeg: University of Manitoba Press.

LaRocque, E. 1999. *Native Writers Resisting Colonizing Practices in Canadian Historiography and Literature.* Unpublished doctoral dissertation, Program of Interdisciplinary Studies, University of Manitoba.

Memmi, A. 1965. *The Colonizer and the Colonized* (Trans. Howard Greenfield). Boston: Beacon Press.

Said, E. 1993. *Culture and Imperialism.* New York: Vintage Books, Random House.

Said, E. 1994. *Representations of the Intellectual.* New York: Vintage Books, Random House.

University of Manitoba Task Force. 1998. Building on strengths. *Task Force Report.* Winnipeg: U of MB.

Vickers, J. 1997. *Reinventing Political Science: A Feminist Approach.* Halifax: Fernwood.

---

[1]   Joyce Green (Ph.D.) is an Associate Professor in the Department of Political Science at the University of Regina.

Long Way From Home

Emma LaRocque[1]

I've walked these hallways
a long time now
hallways held up by
stale smoke
thoughts

I've walked these hallways
a long time now
hallways pallored by
ivory-coloured
thoughts

I've walked these hallways
for a long time now
hallways without windows
no way to feel the wind
no way to touch the earth
no way to see

I've walked these hallways
a long time now
every September closed doors
stand at attention
like soldiers
guarding fellow inmates
guarding footnotes
guarding biases

as I walk by

I do my footnotes so well
nobody knows where I come from
hallways without sun
the ologists can't see
they count mainstreet
bodies behind bars

they put *Ama*'s moose bones
behind glass
they tell savage stories
in anthropology Cree

My fellow inmates
they past us prehistoric
standing in front of us
as if I am not there too
as if I wouldn't know
what they think they show
showing what they don't know
they don't know what they show
they take my Cree for their PhD's
like Le Bank
as my *Bapa* would say
they take our money for their pay

When I first came to these hallways
I was young and dreaming
to make a difference
thinking truth

With footnotes pen paper
chalk blackboard
I tried to put faces
behind cigar store glazes
I tried to put names
behind the stats
of us brown people
us
us brown people
in jails
in offices
in graveyards
in living rooms
but to them it was
just Native biases

I've walked these hallways
a long time now

hallways hallowed by
ivory-towered bents
way too long now

hallways whitewashed with
committee meetings memos
promotion procedures
as fair as war
pitting brown against colonized brown
choosing pretend Indians

When I first came to these hallways
I was young and dreaming
to make a difference

but only time has passed
taking my *Ama* and *Bapa*
my *Nhisis* my *Nokom*
my blueberry hills

I've walked these hallways
a long time now
I wanna go home now
I'm tired of thinking for others
who don't wanna hear anyways

I wanna go home now
I want to see the evening stars
get together for a dance
the northern light way
like *Ama*'s red river jig
I want to see the sun rise
hot orange pink
like *Bapa*'s daybreak fire

no one could see the morning come
as my *Bapa*
no one could scurry in the stars
as my *Ama*

I wanna go home now

but where is home now?

I do my footnotes so well
nobody knows where I come from
my relatives think
I've made it
they don't know
how long I've walked these hallways
my feet hurt
at 43
I wanna play hookey
but I can't
I have credit cards to pay
footnotes to colonize
My relatives think
I've made it
they don't know
who all owns me
they won't lend me money
from their UIC's
my relatives laugh.

Oh I did my footnotes so well
nobody knows where I come from

I've walked these hallways
with them a long time now
and still they don't see
the earth gives eyes
injustice gives rage
now I'm standing here
prehistoric and all
pulling out their fenceposts of civilization
one by one
calling names in Cree
bringing down their *mooneow* hills
in English too
this is home now.

[1]   Emma LaRocque (PhD) is internationally known for her Aboriginal literature. This work is reprinted with permission from *ARIEL: A Review of International English Literature 25(1)*.

Community Participation in Health Research Ethics

Joseph Kaufert, Laura Commanda, Brenda Elias,
Roda Grey, Barney Masuzumi, Kue Young[1]

Abstract

This paper summarizes some of the fundamental issues involved in ensuring the representation of the community within the ethical review of research as they were discussed at an international workshop on "Ethical Issues in Health Research among Circumpolar Indigenous Peoples" held in Inuvik 1995. The participants included representatives of Canadian regional Aboriginal organizations and First Nations and representatives from Canadian universities, research councils and the circumpolar health research community.

Introduction

Current debates over the ethics of research in Aboriginal Canadians and other indigenous communities emphasizes the need for a re-examination of the ethical contracts made between researchers, individual research participants and communities or other collectivities. This paper summarizes some of the fundamental issues involved in ensuring the representation of the community within the ethical review of research as they were discussed at an international workshop on "Ethical Issues in Health Research among Circumpolar Indigenous Peoples" held in Inuvik 1995 (Young 1995). The participants included representatives of Canadian regional Aboriginal organizations, universities, research councils and the circumpolar health research community. The workshop was held to initiate a dialogue between the health research community and indigenous peoples' organizations in the circumpolar nations. Initially, planners anticipated that workshop participants might draft a set of guidelines for health research ethics relevant to Aboriginal and circumpolar peoples, participating research agencies and circumpolar nations. Instead, the meeting served as a forum in which Aboriginal and circumpolar indigenous leaders expressed their opposition to power relationships inherent in previous biomedical and population health research and explored alternative models for balancing research participation.

In the four years since the Inuvik workshop several of the participants have followed up the initial discussions working in informal networks and participating in forums, such as the Tenth International Congress on Circumpolar Health in 1996 and a 1999 workshop exploring ethical issues in the conduct of genetic research in Aboriginal communities. The Inuvik meetings anticipated the attempts of research councils to incorporate the rights of collectivities into research ethics guidelines and identified barriers to co-participation and alternative methods for representing communities and Aboriginal organizations.

Themes and Processes

Researchers and community spokespersons attending the workshop discussed the ethical, methodological and political importance of incorporating cultural values and contemporary political perspectives of Aboriginal communities into the research review process by adopting some of basic principles of participatory research. The major themes in this discussion included: (a) frameworks for protecting and balancing the rights of individuals and the rights of communities; (b) approaches to defining communities; (c) fair representation of alternative stakeholder groups within communities; (d) importance of equal participation of researchers and communities in establishing research priorities; (e) methods of obtaining informed consent at the individual and community levels; (f) problems of assuring confidentiality and protecting the identity of the community; and (g) proposals for protecting communities from risks associated with the research process.

Discussions of the relationships between researchers and Aboriginal communities focussed on the importance of developing a more participatory research process in which both sides would work together on: (a) defining research problems and obtaining funding; (b) training and involving community members in data collection; (c) ensuring the participation of community members and organizations in the analysis and interpretation of research findings; and (d) developing joint controls over the dissemination of results.

Policy Context

The workshop incorporated work on research ethics contributed to by indigenous organizations in Canada, the United States and Australia, including the following documents distributed to participants prior to the meeting: *Dené Tracking: A Participatory Research Process for Dené/Métis Communities,* (Masuzumi and Quirk 1993), the Inuit Tapirisat's *Negotiating Research Relationships in the North* (Inuit Tapirisat of Canada 1993) and the *Ethical Guidelines for Research* adopted by the Royal Commission on Aboriginal Peoples (RCAP 1993). *The Code of Research Ethics* developed by the Kahnawake School Diabetes Prevention Project in 1997 has provided a model for negotiating locally tailored guidelines (KSDPP, 1997). The First Nations and Inuit Regional Health Survey Code of Research Ethics (1997) provided guidelines which balanced local, regional and national interests on ownership, control and access (OCA) to health informants (Tri-Council Working Group 1996). These codes provided standards and process models for evaluating the ethical relationships with communities which sponsor research.

Speakers at Inuvik focused on the problem of reconciling research questions and scientific knowledge frameworks with 'local knowledge' of indigenous communities, noting that conventional ethical guidelines do not engage this issue. They emphasized that local and traditional knowledge is constructed differently than biomedical knowledge. Transmission of traditional or local knowledge is largely done through listening, experience and incorporation of information into oral tradition (Legat *et al.* 1991). Initiatives to assist investigators to understand more generalized Aboriginal knowledge and more specific local knowledge required that the researcher direct not only intellectual, but also spiritual and environmental awareness. Speakers emphasized that the research ethics review process must both engage and treat as valid both forms of knowledge in evaluating the risks and benefits of proposed research.

Research Ethics Review

Critics of current Canadian systems for reviewing the ethical dimension of a research project noted at Inuvik that the responsibility in health research is usually assigned to university-based human subjects committees. These committees usually have no first hand knowledge of local conditions, local needs or priorities. Several speakers commented that central scientific and ethical review processes have limited capacity to assess the potential local relevance of the research product. The scientific contribution of the research to applied and basic science knowledge is also seldom communicated to individual participants or to the community. Speakers at the Inuvik Workshop discussed the perception of research at the community level, suggesting that most projects are seen as having little local relevance. They suggested that much of the social science, health, and natural science research conducted in Aboriginal communities since 1945 was seen locally as not meeting community needs or contributing knowledge relevant to community development (Nahanni 1993). They proposed that the central criteria for accessing distribution of risks and benefits of research conducted in communities should be "whose interest does the research serve". In her plenary address, Martha Flaherty, President of Pauktuutit (Inuit Women's Association), laid out the policy context for the ensuing discussions of the impact of research on issues of local autonomy, scientific hegemony, and geopolitical interests and the need for equal participation in all phases of the research process:

> Real participatory research must include Inuit control over the identification of areas and issues where research is needed and the design and delivery of the methodology. Inuit would participate in the collection and analysis of data and have equal control over the dissemination of the information and research findings. In my view, anything less is not participatory and it is unfair to call it such. (Flaherty 1995)

Flaherty emphasized that health researchers must re-examine the boundaries between themselves and the communities in which they work. This will require rethinking accepted ways of doing scientific research and adoption of new models of participation which more fully meet the needs of indigenous people everywhere (Elias and O'Neil 1995).

Applying Ethical Principles

The importance of differentiating between ethical agreements with individual research participants and agreements with communities was a recurrent theme at the Inuvik workshop. A framework for examining core values in individual and community-based research ethics developed by William Freeman provided a model for participants to discuss the problems of transferring primary principles (such as autonomy, beneficence, consent or distributive justice) from the analysis of individual ethical protection to the challenges of protecting communities (First Nations and Inuit Regional Health 1997). For example in both clinical and research ethics, maximizing individual autonomy is presented as a fundamental principle providing the rational for informed consent agreements, and protocols for maintaining anonymity and confidentiality (First Nations and Inuit Regional Health 1997). In criticizing the application of the autonomy principle at community level several workshop participants noted that most health researchers are concerned primarily with the protection of the individual subject through the use of detailed individual consent agreements. At Inuvik representatives of regional Aboriginal organizations stated that they wanted greater emphasis to be laid on consent at the level of the community as a whole. One of the concerns voiced in relation to reliance on external ethical review committees (REBS) was their lack of a local knowledge base, which limited their capacity to judge whether the process used to obtain community consent was meaningful in local terms.

Informed Consent: the Community and the Individual

Freeman's proposals for negotiating meaningful consent agreements provided a focus for discussion of consent at Inuvik (Freeman 1993). Several spokespersons for Aboriginal organizations argued that the researcher must first secure the consent of the community before moving to obtain consent from individual subjects. They also emphasized the importance of researchers committing time and resources to explaining the risks and benefits of the proposed research initiatives. This process must occur without oversimplification of real risks and benefits and must be made using a format which is culturally and linguistically accessible. It was suggested that if participants are to have access to full information, then all objectives and options, including non-participation, "had to be presented in an accessible format; including oral presentation in community forums, videotapes and documentation printed in Aboriginal languages" (Freeman 1993). The requirements for valid consent agreements usually include: (a) demonstration of subject competence; (b) communication of full information on risks and benefits; (c) assurance that the subject comprehended the information; and (d) guarantees that the individual is able to act independently (Freeman 1994).

Participants endorsed Freeman's proposal that consent forms be brief, comprehensive, clear, easily readable and provide contextual information on the problem and proposed intervention (Freeman 1993). Participants emphasized that research objectives must also be stated in the context of local knowledge because generic references to benefits involving advancing basic science knowledge were not easily interpreted by individuals or community members. Several speakers supported Freeman's suggestion that consent agreements be presented in a more interactive format where the written document provides the script for face to face discussions between potential volunteers and researchers. Consent agreements may need to use alternative media formats including video clips, community meetings and community radio.

Who Speaks for the Community?

Participants at the small group sessions at the Inuvik workshop discussed the process of reaching and representing the full spectrum of community stakeholders. Representatives of Aboriginal organizations commented that community leaders involved in making decisions about research access might not be the ones most affected by a particular research intervention. They also discussed the problems which arise when significant stakeholder groups (such as women or people without treaty status) are disenfranchised from full community participation. Examples were raised of communities in which men dominate decision-making, or in which the elders are not appropriately represented, or where decision-making is controlled by an unrepresentative leader who does not represent the interests of the community or individual constituents effectively.

Although community consent is separate from individual consent, conflicting decisions might be made at individual and community levels. In some cases principles emphasizing individual autonomy may conflict with criteria defining the benefit to the community. Bioethical decision frameworks emphasize maintaining the autonomy of the "unique self" and therefore enshrine, through use of consent agreements where the rights of the individual are weighed as being more "fundamental" than those of the community. However, despite the autonomy principal several participants stated that the rights of individual and the shared interest of the community might be weighted differently in Aboriginal communities.

Participatory Frameworks

Discussion of the emergence of participatory research frameworks, in Aboriginal health research also emphasized the notion of consent as a 'process'. A consent agreement with individuals and communities, negotiated at a single point in time assumes a relatively static relationship between the researcher and the research subject. Speakers commented that negotiation of consent should not be regarded as a single event, but as a process extending from the formulation of the research protocol, through the processes of data collection, interpretation and dissemination of final results. While agreeing on the importance of legal criteria, participants in the workshop wanted these conditions to be achieved by using alternative frameworks and decision-models, such as the Dené/Métis Model Agreement. These models emphasizing participatory research processes were preferred because they defined consent as a mutual contract. This framework was also presented as a more appropriate mechanism for protecting the rights of Aboriginal communities.

Assessment of Risk and Benefit

The introductory session on ethical criteria in health research emphasized that the principles of beneficence and non-maleficence are usually applied to the researchers' relationship with the individual research subjects. For example, ethical review involves application of risk/benefit criteria often are seen as the primary mechanisms for evaluation of beneficence (the obligation to do good) and non-maleficence (the obligation to minimize harm to the subject). Participants in the Inuvik meeting discussed the applying the principles of beneficence and non-maleficence to development of ethical relationships with Aboriginal communities and First Nations. Participants emphasized that the community may be harmed by data which represents only negative dimensions of health status and associated 'social problems' in community research.

Participants from First Nation's communities criticized conventional approaches to explaining the risks and benefits of research to the community emphasizing biomedical concepts. Several health researchers defended research which did not have direct benefit, but produced basic scientific knowledge. Representatives of Aboriginal organizations emphasized that the wider benefits of basic science knowledge were seldom effectively communicated to participants and community leaders. Other speakers emphasized that the biomedical notion of research contracts between mutually trusting and mutually benefitting co-participants were difficult to sustain "when researchers 'parachuted' into a community, collected their data and flew out."

Population health research was also identified as a source of potential risk to individuals and communities. Projects which utilize secondary data from medical records, electronic databases or biological samples collected in the past are often less visible and may escape community oversight. Ethical review of research programs using secondary data is completed by university-based human subject committees which have minimal knowledge of or contact with communities or First Nations. William Freeman described the new protocols being utilized by the Institutional Review Boards of the Indian Health Service, requiring renewal of individual and community consent agreements for research involving access to previously collected data and biological specimens. Other speakers felt that similar agreements requiring individual and community consent should also be developed for other research utilizing data collected for clinical health information systems.

Community Benefits and Distributive Justice

The application of principle of justice in the conduct of community health research evoked significant debate at the Inuvik conference. At the level of the individual, discussions focussed on the specific mechanisms for protecting individual subjects from more powerful researchers and clinicians. Several speakers indicated that participants in health research in northern communities often felt dependent on clinician/researchers because they needed clinical care. Many perceived that refusal to participate in research might have negative impact on people's access to health services. Both individuals and communities lacked awareness of participants' rights. Several speakers pointed to the need for special protection of individuals and communities who were perceived at being at high risk. Participants admonished community leaders to accept the responsibility of protecting their members against high-risk research.

Community Participation in the Research Process

Participants in Inuvik workshop emphasized the need for guidelines which define rights and obligations at both the individual and community levels. The rights of First Nations communities to define research priorities, to be involved in ethical review and ultimately control access was emphasized by the Honorable Nellie Cournoyea, who was Premier of the Northwest

Territories, and Martha Flaherty, who was President of the Inuit Women's' Association in their plenary addresses. Both speakers referred to the sovereignty of First Nations and Inuit communities and emphasized that those involved in research relationships with Aboriginal communities must recognize the legal implications of treaty agreements and contemporary research contracts.

In addressing the issue of community control of health research within the context of Aboriginal communities, participants conceded that the problems of evaluating the ethical dimension of community health research necessitated defining "the community in terms of shared identity, culture and political boundaries". A common point made by participants was that members of a community have an awareness of belonging to an entity which is separate and distinct from their identity as individuals. However, several speakers also acknowledged that there were different definitions of community among urban Aboriginal populations, communities without treaty status, First Nations and Inuit communities.

Speakers at the Inuvik conference addressed the question of who represents the interests of the community. They recommended that ethics committees and funding agencies be asked to require evidence that leadership represented the interests of most individuals in a community or collectivity. They also recommended that processes be developed to ensure that the interests of all stakeholder groups within a community were fairly represented.

Participants at the Inuvik workshop also discussed the impact of the current organizational structure of the system of human subjects review for health research in Canada. Several participants in the Inuvik workshop emphasized that ethical review of health research was currently centered in university-based human subjects committees and monitored by academic research councils. In these forums, the perspectives of individual communities and First Nations governments were seldom adequately represented. Ethics committees and funding bodies customarily determine whether the rights of individuals and communities are adequately protected by reviewing consent agreement and documentation from community councils or regional Aboriginal organizations. Human subjects committees in universities often lack a clear-cut definition of what constitutes the community or 'collectivity'. Speakers emphasized that external human subjects committees cannot access the legitimacy of local participants' claims to represent the community and often misunderstood differences in the political and geographic criteria defining membership. Several representatives of Aboriginal organizations emphasized that to be politically and socially meaningful, definitions of community used in contemporary health research must express the sense of belonging to a collectivity among members. They stated that references to communities, First Nations and other collectivities in new ethical codes must engage the realities of increasing self-determination in Aboriginal communities.

Conclusion

The Inuvik workshop provided a valuable forum for articulating First Nations and Inuit community's demands for participation in problem definition, design, fieldwork, analysis and dissemination results. It also provided researchers a forum for articulating their concerns about changing research relationships and maintenance of academic research priorities. The meetings provided a forum for the expression of the alternative perspectives of Aboriginal communities or organizations and health researchers on issues of process, ownership, benefit and control. The deliberations and contested areas of ethical oversight were not documented in published proceedings and did not result in the production of a 'model code'. Although the workshop did not produce drafts of research guidelines which reflect the priorities of Aboriginal and circumpolar peoples, it did provide a forum for participants representing First Nations, regional Aboriginal organizations, health researchers, ethicists and policy makers to identify a series of problems or issues which must be addressed to develop a more equitable and participatory framework for future research collaboration.

The longer term impacts of the Inuvik workshop on "Ethical Issues in Health Research among Circumpolar Indigenous Peoples" are visible in the: (a) continuing dialogue at national and international conferences focusing on research ethics and cultural property and participatory research processes; (b) development of informal networks of Aboriginal researchers, organizational representatives and ethicists; and (c) attempts to acknowledge the unique perspectives of First Nations and other Aboriginal communities in drafting of new research ethics guidelines in Canada.

Since 1995 many of the participants in the Inuvik workshop have continued the discussion of the rights of Aboriginal people as individuals, First Nations and other collectivities in reviewing the ethical dimension of health research at scientific meetings, such as 10th Circumpolar Health Conference in Anchorage, Alaska in 1996 and at more focused North American meetings dealing with specific ethical

60

problems in genetic research. In addition many of the participants have continued to work in networks to convene a follow-up meeting, organized and sponsored by Aboriginal organizations and researchers. The objective of the follow-up meeting would be to develop structures and processes within First Nations and Aboriginal regional organizations for ethical and community impact assessment. Finally, the concept of the collective rights of First Nations and communities were engaged in the first two working drafts of Canadian Tri-Council Policy Statement (1994, 1996, 1998, Asch 1994).

The final draft of the statement *Ethical Conduct for Research Involving Humans* describing the policies of the Medical Research Council (MRC), the National Sciences and Engineering Research Council (NSERC) and the Social Sciences and Humanities Research Council (SSHRC) included Section 6 "Research Involving Aboriginal Peoples" (Raynolds 1979). However, this section of the document did not include specific provisions related to the rights of Aboriginal peoples and stated that the Councils had not held sufficient discussion with representatives of affected peoples or groups, or with various organizations or researchers involved. Continuation of the process begun at the Inuvik workshop may be one mechanism for developing guidelines acknowledging the role communities and First Nations using a participatory framework.

References

Asch, M. 1994. *A Report on Guidelines Respecting Research with Collectivities to the Tri-council Working Group.* Edmonton: Depart. of Anthropology, University of Alberta.

Elias B. and O'Neil, J. 1995. *A study into the Social, Cultural, and Disciplinary Understanding of Risk Perception and Risk Acceptability of Contaminants in the Canadian Arctic.* Arctic Environmental Strategy Contaminants Program, Indian and Northern Affairs Canada. Northern Health Research Unit, University of Manitoba, June.

First Nations and Inuit Regional Health Survey National Steering Committee. 1997 Akwesasane Mohawk Territory. In *First Nations and Inuit Regional Health Survey National Report* pp. A55-A60). Ottawa.

Flaherty, M. 1995. Address to International Workshop on Ethical Issues in Health Research among Circumpolar Indigenous Populations, Inuvik, June 2

Freeman, W. 1993. Research in rural Native communities. In M. Bass, E. Dunn, P. Norton, M. Stewart, F. Tudiver (Eds.) *Conducting Research in the Practice Setting* (pp 179-196). Newbury Park, CA: Sage Publications.

Freeman W. 1994. Making research consent forms informative and understandable: The experience of the Indian health service. *Cambridge Quarterly* *of Healthcare Ethics 3:*510-521.

Inuit Tapirisat of Canada, 1993. Negotiating research relationships in the north. *Background paper for the Workshop on Guidelines for Responsible Research, Yellowknife, September 22-23, 1993.*

KSDPP (Kahnawake Schools Diabetes Prevention Project). 1997. *Code of Research Ethics.* Kateri Memorial Health Centre, Kahnawake Territory, Mohawk Nations, via Quebec.

Legat, A. *et al.* 1991. *Report of the Traditional Knowledge Working Group: Culture and Communication.* Yellowknife, NWT: GNWT

Masuzumi, B. and Quirk., S. 1993. *Dené Tracking: A Participatory Research Process for Dené/Métis Communities: Exploring Community-based Research Concerns for Aboriginal Northerners.* Dené Cultural Institute (So'bak , Denendeh), September.

Nahanni, P. 1993. Thoughts on Aboriginal knowledge. In P. Ernerk, L. Dorais and L. Muller-Willie (Eds.) *Social Science in the North.* Keynote presented at the Eighth Inuit Studies Conference and First International Congress of Arctic Social Sciences. pp 23-29. Ste-Foy, Quebec: International Arctic Social Sciences Association.

Raynolds, P. 1979. *Ethical dilemmas. Social Science Research.* San Francisco, CA: Jossy-Bass Publications.

RCAP (Royal Commission on Aboriginal Peoples). 1993. *Integrated Research Plan.* Ottawa: RCAP.

Tri-Council Working Group. 1994. *Issues Paper.* November. Ottawa.

Tri-Council Working Group. 1996. *Code of Conduct for Research Involving Humans.* March. Ottawa.

Tri-Council Working Group. 1998. *MRC, NSERC, SSHRC. Section 6: Research involving Aboriginal peoples. Tri-Council Policy Statement: Ethical Conduct for Research Involving Humans* pp 61-64. Ottawa.

Young, K. 1995. International workshop on ethical issues in health research among circumpolar indigenous population. *Northline 2.*

---

[1] Joseph Kaufert (Ph.D.), Medical Services Branch, Health Canada; Laura Commanda, Inuit Tapirisat of Canada; Brenda Elias, Medical Services Branch, Health Canada; Roda Grey, Consultant and Land Claims Officer, Government of Northwest Territories; Barney Masuzumi, Consultant, Dené Institute; Kue Young (Ph.D.), Medical Services Branch, Health Canada.

From the Land to the Classroom: Broadening Epistemology

Emma LaRocque[1]

Abstract

I have been teaching in Native Studies at the University of Manitoba for about 23 out of the 25 years of its existence. As a Native educator who comes from a 'traditional' culture, I take this special publication celebrating '25 Years of Excellence' in Native Studies as an opportunity to reflect on 'traditional knowledge' and its impact on Native Studies and scholarship.

Introduction

As an Aboriginal scholar who has long worked within the university system and liberal arts program, I have been taking keen interest in the recent but rapidly growing research and debate on Indigenous 'traditional ecological knowledge' (TEK). So far, much of the discussion revolves around Traditional Knowledge (TK) with respect to environmental concerns and resource management, with some attempts to clarify the relationship between western science and TK. As a researcher in Canadian historiography and contemporary Native literature, I am interested in the fact that there is now finally some concession by western scientists and researchers that Aboriginal peoples' knowledge, both in fundamentals and practice, is coherent and valuable. Though this may be cause for some celebration for those of us who have long advanced or modelled such a view, certain characterizations of 'traditional ecological knowledge' indicate the limited extent to which Aboriginal knowledge is applied. This paper will generate thoughts on broadening the application of critical Aboriginal epistemology.

There are a number of challenges which confront those of us who are applying Aboriginal epistemology in areas of study or teaching which concentrate on what may be called, for lack of more appropriate terminology, pure intellectual work rather than field research. In addition to the philosophical demands of combining Western and Aboriginal epistemologies, certain associations of 'traditional knowledge' with field research and the Aboriginal 'community' are posing political problems for Aboriginal scholars. I begin with prevailing notions of 'traditional knowledge'.

Defining 'Traditional' Knowledge

TK is largely profiled as 'holistic' land-based knowledge transmitted by the elders through oral Native language and praxis (Colorado 1988, Johnson 1992, Stevenson 1992, Berkes 1993, Gadgil *et al.* 1993, Emery and Associates 1997, Simpson 1999). Hoare *et al.* (1993) provide a fairly typical definition of 'indigenous knowledge' as:

> [T]hc culmination of generations of experience and insight passed down through oral tradition. This knowledge was holistic in nature incorporating spiritual, ecological, human and social experiences into one understanding of Native peoples' place in the universe. (48)

Hoare *et al.* (1993) note that TK is "built on observation, experience and reflection, while its teachings are grounded in the natural world"(48). Invariably, attempts to define TK has lead to valuative comparisons between Traditional Ecological Knowledge (TEK) and Western Science (Colorado 1988, Johnson 1992, Berkes 1993).

While we can appreciate that these are attempts to clarify and even validate 'traditional' knowledge, there are some potential problems and stereotypes with these treatments. With respect to Aboriginal peoples in the United States and Canada, stereotypic images of 'the Indian' (Berkhofer 1978, Doxtator 1992, Francis 1992, LaRocque 1999) have informed many of the notions associated with 'traditional knowledge'. For example, for lack of more precise translations, or research, we have in modern times generalized Native cultures as 'intuitive', 'spiritual', 'qualitative', 'moral' and 'holistic' but these are descriptions subject to oversimplification, particularly in treatments which trait-list Western and Native cultural characteristics (Stevenson 1992, Berkes 1993, Emery and Associates 1997). Charting Native cultural traits in juxtaposition to

Western ones has become deeply embedded in current social and even academic thinking. I have long had serious concerns with this and have recently called for its re-examination in criminal justice applications (LaRocque 1996, 1997), and in literary criticism of contemporary Native literature (LaRocque 1999). Such a re-examination is needed in TK studies but I do not go into a detailed analysis here.

Of course, understanding and treatment of TK is rapidly expanding. Researchers continue to discover that the holistic world view is by no means simple or merely mystical. Aboriginal practitioners of the land do pay exquisite attention to detail (Warry 1990, Ryan and Robinson 1990, Reimer 1993, McDonald et al. 1997), and their spirituality is intrinsic to strategic applications of cultural knowledge with respect to resource use (Riddington 1982, Feit 1986, Colorado 1988, Johnson 1992). It is just that they have used a different 'language' in these developments.

There is certainly a growing appreciation that Native knowledge systems are way more sophisticated, coherent and systematic than heretofore recognized (Colorado 1988, Johnson 1992, Berkes and Henley 1997, McDonald et al. 1997, Simpson 1999). The extent to which Indigenous cultures and peoples of the Americas have contributed to world knowledge, not to mention, to European prosperity, is explored, for example, by anthropologist Weatherford (1988). There is also growing concession that Western Science needs the Aboriginal perspective, approach and knowledge (Knudtson and Suzuki 1992, Gadgil et al. 1993). Nonetheless, it remains that Aboriginal knowledge is still largely limited to 'traditional' and ecological knowledge.

Grounding Aboriginal Knowledge

With some exception (Colorado 1988, Johnson 1992, Stevenson 1992, Simpson 1999), TK theorists have, by inference, treated 'traditional' knowledge not only as the sum total of Aboriginal knowledge but as dying. Indeed, some have pointed to a 'crisis of knowledge' as elders are passing away. Within a certain context, perhaps such concerns may be valid. "It is undoubtedly true that some erosion of TEK has taken place. However, both the research of social scientists and indigenous peoples themselves confirm the continued vitality of their cultures and note that TEK is changing or evolving rather than dying" (Johnson 1992:4). But the call to urgently retrieve and record TEK is reminiscent of the 'Vanishing Indian' line of thought, a well-travelled theme of the perpetually dying

Indian (Francis 1992). This is the view which confines Native peoples and cultures to the typologyzed static 'traditional' culture (a view challenged in LaRocque 1975). In contrast, Western culture is somehow inherently progressive. By definition, Native culture is condemned to die since anything it does is 'traditional', while, by definition, western culture can never die since anything it does constitutes 'progress'. This line of thinking continues to plague not only the study but the very identity of contemporary Native peoples.

In so far as Aboriginal world view is tied to the land and its resources, its basis and collection of knowledge is fundamentally tied to the land. This quite literally grounds Aboriginal knowledge. While this should provide some explanation to non-Native Canadians why it is that the land base is so vital to Aboriginal peoples (the significance of space and place cannot be overemphasized here), it does present us with some significant problems. The implications should be unsettling: if Aboriginal knowledge is confined to non-industrial use of land or language, 'tradition' and 'elders' obviously, it is condemned to limited use and a certain demise! Questions arise as to the wider application and life span of Aboriginal knowledge.

What room is there for contemporary Aboriginal knowledge in all this? This question demands much greater attention than I can give it here. There are many important issues bearing on realities of colonization and decolonization as well as notions of change and tradition within Aboriginal thinking and practice. The fact of change in Aboriginal cultures is a complex thing. Native peoples have experienced forced change through colonization, yet at different times and phases, they have engaged in cultural exchange as peoples with an evolving culture. While it is possible to trace various colonial forces such as the Indian Act, residential schools, and so forth, it is more difficult to discern all the crucial cultural spaces from which Native peoples have freely acted. The fact is, Native knowledge is being transmitted from generation to generation in Native cultures. Aside from the problem of defining 'eldership', it is not only 'elders' who do the teaching in Native homes and communities. Consequently, it is not only 'elders' who have 'traditional' knowledge. Many younger people also have 'traditional' knowledge in terms of their relationships to ecology and in terms of their world views, languages, and land-based expertise.

But is this all there is to Aboriginal knowledge, that is, that it can only be practised 'traditionally' on the land, whether 500 years ago or today? What about all the knowledge and experience gained over the last 500 years? What about Native persons who live modern lives both on the land or in cities? For example, my brother who is in his early 40s not only knows, practices and lives a land-based (Cree-Metis) way of life, he also knows and practices contemporary languages and skills. He has not suffered from cultural dislocation in his process of translating ancient knowledge into contemporary meaning. Then there are those who live in cities and have jobs such as teaching in mainstream Canadian classrooms. We practice contemporary languages and skills, yet carry within us and continue to transmit our languages, oral literatures and land-based ways. Many of us also have close connections to the land or to those in our communities who chose to stay and keep on living off the land (as much as is feasible). Like my brother, we too are translating 'traditional' knowledge into contemporary meaning without suffering any necessary cultural dislocation.

Among other things, if Native peoples have not moved into industrial centers, the industrial has long moved into their worlds. As one who grew up in the bush (with all that this implies in terms of ecological cultural knowledge and practice) complete with gardens, clocks, radios, steel tools, trains, towns and schools, I often feel a time-warp when reading about 'traditional knowledge'. For the most part, as their parents before them, my parents and their generation of hunters and trappers integrated non-industrial and industrial worlds quite comfortably, as long as they had a resource base and choice to exercise their cultural knowledge. In many respects, ideas on 'traditional knowledge' today are both primitivist and eclipsed, perpetuating a static version of Aboriginal cultures and peoples. This is not to mention that Native identity today cannot be confined to those with linguistic and/or land connections. Those of us who were privileged to have grown up immersed in a Native language in a land-based lifestyle are challenged to open our minds and hearts to a whole new generation of 'Aboriginals'.

Re/Constructing Aboriginal Knowledge

We face challenges we have not even thought about in our attempts to re/construct Aboriginal knowledge meaningful in today's realities. We must avoid portraying Aboriginal cultures and knowledge in that fixed romanticized sense of the treatment. The surest way to freeze any culture is to package it in a formulaic container of traits. The ossification of Native cultures is a real concern to those of us who must struggle to get a hearing as contemporary Native peoples, both on the lands and in the classrooms. There is every historical and anthropological evidence Aboriginal cultures of the Americas were and are dynamic (Weatherford 1988, Dickason 1992,

Morrison and Wilson 1995). What will keep Aboriginal knowledge vibrant and meaningful is our ability to translate it into contemporary terms from generation to generation.

Colonization has disturbed Native cultural development and decolonization will enable Native cultures and peoples to carry on into future generations. As long as Native peoples have self-determination and as long as they have the ground and means of "doing things together" (Puxley 1977: 111), they have the potential to exercise and translate 'old' Native science into meaningful modern terms. Our ground of knowledge and experience must include our contemporary realities. We must recover that which is dynamic and inherently portable in Aboriginal epistemologies. Even though Native peoples have suffered from colonial shock, they have displayed remarkable cultural resilience. My idea of colonial shock is perhaps best understood as a response to 'collective trauma' (Shkilnyk 1985) experienced under sustained colonial assaults. For far too long such trauma has been mistaken or whitewashed as mere 'culture shock', suggesting that there was something innately weak about 'traditional' cultures. It is imperative we locate the root of the issue in our discussions of Native cultural changes and responses. Adaptive strategies should not be mistaken for total assimilation. I believe the greatest strength of the Aboriginal *weltanschauung* is its ethical basis (Deloria 1973, Cardinal 1977, Colorado 1988, Soui 1996). Native knowledge is informed by an ethical and spiritual basis which is intimately linked with Aboriginal people's relationship with each other, and with the land and its resources.

The ethical basis and the ethos of Aboriginal epistemologies have sustained cultural survival. The more obvious ways we 'carry' our cultures are through our languages, upbringing and training, but we also carry our world views in infinitely subtle ways. All these ways are expressed in our contemporary epistemologies. This means that our bases and approaches to knowledge, and to the gathering, use and dissemination or teaching of knowledge may be quite different from Western conventions. These differences though are much more complex, profound and potentially reconstructive than any cultural typologies which have become current in comparisons between Aboriginal and Western ways of knowing. Equally, it must be emphasized that though our epistemological bases may be 'different', both systems require "thoughtful and systematic observation" (Johnson 1992:3), and "rigour, reliability and validity" (Colorado 1988:51). There are important meeting points between Western and Aboriginal systems, if only they were not clouded by political inequalities.

Much like my parents but in a different context, of course, I have integrated western and Aboriginal knowledge systems. But I did not always have a language to frame what I have modelled as a contemporary Native educator. The relatively recent surge of interest and research on TK has been an affirming addition to my work of revisiting Aboriginal and colonial languages in a post-colonial world. Throughout the years, I have come to identify and 'name' key elements of both Aboriginality and coloniality in the way that I teach and pursue knowledge and research. A post-colonial Aboriginal epistemology necessarily entails deconstruction and reconstruction. For Aboriginal scholars, it has meant, among other things, dismantling stereotypes and uncovering the covert but dominant narrative in western scholarship. For me, this has entailed actually modelling the use of overt voice. I not only teach students to become critically aware of the numerous techniques of impartiality in western history and literature, I do not remain distant or alienated from both my research and my community of origin. As a matter of principle, I have avoided aloofness and mystification of English (both often mistaken for objectivity and height of scholarship) in the classroom or in my writing. And of course, the Native perspective and experience necessarily provides the hub in the wheel of our teaching in the field of Native Studies. In ways beyond words, we have been advancing the legitimation of Indigenous knowledge.

TK and Native Studies

But there is a marked difference between the ways our knowledge is received and the ways 'traditional knowledge' provided by 'elders' is being received. The characterization of TK has created a hierarchy (not to mention, a stereotype) of Aboriginal knowledge with 'elders' and 'traditional knowledge' on top and academic and contemporary knowledge on the bottom. How TK is conceived and priorized does not always or universally bring happy results to either Native Studies or to Native scholars.

In a number of respects, 'Native Studies' is currently in the process of being segregated. It is an irony that as appreciation for 'traditional' knowledge is gaining, the process is marginalizing Aboriginal scholarship to TEK, PAR, linguistics and legends, spirituality and healing and 'community'. This does not bode well for Aboriginal scholars who do not adopt a language identified with 'traditional knowledge', or whose work is centrally intellectual and whose disciplines are in the arts and humanities. Such scholars may find their perspectives and work questioned. They may be criticized for not having an 'Aboriginal perspective', making them vulnerable to politically-motivated opinion and ideological control.

There is also the new political pressure for scholars to have their research and findings go through scrutiny and authentication by Aboriginal communities. I note that university funding agencies are moving in this direction as well. I fully support Native control of cultural knowledge and resources for those engaged in field research in Native territories. Because unequal power relations exist between western scientists/agencies and communities, Native peoples have every reason to be vigilant in protecting their lands as well as their cultural and intellectual properties. Ethical guidelines for responsible research are being developed (Colorado 1988, Berkes 1993, Masuzumi and Quirk 1993, Reimer 1993, Carpenter 1993, Inuit Tapirisat of Canada 1993, Flaherty 1994, Oakes and Riewe 1996). However, I worry about the direction universities are moving concerning the application of community control in our classrooms, research and even staffing. For example, I am concerned about extending 'community' control into our hiring policies and practices in departments or programs having to do with 'Native Studies'. Over the last several years, most university and college ads for teaching or administrative jobs in Native-focused academic programs and departments stipulate that a successful candidate must have some kind of community connection or expertise. Often, the ads require that community expertise must include fund-raising capabilities. I view such requirements as part of putting pressure on Native academics and Native communities to provide their own funding or do their own fund-raising for programs that are within universities! This neatly takes financial responsibility away from universities in the guise of community support but I do not see mainstream scholars being made to do their own fund-raising for their departments. In what way is this being supportive to Native scholars who should be free to teach and pursue knowledge without having to expend time and energy around funding? The biggest concern I have, though, centers around notions and uses of 'community' which is placing an extra 'burden of proof' on Native candidates. This is especially true for those who do not do field or 'traditional' work but are otherwise perfectly qualified academics. Add to this the fact that the majority of field and TEK researchers are not Native.

The notion of 'community' is quite amorphous and certainly vulnerable to political manipulation. There are so many different cultural and interest groups within the four different Native umbrella groups (Status, non-Status, Métis, Inuit) that some measure of community identification and accountability must be put in place in our hiring procedures. Further, 'community' is increasingly limited to 'traditional knowledge', elders and spirituality, even though the Native population is culturally diverse, and increasingly young, English-speaking and urbanized (Dickason 1992, Frideres 1998). If community opinion is going to be used as a major consideration in university hiring, then we must be very clear and careful as to who and what we define as 'community'. Obviously, there are jobs which should require community expertise but should this be so in *academic-based* university departments especially within the liberal arts faculties? This question takes on a sombre significance when we see that mainstream university departments such as history, sociology, psychology, political science, english, and so forth, do not place an extra dimension of community responsibility or authentication on their scholars for their teaching positions. To put it more starkly, are mainstream non-Aboriginal scholars made to go to *their* (non-Aboriginal or 'White') communities for permission and cultural validation in order to qualify for teaching and/or administrative jobs, research grants or promotions?

The 'community' situation that faces Native academics is not the same as what faces most other Canadian intellectuals. Most Native scholars of my generation were not born into their stations, and so we as 'engaged researchers' tend to identify ourselves as part of 'the community', not estranged from it in the way mainstream intellectuals often are (LaRocque 1990, 1999). To make us prove our 'communitability' is redundant. But education is a two-edged sword for Native peoples. The irony is that my generation of Native scholars entered universities without community support. Even today Native scholarly knowledge is neither understood nor given the same respect as other kinds (traditional, elders) of knowledge in many Native communities. But as more First Nation, Métis and Inuit students enter universities, Aboriginal scholarship will take on greater significance.

What responsibilities (and to whom) do Native scholars have? Are they to be treated as mere mouthpieces of 'community' needs or belief systems? Scholars in Native Studies have "an extra-ordinary mandate" (as our Native Studies mission statement states) to reflect sensitivity to Native perspectives and experiences, and I have long advanced such a mandate, however, it cannot mean subjecting scholars to ideological or political control, or to evaluations outside of university protocol. Aboriginal scholars must have as much academic freedom and as fair treatment as our non-Aboriginal colleagues. Scholarship directs us to aspire for "that critical and relatively independent spirit of analysis and judgement ought to be the intellectual's contribution" (Said 1996:86).

Aboriginal Scholarship and the University Classroom

The effects of colonization on both white and Native scholars and scholarship in Canada is barely beginning to be investigated but it is clear that colonization affects our respective pursuits of research and theory as well as our pedagogies and ranking in academia. It is still largely the case that the "globalization of knowledge and Western culture constantly reaffirms the West's view of itself as the centre of legitimate knowledge, the arbiter of what counts as knowledge and the source of 'civilized' knowledge" (Smith 1999: 63). My observation and experience is that the university community including students, colleagues and administration has not known how to respond to or even recognize Aboriginal pedagogics within western systems, especially those which combine cultural ethos with critical analysis. Although this is in the process of changing, especially within Native Studies, we do still face resistance in the way our knowledge base and cultural information as well as our decolonized methodologies are received (LaRocque 1990, Acoose 1995, Monture-Angus 1995, Smith 1999, Green 2000).

Our teaching faces extra-ordinary challenges as well, especially for those of us engaging more in critical intellectual work than in cultural portraiture. Because we serve fairly disparate (in culture, colonial experience, economic status, educational heritage and system facilitation) student communities, and therefore, expectations, we are vulnerable to multi-pronged criticisms. Native students may require and demand culturally-appropriate pedagogies. Recently, in a class of Native adults, a number of students assuming the role of 'elders' challenged me concerning the basis of knowledge, and by implication, academic evaluation. We had an engaging discussion on legitimation of knowledge. How do we really deal with the western hegemonic canons which have a direct bearing on scholarship refashioned by non-western experience? Is academia willing to make any real changes to accommodate different knowledge systems?

Politics enters our classrooms as well when students (both Native and Non-Native) deeply conditioned to assume the universality and objectivity of the Western narrative, do not or will not understand the political nature of history, representation and epistemology. In the context of teaching English literature from a non-western view, Mukherjee (1994) reports similar experiences in her classrooms. Stereotypes about 'traditional knowledge' and how this is expected to function in 'Native Studies' or in Native instructors have played no small role in this. Schools and society have failed to prepare most students for critical and cross-cultural or multi-racial education. While White students may react to a critical treatment of Canadian history or popular culture, Native students may feel threatened by critical treatment of gender roles or spirituality, for instance. Some students may not recognize or accept Aboriginal epistemology when Aboriginal scholars use 'voice', encourage group work, encourage multidisciplinary and interdisciplinary research and perspectives, provide documentation on colonization or insist on academic excellence. Such students may resort to techniques of backlash by accusing us of bias or even reverse discrimination in their evaluations. Most evaluations in universities are based on standardized western notions and expectations. Such evaluations fail to take into account cross-cultural or multi-racial realities in classrooms. There are no culturally-appropriate evaluations. For that matter, there are no critically-appropriate type of evaluations. As a number of post-colonial scholars have pointed out (Ashcroft *et al.* 1995), there is little, if any, systemic support for non-western critical pedagogies in universities. We are directed through "sanctioned ways of writing" and "publishing in the right places" (Mukherjee 1994:xiii), and I would add, we are evaluated through sanctioned ways of thinking and teaching. Standardization, then, has direct implications in our promotions and ranking (Mukherjee 1994, Christian 1995).

Conclusion

The onus is often put on Aboriginal scholars to 'prove' themselves within (and now outside of) the academic community. After 25 years, we must now ask some tough questions in return. What have mainstream universities learned from Aboriginal scholars over the last 25 years? What have they done to not only accommodate but actually facilitate both Native Studies and Native scholars and/or scholarship? How many unsegregated Native Studies departments are there across Canada? How many Native instructors and administrators are there in these departments? How many graduate programs are there in these departments? How many Native instructors have tenured faculty ranking consistent with their publications, years of teaching, intellectual output and Aboriginal knowledge-base? Why do we not recognize Aboriginal intellectuals who not only bring western academic excellence but equally, Aboriginal epistemological excellence? We give degrees to those who fulfil western-defined programs but there are no symbols or avenues of legitimation for those Native individuals who not only go through rigorous academic training in western scholarship, but also bring with them Aboriginal ethos and knowledge systems into the classrooms. This part of our expertise is taken for granted. There are no increments for this knowledge, neither in pay nor promotions. There are some exceptions. For example, Native linguists, lawyers and Elders are gaining facilitation in academic systems.

In large part, the advancement of TK has taken place within the context of decolonization. In order for me to practice decolonization, I have had to create a discourse built on all my intellectual heritages. Resistance scholarship and the contemporarization of Aboriginal epistemology is a complex topic. In the context of Native resistance literature, I treat the discussion in some interdisciplinary (History/English) depth in my recently completed dissertation: *Native Writers Resisting Colonizing Practices in Canadian Historiography and Literature* (LaRocque 1999). As resistance Native scholars we have both a cultural and colonial experience from which to build our discourse, and this does take us to the cutting edge of what is circumscribed as 'scholarly' or as 'traditional'. The task is to create a space and place to be able to enter into the particular discourse of western thought and format without having to internalize its coloniality or to defy our personal and cultural selves. How we integrate these worlds within scholarship remains a tug of war but it is an issue about which Native scholars are in the process of forging. It is within the context of challenging the assumptions, methodologies and uses of western 'science' that traditional Aboriginal knowledge has been 'discovered' and in some fields, increasingly validated. Our contemporary Aboriginal epistemologies and educators also need to be validated. It remains for universities to recognize, in theory and in practice, our unique and substantially original contributions.

References

Acoose, J. 1995. *Iskewawek: Kah'Ki Yaw Ni Wahkomakanak.* Toronto: Women's Press.

Ashcroft, B. and Griffiths, G. and Tiffin, H. (Eds). 1995. *Post-Colonial Studies Reader.* London and New York: Routledge.

Berkes, F. 1993. Traditional Ecological Knowledge in Perspective. *Traditional Ecological Knowledge: Concepts and Cases*, J.Inglis, J. (Ed.) Ottawa: Canadian Museum of Nature.

Berkes, F. and Henley, T. 1997. Co-Management and Traditional Knowledge: Threat or Opportunity? *Policy Options* 18(2) 29-31.

Berkhofer, R. 1978. *The White Man's Indian.* New York: Random House.

Cardinal, D. 1977. *Of the Spirit.* G. Melnyk (Ed.) Edmonton: NeWest Press.

Carpenter, W. 1993. *Guidelines For Responsible Research in Northern Canada: Discussion Paper, ACUNS Conference.* October 2, Ft. Smith, NWT.

74

Christian, B. 1995. The Race For Theory. In B. Ashcroft, G. Griffiths and H. Tiffin (Eds.). *Post-Colonial Studies Reader*. London&NY: Routledge.

Colorado, P. 1988. Bridging Native and Western Science. *Converg.* 21(2/3): 49-67.

Deloria, V. 1973. *God Is Red*. New York: Dunlop.

Dickason, O. 1992. *Canada's First Nations: A History of Founding Peoples From Earliest Times*. Toronto: McClelland & Stewart.

Doxtator, D. 1992. *Fluffs and Feathers*. Brantford: Woodland Cultural Center.

Emery, A. and Associates. 1997. *Guidelines for Environmental Assessments and Traditional Knowledge*. A Report from the Centre for Traditional Knowledge. Hull, QC: Can. Int. Dev. Agency and Environment Canada.

Feit, H. 1986. Hunting and the quest for power: The James Bay Cree and whitemen in the 20th Century. In R. Morrison and C. Wilson (Eds.) *Native Peoples: The Canadian Experience*. Toronto: McClelland & Stewart.

Flaherty, M. 1994. *Freedom of Expression or Freedom of Exploitation*. Speech to the Association of Canadian Universities for Northern Studies 4th National Students' Conference on Northern Studies, Nov. 27, Ottawa.

Francis, D. 1992. *The Imaginary Indian*. Vancouver: Arsenal Pulp Press.

Frideres, J. 1998. *Aboriginal Peoples in Canada: Contemporary Conflicts*. Scarborough: Prentice Hall Allyn and Bacon Canada.

Gadgil, M., Berkes, F. and Folke, C. 1993. Indigenous Knowledge for biodiversity conservation. *Ambio* 22(2-3): 151-156.

Green, J. 2000. Transforming at the margins of the academy. In J. Oakes, R. Riewe, M. Bennett and B. Chisholm (Eds.) *Pushing the Margins: Native and Northern Research*. Winnipeg: Native Studies Press.

Hoare, T. Levy, C. and Robinson, M. 1993. Participatory Action Research in Native communities: Cultural opportunities and legal implications. *The Canadian Journal of Native Studies* 13(1):43-68.

Inuit Tapirisat of Canada. 1993. *Negotiating Research Relationships in the North: A Background Paper for a Workshop on Guidelines for Responsible Research*. Yellowknife, NWT.

Johnson, M. 1992. Dené Traditional Knowledge. Excerpt from *Lore, Capturing Traditional Environmental Knowledge*. Ottawa: Dené Cultural Institute/ International Development Research Centre.

Knudtson, P. and Suzuki, D. 1992. *Wisdom of the Elders*. Toronto: Stoddart

LaRocque, E. 1975. *Defeathering The Indian*. Agincourt: Book Society of Canada.

LaRocque, E. 1990. Preface: Here are our voices. In J. Perreault and S. Vance (Eds.) *Writing The Circle: Native Women of Western Canada*.Edmonton: NeWest Publishers.

LaRocque, E. 1996. The Colonization of a Native Woman Scholar. In C. Miller and P. Chuchryk (Eds.). *Women of the First Nations: Power, Wisdom, and Strength*. Winnipeg: University of Manitoba Press.

LaRocque, E. 1997. Re-examining Culturally Appropriate Models in Criminal Justice Applications. In M. Asch (Ed.). *Aboriginal and Treaty Rights in Canada: Essays on Law, Equality and Respect for Difference*, UBC

LaRocque, E. 1999. *Native Writers Resisting Colonizing Practices in Canadian*

Historiography and Literature. Ph.D. Dissertation. Univ. of Manitoba.

Mazusumi, B. and Quirk, S. 1993. *Exploring Community-Based Research Concerns for Aboriginal Northerners.* Dene Tracking.

McDonald, M. Arragutainaq, L. and Novalinga, Z. 1997. *Voices from the Bay: Traditional Ecological Knowledge of Inuit and Cree in the Hudson Bay Bioregion.* Ottawa: Canadian Arctic Resources Committee and Environmental Committee of Municipality of Sanikiluaq.

Monture-Angus, P. 1995. *Thunder in my Soul: A Mohawk Woman Speaks.* Halifax: Fernwood.

Morrison, B. and Wilson, C. 1995. *Native Peoples: The Canadian Experience.* Toronto: McClelland & Stewart.

Mukherjee, A. 1994. *Oppositional Aesthetics: Readings from a Hyphenated Space.* Toronto: TSAR.

Oakes, J. and Riewe, R. 1996. Communicating Inuit perspectives in research. In J. Oakes and R. Riewe (Eds.) *Issues in the North*, Vol. I. Edmonton: Canadian Circumpolar Institute.

Puxley, P. 1977. The colonial experience. In M. Watkins (Ed.) *Dené Nation - The Colony Within.* Toronto: University of Toronto Press.

Reimer, G. 1993. 'Community-based' as a culturally appropriate concept of development: A case study from Pangnirtung, NT. *Culture* 13(2):67-74.

Riddington, R. 1982. Technology, world view, and adaptive strategy in a northern hunting society. *Can. R. of Sociology & Anthropology* 19 (4):469-480.

Ryan, J. and Robinson, M. 1996. Community participatory research: Two views from Arctic Institute practitioners. *Practising Anthropology* 18 (4): 7-11.

Said, E. 1996. *Representations of the Intellectual.* New York: Vintage Books.

Shkilnyk, A. 1985. *Poison Stronger Than Love: The Destruction of an Ojibwe Community.* New Haven: Yale University Press.

Simpson, L. (1999). *The Construction of Traditional Ecological Knowledge: Issues, Implications and Insights.* Ph.D. Dissertation. U. of Manitoba.

Soui, G. 1992. *For An American Autohistory.* Toronto: McGill-Queens.

Smith, L. 1999. *Decolonizing Methodologies: Research and Indigenous Peoples.* London: Zed Books.

Stevenson, M. 1992. In Search of Inuit Ecological Knowledge: A Protocol for Its Collection, Interpretation and Use. Paper for Dept.of Renewable Resources, GNWT, Qikiqtaaluk Wildlife Board, and Parks Canada.

Warry, W. 1990. Doing Unto Others: Applied Anthropology, Collaborative Research and Native Self-Determination. *Culture* 10(1):61-73.

Weatherford, J. 1988. *Indian Givers: How The Indians of the Americas Transformed The World.* New York: Ballantine Books..

[1]   Emma LaRocque (PhD.) is a Métis scholar from Big Bay, Alberta and a professor in the Department of Native Studies, University of Manitoba. She specializes in Native-White relations, focusing on the impact of colonization on cultural production, history, literature, identities and gender roles.

An Aboriginal Perspective on TEK and Western Science

Earl Stevenson[1]

Abstract

Traditional Ecological Knowledge (TEK) has become a popular information base utilized by Scientists and Natural Resource Managers. However, the pursuit of TEK has lead to a lack of understanding by the mainstream. This paper addresses this issue and the meaning of TEK from the perspective of an Aboriginal student.

Introduction

Western science, in its hierarchical world, places its paradigms and world views as the epitome of human thought, resulting in the opinion that 'true' scientific discourse can only take place through the experiments and methodologies of the science that Western societies adhere to (Petch 2000). I dissuade people from accepting this arrogant attitude. In this paper I show a counter-balance to the Western ideals of Traditional Ecological Knowledge (TEK) and offer an Aboriginal perspective or a window into the Original Peoples world views.

TEK Defined?

In order to understand the context of this paper, an understanding of TEK is necessary. However, one must first understand that TEK is a Western scientific concept "that came into widespread use only in the 1980s" (Berkes 1999:4). This is a definition or term put forth by the scholars of Western academia in an attempt to understand TEK (Stevenson 1996).

Berkes (1999:8) states that TEK is "a cumulative body of knowledge, practice, and belief, evolving by adaptive processes and handed down through generations by cultural transmission, about the relationship of living beings (including humans) with one another and with their environment". Petch (2000:139) describes TEK as "the accumulation of information about a particular ecological setting which has resulted from experience and observation and which has been passed down from one generation to the next, through oral tradition and by learned behaviour".

TEK definitions fail to incorporate the spiritual and intimate interactions between Aboriginal peoples and the land (AFN 1995). Central to this 'Cosmological Understanding', as Linklater (1997), a Cree scholar, refers to Traditional Knowledge, is that the traditional landscape cooperating with the Oral Tradition serves as the mediums for Aboriginal inquiry into the Natural World.

> Native American teachings describe the relations all around-animals, fish, trees, and rocks-as our brothers, sisters, uncles, and grandpas. Our relations to each other, our prayers whispered across generations to our relatives, are what bind our cultures together (LaDuke 1999:2).

LaDuke, an Anishinaabekwe, discusses the intimacy that Aboriginal people have with the land; in Western science there is no intimacy whatsoever with regards to the natural environment. Western orthodox sciences reduce the natural environment into small segment. Ball (2000), likens Science as being amoral. Berkes (1988:8) points out "that our (Western) cosmology is based far too heavily on empiricism and scientism, and is insufficiently based on humanistic notions and morality towards nature". However, unlike Western doctrines, Aboriginal science is a holistic framework; it examines the natural environment as well as the spiritual and cosmological components of Aboriginal world views. I hesitate to use the phrase Aboriginal science for fear of reducing the Aboriginal world views into a singular discipline. It is a complete arrangement of disciplines woven together completing the circle of Aboriginal knowledge. For a grounded, holistic understanding of TEK, one has to be borne with the inherent spirituality of an Aboriginal person. That is a strong statement, however, should we accept the definitions of TEK from someone who is not a practitioner of TEK? Can the Western academic deliver a complete and justifiable result of TEK without having lived life's experience as an Aboriginal person? The Arctic Institute of North America and Joint Secretariat-Inuvialuit Renewable Resource Committee said:

> Traditional knowledge is an accumulated body of knowledge that is rooted in the spiritual health, culture, and language of the people and handed down from generation to generation. It is based on intimate knowledge of the land, water, snow, ice, weather, and wildlife, and the relationships between all aspects of the environment The wisdom comes in using the knowledge and ensuring that it is used in good ways. It involves using the head and heart together. Traditional knowledge is dynamic, yet stable, and is shared in stories, song, dance, and myths. (1996:114)

For too long Aboriginal societies have endured the inquisitions, inquiries and other scientific research into their ways of living. Deloria (1995:17), a Native American scholar at the University of Colorado, states:

> Institutionalization of science . . . meant that scientists would come to act like priests and defer doctrine and dogma when determining what truths would be admitted, how they would be phrased, and how scientists themselves would be protected from the questions of the mass of people whose lives were becoming increasingly dependant on them.

Aboriginal scholars' primary complaint towards Western science is the lack of respect and honour shown towards TEK (Deloria 1995). This lack of respect is evidenced by Nadasdy (1999:3) who wrote how biologists said "that 'traditional knowledge' is simply a political ploy invented by aboriginal people to wrest control of wildlife from 'qualified' scientific managers". This is a first hand description of the racist attitudes that some non-Aboriginal scientists possess towards the Aboriginal knowledge keepers.

TEK Verified?

Implicit in many Western scientists' views of TEK is the question how is this knowledge verified? What constructs or tools does the Western academic utilize in order to 'classify', 'quantify' or 'verify' TEK? According to Proctor (2000:161) "TEK is forced into the two categories of 'truth' (as empirical facts) and 'spirituality' (as non-truths) in positivist thinking. The dominant culture often judges other knowledge through positivist criteria." Underlying in the Western paradigm is the issue of inquiry, how it is performed, whether it meets the standards proposed by these paradigms, and how it is verified. Aboriginal knowledge keepers carry 'truth', Indigenous systems of verification are in place to maintain the 'truth'. They pass on this 'truth', it is a part of their life, their belief system, their world views. Western academics, when they question the validity of TEK, attack the integrity and honesty of the Aboriginal knowledge holder. 'Truth' is a basic tenet in Aboriginal world views, it is a sacred teaching, to not tell the truth is to not honour the Creator! Deloria (1995:47) states "scientists placed themselves in the posture of knowing more, on the basis of their own very short-term investigations, than the collective remembrances of the rest of humankind".

Skead (1999), an Ojibway Elder, who has left this world and has since entered into his next journey, said:

> The Sweat Lodge teaches me a lot of things. It comes from the Mother Earth. How everything gets to be together, how important it is that the great teachings of Mother Earth, the things that are growing, the trees, water, and the birds and the animals that are four-legged. Even the bugs, everything, everything in this life. We learn, I learn that I am not any better than all these things. They are all equal, that's life. (168)

In my humble opinion respect is crucial in understanding Aboriginal knowledge, in order to respect this knowledge, one should not have to scrutinize the wisdom held by the Elders. All aspects of the natural and spiritual environment serve as teachers for traditional Aboriginal knowledge. Skead mentioned equality, as a result, we see no hierarchical process in his knowledge. Implicit in his wisdom is humility, and the power of Nature (Mother Earth). A deep respect resides in Aboriginal knowledge for all ingredients of the natural and spiritual environment.

During a class discussion, as the only Aboriginal student, I was asked about TEK and whether I considered myself as a holder of TEK. I had to consider this query for a few moments, then I replied that yes, I do carry this knowledge with me. However, I also pointed out that since

I attend university in an urban setting, this does not allow me as much of a chance to attain more knowledge about our natural and spiritual worlds. Regardless, I also had to mention that wherever I am, I will always carry some Aboriginal knowledge with me, be it in a University classroom or out on the land with my father. In addition, I pointed out that I will not have as much knowledge of our heritage landscape as someone who may have spent a considerable more time on the land than me.

Is TEK Uniform?

World views of the hundreds of Aboriginal Nations in North America are similar in many respects, but each has their own unique systems of learning. When Western academics attempt to define TEK, they generalize and imply that it is uniform. LaRocque (2000), states that in academia there is a 'trait listing' implying that Aboriginal knowledge is similar across the landscape, this is, of course untrue. Furthermore, Colorado (1988:49) mentions, "research has been perceived and presented as mono-cultural, thus not accepted by the Native community. All peoples, including Native Americans, have some way of coming to knowledge. Each tribe has its specific methods".

We have to use caution when we encounter the characterizations of TEK being applied by Western scholars. Simpson (2000a:166) reflects, "Positivist social scientists failed to recognize that their inquiries were rooted in their own belief systems and world view and justified silencing those people who possess the greatest insights into their own state of affairs in the name of objectivity". Further to this, "According to the post-positivist scientist, this inevitably rendered their results epistemologically unsound" (Kirby and McKenna 1989 in Simpson 2000a:166). Consequently, we witness inconsistencies in the interpretation of data by these two modes of understanding.

As an Aboriginal student, I am in a unique position in that I can derive personal insight into the discussion on TEK. Nonetheless, I cannot take this insight into TEK lightly. Simpson (2000a:169) notes, "One of our responsibilities as Aboriginal academics is to use our privileged formal education to reinforce Aboriginal traditional social structures, world views and ways of knowing within the walls of academe. Post-positivist Aboriginal scholars need to begin to follow our own cultures' rules and assumptions regarding conduct of inquiry". It is in my own best interests, and those of my people, to respect and honour the knowledge that is passed onto me. Due diligence must be taken to protect the intellectual property rights of the Aboriginal knowledge holders.

On my academic journey through Natural Resources Management, I am also learning that Western doctrines should be critiqued. Simpson (2000b:188) advises her students to "use science, but they are also aware of its limitations, its biases and its dominance. I teach them how to use science, but also how to resist and challenge science as a knowledge system". Throughout my university career I have lamented the fact that there was not strong Aboriginal content in many of the courses which I attended. University programs would be much richer if teachings from the people who are most intimate and knowledgeable with the land, our Elders, were included.

Although I am disappointed to see that Western science fails to give proper accord to TEK, it heartens me to see Aboriginal academics such as Simpson advocating for Aboriginal knowledge. What the scientific community needs is to recognize the efforts of Aboriginal scholars and their respective ways of knowing. Deloria (1995:161) mentions:

> It is almost impossible to get non-Indian scholars pried loose from their own cultural presuppositions to do careful interpretive work on Indian traditions. While they may loudly declare that the two cultural traditions are dissimilar, most of them do not seem to know what that really means.

Western scholars construct inadequate interpretations of Aboriginal Peoples' knowledge and beliefs. A case in point are the two definitions on TEK provided by Berkes and Petch earlier in the paper.

Can TEK and Western Science Have Equal Status?

Many scholars, Aboriginal and non-Aboriginal have stated that Aboriginal knowledge can continue to be used. Usher (1993:117) spoke of 'harmonization' between Western science and Aboriginal knowledge. Riewe and Gamble (1988:35) support the fact that Aboriginal knowledge is crucial, "Cooperative management can not simply mean an advisory role for the Native users; rather the users must be fully involved in the design and production of the wildlife management schemes". In a similar argument, Deloria (1995:60) contends:

> Two things need to be done. . . . First, corrective measures must be taken to eliminate scientific misconceptions about Indians, their culture, and their past. Second, there

82

needs to be a way that Indian traditions can contribute to the understanding of scientific beliefs at enough specific points so that the Indian traditions will be taken seriously as valid bodies of knowledge.

Care and attention must be used when Aboriginal knowledge is utilized. A power relationship develops when Western scholars document TEK, the ability by the Aboriginal knowledge keeper to safeguard this knowledge is then reduced. Simpson (1999:87) continues:

> Indigenous Knowledge systems control the transmission of knowledge in a much different manner than does the dominant society, yet those can only remain intact under oral systems of transmission because they require reciprocity and interaction. When Indigenous Knowledge holders lose control over their knowledge it can lead to the marginalization and appropriation of their knowledge.

Final Remarks on the Debate

The TEK and Western science debate raises doubts over whether this knowledge should be available to the public. Sensitive information definitely should not be made available. Intellectual property rights of the Aboriginal knowledge holders must be maintained and honoured. However, my Aboriginal heritage is based on sharing. My ancestors have always shared with whomever asks from them, as long as it was asked in the spirit of honour. I too would like to share my research experiences, but at what cost? Will I be making the heritage of my people a commodity? Questions that I must ask not only myself, but also my community!

References

AFN. 1995. *The Feasibility of Representing Traditional Indigenous Knowledge in Cartographic Pictorial or Textual Forms.* Ottawa

Arctic Institute of North America and Joint Secretariat-Inuvialuit Renewable Resource Committee. 1996. *Circumpolar Aboriginal People and Co-management Practice: Current Issues.* Calgary:AINA.

Ball, T. 2000. Pers.Com. Retired Professor of Geography, U of Wpg. Feb. 9.

Berkes, F. 1999. *Sacred Ecology: TK and Resources Management*. Phil: Taylor and Francis.

Berkes, F. 1988. Environmental philosophy of the Chisasibi Cree people of James Bay. In M. Freeman and L. Carbyn (Eds), *TK and Renewable Resource Management in Northern Regions*. pp. 7-21. Ed: Boreal Institute.

Colorado, P. 1988. Bridging Native and Western Science. *Conv.*(2/3):49-86.

Deloria, V. 1995. *Red Earth, White Lies: Native Americans and the Myth of Scientific Fact*. Golden, CO: Fulcrum Publishing.

Kirby, S. and McKenna, K. 1989. *Experience, Research and Social Change: Methods From the Margins*. Toronto: Guimond Press.

LaDuke, W. 1999. *All Our Relations: Native Struggles for Land and Life*. Cambridge, MA: South End Press.

LaRocque, E. 2000. Pers. Com., Aboriginal scholar and Professor, Dept. of Native Studies, U of M. Feb. 10.

Linklater, E. 1997. Archaeology, historical landscapes and the Nelson House Cree. *Manitoba Archaeological J.* 7(1):1-44.

Nadasdy, P. 1999. The politics of TEK: Power and the "integration" of knowledge. *Arctic Anthropology* 36(1-2):1-18.

Petch, V. 2000. TEK: An anthropological perspective. In J. Oakes, R. Riewe, S. Koolage, L. Simpson, and N. Schuster (Eds.), *Aboriginal Health, Identity and Resources*. pp. 137-149. Winnipeg: University of Manitoba.

Proctor, A. 2000. TEK: An analysis of the discourse. In J. Oakes, R. Riewe, S. Koolage, L. Simpson, and N. Schuster (Eds.), *Aboriginal Health, Identity and Resources*. pp. 150-164. Winnipeg: University of Manitoba.

Riewe, R. and L. Gamble. 1988. The Inuit and wildlife management today. In M. Freeman and L. Carbyn (Eds.), *TK and Renewable Resource Mgt Northern Regions*. Edmonton: Boreal Institute for Northern Studies.

Simpson, L. 2000a. Anishinaabe ways of knowing. In J. Oakes, R. Riewe, S. Koolage, L. Simpson, and N. Schuster, (Eds.), *Aboriginal Health, Identity and Resources*. pp.165-185. Winnipeg: University of Manitoba.

Simpson, L. 2000b. Indigenous knowledge and western science. In J. Oakes, R. Riewe, S. Koolage, L. Simpson, and N. Schuster, (Eds.), *Aboriginal Health, Identity and Res.* pp. 186-195. Wpg: University of Manitoba.

Simpson, L. 1999. *The Construction of Traditional Ecological Knowledge: Issues, Implications and Insights*. Winnipeg: University of Manitoba.

Skead, A. 1999. It's just like reading a book when I am talking to you. In P. Kulchyski, D. McCaskill, D. Newhouse (Eds.), *In the Words of Elders*. Toronto: University of Toronto Press.

Stevenson, M. 1996. Indigenous knowledge in environmental assessment. *Arctic* 49(3): 278-291.

Usher, P. 1993. The Beverly-Kaminuriak Caribou Management Board: An experience in co-management. In J. Inglis, (Ed.), *Traditional Ecological Knowledge: Concepts and Cases*. pp.111-120. Ottawa:IDRC.

---

[1]   Earl Stevenson is from the Peguis First Nation in Manitoba and is a graduate student attending the Natural Resources Institute at the University of Manitoba.

Traditional Ecological Knowledge and University Curriculum

Melanie Van Gerwen-Toyne[1]

Abstract

In recent decades an attempt has been made to integrate Traditional Ecological Knowledge (TEK) and Science. Today there are ongoing problems and new issues that bring light as to why the integration has not been very successful. This paper reviews the literature on TEK and provides thoughts regarding the importance of updating University curriculum to meet today's changing procedures of resource management.

Introduction

Aboriginal communities have lived with their land for centuries, developing an intimate knowledge about the land. Recently, ecological researchers have become interested in Aboriginal experiences and the study of Traditional Ecological Knowledge (TEK). Some because of genuine hope of improving resource management, others because they had no choice since the settlement of land claims gave more control of research to the First Nations. However, the path by which TEK has developed is unsatisfactory to First Nations. Today more researchers are realizing the flaws in the TEK procedures and are attempting to correct them, and more communities are attempting to strengthen their cultural traditions. Universities must also realize the changes occurring in resource management and upgrade their curriculum to better prepare graduating students to work in co-management with First Nations.

Pre-TEK: Before 1980's

Aboriginal people lived in and adapted to the Arctic environment for thousands of years, developing intimate relationships with their surroundings, be they human, animal, plant, soil, or inanimate (Gunn *et al.* 1988). Their social and spiritual rules and taboo's, harvesting techniques, nomadic lifestyle and sharing ethics enabled them to maintain animal populations, ensuring food for the future (Gunn *et al.* 1988, Riewe and Gamble 1988, Oakes and Riewe 1996). In today's terms, they were efficient renewable resource managers. In this diverse and creative way, Aboriginal people lived on the land, with the land, for centuries before contact with southern modernization. Upon contact, Aboriginal people took advantage of southern technologies like rifles and eventually snow machines. They also taught southern visitors skills regarding dog handling, navigation, shelter building, hunting and fishing, food preparation, recreation, health care, clothes making, governmental organization and more (Oakes and Riewe 1996, Simpson 2000, Proctor 2000).

In the last 50 years, some ecological researchers developed an interest in Aboriginal knowledge regarding resource management (Proctor 2000). However, the majority of researchers disregarded First Nation advice stating that Aboriginal ideas of resource management were unscientific, anecdotal, without method, folklore, unreliable, inferior, inefficient, or subjective, and therefore ignored (Hobson 1992, Agrawal 1995, Lapadat and Janzen 1995, Simpson 1999).

The Birth of TEK: 1980's to mid-1990's

In the 1980's the number of ecological researchers interested in Aboriginal knowledge grew dramatically. For some the interest was genuine, for others it was forced due to land claim settlement and First Nation control over research. Researchers labelled Aboriginal experiences as Traditional Ecological Knowledge or TEK and attempted to integrate it into scientific methodologies. It was hoped that the integration would increase access to Aboriginal knowledge and provide answers to present ecological questions (Freeman 1992, Hobson 1992, Wolfe *et al.* 1992, Stevenson 1996). However, problems associated with the integration of TEK and Science were soon discovered. Characteristics of TEK and science were seen as conflicting (Gunn *et al.* 1988, Bielawski 1992, Freeman 1992, Johnson 1992, Wolfe *et al.* 1992, Berkes 1993, Agrawal 1995). Some researchers refused to accept TEK as valid without scientific verification (Gunn *et al.* 1988, Riewe and Gamble 1988, Freeman 1992, Hobson 1992, Johnson 1992, Wolfe *et al.* 1992, Agrawal 1995, Oakes and Riewe 1996). Aboriginal peoples hesitated to share TEK due to a lack of control over the scientific methodology and mistreatment by researchers. Aboriginal people found that when they agreed to share their knowledge with researchers (to document it for future generations and to help researchers treat resource management more holistically), many researchers treated TEK as a database without showing proper respect to the original knowledge owners (Oakes and Riewe 1996, Stevenson 1996).

TEK in 2000

The same issues continue and new issues are identified, including language barriers, First Nation control, and the potential loss of TEK. Language barriers, such as: the difficulty of defining terms in TEK (Stevenson 1996, Nadasdy 1999, and Petch 2000), the lack of English words for an accurate explanation of First Nations spirituality and beliefs, researchers difficulties in representing what they learned from First Nations (Nutall 1998, Petch 2000), and researchers use of scientific technical terms (Nadasdy 1999, Petch 2000) lead to mis-communication. Another issue is that the process of defining and documenting TEK provides scientists with more control than to the original knowledge owners (Nadasdy 1999, Simpson 1999, 2000, Proctor 1999, 2000). This occurs when TEK is reduced to factual information without the original cultural and spiritual contexts. The assimilated version is often barely recognizable to the original owners and therefore has little meaning to the people it represents. As a result, TEK has become a commodity, alienated from its original owners and used by others for purposes that may not benefit the community.

First Nations fear that once their knowledge is assimilated into scientific reports, they will lose their decision-making powers. Science has defined what TEK is, influenced how it is documented, questioned what is authentic knowledge (Nadasdy 1999) and taken the role of identifying whether or not TEK is lost. According to Wolfe et al. (1992), young people must go through stages of maturation processes of learning in order to acquire TEK; without this process TEK is lost as the Elders pass on. Many communities today are not acquiring this level of learning due to western modernization and lack of teaching from Elders (Gunn et al. 1988, Riewe and Gamble 1988, Wolfe et al. 1992). Does this truly mean that TEK is lost? In 2000, communities and researchers are placing large amounts of efforts towards resolving issues related to integrating TEK and science; co-management is the expected way of research. Universities must address this issue so that future resource managers will be better trained to work with First Nations in a mutually beneficial manner.

Reflections from a Future Scientist

The well established university-level courses for resource management science degrees were acceptable in the past, however, current and future resource managers require additional course work to develop the background and skills needed to work in co-management with First Nations. Currently, the undergraduate degree of a typical science student includes courses in biology, ecology, statistics and other science topics essential to the degree, not even one course with significant Aboriginal content is required yet many biologists get jobs working with First Nations and using TEK. With the settlement of land claims, First Nations decide what research will be performed in their area. Future resource managers must therefore know how to work *with* First Nations in co-management projects to obtain mutually satisfactory goals. In order to do this, the resource manager must understand and respect the lifestyle, beliefs, values, culture and language of First Nations. Co-management and the use of Traditional Ecological Knowledge is becoming the way of the future for resource management.

As a Master of Science student, I found myself confronted with the question of how to work with First Nations in a mutually beneficial fashion without any training in this area, nor with any introduction to the co-management process at the undergraduate level. During my field work in an Aboriginal community and two courses I then took relating to Northern Studies I realized I was only just beginning to think about Aboriginal people's perspectives instead of theories and statistics. I also realized that many of my peers were entering the work force and research arena in areas that would certainly affect First Nations, without any idea of the impact of their work on First Nations, the need to involve the community, or how to involve the community. Universities must acknowledge this significant gap in training and revise curriculum at the undergraduate and graduate level to ensure that graduates in all disciplines have at least a basic understanding of First Nations world views.

The undergraduate science degree prepared me to deal with the *science* of resource management but the *reality* of resource management is changing, moving towards co-management. Universities must adapt to this change and update the undergraduate curriculum to better prepare graduating resource management students to deal with these new issues in a respectable and mutually beneficial fashion.

References

Agrawal, A. 1995. Dismantling the divide between indigenous and scientific knowledge. *Development and Change 26:* 413-439.

Berkes, F. 1993. Traditional ecological knowledge in perspective. In J. Inglis (Ed.) *TEK: Concepts and Cases* pp. 1-11. Ottawa: IDRC.

Bielawski, E. 1992. Inuit indigenous knowledge and science in the arctic. *Northern Perspectives 20*(1): 5-8.

Freeman, M. 1992. The nature and utility of traditional ecological knowledge. *Northern Perspectives 20*(1): 9-12.

Gunn, A., Arlooktoo, G. and Kaomayok, D. 1988. The contribution of traditional ecological knowledge of Inuit to wildlife management. In M. Freeman and L. Carbyn (Eds.) *Traditional Knowledge and Renewable Resource Management in Northern Regions* pp. 22-30. Edmonton: IUCN Commission on Ecology, Boreal Institute. Occasional Pub. 23.

Hobson, G. 1992. Traditional knowledge is science. *Northern Perspectives 20*(1): 2.

Johnson, M. 1992. Dené traditional knowledge. *Northern Perspectives 20*(1): 3-5.

Lapadat, J. and Janzen, H. 1995. Collaborative research in northern communities: Possibilities and pitfalls. *BC Studies 104*: 6-83.

Nadasdy, P. 1999. The politics of TEK: Power and the "integration" of knowledge. *Arctic Anthropology 36*(1-2): 1-18.

Nutall, M. 1998. Critical reflections on knowledge gathering in the arctic. In J. Dorais, M. Naggy and L. Mueller-Wille (Eds.) *Aboriginal Environmental Knowledge in the North* pp. 21-36. Quebec: GETIC, University Laval.

Oakes, J. and Riewe, R. 1996. Communicating Inuit perspectives on research. *Issues in the North 1*: 71-79.

Petch, V. 2000. Traditional ecological knowledge: An anthropological perspective. In J. Oakes, R. Riewe, S. Koolage, L. Simpson and N. Schuster (Eds.) *Aboriginal Health, Identity and Resources*. Winnipeg: University of Manitoba , Depts. of Native Studies and Zoology, and Faculty of Graduate Studies.

Proctor, A. 1999. *Definitions and the Defining Process: "Traditional Ecological Knowledge" in the Keewatin Region, Nunavut*. Unpublished Masters Thesis. Winnipeg: University of Manitoba, Natural Resources Institute.

Proctor, A. 2000. Traditional environmental knowledge: An analysis of the discourse. In J. Oakes, R. Riewe, S. Koolage, L. Simpson and N. Schuster (Eds.) *Aboriginal Health, Identity and Resources*. Winnipeg: University of Manitoba , Depts. of Native Studies and Zoology, and Faculty of Graduate Studies.

Riewe, R. and Gamble, L. 1988. The Inuit and wildlife management today. In M. Freeman and L. Carbyn (Eds.) *Traditional Knowledge and Renewable Resource Management in Northern Regions* pp. 31-37. Edmonton: IUCN Commission on Ecology and Boreal Institute. Occasional Publication #23.

Simpson, L. 1999. *The Construction of Traditional Ecological Knowledge: Insights, Issues and Implications*. Unpublished Interd. Ph.D. Dissertation. Winnipeg: U of MB, Zoology, Native Studies and Anthropology.

Simpson, L. 2000. Indigenous knowledge and western science: Towards new relationships for change. In J. Oakes, R. Riewe, S. Koolage, L. Simpson and N. Schuster (Eds.) *Aboriginal Health, Identity and Resources*. Winnipeg: University of Manitoba. Native Studies and Zoology, and Graduate Studies.

Stevenson, M. 1996. Indigenous knowledge in environmental assessment. *Arctic* 49(3): 278-291.

Wolfe, J., Bechard C., Cizek P. and Cole, D. 1992. *Indigenous and Western Knowledge and Resources Management Systems*. University of Guelph: Rural Planning and Development.

[1]   Melanie Van Gerwen-Toyne is a graduate student in the Department of Zoology at the University of Manitoba and is currently working with the Gwich'in on a fisheries co-management project.

Transforming at the Margins of the Academy

Joyce Green[1]

Abstract

In this paper I examine the tensions that Aboriginal women academics must negotiate in the course of professional life, in the context of societal and academic institutions that are profoundly sexist and racist. These tensions make academic life much harder for Aboriginal women than it is for the prototypical white male academic.

Introduction

The conflictual academic experience of Aboriginal women has been my reality as well as an intellectual interest. Personal experience does not place our analyses beyond critique, but personal experience can be central to both theory and analysis (Ng 1999, Overall 1998). My heritage includes both settler and Aboriginal peoples, and so my personal social, familial and political context includes all of the tensions that I will address here. This context is both a social location and an experience of an unequal dialectic of conflict, configured by dual racism, colonialism, sexism, and marginalisation. The category of Aboriginal academics is very small and predominately located in Native Studies programs, in designated Native focus components of other programs, and scattered across disciplines. It is statistically insignificant in relation to the universe of academics, and it is further reduced by controlling for sex. Why? Institutions, even those that promote equity hiring, do not hire, retain and promote Aboriginal academics. Under ameliorative measures, such as the University of Alberta's "Opening Doors" policy designed to improve representation of designated groups, representation dropped in all categories. However, the existence of the policy produced a furore among some on campus, who charged that principles of merit would be violated, as worthy (implicitly white male) candidates were trumped by (implicitly unworthy) candidates who fit the designated groups.

Even in the arena into which Aboriginal scholars are expected to flow (Native Studies) it is difficult to obtain a doctoral degree in Canada. Trent University now offers a doctoral program and the University of Manitoba offers an interdisciplinary doctoral program in Native Studies. Students with Native Studies majors re-qualify in another discipline (this is how I wound up in Political Science) and contend with professors and students who expect them to be Indian experts. Native Studies programs, professors, and students are poorly integrated into the university; are under-funded; have poor visibility; tend to be ignored by related disciplines and scholars (for example, political science, sociology, economics, law and philosophy); and overlooked by students who fail to see this study as a vital part of their education. Few staff and students encounter the minuscule numbers of Aboriginal women academics, and so they neither get the benefit of our scholarship nor do they get to see us as Aboriginal, in academic positions. For Aboriginal academics in the 'regular' disciplines, institutional and collegial support is substantially lessened, and visibility is less than in Native Studies. In addition, Aboriginal sociologists, political scientists and biologists (to name a few) are expected to be 'Indian experts' regardless of their research focuses. Finally, the combination of low numbers of women academics, the dynamics of academic politics, institutional racism, and the lower numbers of other women and Aboriginal male academics with whom to build solidarity, results in a lonely, isolating and implicitly hostile workplace.

Inclusive Structures and Transformative Potentials
In this section I describe the structures that shape our inclusion while they perpetuate our subordination and our radical transformative potential. Many Aboriginal academics (and many female academics, and academics from other minorities) find themselves in the curious position of being marginal and tokenized at the same time as we seek space in the academy for our physical presence, our intellectual freedom, and for our political and pedagogical perspectives (Kelly 1998, LaRocque 1996, Ng 1999, Razack 1998, Stalker and Prentice 1998). These stances are often informed by our experiences and analyses of oppression: they exemplify that 'the personal is political'. They are often viewed as illegitimate, radical, unacademic, or threatening to colleagues, students, administrative

processes; to the notion of meritocratic tenure in the academy; and to disciplinary canons.

Here, three things happen to Aboriginal women and marginalised others in the academy. First, we embody difference from the dominant institutional norm, which is thoroughly constructed for male, colour and class privilege. (In this context we should consider sexuality and disability as well.) This physical representation of difference exists regardless of our personal intellectual or political pursuits! This results in the Never Fitting In phenomenon, or in its counterpart, the phenomenon of self-annihilation: fitting in by rejecting one's particularity and the analysis I present here, in favour of conformity with the existing institution. This is manifest in women who are as patriarchal as men; in marginalized others who deny the existence of or their personal experience with racism; and in beliefs that there is a neutral meritocracy which recognizes a scholastic excellence that may be equally pursued by all.

Second, assuming that we make our way through social and institutional filters into the student or faculty body, we are sometimes explicitly and sometimes implicitly expected to serve as representatives of those whose attributes we share. Thus, our markers of difference (that is, our visibility, which is different than consciousness of the political significance of difference) become an asset for the institution, which too often overloads us as individuals with committees and courses designed to benefit from our tokenistic appointment, sometimes with no regard for the unrelated nature of our scholarship! But while the institution tokenizes us in this fashion, it is much less willing to endorse the different pedagogical, methodological, and theoretical practices that we bring with us. For those of us who teach and study critical, anticolonial, and feminist theory and practice, there are continual challenges to our centrality to curriculum and to particular disciplines, and to our scholarly significance.

Third, we are always asked to bear too many burdens that mainstream, male-stream scholars need not bear: representation, voice, mentorship, and so on as Aboriginal and as female. That is, we are asked to legitimate the oppressive academy as inclusive; we are asked to explain the Other to the privileged; we are asked to recruit and promote Our Own, while simultaneously being asked to conform to the not-so-neutral academic career path, disciplinary curriculum, and institutional practices. Some of this is chosen by us, but much of it is imposed by institutions and colleagues who choose not to change. Educating the ineducable about gender and Aboriginal questions exhausts and enrages at least some of us (LaRocque 1999).

Resistance to marginalized others within the academy comes

from two primary factors. The first is the intuitive reaction by those who are dominant against the inclusion as equals of those who have been subordinate by definition. The historic, cultural and intellectual foundation of the academy is deeply imbued with patriarchal, racist and colonial assumptions and practices which circumscribe the conditions of intellectual life. The components of what it means to be excellent rest on these assumptions and practices. It is no surprise, when our inclusion in the academy draws a visceral reaction, particularly from those who have not investigated their own assumptions. Let me rephrase this: we (all women, Aboriginal peoples, and marginalized others) are 'always, already' suspect to those whose privilege and knowledge rest on our subordination. The 'always, already' formulation is used by some scholars to capture the process of the racist gaze upon those constructed as 'other', who are marked by their physical particularity as always, already subordinate. The second factor is a logical consequence of the implications of our inclusion: power relations, life expectations, forms of knowledge and so on, will be challenged and there will be change. Despite our marginal and suspect status, we are potentially transformative. The operation of this second factor destabilizes everything the beneficiaries of the existing academy have been led to believe about excellence, the process of knowledge production, and the recruitment of students and colleagues. Most of all, it threatens their own sense of entitlement on the basis of what they have learned to be the criteria for advancement.

These two factors trigger the reactive, hostile counter-arguments to our inclusion known as "the backlash", accompanied by reactionary calls for freedom from "political correctness" (Overall 1998:44-52). In this formulation, those of us who name and object to our oppression, or who stand in solidarity with marginalized others, are transformed by our stance into the oppressors of those whose privilege we challenge. Let me rephrase: the backlash and the dismissive label 'political correctness' construct marginal, subordinated people as dominating oppressors. At the same time, the accompanying hostility produces what many of us have experienced: the Chilly Climate. Institutional intransigence and colleagues' hostility and derision freeze many of us out of the academy. The exclusionary western canon that is taught in the core disciplines reproduces the kinds of scholarship that affirm the existing relations of dominance and subordination. Theory and practice that dispute this and produce alternative accounts of reality are subversive, and are barely tolerated by the academy. To the extent that the academy is grounded in race, sex and class privilege, it reproduces these relations and the legitimations of them. And it has limited toleration of women's studies,

Aboriginal studies, and class analysis. This exclusion ranges from the low numbers of academics who are marginal by definition (women, racialized people, 'out' gays and lesbians) and by their exclusion as subjects from the canon.

How does all of this play out for Aboriginal women? First, it means that those who are able to gain access to the academy are excellent by definition. We have persevered in the face of implicit and explicit challenges to our inherent legitimacy. We have endured and learned core curricula that ignore, exclude, racialize, or sexualize, our histories, cultures, and persons. Then, after meeting the institutional requirements on this score, and despite the lack of financial and institutional support, have pursued scholarship that challenges precisely these kinds of exclusions and generates a more complete knowledge. We know we are good scholars.

We also know, from simple observation, that the existing not-so-neutral system of recruitment and promotion in the academy is in fact an affirmative action program for mediocre white men. Aldea Landry, a cabinet minister in Frank McKenna's 1989-1991 Liberal government in New Brunswick, put it this way: "Women haven't [yet] earned the right to be mediocre" (Desserud, 1997:270). This is not an allegation that all white males are mediocre: many are excellent. But the presence of substantial numbers of mediocre colleagues suggests that the primary criteria is maleness and race how otherwise to explain the homogenous character of the academy? Inclusion of others fosters real measures of merit by requiring demonstrated excellence, not just sex and race privilege. Second, we are transformative. From the fact of our presence and the original and radical nature of our work, we challenge the academy to confront its particular forms of privilege and its bases of exclusion. This process is conditional, continual, and far from over. Mary Daly (1973), a feminist philosopher, observed that we hold the most transformative power when we are engaged in "creative existence on the boundary" of dominating (patriarchal, colonial) institutions. Our work is fraught with complications and contradictions, we must negotiate the racist, sexist relations within the academy, plus the politics and strategies of divergent Aboriginal communities. This subjects us to serious political pressure if we obtain any profile, and if our analyses or work does not suit particular individuals or organizations. Feminist Aboriginal women, and women who have contested existing power relations, have ample evidence of this repressive impulse, and it is injurious and incompatible with our work as academics. Aboriginal women academics negotiate multiple and contradictory considerations in which we are never, ever, allowed to be neutral. Third, we are mentors: Aboriginal and many female students find in our existence some solidarity, and sometimes in our scholarship, inspiration and enlightenment. These students become part of the transformative yeast in the academy and in their own communities. Fourth, we are colleagues, and some of our non-Aboriginal and male colleagues resist us. Others are curious. Some are in solidarity with us. Again, to the extent that we contest what knowledge is, how it is evaluated, and what the power relations are that configure it, we instigate academic excellence and social transformation.

All this happens at some expense. It's hard, painful and dangerous to take on consolidated power relations. Some of us are eliminated. In my own discipline, political science, many departments are considered to have Chilly Climates. But some of us are here, and we demonstrate that we are not homogeneous; we can be subversive of existing power relations; we are excellent; we are controversial; we are in solidarity with many others; and we are your colleagues. We contribute through teaching, through research, and through critique. To uphold the best elements of scholarly excellence, both administrations and individual scholars must confront the academy's racist and sexist foundations and assumptions. Further, they must incorporate those who critique these foundations, without demanding an assimilative conformity.

References

Daly, M. 1973. *Beyond God the Father*. Boston: Beacon Press.

Desserud, D. 1997. Women in New Brunswick politics In J. Arscott and L. Trimble (Eds.) *In the Presence of Women*. pp.254-277.TO: Harcourt Brace.

Kelly, J. 1998. *Learning to be Black in White Society*. Halifax: Fernwood.

LaRocque, E. 1996. The Colonization of a Native woman scholar. In C. Miller and P. Chuchryk (Eds.) *Women of the First Nations: Power, Wisdom, and Strength* pp. 11-18. Winnipeg: University of Manitoba Press.

LaRocque, E. 1999. *Native Writers Resisting Colonizing Practices in Canadian Historiography and Literature*.Unpub. doctoral dissertation,Uof MB.

Ng, R. 1999. Sexism and racism in the university. In A. Beer (Ed.) *Can. Woman Studies*. pp. 370-379. Toronto: Inanna Publications and Education.

Overall, C. 1998. *A Feminist Reflections from Academia*. Peterb.,ON: Broadview.

Razack, S. 1998. *Looking White People in the Eye: Gender, Race, and Culture in Courtrooms and Classrooms*. Toronto: University of Toronto Press.

Said, E. 1994. *Representations of the Intellectual*. New York: Random House.

Stalker, J. and Prentice, S. 1998. *The Illusion of Inclusion: Women in Post-Secondary Education*. Halifax: Fernwood Publishing.

[1]   Joyce Green (Ph.D.) is an Associate Professor in the Department of Political Science at the University of Regina.

The "Dating" Game:
Who Should Date Who?

Drew Hayden Taylor[1]

The last time I was in Edmonton I got asked it again. It's a question I find myself getting asked quite frequently, as if I am the spokesperson for all Native men in Canada (if I am, I want a better salary). And to tell you the truth, it's getting annoying. This time it happened on a radio talk show hosted by a Native woman. Logically, it is always a Native woman who asks this question.

"Why is it that Native men, when they reach a certain level of success and power, end up dating and marrying only white women, and not Native women?"

Often they point to Ovide Mercredi, Graham Greene and Tom Jackson as examples. All well known, prosperous men who's partners are of the Caucasian persuasion. This is a question and issue that is of specific interest to many Native women, who regard this practice as a rejection of them, and the preservation of Native society.

Many Aboriginal nations are either entirely or directly matriarchal, or have elements involving strong female interaction embedded in the culture. There is a belief that women are the protectors and teachers of the culture, especially when it comes to raising children. So when a non-Native woman enters the scene, it can disrupt what some see as the continuing cycle of cultural preservation.

But understanding that, is their question still a valid one? True, you go to many functions and social gatherings where the intelligentsia or successful Aboriginal gather, and it does seem like the majority of the Native men do sport non-Native spouses. Jordan Wheeler, Native writer for SIXTY BELOW and THE REZ (who's wife by the way is a lovely Native woman) blames it on the circles "prosperous" Native people are forced to circulate.

Since there are more "successful" white people than Native people, relatively speaking, and more "prominent" Native males then females, again I use the term loosely, the individuals one is likely to meet, interact and develop relationships with will have a mathematical probability of being non-Native female. Unfortunate but true.

However, I do seriously doubt this is the only reason. Life is not that simple. Some who like to dabble in amateur (or not so amateur) sociological examination believe there is a deeply subconscious (or maybe not so deep) belief that a non-Native girlfriend is a symbol of success, of achievement in both white and Native society. Or then there's the theory that white women are just easier to find in the dark. I don't know which is the correct answer, or even if there is an answer. One could say that maybe two people just fell in love, but for reasons I've quoted above, this issue has taken up a political taint to it.

If snuggling with people of no definable Native heritage is a crime, then it is one I am guilty of. Rightly or wrongly, I am a graduate of the "color-blind school of love". But taking into account the last four girlfriends I have had, I've noticed a disturbing trend developing in my personal life. One that on the surface, may lend credence to the argument.

One of the first serious relationships I ever had was with a Native woman, then sometimes afterward I fell in love with a woman who was a half breed like myself, then I found myself with a Filipino woman (still technically a visible minority but not Native and not Caucasian). Then finally, I spent several years with a white woman. If this trend keeps up, my next girlfriend will either be an albino or an alien.

To the best of my knowledge, none of these relationships were politically or socially motivated. I'm not that bright or ambitious. They just developed as most relationships do. You see each other in a room, make eye contact, you mumble to yourself "oh please God, please", and the rest I'll leave to your imagination.

One older Native woman, a strong proponent of Native men marrying Native women, even verbally chastised me for dating a white girl, urging me to break up with her and start seeing a Native woman she had just recently met. Even though her three daughters had married, had children by, or were simply dating white men, I was at fault here. The irony of the situation was not lost on me.

This begs a different consideration to the original dating question. Why is it never questioned why successful Native women, such as Buffy Ste. Marie or Tantoo Cardinal, marry white men? Granted the ratio is substantially different but still I think it is a valid issue. I even posed that question to the hostess on the radio show. She looked at me blankly for a moment before answering "I don't know. I don't have an answer for that."

And is it only the white culture that's at question here? The issue of the dominant culture absorbing and sublimating the much smaller Aboriginal culture? What about, for sake of argument, Black people? There was no noticeable reaction to my relationship with my Filipino girlfriend, in fact many people jokingly commented that she looked more Native then I did. What about the Asians, both South (the real "Indians"!) And East? And if you really want to throw a wrench into the works, what about the Sami, the Aboriginal people of Scandinavia, otherwise known as the Laplanders? They all have blonde hair and blue eyes but are recognized as an indigenous people. I've been claiming to be half Sami, half Ojibway for years.

And does this question only relate to procreative couples? What about gay and lesbian relationships? I've never heard of any grief being given or received over an inter-racial relationship in either community. It all gets so confusing.

So I sit here, a single man, afraid to pick up the telephone and call somebody. For depending on who I phone, I will no doubt be making a very important and major political statement. I just want somebody to go to the movies with.

---

1   Drew Hayden Taylor (Curve Lake Reserve, Ontario) is one of the most prolific Aboriginal playwrights and columnists in Canada. His collection of stories are published in *Funny, You Don't Look Like One* and *Further Adventures of a Blue-Eyed Ojibway*.

How Native is Native if You're Native?

Drew Hayden Taylor[1]

Within the growing and diverse Native community, there seems to be an ongoing ideological battle raging. One that seems to have reversed itself from what was practiced decades ago. I remember growing up, that the more "Native" you looked, for example, dark skinned with prominent Aboriginal features, the lower you were on the social totem pole (no cultural appropriation of West Coast symbols intended).

White was in and Native people (and no doubt many other ethnic) tried to look it, dress it or act it. Those that didn't were often made fun of. Being dark was no lark. In the Caucasian world, people who's family history included a drop or two of Native blood bent over backwards to keep the scandal a secret. The skeletons in those closets would thrill anthropologists and museums the world over.

These days, it's a completely different ball game. Native is in. The darker you are, the more you are embraced, the more "Indian" you are thought to be. The lighter your skin, the more difficult it sometimes is to be accepted by your Aboriginal peers (and the non-Native world). White is no longer right. And heaven forbid, those in the dominant culture with some barely remembered ancestor that happened to tickle toes and trade more then some furs and beads with a Native person, should let a conversation slip by without managing to mention at least four of the 24 chromosomes in their body don't burn in the summer sun.

But its often more then simply how you look. It's how you think, act, where you live, and point with your lower lip. Consequentially, something more representational of the existing philosophical schism is the difficult question of determining "what makes a Native a Native?" What set of qualifications or characteristics will allow an individual to speak as a Native person, or have an opinion representative of the larger Indigenous population? Sure as Hell beats me. But as sure as there's a hundred "Xena - Warrior Princess" web sites on the Net, there are a vast number of "experts" existing in this world eager to tell you what defines a Native and would more then happily tell you whether you fit into that category.

Personally I think it must be so great to have all the answers. My ambition in life is to be such an expert. I have done the necessary amount of research. God (or the Creator) knows my blueish-green eyes have allowed me a unique entry into such discussions. Drew Hayden Taylor - Aboriginal Attitude and Attributes Assessor (DHT - AAAA).

One such example of the broad spectrum of Aboriginal acceptance involves the world of education. Many Reserves and Native educational organizations are constantly encouraging and extolling the virtues of education to the youth.Yet, there are many individuals in these communities who believe that the more education you become, the less "Native" you will be. They scorn and disdain those who want to or have gone through the educational process. Evidently, knowledge and learning deprives an individual of their cultural heritage. I must have missed that in the sweat lodge.

Conversations with Elders and traditional teachers have convinced me that this is not a traditional teaching. Many Elders urge and encourage the pursuit of education. In fact, the two worlds of tradition and scholastic education can, and often do, travel the same roads, albeit one on horseback and the other on a vintage 1953 Indian Scout motorcycle. In fact, those that are often wary of formal education are usually locked somewhere between both worlds, neither traditional, nor particularly well-educated. Unfortunately, it is their own insecurity that is being presented - thus proving the need for educated Native psychologists.

Another example on the flip side involves the disquieting story a Native educator told of a Reserve education counsellor in a southern Ontario community. Practically every year this person would ask at least one and who knows how many off-Reserve students, "why should you continue going to University?" She would then strongly hint that this student almost owes it to the community to quit school, saving the Reserve money.

So if some students on the Reserve are being urged not to go to University, but all the money is being reserved for them to go, where is all this money going? That is what is called the I-don't-know-if-I-should-go-to-school-or-stay-home-and-collect-welfare-or-possibly-scratch-out-a-living-telling-students-what-to-do Paradox.

I have a column in a Regina newspaper/magazine jokingly called "The Urbane Indian". I was telling this to a Native woman at a meeting and she asked me what urbane meant. I told her it was similar to sophisticated, refined or knowledgeable. She thought for a moment before responding "I hope I never get like that." Evidently being suave and debonair (or as we say on the Reserve - swave and debone-her) is not a Native characteristic worth having.

There are also those who believe the more successful you are, the less Native you are considered. If you have money, toys, a nice house, two accountants and have a vague idea where the Caribbean is, then you are obviously not one of the Indigenous people. I remember reading an interview with a successful Prairie business man who was looked down upon by his brethren because he had made a financial success of his life. And he rationalized it out as "If being Indian means being poor, then I don't necessarily want to be Indian." A harsh statement indicating the man did not think there was a middle ground. I know many successful Aboriginals who are every bit as "Native" as those who still subsist on Kraft dinner and 1974 Dodge pickups.

Taking all of this into consideration, I guess this means the only true "Native" people are uneducated, poor people with poor vocabularies.

As cliched as it may sound, I think everybody has their own unique definition of what being Native means. Very few of us exist in the world our grandparents lived in, where their definition was no doubt far from ours. And this definition will no doubt further evolve in the coming Millennium. My career as a DHT - AAAA will have to wait because I don't have all the answers. I don't know the boundaries and necessary factors for such important decisions like these. To tell you the truth, I don't even care anymore.

I do know one thing though. Passing judgement on other people isn't a particularly Aboriginal thing to do. I know this because an eagle came to me in my dreams, along with a coyote and a raven, they landed on the tree of peace, smoked a peace pipe, had a baloney sandwich, played some bingo, then told me so.

That should shut them up.

---

[1]   Drew Hayden Taylor is an Ojibway from the Curve Lake Reserve in Ontario. His plays, including *Toronto at Dreamers Rock*, *Only Drunks and Children Tell the Truth* and *Someday*, have been produced numerous times throughout Canada. His collection of stories are published in *Funny You Don't Look Like One* and *Further Adventures of a Blue Eyed Ojibway*.

Issues of Hybridity in Ian Ross' *fareWel*

Chris Johnson[1]

Abstract

Ian Ross is frequently concerned with issues of 'hybridity'. In fareWel, Ian constructed a hybrid identity, one which allows him to transgress several boundaries, between white and Native, comic and serious, clear-sightedness and hopefulness. Ian Ross began by drawing on his non-Aboriginal heritage. Work on fareWel, and work with Aboriginal actors and Aboriginal characters, created a balance derived in part from learning what his characters learn.

Introduction

Winnipeg playwright Ian Ross was brought up in and to some extent continues to live in two worlds. He is the son of a status Native woman and a Métis father, and he spent the first few years of his life in the Métis community of Kinosota. His family moved to Winnipeg when he was five. He has spent a good deal of time on his mother's reserve, Fairford, where he has family, and that experience is an important part of who he is. On the other hand, he was brought up in multi-cultural Winnipeg and was educated in a Euro-centered school system. His first theatrical loves, acquired as a Film and Theatre student at the University of Manitoba, were Shakespeare, Ibsen, and Mamet (all of whom, incidentally, influence *fareWel*); only later did he come to admire the writing of Native playwrights like Tomson Highway (who is also an influence on *fareWel*). Little wonder then that his writing is frequently concerned with issues of "hybridity".

I use the term "hybridity" as it has been employed by the theorists of postcolonialism. "Postcolonial studies have been preoccupied," says Loomba (1998:173), "with issues of hybridity, creolization, *mestizaje*, in-betweenness, diasporas and liminality, with the mobility and cross-overs of ideas and identities generated by colonialism." Ironically, the phenomenon which has come to be thought of as "hybridity" originated in colonial strategies of subjugation and assimilation; through interbreeding and education, the "native" (and here we use the term generically) was to be Europeanized. That is, "improved" but nonetheless kept in the position of "other". As Loomba (1998:173) says, "The underlying premise was, of course, that Indians can mimic but never exactly reproduce English values, and that their recognition of the perpetual gap between themselves and the 'real thing' will ensure their subjection." However, Loomba (1998:174) continues, "In practice it did not necessarily work in that way: anti-colonial movements and individuals often drew upon Western ideas and vocabularies to challenge colonial rule. Indeed they often hybridized what they borrowed by juxtaposing it with indigenous ideas, reading it through their own interpretative lens, and even using it to assert cultural alterity."

Cultural Alterity and fareWel

fareWel "borrows" the form of Eurocentric theatre, even techniques particular to individual European writers, juxtaposes it with indigenous ideas, and, ultimately, asserts a cultural alterity while at the same time examining the nature of that alterity. Most of the characters in the play are caught between two worlds, and must learn to derive strength rather than stasis from their "in betweenness". Ian started fareWel believing that he had some answers. The first draft strongly embodied his conviction that self-government would lead Aboriginal people into an even deeper state of despair. It concluded with Rachel weeping; that ending was the first image of the play to come into his mind. The first draft also reflected Ian's Christian background in that the Christians in the story were more in control of their lives than were the characters who followed traditional Native spiritual beliefs -- the Christians don't drink. Again in retrospect, Ian feels that he was rather too doctrinaire, pointing out that those who follow the traditional beliefs don't drink either, that it is the people without any belief system at all who are the most vulnerable to substance abuse. On his own reserve, he says the traditional aspect of the culture was so suppressed that he was never really aware of it, except through "superstitions" that crept into Christianity.

Early versions of the play were also strongly critical of Native leadership, indeed suggested that there was no real leadership at all. Finally, Ian said, his answer was: "It's all fucked, and nothing's going to get better." Over the three years it took to write the play, he came to realize that he didn't want to say it's hopeless, that he didn't really believe that, and that he wouldn't be writing about Aboriginal people if he did. More and more, he wanted a note of hopefulness, but in a way that didn't compromise the problems, and that didn't contrive a Hollywood optimism. "I'm not going to say that Rachel changes everything, that everyone's going to school, that Melvin stops sniffing gas, because that's not true." Nonetheless, the play as produced and published ends with everyone getting something of what he or she wants; often that doesn't amount to much, but it is something. So Nigger gets a new sock. And Rachel, after wanting a smoke for the entire play, finally gets a cigarette. And she doesn't weep.

History, Humour and Balance

Ian's theatrical education entered a new dimension when the play was workshopped three times, twice at the Prairie Theatre Exchange and once at Banff, and as the actors involved in the PTE workshops were Native, Ian found himself working with other Aboriginal theatre artists for the first time. When *fareWel* was in its early stages, there was some anxiety in Winnipeg's Aboriginal community, especially among Aboriginal artists, that the play might be damaging to that community's image and political hopes, that it was a bad idea, even disloyal, to expose Native "dirty laundry". However, given the difficult and complicated history of the Aboriginal peoples over the last few centuries, it would be surprising if there weren't in life as well as in Ian's play divisions of opinion and disputes within the community as to what should be done to construct a better future, achieve justice, heal the many nations. As work on the play went on, Ian did take some of these anxieties into account, while never abandoning the ambition to look at the problem whole, not papering over the cracks but showing a community struggling with a hard past and an uncertain future, having to work to equip itself to participate in the debates, showing the fears experienced by smaller groups within the larger, for example the determination felt by many Aboriginal women to avoid replacing one political system from which they are excluded with another political system from which they would be excluded. The Aboriginal actors with whom Ian worked challenged Ian's overly narrow and rigid initial "answers", bringing other Aboriginal experiences to the play. With them came what Ian calls "balance", and more questions, and the questions, Ian found, were more interesting than the answers. Now, he says, "My job is to raise questions; if I thought I had answers, I'd be a politician." The play was also becoming funny, if often in a rather disturbing way. As the overly rigid answers moved aside, there was room for the absurdity of the rez situation to assert itself, and also room for a kind of joy achieved against all obstacles. Like Highway before him, Ian was now committed to demonstrating that Aboriginal perspectives are frequently comic perspectives.

The events in *fareWel* are precipitated by the temporary collapse of a colonial system "the welfare cheques don't show up" at the fictional Partridge Crop reserve in the Interlake region of Manitoba. The residents of the reserve are thus compelled to immediately construct a "post-colonial" mode of living, and to do so must mediate between the claims of the past, what Rabillard (1993:6) calls "an essential and definitive purity", and the vicissitudes of a complex and unstable present. When Teddy Sinclair launches his political movement aimed at self-government, he significantly does so in Saulteaux. In large part, Teddy's speech calls on the authority of an authentic, and unmixed past: he proposes to ban "blonde-haired, blue-eyed Bill-C31ers", and to return to "Indian religion" (Ross 1997:57). At the same time, apparently unaware of the contradictions, Teddy draws on the values and characteristics of the dominant culture to solve the problems of his reserve: casino revenue, political patronage, and, most significantly, the silencing of women. He tries to refuse both voice and vote to the women present at the meeting. Even the form of Teddy's call for "purity" is in effect hybrid: in the midst of torrents of Saulteaux, English words leap out, their presence made all the more apparent by the contrast, the significance of their values underlined by the fact that there is no Saulteaux word to express the thoughts and judgments they carry: "Las Vegas", "wheels of fortune", "blackjack", "slot machines", "Bill C-31", "blond hair", "Bazooka Joes", "Nigger", "gravel", "hooker".

It is primarily Rachel who sees through Teddy's political platform and recognizes that while Teddy's anger is certainly genuine, his plan is also patriarchal, neo rather than post colonial, and ultimately a grab for personal power. She abandons her plan to go back to Winnipeg, where she had lived in the past, and stays in Partridge Crop to fight for her version of the future, one which, would include women, would not ban the Christians in the name of traditional values, nor the C-31ers for their matrilineality and hybridity. In the climactic confrontation of the play, she puts on a dance costume traditionally reserved for men, confronts Teddy, and dances, her breasts bared "the gaze is disrupted and turned back on itself" as a forceful theatrical image of female power. Rachel's defiant dance is a gender transgressive act that calls into question the validity of Teddy's dubious appeal to the 'authentic'. "It's time to put things right" she tells Teddy, "To say goodbye to the things that keep us down. Our people's future comes from the past. Not male or female. Pure or mixed.

Christian or Traditional. It's all these things. Together. Respected." (Ross 1997:88). Rachel's inclusive vision embraces the recent as well as the distant past: to find an identity that neither rejects nor confines itself to tradition. Partridge Crop must accept and recognize not only some values of pre-contact culture, but also what has since happened to that culture, the consequences of its encounter with the dominant culture and of its colonization.

The past is gone, but it can still exert an influence, can still be called on to resist assimilation. Rachel herself refers to tradition and to traditional practice in constructing this new course for herself as a Native woman: before she commits her act of gender defiance, she goes to an elder to have the dance outfit blessed. But, pragmatically and obviously, she must go to the only elder available, Sheldon, or "Nigger" Traverse, hardly the noble savage and wise old man of romantic myth. "How come you're asking me?" Nigger asks. "Because. You're an Elder." "No one's said that to me before. That I'm an Elder." "Can I use this?" Rachel asks, referring to the dance outfit. "What does your heart tell you?" "Yes." "OK then" (Ross 1997:81). Before Rachel leaves, she offers him two cigarette butts, the only tobacco she has, and calls him "Sheldon", addresses him by his name rather than the habitual, defining nickname or label. Among other things, Rachel is reviving and rehabilitating the traditional institution of the Elder, a deference to experience, but real experience in the real and present world rather than an authority derived from myth, and certainly rather than myth reinterpreted by someone else's culture.

For Ian, Nigger personifies what he sees as the most important characteristic of Native people: the ability to survive. Every accident that can befall a human being seems to happen to Nigger: dogs chase and bite him, a chain saw falls on his leg, he gets caught in a garbage truck compactor, he accidentally shoots himself, he sets himself on fire by smoking when he tries to sniff gasoline, he gets run over by a police car. But still he keeps coming back.

Among other things, Nigger, including his nickname, is a dramaturgical ambush, as indeed are most of the other characters in the play, an invitation to succumb to stereotype followed by a subversion of the stereotype. In many respects, Nigger resembles an Aryan Nations racist caricature of the Indian bum: he depends on Welfare, is none too clean, smells, lives in the present and for the moment, is child-like, naive, impulsive, careless, improvident, and accident prone. We learn that in the past, Nigger lived on Winnipeg's Skid Road and subsisted as a panhandler until he was run over by a police car, was awarded $10,000 in compensation, returned to Partridge Crop, sobered up, and gave his money away to other residents of the reserve. Nigger is the sort of Indian most white members of the audience would avoid if they encountered him on the street. He suggests as strategies for approaching Ottawa the tactics that worked for him as a panhandler: "look really pitiful" and "bug the shit out of someone".

When Nigger is trying to comfort a mixed up young man by reciting the advantages of being Indian, he mentions first that Indians don't go "bald headed". He then adds that Indians taught the white man to eat turkey, and that's how Thanksgiving came to be, "except they don't share our turkey with us anymore." "Indians are teachers," he says, "We're gonna teach the white people again how to live." We in the audience get set for a "my heart soars like a hawk" speech, words of wisdom from the culturally pure Other, the voice of one "close to nature". Instead, we get: "Lots more white people are gonna be poor. And they're gonna be on welfare. And because we already know how to live on welfare. We're gonna teach them how to live again" (Ross 1997:74). The dislocation of our expectations is funny, but the real joke is that Nigger is right, as he often is in the play. The character who is funny and likable but nonetheless apparently dismissible in his resemblance to devaluing stereotype is in fact very perceptive, an Elder whose wisdom derives from a long and relatively successful struggle with life, as Rachel recognizes, a wisdom more often than not expressed in unassuming, vernacular Amerindian English.

Late in the play, it would appear that Nigger has finally been killed, struck by a truck and knocked into the ditch. I've seldom seen an audience so upset and moved by the apparent death of a fictional character "audible" Oh no's, followed by a tangible hush and stillness on the part of white and Native audience members alike. Great relief when he returns, even more battered than he was before, but still very much alive. And it's not an arbitrary sentimental reversal "we've been told, shown, that he always survives." At Nigger's return, we realize that we've come to love him, for who he is now, and that affection extends to characteristics stereotype teaches us are reasons to despise him. Good ambush. This is the Elder in a new form, a figure of great transgressive power, and yet another way in which the spirit of the Trickster can manifest itself in the world.

Similarly, Rachel too is linked to racist stereotype, and to sexist stereotype as well -- it's revealed that in her Winnipeg past, she was a prostitute, and significantly, Teddy holds against her not only her former trade, but her insufficient "Indianness": "I would never sleep with this disease. She's not even proud of her own hair. Look at it. It's dyed. Indian hair. Black hair. She's embarrassed of it." "Get your black ass off my reserve" (Ross 1997:59). As Loomba notes, "Colonialism intensified patriarchal relations in colonized lands, often because native men, increasingly disenfranchised and excluded from the public sphere, became more tyrannical at home" (Loomba 1998:168). Here, Teddy is trying to reclaim the public sphere through Native self-government, and refuses to share, to include a woman, especially a "fallen woman", by exerting patriarchal power. But Rachel is not to be dismissed or diminished, either by Teddy, an erstwhile client, or us: "I was a whore. I've been fucked many times. It's made me strong" (Ross 1997: 88).

Melvin, the C-31er unsure of his identity as an Indian, the character in this play with whom Ross most identifies, is a habitual sniffer of gasoline. Substance abuse, like destitution and prostitution, is shown to be more than a stereotyped attribute, but the material consequence of economic and political facts, one of an individual's many responses to those facts rather than the entire individual. This is not something to be evaded but the recent part of a history which must be accepted in its entirety if it is to be used as a source of strength: in order to recover parts of the distant past, one must work through the recent past.

Melvin is the character in the play least sure of his identity as an Aboriginal, the site where claims of the culturally pure past and the hybridized present are most vigorously contested. Much of the confusion arises from the dominant culture's historical and political attempts to define who is and who is not Aboriginal, to contain the "other" through legal inscription. C-31 is the federal legislation passed in 1985 which restored legal Indian status and concomitant rights to Native women who had lost their status by marrying non-Native men. Previously, only Native men retained their status when they married a non-Native, and furthermore their non-Native wives acquired status through the marriage.

Ian Ross sees C-31 as positive in a number of respects. It restored rights to women who had lost them (like Ian's mother, as Ian's father is a non-status Métis), and also to their children (like Ian). He sees the political struggle leading up to the passing of C-31 as an example of Aboriginal women standing up for themselves, rejecting roles attributed to them by both gender and race, as Rachel does in his play. He also sees the tactics involved, going outside the country for assistance from international bodies like the United Nations, as a forerunner of the political future of Native Canadians, for he believes that only through Aboriginal people's going outside Canada for allies can enough pressure be put on the Canadian government and the non-Native Canadian public to persuade them to recognize treaty rights and rectify other injustices.

He draws parallels to the international pressure put on the apartheid regime in South Africa.

On the other hand, the effects of C-31 have exacerbated social problems on a number of reserves, and is itself a contentious issue in many Aboriginal communities. Some reserve lists literally doubled overnight, but as resources and financial support have not been increased proportionately, that has meant less for all. There is conflict and resentment about whether those who are on the list by virtue of C-31 but who do not reside on the reserve should have the same treaty rights as those who have lived on the reserve all their lives, whether, for example, education funds should go to non-residents with, perhaps, higher grades, at the expense of reserve kids. A set of white laws and revisions, the Indian Act, originally promulgated to achieve racist ends, has created a kind of racism on the Reserves.

Teddy has learned misogyny, and has internalized racism. He is the most virulent example of a racism that, in the unstable present, is a demonstrable part of current reserve culture: hybridity is not necessarily entirely benevolent. On one hand, Nigger is called "Nigger" because his skin is darker than that of most "he is almost too Indian", a compendium of those characteristics which his neighbours believe are the reasons the dominant culture looks down on all Indians. Melvin, on the other hand, is not Indian enough. Teddy taunts Melvin with being a C-31er, unworthy of the group's acceptance, even of gravel on the road in front of his house. "All you got is a card and some bullshit treaty number" (Ross 1997:58). "Race" and "purity", concepts historically used to exclude and dehumanize Aboriginals, are now used by some Aboriginals to deny hybridity and thus maintain the rigid definition and division of cultures.

The white government says that Melvin is an Indian, but that isn't good enough for Melvin nor for some other residents of the Partridge Crop Reserve. Teddy not only taunts Melvin with his C-31 status but denies him work with the new band council: "You're lucky I even let you stay here [on the Reserve]. I can get rid of all you Bill-C31ers. You're just a bunch of mooches. Taking away from us real Indians" (Ross 1997:77). Note how he mirrors the vocabulary of racist slurs directed against Indians by right-wing whites. Teddy also uses Melvin's racial insecurity to coerce the young man into illegal and dangerous activity. If Melvin 'borrows' a truck Teddy needs to move some gambling equipment, Teddy will make Melvin an Indian: it's a "spiritual thing" says Teddy, and besides, "Indians don't chicken out from nothing" (Ross1997: 78). (It is this truck, with Melvin at the wheel, that almost kills Nigger.)

Typically, it is Nigger who is most willing to accept Melvin as an Indian. He will teach him Saulteaux. He gives Melvin the lesson about Indians being teachers. Furthermore, Melvin is an Indian, Nigger says, because Nigger recognizes him as an Indian: "Indians know other Indians Even if they're part white. We're brothers and sisters" (Ross 1997:73). Thus Nigger's understanding of Aboriginality, like Rachel's, includes and embraces hybridity. By the end of the play, Melvin learns that the most important definition of "Indian" is his. When the welfare cheques fail to show up again, Melvin gets angry: "You fuckers. Where the hell's our money? You're making us starve and live in shit. I'm sick of it. You hear that? Are you hearing me? I'll kill you. I'll kill all of you. You fuckers. I hate this. Do you hear me?" (Ross 1997:89), and he rips up his treaty card. Later he realizes that getting mad made him feel good: "It made me feel like . . . an Indian" (Ross 1997:90). The defining emotion is more authentic, more to the point, than the treaty card.

By the end of the play, then, Melvin feels like an Indian. Nigger discovers that people regard him as a "good man" and that he doesn't have to die for people to feel that way. Rachel and Teddy accept each other for who they are, a Native woman and a Native man, freed from the definitions imposed upon them by the dominant culture and from expectations created by a past to which they cannot return. The Partridge Crop Pentecostal Church, which Teddy turned into the "Creator's Church", is finally the "Partridge Crop Pentecostal Church of the Creator", with room for both Christians and Traditionalists. While it is true that by the end of the play, colonialism has returned in the form of Welfare, or fareWel, the people of the Partridge Crop First Nation have changed, a little, during the ellipsis, and now dare to think in terms of a permanently post-colonial culture. Most of the changes move in the direction of rejecting hierarchy and rigidity, of transgressing boundaries regardless of the origins of those borders, of accepting and growing a hybrid culture.

Conclusion

In writing this play, Ian Ross constructed for himself a hybrid identity, one which allows him to transgress several boundaries, between white and Native, obviously, but also between comic and serious, between clear-sightedness and hopefulness -- "I'm either a romantic cynic or a cynical romantic," he says. When I first knew him (Ross 1996), he leaned more towards the "white" component of his heritage, but the work on the play, work with Aboriginal actors and Aboriginal characters, created the "balance" to which he refers; this balance derives in part from learning what his characters learn. To paraphrase Loomba, he, like his characters, can now hybridize what he borrows [from Mamet, for example, or from my theatre history courses] by juxtaposing it with indigenous ideas, reading it through his own interpretative lens, and using it to assert cultural alterity.

References

Loomba, A. 1998. *Colonialism/Postcolonialism.* London and New York: Routledge.

Rabillard, S. 1993. Absorption, elimination, and the hybrid: Some impure questions of gender and culture in the trickster drama of Tomson Highway. *Essays in Theatre* 12(1):3-27.

Ross, I. 1997. *fareWel.* Winnipeg: Scirocco Drama.

Ross, I. 1996. Interview with Chris Johnson, February.

[1]   Chris Johnson is a Professor of theater in the Department of English at the University of Manitoba.

The Medicine Wheel:
An Examination of Its Use and Purpose

Jonathan Ellerby[1]

Abstract

This paper explores the contemporary and historical use of the medicine wheel. Academic contentions surrounding its origins and Aboriginal understandings of its place in spiritual tradition are addressed. The use of more culturally specific symbols and teachings which more accurately represent the unique culture and history of different Aboriginal communities are suggested.

Introduction

The medicine wheel has become a prevalent symbol in Aboriginal and non-Aboriginal Canadian society today. It is found wherever Aboriginal specific programs exist: from the halls of hospitals, to the walls of prisons and on to the recovery programs common to Aboriginal communities. The medicine wheel image is also integrated into spiritual literature (Meadows 1989), public logos, and the new age iconography of the late twentieth century (Eaton 1982, Sun Bear and Wabun 1992). Western scholars (Haack 1987, Moore 1973, Townsend In Press) have challenged the origins of the medicine wheel and the Aboriginal right to claim its historicity. Aboriginal scholars and spiritual leaders have also brought into question its present use and the many claims of its origin (Moore 1973). The common presence of the medicine wheel in "new age" philosophy in particular has created a distinct area of concern in Aboriginal circles (Churchill 1988, 1994).

The medicine wheel is now central to the teaching models, religious education, and therapeutic approaches found commonly among Aboriginal people across the Canadian prairies and elsewhere. Widespread use alone has justified its validity (Brink 1990). The questions explored in this paper are: "What are the effects of this 'pan-Indian' usage? What are the negative consequences of the popularization of the medicine wheel image? And, what are the challenges it presents for the future?" Though final conclusions may be impossible, we must begin the important dialogue about the future development and change in the representation of Aboriginal identity and cultural philosophy.

Basic Medicine Wheel Designs

The term medicine wheel generally refers to the visual image of a circle divided equally into four quadrants. The explanation of the symbolism and meaning of this image varies among authors and Aboriginal communities. Common interpretations include the medicine wheel as representative of a cosmology that is divided into four, including: four directions of the world, four seasons, four aspects of the human (mind, body, heart and soul), and four stages of life (infancy, adolescence, adulthood, old age) (McGaa 1990). Understood as both a cyclical model and a holistic representation, the medicine wheel symbolizes various levels and systems of human experience and belief (Bopp *et al.* 1984, McFarland 1993).

Usually, Aboriginal instruction on the symbolism of the medicine wheel includes colour and animal associations with each of the directions. The colours are based on pre-existing cultural patterns and beliefs, while the animals are symbolic of the human qualities and lessons attributed to each particular quadrant. As a hypothetical example, the eagle may be associated with the north, as well as wisdom, old age and winter. The medicine wheel can be extremely complex in its interrelated layers of symbolism, religious meaning, and didactic representation.

The Medicine Wheel as a Pedagogical Tool

Outside of non-Aboriginal New Age appropriation, applications of the medicine wheel that directly involve Aboriginal people are either used as a pedagogical tool or a cultural analogy. Each of these usages contributes significantly to Aboriginal culture and social health, as well, each use has a number of inherent problems.

As a pedagogical, or instructive tool the medicine wheel serves as a framework for delivering educational or therapeutic approaches within the contexts of western based institutions and Aboriginal communities (Bopp *et al.* 1984, Ellerby and Ellerby 1998, Waldram 1997, White 1996). Many Canadian institutions incorporate the medicine wheel framework in previously non-Aboriginal focussed material and programs. This is usually done through Aboriginal program providers and developers. Occasionally, non-Aboriginal individuals or programs develop an application of the medicine wheel. For example, the medicine wheel is used in Aboriginal curriculum design (White 1996). By mapping the instruction of a course on the medicine wheel framework, the subject material is made psychologically and spiritually relevant through its association with an image that is perceived as distinctly Aboriginal. Another example is the use of medicine wheel frameworks for treatment models in correctional institutions in an effort to make therapeutic group work more relevant to Aboriginal offenders (Ellerby and Ellerby 1998, Waldram 1997). Through the use of the medicine wheel, non-Aboriginal psychological approaches are integrated with Aboriginal concepts and cultural teachings. By making educational and therapeutic opportunities relevant and more meaningful to Aboriginal people, the medicine wheel is an important contribution to Aboriginal culture and social health.

Some academics state there is absolutely no historical presence of the medicine wheel image in any Aboriginal culture (Townsend In press). Others observe many cultural groups with similar images and teachings such as the *changleshka wakan*, or sacred hoop, used by Dakota/Lakota Nations of the North American plains (Brown 1953, Powers 1986, Stolzman 1986). The Dakota/Lakota traditionally incorporated a symmetrical cross, generally representing the four directions, within a circle of equal diameter to create a symbol identical to the contemporary medicine wheel. In a few locations in the great plains region of the United States and the prairie and western Great Lakes region of Canada, ancient patterns of stones are laid out on the ground in a fashion that replicates a medicine wheel-type of design (Calder 1977). The archeological and anthropological conclusions on these finds remain tentative (Eddy 1974, Haack 1987, Kehoe and Kehoe 1977). Like the academic community, in Aboriginal communities there remains a range of opinions, even among communities located near actual archeological "medicine wheel" sites. Some state these designs prove the historicity of the medicine wheel. Others, noting that the configurations of stone pre-date most oral histories and traditional knowledge, state an absence of certainty or any conclusions what so ever.

Other degrees of cultural relationship also exist. The medicine wheel is traditionally referred to in the religious ceremonies and spiritual didactics of many Aboriginal communities, like the Ojibway communities of southern Manitoba and Northwestern Ontario. In these cases, the medicine wheel is fully integrated as a sacred and central symbol for spiritual and holistic instruction (Morrisseau 1998, Nabigon and Mawhiney 1996). Community members and religious leaders state their use of the medicine wheel is historically specific to their culture. In contrast, some academics refute the visual medicine wheel construct, not its component philosophies, which are clearly documented in ethnographic accounts of the importance of the four directions and quadratic paradigms (Brown 1953, Landes 1968). This raises the critical issue of cultural invention. The new use of a symbol does not mean it is not "authentic" or a discontinuation from historical notions and practices (Hobsbawm 1983, Jaimes 1994). Cultural invention is central to Aboriginal cultures and traditions which come from historical, as well as spiritual intervention and inspiration (Irwin 1994). Examination of the degrees of cultural relationship to the medicine wheel is needed to better address the claims of the medicine wheel's existence as a pure contemporary cultural invention.

Regardless of archeology or religious integration, the use of the medicine wheel in Aboriginal communities is strongly related to its use in institutions. Much of the pan-Indian identity gained through Aboriginal educational, recovery and rehabilitation programs is maintained by the individuals that return to their communities. Particularly among community-based treatment programs and providers, the use of the medicine wheel is common and largely informed by institutional experiences and workshops. The institutional dissemination and pan-Indian nature of the medicine wheel presents its major pedagogical problem in an age of cultural vulnerability: the medicine wheel undermines the representation and empowerment of individual communities and their unique cultural symbols.

While the medicine wheel has had a powerful effect in empowering Aboriginal peoples, its pan-Indian and cross-culturally transferable nature leads to a form of cultural homogenization. The common use of the medicine wheel underscores the commonalties of Aboriginal philosophies and issues. It suggests that the way to create an "Aboriginal approach" to education, treatment or any non-Aboriginal concept is to re-articulate it in the framework of the medicine wheel. This undervalues and ignores the distinct variations among Aboriginal cultural groups by implying that they can all be philosophically reduced to the same models. The extensive use of the medicine wheel maintains a lack of attention to community specific symbols and the potential for new pan-Indian images which might suggest diversity in a better way.

The pedagogical use of the medicine wheel to "Indigenize" non-Aboriginal forms of programming masks the maintenance of non-

Aboriginal control and philosophical dominance. For example, a prison rehabilitation program remodelled on the medicine wheel framework still maintains an agenda based on institutional authority. The use of medicine wheels to create cultural familiarity and sensitivity within institutions, or in the passing of information in any way, is often a symbolic and superficial gesture with little regard to the important issues of social control, authority or self-direction (Havemann 1988, Kellough 1980).

The Medicine Wheel as a Cultural Analogy

The medicine wheel is also used as a visual representation of Aboriginal philosophy which is often within the context of institutional pedagogical settings. As a cultural analogy, the medicine wheel is used to express the nature of Aboriginal philosophy or cosmology suggesting that the worldview or psychological reality of an Aboriginal community or individual can be expressed in terms of the medicine wheel design. When the medicine wheel is used as a framework, there is a sense of utility and separation between the information and the model. When it is used as a religious teaching tool there is a sense that it is a construct, a rich symbolic element within a larger tradition. In contrast, there is a danger when the model itself is expressed as *representative* of Aboriginal experience or philosophy.

The medicine wheel may represent *parts* or *elements* of an Aboriginal worldview, however, it does not represent the *relationship* or *experience* of those elements with any degree of sophistication. A common example of this inadequacy can be seen when the medicine wheel is used to represent Aboriginal philosophy of human nature (Bopp *et al.* 1984, Nabigon and Mawhiney 1996). In this application, each quadrant of the medicine wheel represents a part of the "self". This model generalizes the Aboriginal belief in the mental, emotional, spiritual, and physical elements of human beings, as well as the holistic nature of experience. It does not, however, represent the *relationship* between these elements correctly.

Spirituality is not a sub-categorical *element* of reality; rather, it is the *foundation* of all things (Beck *et al.* 1992, Deloria 1994, 1995). This relationship would be more accurately represented in other models where the visual image actually reflects a distinctly Aboriginal view in which spirituality is represented as the core. The medicine wheel model of the "self" is based on a Western, or Cartesian, notion of reality which divides the natural world into parts (Wilber 1998). In fact, the most central distinction between Cartesian and Aboriginal thought is the very specific understanding of the *relationship* between the parts of human beings. This difference is the central flaw in the medicine wheel model. In the representation of Aboriginal belief and experience the medicine wheel is inappropriate and misleading. The widespread application of the medicine wheel is largely due to its capacity to reorganize *non-Aboriginal* constructs and not because it represents distinctly Aboriginal ones.

Conclusions: Old Ways, New Visions

The medicine wheel has played an important role in the revitalization of Aboriginal tradition and identity. Where Aboriginal representation in Western institutions has been minimal, the use of the medicine wheel has introduced the notion that Aboriginal people may be better served with their own manners of education and treatment. The medicine wheel has recently been instrumental in infiltrating Western institutional paradigms in an attempt to support Aboriginal identity and to make non-Aboriginal conventions relevant and engaging for Aboriginal people. In contrast, for some communities, the medicine wheel has long been an important symbolic element of Aboriginal spirituality and continues as such today. In any case, the contemporary merits of the medicine wheel are clear (Brink 1990).

Now it is time for Aboriginal educators and programming representatives to re-evaluate the role and function of the medicine wheel, and for Aboriginal communities to examine the way this symbol reflects their distinct cultural heritage. The rich symbolism and cultural images common to the Aboriginal communities are obscured by the popularization of this pan-Indian symbol. The stereotypes and reductionist attitudes of non-Aboriginal people have only been perpetuated by the widespread use of a single framework for Aboriginal thought.

Though pan-Indian movements have served to strengthen a broad social Aboriginal identity, they also "Indigenize" forms of non-Aboriginal education, rehabilitation and social control. The improvement of Aboriginal services is critical, however, so is the need for *distinctly* Aboriginal control and development. Medicine wheels are not enough. Each community must begin to manifest their own distinct identity and their own future. The revitalization of Aboriginal culture must come from a celebration of the beautiful diversity in Aboriginal communities.

In addition, non-Aboriginal and Aboriginal scholars must critically challenge the use of the medicine wheel as a representation of Aboriginal paradigms of thoughts, experiences, and worldviews. The publication of mis-representative models only serves to perpetuate false conceptions of Aboriginal peoples. We must begin developing visual representations that indicate, explicitly, the radical differences that exist between Aboriginal and non-Aboriginal thought. The articulation of one worldview in terms of another remains complicated. This is not, however, a conclusive act, rather it is a process. In the movement towards autonomy and independence in Aboriginal communities, the expression of worldview and community identity remains central. Only through these articulations can cross-cultural exchange and understanding begin. In this way individual Aboriginal traditions will be acknowledged for the profound and original contributions they offer pan-Indian and non-Aboriginal thought and society.

References

Beck, P., Walters, A., and Francisco, N. 1992. *The Sacred: Ways of Knowledge, Sources of Life.* Tsaile, AZ: Navajo Community College Press.

Bobb, J., Bobb, M., Brown, L. and Lane, P. 1984. *The Sacred Tree.* Lethbridge, AB: Four Worlds Development Project, University of Lethbridge.

Brink, N. 1990. The healing powers of the Native American medicine wheel. In J. Shorr and P. Robin (Eds.) *Imagery: Current Perspectives* pp. 45-54. New York: Plenum Press.

Brown, J. (Ed.) 1953. *The Sacred Pipe: Black Elk's Account of the Seven Rites of the Ogalala Sioux.* Norman, OK: University of Oklahoma Press.

Calder, J. 1977. *The Majorville Cairn and Medicine Wheel Site Alberta.* Ottawa: National Museum of Canada.

Churchill, W. 1988. A little matter of genocide: Native American spirituality and New Age hucksterism. *Bloomsbury Rev.* September/October: 23-24.

Churchill, W. 1994. *Indians Are Us?* Toronto:Between the Lines Publishing Co.

Deloria, V. 1994. *God is Red.* New York: Delta Books.

Deloria, V. 1995. *Red Earth, White Lies.* New York: Scribner.

Eaton, E. 1982. *The Shaman and the Medicine Wheel.* Wheaton,IL: Theosophical.

Eddy, J. 1974. Astronomical alignments of the Big Horn medicine wheel. *Science* *184*(4141): 1035-1043.

Ellerby, L. and Ellerby J. 1998. *Understanding the Role of Elders and Traditional Healers in the Treatment of Aboriginal Sex Offenders.* Ottawa: Aboriginal Peoples Collection.

Haack, S. 1987. A critical evaluation of medicine wheel astronomy. *Plains Anthropologist* 32:77-82.

Havemann, P.1988.The Indignization of social control in Canada. In B. Morse and G. Woodman (Eds.) *Law & Society* pp. 71-100. Providence,RI: Foris.

Hobsbawm, E. 1983. Introduction. In E. Hobsbawm and T. Ranger (Eds.) *The*

Invention of Traditions pp. 1-14. Cambridge: University Press.

Irwin, L. 1994. *The Dream Seekers.* Norman, OK: University of Oklahoma.

Jaimes, M. 1994. Pan-Indianism. In M. Davis (Ed.) *Native North America in the Twentieth Century* pp. 538-541. New York: Garland Publishers.

Kehoe, T. and Kehoe, A. 1977. Stones, solstices, and Sun Dance structures. *Plains Anthropologist* 22(76): 85-95.

Kellough, G. 1980. From colonialism to economic imperialism: The experience of the Canadian Indian. In J. Harp and J. Hofely (Eds.) *Structured Inequality in Canada* pp. 343-376. Scarborough, ON: Prentice-Hall.

Landes, R. 1968. *Ojibwa Religion and the Midewewin.* Milwaukee: University of Wisconsin Press.

McFarland, R. 1993. Indian medicine wheels and placentas: How the tree of life and the circle of life are related. *J. of Psychohist. 20* (4): 453-464.

McGaa, E. 1990. *Mother Earth Spirituality.* New York: Harper.

Meadows, K. 1989. *Earth Medicine.* Rockport, MA: Element.

Moore, J. 1973. Review of *Seven Arrows* by Hyemeyohsts Storm. *American Anthropologist 75:* 1040-1043.

Morrisseau, C. 1998. *Into the Daylight: A Wholistic Approach to Healing.* Toronto: University of Toronto Press.

Nabigon, H. and Mawhiney, A. 1996. A Cree medicine wheel guide for healing First Nations. In Turner, F. (Ed.) *Social Work Treatment: Interlocking Theoretical Approaches* pp. 18-36. New York: Free Press.

Powers, W. 1986. *Sacred Language: The Nature of Supernatural Discourse in Lakota.* Norman, OK: University of Oklahoma Press.

Stolzman, W. 1986. *The Pipe and Christ: A Christian-Sioux Dialogue.* Chamberlain, SD: Tipi Press.

Sun Bear and Wabun.1992. *The Medicine Wheel: Earth Astrology.* NY: Simon & Schuster.

Townsend, J. In press. Shamanic spirituality: Core shamanism and neoshamanism in contemporary western society. In S. Glazier (Ed.) *Readings in the Anthropology of Religion.* Westport: Greenwood Publishing.

Waldram, J. 1997. *The Way of the Pipe.* Peterborough, ON: Broadview Press.

White, L. 1996. Medicine wheel teachings. In S. O'Meara and D. West (Eds.) *From Our Eyes* pp. 107-122. Toronto: Garamond Press.

Wilber, K. 1998. *The Marriage of Sense and Soul: Integrating Science and Religion.* Toronto: Random House.

---

[1]   Reverend Jonathan Ellerby (MA) has worked for many years with Aboriginal and Indigenous spiritual leaders learning traditional Aboriginal spirituality and healing.

Deconstructing Tourism Image of a National Park

Kelly MacKay [1]

Abstract

This inquiry considered a First Nation community's interpretation of a national park's image. Data were collected through a focus group using free elicitation and destination visuals. Destination image was interpreted through a deconstructionist framework. Findings indicated distinct and conflicting place images when the Aboriginal group is not clearly defined in a tourism host or guest role.

Introduction

Cultural identity frequently assumes an association or a personal attachment to geographical locations of birth or early socialization (Proshansky *et al.* 1983). The inseparability of nature and culture in many Aboriginal cultures strengthens this sense of place even more. Although Aboriginal cultures are not monolithic, the sacred concept of place percolates throughout (Hinch 1998, Hollinshead 1992). Furthermore, aesthetic landscape values have been linked to cultural identity through their symbolic representations (Bourassa 1990). Tourism destination image advertising has been linked to both cultural identity and political propaganda (Duncan 1991, Papson 1981). Official imaging of distinctive natural features has contributed to the success of many tourist destinations. It is a common symbolism for opposition to or escape from everyday life (Hummon 1988). Over one third of tourist destination brochure content is typically devoted to landscape (Dann 1996a). What is depicted or not depicted in destination image advertising, and on whose authority it is selected, involves a complex question of what comprises the destination and who has the power to define its identity. Cultural analysis of tourism as a secular ritual (MacCannell 1976, Graburn 1983) has revealed tourism advertising as a culturally significant symbolic text (Hummon 1988). The overall goal of this case study was to enhance understanding of place image in the context of a natural tourism destination based on interpretation of promotional visuals by a First Nation community. This inquiry considered the case of one First Nation community's interpretation and evaluation of destination image, as it is conveyed through symbolic aspects of a destination.

Visual Image, Culture, and Nature

Since tourism is uniquely visual, photographs are considered paramount to successfully creating and communicating an image of a destination. In tourism brochures over 75% of the content is pictorial (Dann 1996a). Olson *et al.* (1986) reported that visual content of advertisements affects the perception of vacation experience through association of certain types of pictures with certain types of experiences (e.g. natural scenery interpreted as conducive to a romantic vacation). As such, photographs have been used to understand the process with which tourist destinations are represented (Albers and James 1988). Although destination image advertising relies heavily on visual elements, there is a paucity of research on its pictorial content relating to messages conveyed (e.g., image) through pictures as opposed to the primary (verbal) discourse. Although destination image is conveyed through multiple channels, including verbal messages and managerial practices, photographic and video technology have dominated the communication and perception of destination image (Dann 1996a).

Visuals are one technique of the language of tourism and are paramount in tourist destination promotion and image creation. Image formation models typically correspond to either person-determined image or destination-determined image (Crompton 1977). Person-determined image reflects the individual differences in information processing and interpretation; where as, destination-determined image reflects the actuality of the destination. The nature of the inputs that contribute to individual's image of a destination have been classified as organic and induced (Gunn 1972). Organic refers to the communication not developed by the destination (e.g. news reports) and includes actual experience with a destination. Induced refers to purposeful, targeted marketing efforts devised by the destination. Extensions on Gunn's fundamental conceptualization of image have been offered by several researchers and build on the notion of multidimensionality of image portrayal and formation (Echtner and Ritchie

1993, Fakeye and Crompton 1991, Gartner 1993).

Typically destination image is measured using attribute scales and a structured semantic differential and/or Likert-type methodology (Calantone *et al.* 1989, Crompton 1977, Gartner and Hunt 1987, Hunt 1975, Phelps 1986). Recent departures from this method of inquiry include Dann's (1996b) qualitative analysis of linguistic content of mental images utilizing pictorial stimuli, and Echtner and Ritchie's (1993) multidimensional definition and measurement approach to destination image. Echtner and Ritchie (1993) used both structured and unstructured methods to reveal three underlying dimensions of destination image: attribute-holistic, functional-psychological, and common-unique. Their findings suggested that both symbolic and tangible features play a role in defining image of a place, and that measurement techniques need to be sensitive to multidimensionality of destination image.

Culture is purported to have an influence on how people interpret and experience the natural environment (Kaplan and Kaplan 1989, Kaplan and Talbot 1988, MacKay and Fesenmaier In Press, Ulrich 1983). However, exploration of Aboriginal perspectives on this issue has rarely and only recently occurred (Hinch 1998, MacDonald and McAvoy 1997). The majority of attention relating to Aboriginal peoples and tourism focuses on indigenous cultural tourism product (Colton and Hinch 1999, Hinch and Butler 1996, Hinch and Delamere 1993, Walle 1993, Zeppel 1992) rather than Aboriginal perspectives on tourism representation. This study concentrates on the visual elements of tourism advertising, with the objective of exploring a First Nation community's image of a proximal national park as conveyed through pictorial representations of it.

Research Methods

The problem with this research, like much other qualitative research, is how to best describe the experience of others (Lincoln and Denzin 1994). The researcher is not an objective, neutral observer and is positioned in his/her own socio-political context. The purpose of this case study was not to provide an ethnography; however, it is not possible to write the research report without the presence of the author being felt. The author acknowledges her membership outside the Aboriginal community, her roles and experience as a white female, and the potential influences and interpretations that may result. The intent is to provide voice and elucidate experience as provided by the research participants and as understood by the researcher (Altheide and Johnson 1994). The poststructural approach to this work attempts to examine how power and ideology percolate through the discourse of tourism advertising. The symbolism and meaning of destination image is interpreted through a deconstructionist analysis of tourist destination advertising. Deconstruction is used as a strategic devise to question when authority emerges (Leitch 1983). Deconstruction appears intuitively suitable for this case analysis as it is frequently used to comment on postmodern culture and to question commonly held truths and values. It has been termed a criticism of received ideas (Norris 1991).

The technique of photo elicitation is one way to improve the cultural meaningfulness of questions (Harper 1994). Used as a guide to stimulate discussion, the researcher's interpretation of the pictures (e.g., pre-selected categorizations) is challenged by those asked to interpret them. More specifically, the research participants realize that the researcher does not necessarily share their interpretations and understanding of the pictures. Harper (1994) espouses the use of photo elicitation as a means to redefine the research relationship and as a method to advance ethnographic inquiry. The post-structural paradigm examines the repression of race and class, and the exclusion of voices of marginalized groups (Kincheloe and McLaren 1994). Photography, traditionally, has been perceived as part of the power and domination that lie behind the relationship of dominant culture to minority culture (Harper 1994) and thereby makes it a highly suitable device for the deconstruction and reconsideration of destination visuals as "networks" of power and place representation.

Post-structuralism urges reconsideration of pictures, their formulation, constitution and conventional interpretation. The visual is an occasion for the interplay of multiple meanings/interpretations. Deconstruction is a means to examine the politics of image, to reveal destinations as authors of this image, and to provide a framework for uncovering the implications of promoting destinations based on idealized images. MacCannell (1992) suggests that national parks are museumized nature. Nature has been marked off and interpreted, controlled and staged. Authentic nature has been relegated to that which has been designated as such, pragmatically by legislation and conceptually by sacralization (MacCannell, 1992). The deconstruction framework engaged in this paper examines destination image formation by utilizing relevant comparisons with museums and display (Crew and Sims 1991, Fesenmaier and MacKay 1996). The key comparatives focus on institutional power exercised in terms of creating and controlling image through authoritative voice, recontextualization, authenticity, and created meaning. A focus group is used to explore these issues.

Assessing Place Image

This research,part of a larger study on image of Riding Mountain National Park (RMNP) (MacKay and Fesenmaier 1997), focuses on the results of a focus group conducted with Ojibway (Saulteaux) members of Rolling River First Nation in Erickson, 25 kilometers south of RMNP. Participation by Rolling River First Nation was facilitated through West Region Economic Development Corporation and the community's volunteer association. Arrangements for the focus group to occur at the reserve were made through the third party organization. The contact person was a former resident of Rolling River and assured the researcher that use of English would not be problematic and the general focus group protocol would be acceptable and appropriate for the participants. The focus group technique allowed the researcher to collect a concentrated set of interactions that would not have been accessible to her using other qualitative (e.g., observation, interview) or quantitative methods (e.g., survey) (Morgan 1997). Procedures for the focus group followed Krueger (1994).

The focus group meeting was held on the Rolling River First Nation Reserve at the Band Office/Community Centre. The twelve members of the focus group were all current residents of this First Nation community and spoke English. The group consisted of five women and seven men between the ages of 18 and 64. Participants were provided with refreshments and a monetary donation was made to their volunteer association. After the introductions were made, the research purpose, review of proposed procedures, and negotiations for participant compensation were discussed. The discussion was recorded on flip charts to stimulate group interaction and richer descriptions of the generated responses that may not otherwise have been offered. All follow-up arrangements were handled over the phone with confirmation letters sent by the researcher to the liaison person.

The focus group was designed to assess both organic and induced image. Firstly, participants were asked about their (organic) image of RMNP using questions guided by the multiple dimensions of destination image suggested by Echtner and Ritchie (1993) and administered according to the free elicitation of descriptive adjectives for tourism image assessment technique (Reilly 1990). Specifically participants were asked to provide three words that best describe: the Park to you; the Park as a vacation destination; the mood or atmosphere experienced or expected to be experienced at the Park; and any distinctive or unique attractions at Riding Mountain National Park. With this technique the respondents (rather than the researcher) provide the image dimensions, and a lack of image is revealed through the inability to provide descriptors. Although the discussion of findings from this technique sometimes refers to numbers of responses, the critical focus was on themes emerging from discussions of the evoked image words, the context of the remarks, and their underlying meanings.

Table 1. Responses to Visuals

Slide No.	Description of Visual	Remarks by Group Members
1	Forest	devastation, trees, ravine, creek, flowers, undisturbed, lost, growth, bugs
2	Forest background, canoeists on lake	calm, Europeans coming, togetherness, beaver dam, clear water
3	Signage for a commercial recreation establishment	money, "establishment's name", for sale, useless drive-in, money trap for parents, expensive, fun, recreation, clean cars
4	Chamber of Commerce Information Center building	useless, info centre, waste, meeting place, all alone, lonely, disturbed land
5	Bird on a branch	bird, like to listen to bird, what is bird thinking by himself, dry stick, unhappy bird
6	Children on a marsh boardwalk	destruction of natural environment, tourists, white folk, pollution, manmade bridge, dead spruce, pails to take something out of swamp, disturbing the environment, cattails, warm weather, clear skies, algae/scum on water
7	Hiker overlooking an escarpment	breathtaking view, nice, Bald Hill?, Highway 19, no safety guardrail, tourist, beauty, nice out there, (tree) root out of ground
8	Townsite main street - winter scene	cold, snow, mother nature at her finest, quiet, deserted, closed
9	Canoeists preparing to portage at edge of forest	trouble, beautiful, fall, park employees killing time, fall scene, fresh water, ready to blow up beaver dam, destruction
10	Park Visitor Reception Centre building with children sitting by sign	big sign, pollution, tourists, beyond picture: interpretive centre that is not being properly interpreted, bikes on lawn, kids fighting, used to be a tree there instead of sign
11	Woman and child at beach	not facing camera, no First Nation's people in photos, all tourists in photos
12	Two men playing golf	golf, disturbed soil, possible Oka, bench shouldn't be there, change to natural environment, #4 green, tourist, busy, people waiting, fun, determined, taking his time

Table 1. Responses to Visuals (continued)

Slide No.	Description of Visual	Remarks by Group Members
13	People at Clear Lake beach	itchy, pollution, lots of white people, sand, water, very busy, shopping, no lifeguard, enjoyment
14	Toddler being paddled in a canoe	white boy in canoe, wearing lifejacket, safety, relaxing, clear weather
15	Motor boats moored in lake	anger, pollution, disruption of natural environment, making money on boat rentals, loss of traditional use of lake by First Nations, Canadian flag, asphalt, lumber, buoys, gas boat, killing fish, hydro line to manmade bay, water murky, highly recreational area to waste time if you have money and nothing to do
16	Elk at edge of forest; a canoe with two paddlers	nice, elk, food, dried meat, tourists, damn white people again, beauty, upsetting, people canoeing in environment, autumn leaves, dead trees
17	Woman feeding bird from her hand	whiskey jack, conned whiskey jack with food, not supposed to feed animals, pointless picture, snowplough invasion of nature by man, cold
18	Moose standing under a road sign	skinny moose, pollution, asphalt in Park, man on sign, structure spoils natural beauty of environment, broken up soil, pavement, flowers, moose deciding where to go?
19	Deer on roadside with approaching car	car hitting deer, road kill, wires, fall - deer is gray and fat, pollution, speeding, signage
20	Family riding bicycles in town	destruction of soil & land, museum has changed inside, pollution, people walking on grass, damn white people. flowers, rain on pavement, ranger truck, cyclists, asphalt, dog, government in the hole trying to support the Park - should return it to Native people, lack of proper bicycle safety

Responses to questions about the image of RMNP ("What three words best describe Riding Mountain National Park to you?") often referred to beauty of the natural scenery or to historic federal government expropriation of land from Aboriginal people for a national park ("stolen", "lost", "anger"). Recreational activities, wildlife, and "nice" and "good" were also used to describe RMNP as a Park and also to describe it as a vacation destination. It was a "fun" place for tourists, "commercial" and "expensive". It was not seen as a vacation destination or park for

Aboriginal people. Park mood or atmosphere was described in two ways: "peaceful", "relaxing" and focused on activities for tourists; or "anger" and "loss" reflecting the resentment toward paying a fee to enter land that was traditionally theirs. Several natural (e.g. Clear Lake) and manmade (e.g. Gray Owl's Cabin) features of Riding Mountain National Park were noted as unique; however, many participants couldn't name three unique features of the Park, suggesting that this image dimension may not be as salient. Overall, the participants held an organic image of the Park that was positive with descriptions of beautiful scenery and "fun", "beautiful", "relaxing", and "nice". References to the land being "stolen" or "lost" suggested an undercurrent of negativity toward the Park.

At this point, induced image was assessed. Participants were shown 20 slides representing five categories of visuals adapted from Olson *et al.* (1986): natural landscapes and scenery; people; recreational activities; human-made landmarks and buildings; and wildlife (Table 1). The visuals were obtained from the Parks Canada regional slide bank used for destination (Park) publications and promotions. Visuals were shown for three minutes each or until discussion had lapsed. Group members were asked questions such as: "what images or characteristics come to mind when you look at this picture?" and "how would you describe the atmosphere or mood of this picture?". The critical focus was on themes emerging from discussions rather than individual points made by participants. Issues emergent from responses to visuals are discussed below using authoritative voice, recontextualization, authenticity, and created meaning as the conceptual guideposts for understanding the layers of meaning evoked through destination visuals. Although each is analyzed separately, these constructs are not independent of one another.

Authoritative Voice

Authoritative voice is employed to achieve authenticity (Crew and Sims 1991). When responding to the slides, Rolling River First Nation members offered few comments. There were often silences in spite of prompting, and before the three minutes had elapsed. The three slides that generated the most commentary (numbers 6, 15, and 20) showed Caucasian children on a boardwalk over a marsh; several sail and power boats anchored in the lake; and a Caucasian family riding bikes in the centre of town. Although respondents did describe the obvious physical features and the likely intended "tourist/visitor" atmosphere of the visuals, they made further historical references to their loss of access to and traditional use of the land. Typical Park scenes portrayed in several visuals were associated repeatedly with "disturbance", "devastation", "intrusion" and "pollution". People in visuals were identified as "tourists" and wildlife as "food". Resentment toward a singular representation of people was observed. The group members observed and noted a lack of Aboriginal people in the pictures.

Ideally, image projection would involve multiple voices. However, the commodification of tourism hinders multiple authoritative voices and destination marketing efforts can perpetuate such commodification. Tourist destinations commonly dramatize the values of selected sights so that the travel consumer is directed to what attractions ought to be seen, for example in the RMNP pictures; the lake, the golf course, the information centres, and wildlife. The packaging of attractions in brochures and advertisements blends natural, recreational, and cultural elements into a singular experience called "the tour" (MacCannell 1976). Both attention to and exclusion of certain markers can play a part in authoritative voice. Markers have been described as information about a site and as highly recognizable carriers of desired connotations (Adams 1984). Through their display of words and pictures, brochures and advertising facilitate marker involvement (MacCannell 1976). Tourism promotional material elaborates on markers which are already in existence (Adams 1984). The exclusion factor (e.g., no Aboriginal people in pictures) has been referred to by Dann (1996a) as a significant omission that informs what to expect by what was omitted.

Recontextualization

Place image (without the pictorial prompts) was commonly described as "fun"; however, the pictures of park activities and interpretation of the Park were constantly challenged. Words such as "useless", "trouble", "pollution", and "disturbing" were used to characterize pictures of canoeing, hiking, and the information centres. Elaborations about the visuals occurred based on associations with other images, feelings, or physical features; that is, participants projected beyond the visual. For example, upon seeing the picture of the visitor reception centre, one person remarked "beyond the picture I see an interpretive centre that is not being properly interpreted". These examples illustrate the challenge to the actual content of the picture and reveal its metaphor like message (Albers and James 1988, Dann 1996a). Photography represents a key vehicle for manipulating imagery by molding what and how things are viewed. What is seen as a replication of the real and as a credible source of information is instead a "subjectively mediated content and composition"

(Albers and James 1988:139). Hanson (1996) frames the issue of place recontextualization in terms of exclusion. She questions who has the power to determine nature and submits that boundaries (in National Parks, for example) serve to limit the meanings assigned to place. As such, the recontextualization of place projected through photographic imagery becomes a decontextualization of the peoples involved (i.e. Aboriginal peoples from tourists).

Authenticity

Much of the issue surrounding authenticity in tourism has been a definitional one. Authenticity has generally been defined in two ways; firstly in terms of an original; and secondly in terms of authority. In this case setting, the Park no longer appears to be an authentic place for this First Nation community. The original has been "devastated", "disrupted", "destroyed". References were made to "what used to be..." prior to Park development and "commercialization". MacCannell's (1976) discussion of authenticity centered on structural aspects of the tourist setting and used the framework of Goffman's "front and back" regions to illustrate the concept of staged authenticity.

Staged authenticity involves a progression from front to back, with the back regions being the most authentic, the most desired by tourists, and the least accessible to them. Given the depiction of RMNP by First Nation members, the Park encountered by tourists provides an example of staged authenticity. The "fun", "beautiful" place that is the vacation image projected for visitors was not the same place image evoked for these Aboriginal people. History had been removed, authenticity of the past not represented. However, recently the Western Regional Economic Development Corporation has assumed management of one Park campground. It includes a re-creation of an Anishinaabe Camp, including an interpretative program. Critical tourism (Bruner and Kirshenblatt Gimblett 1994) and emergent authenticity (Cohen 1988) would suggest that this offers an opportunity for self-representation and cultural reproduction to be integrated into the production of tourism at the Park. These perspectives reflect authenticity not as a determination or judgement but more as an area of study to understand the processes of cultural (re)production for tourists and their interpretation. Both reflect the dynamic nature of culture and tourism.

Created Meaning

Image by its very definition and construction is subjective, partial, and plural in meaning and ideology. Hummon (1988) in his examination of state tourist brochures provided illustrations of created meaning in tourist destination images; for example, the city as a symbol of play and leisure, history as a consumable escape, and natives as the exotic other. The reactions of focus group participants to the visuals portraying natural scenery may imply experiencing nature - "undisturbed" or exploiting nature - "devastation". Portrayal of landmarks and historic sites may indicate heritage appreciation - "meeting place" or painful memories - "useless". The potential symbolic interpretation and the evaluation of that interpretation are plural. Additionally, participants frequently labelled the people in the visuals as "tourists". Destinations often use photographs that include people so that the potential tourist can envision him/herself at the destination. Informal discussions with some participants after the focus group concluded revealed that they did not feel welcome in RMNP. The promotional visuals reinforced this notion. Papson (1981) suggests tourism image advertising reconstructs reality. One of the more negative elements has focused on the stereotyped portrayal of ethnic people and their function as an object of the tourist gaze (Urry 1990). The expressed absence of First Nation peoples - "no First Nation's people in photos"; "lots of white people"; "white boy in canoe" - may suggest denial of their existence, removal of relationships between the visiting and Aboriginal culture, or lack of opportunity for First Nations people to experience the Park in a touristic or recreational context. Reduction or absence of people in promotions may suggest distance between Aboriginal people and (other) park visitors.

Conclusion

Image is purported to represent and convey a destination as it is expressed by a selective authoritative voice. As a result, image is a simplified impression of a place for which cues are used to trigger inferences and influence attitudes. Sometimes these cues have unintended as well as intended symbolic value. Regardless of how consistent or controlled the projected visual, there are multiple interpretations of it. Destination marketing organizations emit an authoritative voice in the visual and verbal context of their advertisements and travel brochures. In doing so, not all voices are heard. This case provides an example of how local and/or indigenous voices are not often involved in the formulation of markers either on or off site (Dann 1996a). Control by Parks Canada and other political entities (e.g. town Chamber of Commerce) over Park representation emits the authoritative voice for destination image establishment. Photographic elements presented in advertisements and brochures can be out of context and recontextualized to suggest an interpretation. Albers and James (1988) proposed that the content of a photograph may be authentic but it is the organization that gives it symbolic meaning.

It is the dominant cultural manifestation of a vacation experience that is commonly and visually presented in destination image advertising. The separation by a First Nation community of their place image from those of a Park visitor's destination image suggests distinctions that question authenticity. There is plurality in what people see and how they interpret and experience it. The distinctions made by the participants between a place for tourists and a place for them, questions the conceptual relevance and authenticity of a vacation as (visually and otherwise) endorsed by dominant North American cultural values. Furthermore, focus group participants from this First Nation community discounted RMNP as a potential vacation destination for them. Possible explanations relate to the Park specifically, and more generally to conceptualization of natural tourism places. Regarding RMNP specifically, members of the focus group expressed resentment toward the federal government regarding their loss of traditional land use. This sense of resentment, destruction, and loss that percolated through many reactions to the slides would likely remove RMNP as an option in a vacation destination choice set. Even if RMNP was perceived as a vacation destination, a history of federal government - Aboriginal land claim issues would probably hinder enjoyment of RMNP as a holiday or recreational experience. Whether this negativity is idiosyncratic to RMNP and its proximity to Rolling River First Nation Reserve or would be present for other national parks or nature-based vacation destinations is a question that warrants further investigation.

In conclusion, the findings presented are from a single case study of one First Nation community and one tourist destination location, and as a result, there are limitations. However, the intent was not to represent Canadian Aboriginal culture in any general sense but to initiate dialogue on respondent-based image when the respondent is not of the dominant host or guest culture. Image-makers actively select, organize, combine, and edit what is produced and distributed. A reorientation of image that balances the scale between nature and culture may contribute to a more realistic depiction. Regardless, the selecting or not selecting of a destination's cultural heritage to promote for tourism sends a message about the destination's identity that is received by tourist, Aboriginal, and dominant culture populations. Destination marketing organizations play an active role in reinforcing the consumer image with information and visuals supplied to tour operators and other industry representatives. "No picture can be considered final when the perspectives and narratives of so many are missing, distorted or subordinated to self-serving dominant majority interests" (Lincoln and Denzin 1994: 581).

The strength of image development based on recreation and nature needs to be investigated from both a tourist and First Nation experience. Culture and tourism both have been conceived as processual and mutually contributory (Bruner 1986). Tourist destination advertising discourse, visual imagery and their consequences are examples of the reformulation of destinations work. Tourism has reorganized, "incorporated" nature into an itinerary of approved sights designed to enhance humankind's relationship to itself, as well as to nature (MacCannell 1976). Tourist advertising represents an idealized reality (Hummon 1988). The photographic images presented in advertisements and brochures are like objects displayed in a museum. Both are out of context and recontextualized to suggest an interpretation. The authoritative voices of the display and destination promotion provide the interpretation and authentication (Crew and Sims 1991). Authoritative voice, however, cannot singularly represent a destination image. The viewers of the image are also involved in creating meaning both literal and symbolic. Further investigation is required to document and understand the conflicting destination image when the Aboriginal group is not clearly defined or accepted in either a traditional tourism host or guest role.

References

Adams, K. 1984. Come to Tana Toraja, land of the heavenly kings: Travel agents as brokers in ethnicity. *Annals of Tourism Research 11*: 469-485.

Albers, P., and James, W. 1988. Travel photography a methodological approach. *Annals of Tourism Research 15*:134-158.

Altheide, D., and Johnson, J. 1994. Criteria for assessing interpretive validity in qualitative research. In N. Denzin, and Y. Lincoln (Eds.) *Handbook of Qualitative Research* pp 485-499. Thousand Oaks, CA: Sage.

Bourassa, S. 1990. A paradigm for landscape aesthetics. *Environment and Behavior* 22:787-812.

Bruner, E., and Kirshenblatt-Gimblett, B. 1994. Maasai on the lawn: Tourist realism in East Africa. *Cultural Anthropology 9*(2):435- 470.

Bruner, E.1986. Experience and its expression. In V. Turner, and E.Bruner (Eds.) *The Anthropology of Experience* pp. 3-32. Urbana, IL: University of Illinois Press.

Calantone, R., DiBenedetto, A., Hakam, A., and Bojanic, D. 1989. Multiple Multinational Tourism Positioning Using Correspondence Analysis. *J.of Travel Research 28:*25-32.

Cohen, E. (1988). Authenticity and commoditization in tourism. *Ann.of Tourism Res.15*:371-386.

Colton, J., and Hinch, T. 1999. Trap-line based tours as indigenous tour products in northern Canada. *Pacific Tourism Review 3*(1):1-10.

Crew, S., and Sims, J. 1991. Locating authenticity: Fragments of a dialogue. In I. Karp, and S. Lavine, (Eds.) *Exhibiting Culture: The Poetics and Politics of Museum Display* pp. 159-175. Washington, DC: Smithsonian.

Crompton, J. 1977. A systems model of the tourist's destination selection process with particular reference to the role of image and perceived constraints. Ph.D. dissertation, Texas AandM University, College Station.

Dann, G. 1996a. *The Language of Tourism. A Sociolinguistic Perspective.* Oxon, UK: CAB International.

Dann, G. 1996b. Tourists' images of a destination - an alternative analysis. *Journal of Travel and Tourism Marketing 5*:41-55.

Duncan, C. 1991. Art museums and the ritual of citizenship. In I. Karp, and S. Lavine (Eds.) *Exhibiting Culture: The Poetics and Politics of Museum Display* pp. 88-103. Washington, DC: Smithsonian.

Echtner, C., and Ritchie, B. 1993. The measurement of destination image: An empirical assessment. *Journal of Travel Research 32*: 3-14.

Fakeye, P., and Crompton, J. 1991. Image differences between prospective first-time and repeat visitors to the Lower Rio Grande Valley. *Journal of Travel Research 30*:10-16.

Fesenmaier, D., and MacKay, K. 1996. Deconstructing destination image construction. *The Tourist Review 2*:37-43.

Gartner, W. (1993). Image formation process. *Journal of Travel and Tourism Marketing.* 191-216.

Gartner, W., and Hunt, J. 1987. An analysis of state image change over a twelve year period (1971-1983). *Journal of Travel Research 16*:15-19.

Graburn, N. 1983. The anthropology of tourism. *Annals of Tourism Research 10*:9-33.

Gunn, C. 1972. *Vacationscape: Designing Tourist Environments* Austin: University of Texas.

Hanson, L. 1996. Reconstituting the boundaries of nature: The discursive formation of nature in the debate over the management of Banff National Park. *Avante 2* (2):1-16.

Harper, D. 1994. On the authority of the image: Visual methods at the crossroads. In I. Karp, and S. Lavine (Eds.) *Exhibiting Culture: The Poetics and Politics of Museum Display* pp 403-412. Wash., DC: Smithsonian.

134

Hinch, T. 1998. Ecotourists and indigenous hosts: Diverging views on their relationship with nature. *Current Issues in Tourism 1*(1):120-124.

Hinch, T., and Butler, R. 1996. Indigenous tourism: A common ground for discussion. In R. Butler and T. Hinch (Eds.) *Tourism and Indigenous Peoples* pp. 3-19. London: International Thompson Business Press.

Hinch, T., and Delamere, T. 1993. Native festivals as tourist attractions: A community challenge. *Journal of Applied Recreation Research 18*:131-142.

Hollinshead, K. 1992 'White' gaze, 'red' people - shadow visions: The disidentification of 'Indians' in cultural tourism. *Leisure Studies 11*:43-64.

Hummon, D. 1988. Tourist worlds: Tourist advertising, ritual, and American culture. *The Sociological Quarterly 29*(2):179-202.

Hunt, J. 1975. Image as a factor in tourism development. *Journal of Travel Research 13*:1-7.

Kaplan, S., and Kaplan, R. 1989. *The Experience of Nature: A Psychological Perspective.* Cambridge: Cambridge University Press.

Kaplan, R., and Talbot, J. 1988. Ethnicity and preference for natural settings: A review and recent findings. *Landscape and Urban Planning 15*:107-117.

Kincheloe, J., and McLaren, P. 1994. Rethinking critical theory and qualitative research. In N. Denzin, and Y. Lincoln (Eds.) *Handbook of Qualitative Research* pp.138-157. Thousand Oaks, CA: Sage Publications.

Krueger, R. 1994. *Focus Groups.* Thousand Oaks, CA: Sage Publications Inc.

Leitch, V. 1983. *Deconstructive Criticism an Advanced Introduction.* New York: Columbia University Press.

Lincoln, Y. and Denzin, N. 1994. The fifth moment. In N. Denzin, and Y. Lincoln (Eds.) *Handbook of Qualitative Research* pp.575-586. Thousand Oaks, CA: Sage Publications.

MacCannell, D. 1976. *The Tourist: A New Theory of the Leisure Class.* New York: Schocken Books.

MacCannell, D. 1992. *Empty Meeting Grounds the Tourist Papers.* London: Routledge.

MacDonald, D., and McAvoy, L. 1997. Racism, recreation and Native Americans. Abstracts from the *National Recreation and Parks Association 1997. Symposium on Leisure Research.* Ashburn, VA: National Recreation and Parks Association.

MacKay, K., and Fesenmaier, D. In Press. A cross-cultural exploration of destination image assessment. *Journal of Travel Research 38.*

MacKay, K., and Fesenmaier, D. 1997. Pictorial element of destination promotions in image formation. *Annals of Tourism Research 24*(3):537-565.

Morgan, D. 1997. *Focus Groups as Qualitative Research.* Thousand Oaks, CA: Sage Publications.

Norris, C. 1991. *Deconstruction Theory and Practice.* London: Routledge.

Olson, J., McAlexander, J., and Roberts, S. 1986. The impact of the visual content of advertisements upon the perceived vacation experience. In W. Joseph, L. Moutinho and I. Vernon (Eds.) *Tourism Services Marketing: Advances in Theory and Practice 2*:260-269. AMA: Cleveland State

University.

Papson, S. 1981. Spuriousness and tourism, politics of two Canadian provincial governments. *Annals of Tourism Research 8*:220-235.

Phelps, A. 1986. Holiday destination image - the problem of assessment. An example developed in Menorca. *Management Tourism September*:168-180.

Proshansky, H., Fabian, A., and Kaminoff, R. 1983. Place identity: Physical world socialization of the self. *Journal of Environmental Psychology 3*:57-83.

Reilly, M. 1990. Free elicitation of descriptive adjectives for tourism image assessment. *Journal of Travel Research 28*:21-26.

Ulrich, R. 1983. Aesthetic and affective response to natural environments. In I. Altman and J. Wohlwill (Eds.) *Behavior and the Natural Environment 6*:85-125.

Urry, J. 1990. *The Tourist Gaze*. London: Sage Publications.

Walle, A. 1993. Tourism and traditional people: Forging equitable strategies. *Journal of Travel Research 31*:14-19.

Zeppel, H. 1992. *Cultural Tourism in Australia: A Growing Travel Trend*. Conference Series of the Institute of Industrial Economics 19:127-150. East Perth: New Generation Print and Copy.

[1]   Kelly MacKay (PhD.) is an Associate Professor in Recreation Studies at the University of Manitoba with a joint research appointment with Parks Canada Client Research, Western Canada Service Centre and the Health, Leisure and Human Performance Research Institute.

Aboriginal Women and Integrative Feminisms

Shannon Simpson[1]

Abstract

This paper outlines the traditional place of Aboriginal women and ways 'Integrative feminisms' support Aboriginal women in their struggles to bring communities back to the traditional teachings. Integrative feminisms will allow and promote a male-inclusive, community-based feminism, which Aboriginal cultures insist on. Obtaining a relationship of balance and support with feminism can benefit Aboriginal women and Aboriginal communities as a whole.

Introduction

Numerous attempts made by feminist organizations to incorporate the agendas of Aboriginal women have been instigated primarily by white, middle class feminists with a focus on 'speaking for' Aboriginal women, instead of a creating a space within feminism for Aboriginal women's voices. Resistance by Aboriginal women (and women of colour), and an increased awareness in white feminists, has changed feminism's agenda to become more inclusive. Although it is important to remember and respect the diversity of Aboriginal Peoples across the many nations, I will focus here on the commonalties that bring Aboriginal women together regardless of nation. As the diversity of Aboriginal nations must be recognized so too must the diversity of feminisms. There are many different forms of feminism with diverse goals and agendas. Only a feminism that acknowledges the social structure in which a society is embedded, including issues of race, class, and sexuality will be beneficial to Aboriginal peoples. Feminisms will be pluralized throughout to acknowledge these many branches of feminisms and the possible differences even from within branches.

Based on past experience, Aboriginal women often associate feminism with an agenda that reaches few of their needs. Feminism is sometimes seen as an extension of colonialism by Aboriginal women, meant now to further coerce Aboriginal women into white ideals. Of the many forms of feminism, integrative feminisms lends itself to an all inclusive agenda with the goal of benefiting and supporting all women, globally. Integrative feminisms' insist on inclusivity and promotes agendas reaching all women. Integrative feminisms can support a culturally-focussed, male included, community-based approach which will benefit not only Aboriginal women but Aboriginal Peoples as entire communities.

Women were highly valued and respected in many traditional Aboriginal societies; their thoughts and views were sought before decisions affecting the community were made (Royal Commission on Aboriginal People, [RCAP] 1995). Women and men worked without conflict or strict boundaries, allowing for fluidity between often loosely defined gender roles (Indigenous Women's Network 2000). A feminism which supports Aboriginal women must leave room for cultures and traditions that are traditionally women-positive, not presumed patriarchal. Mainstream feminists often believe that no one has ever experienced the kind of society that empowered women and made that empowerment the basis of its rules of civilization (Allen 1986a). Women were the core of Indigenous resistance to genocide and colonization since the first conflict between "Indians" and invaders (Jaimes with Halsey 1992). In my opinion, it is only with colonization that negative ideals of women were imported and forced upon our people. For the first time, Aboriginal women were experiencing sexist attitudes from others, and for the first time, our men were perpetuating these patriarchal ideals.

The experience of Aboriginal women varies from nation to nation, among status and non-status, and between those living on or off reserve. While some struggles facing Aboriginal women are for self-determination and the greater good of Aboriginal Peoples, others are for pure physical survival:

> Currently our struggles are on two fronts: physical survival and cultural survival. For most women this means fighting alcoholism and drug abuse (our own and that of our husbands, lovers, parents, children); poverty; affluence - a destroyer of people who are

not traditionally socialized to deal with large sums of money; rape, incest, battering by Indian men; assaults on fertility; high infant mortality due to substandard medical care, nutrition, and health information; poor education opportunities or education that take us away from our tradition, language, and communities; suicide, homicide, or similar expressions of self-hatred; lack of economic opportunities; substandard housing; sometimes violent and always virulent racist attitudes and behaviours directed against us by an entertainment and educational system that wants only on thing from Indians: our silence, our invisibility, and our collective death. (Allen 1986a:191)

Feminisms must acknowledge the racist core of Western society because this is the experience of Aboriginal women. Feminism, must accommodate the struggles of basic survival and basic human rights necessitated by colonization. It is unreasonable to expect a woman to fight for a larger cause when she struggles daily to feed, house and cloth her family. A racist and colonialist society, has left our women in such a disadvantaged social and economic state that we must begin our focus at the very structures that inform Aboriginal women's place in this society.

Applying Integrative Feminisms to Aboriginal Women

Many Aboriginal women associate the word feminism with just another forum to have our agendas 'spoken for' and our voices silenced. Skonaganleh:ra writes, "I am very *tired* of having other people interpret for us, other women empathize for us, other women sympathize with us, I am interested in articulating our own directions, our own aspirations, our own past, *in our own words*" (Skonaganleh:ra and Osennontion 1989:7). Many feminisms still perpetuate colonial ideals; however, integrative feminisms can support the struggles of Aboriginal women:

The alternative value core of integrative feminisms in all their variety is the holistic, egalitarian, life-centred rejection of dominant androcentric, dualistic, hierarchical, profit-centred ideology and social structures. These feminisms refuse the oppositions that patriarchal relations presume and structure between the personal and the political, public and private, means and ends, reason and emotion, psychological and social, knower and know, production and reproduction, individual and community, society and nature. Committed to developing new political forms that reflect their holistic values, they attempt to integrate these oppositions as part of their struggles to build a new world. Integrative feminisms affirm both women's equality with men and their differences from men, that is, both *women's equality* and *women's specificity*. (Miles 1996:xi-xii)

Integrative feminisms, promote Aboriginal women's reality and experience within not only Aboriginal communities, but within the society at large, using a holistic approach which integrates Aboriginal women with men, community, traditions and the natural world. Most importantly it will promote the importance of recognizing difference between women and men and how this leads to distinct but balanced roles.

White women from within the integrative feminism framework must not forget or ignore their privileged positions and must be aware of their actions. In the past, white women have often failed to acknowledge their positions of power and this has led Aboriginal women to question the benefits of such an unbalanced relationship. To alter conduct and attitudes requires a fundamental change in behaviour. It requires that white women consciously test their motives, question their actions and test their attitudes consistently in their relationships with Aboriginal women. It also requires that Aboriginal women (and women of colour) differentiate between patriarchal styles of work and racism (Maracle 1996).

Aboriginal Women: Thoughts on Feminism

A feminism that supports Aboriginal women must not only benefit our women, but entire communities and the natural world. Aboriginal women strive for balance among our families and within our communities, integrative feminisms could assist us in achieving that balance by supporting our women in the process of healing our communities and in eliminating the use of patriarchy some of our men have taken on. In traditional Aboriginal society, it was women who shaped the thinking of all the members in a loving, nurturing atmosphere within the family unit. In such societies, the earliest instruments of governance and law which ensured social order came from quality mothering of children (Armstrong

1997). It is therefore only natural that we begin this process of healing with our women. By building solidarity amongst all women, Aboriginal women can use feminism as a network of support in order to motivate Aboriginal communities to work towards coming back to the traditions and teachings that clearly depict the power, respect, and honour of women.

Once our basic human needs are met and our physical survival is not a daily struggle, we can begin to focus our energies on the larger picture. One of the most basic things feminism must allow for is the inclusion of Aboriginal men. Traditionally, Aboriginal men were respectful to us, they held women's thoughts and opinions in high esteem. Maracle (1996:139) states, "let us deal with our men-folk and the refuse of patriarchy they borrowed from white men". For most Aboriginal cultures patriarchy is not, and has never been our traditional way (RCAP 1995). It is just another form of destruction left with us as a result of colonization, that still permeates Western society. We must work with our men, heal our men in order to break the cycles of violence and abuse that have saturated our communities. It is the spirit of the female, holding in balance the spirit of the male, in a powerful co-operative force that is at the core of family and community (Armstrong 1997). We will be a healthier, more balanced society when we use the skills and insights of a wider range of people in dealing with any economic, political, or social issue (Flaherty 1994). It will take the entire community, with the balanced efforts of women, men, children and Elders, to heal our communities.

Feminism can be an asset to Aboriginal women if it supports our women to bring our communities back to the traditions. Respect for women and all that we bring to the community is ingrained in Aboriginal knowledge and teachings. If time and energy is focussed on traditional Aboriginal values, in a community-based framework, respect for not only women, but men, children and Elders, will naturally come back to the communities. Our traditions teach us to have respect for all living beings be they plants, animals or humans. We are taught to consider our actions holistically for the good of the community. Therefore feminism must support our male-inclusive community-based strategy. With this understanding we will be able to work in balance as a community to heal our people, so that we are able to work as a community for the greater good of our people.

Towards a Healthy Relationship with Feminism

There can be much power and strength gained from solidarity amongst all women in a global framework. Regardless of race, class, ethnicity, social status, sexuality, on a global level, all women are at a disadvantaged state. No matter how connected one is with their culture and traditional ways, it is impossible to escape the effects of the world that surround us. Lorde reminds us, "the women's movement is all about the liberation of humanity from the yoke of domination. It is all about the fight against racism and sexism and their effects of our consciousness, no matter what colour we are. It is all about the struggle for unity between oppressed women and men" (Lorde in Maracle 1996:138). Therefore, as Aboriginal women, we must recognize that even if our communities were functioning positively and respectfully as they traditionally were, we cannot escape the patriarchal world that we are embedded in - Western society. We must keep in mind that Aboriginal women's place within their cultures, can differ greatly from Aboriginal women's place within mainstream society, and women's place, on a global scale, and the importance of feminism for *all* women, cannot be ignored. Finding a common bond with non-Aboriginal women will strengthen movement among all women, regardless of race and social indicators, living within the same basic patriarchal structures:

> Yet so humiliated are women of colour by racism and so humiliated by sexism are white women that modesty between ourselves is the very thing we lack. We are mutually influenced by patriarchal styles of work. Our mutual survival requires that we cut the strings that tie us to patriarchy and find a new thread to bind us together. (Maracle 1993:158)

Given that Native Americans comprise about 0.6 percent of the North American population, and the magnitude of the problems we face, it would seem imperative that we attract support from non-Indian groups, forming alliances and coalitions with non-Aboriginal groups where possible on the basis of some mutually recognized common ground (Jaimes with Halsey 1992). Forming alliances with other women allow Aboriginal women to increase the knowledge base of feminist thought. Integrative feminisms strive for a complete restructuring of the very way Western society functions, on social, economic and political levels. Similarly, Aboriginal peoples strive for their traditional ways to be recognized and respected, which in turn insists a complete restructuring of Western society in the same ways desired by integrative feminisms. Then, not only can women benefit from unity amongst themselves, but the entire society could benefit from the restructuring desired by Aboriginal Peoples and by feminists. It is important to recognize this (unity) and common agenda as a source of strength and power, and not as a detriment to either community:

> If American society judiciously modeled the traditions of the various Native Nations, the place of women in society would become central, the distribution of goods and power would be egalitarian, the elderly would be respected, honored and protected as a primary social and cultural resource, the ideals of physical beauty would be considerably enlarged (to include "fat," strong-featured women, gray-haired, and wrinkled individuals, and others who in contemporary American culture are viewed as "ugly". . . . [T]he spiritual nature of human and nonhuman life would become primary organizing principle of human society . . . war would cease to be a major method of human problem solving. (Allen 1986b)

Conclusion

> We survive war and conquest; we survive colonization, acculturation, assimilation; we survive beating, rape starvation, mutilation, sterilization, abandonment, neglect, death of our children, or loved ones, destruction of our land, our homes, our past, and our future. We survive, and yet we do more than just survive. We bond, we care, we fight, we teach, we nurse, we bear, we feed, we earn, we laugh, we love, we 'hang in there', no matter what. (Allen 1986a:190)

The strength of Aboriginal women is evident in all the turmoil we have survived. It is not only the result of colonization we are left with, but a society that fully perpetuates colonialist ideals. As long as colonialist ideals persist, our struggles will also persist. The patriarchal ideology, imported by colonization manifests itself in some of our men. We must work together to ensure patriarchy has no place within our nations and communities. Integrative feminisms can help to unify women and support Aboriginal women, providing that white women from within these movements acknowledge their privilege and are able to respectfully share their power and voices.

We are striving for a way to live in today's world in a way that is embedded in Aboriginal traditions. We are not trying to exclude our men, but to focus on our ways that insist on the power, respect and honour of women. We are striving for a balance between all aspects of our community including the natural world. With integrative feminisms supporting Aboriginal women and Aboriginal world views we can work together, towards a common goal of restructuring the foundations that inform the society we live in. The end result will be a better world for Aboriginal women, Aboriginal communities and the worlds that surround us.

References

Allen, P. 1986a. Angry women are building. In *The Sacred Hoop* pp.189-193. Boston: Beacon Press.

Allen, P. 1986b. Who is your mother? Red roots of white feminism. In *The Sacred Hoop* pp. 209-221. Boston: Beacon Press.

Armstrong, J. 1997. Invocation: The real power of Aboriginal Women. In C. Miller and P. Chuchryk (Eds.) *Women of the First Nations: Power, Wisdom and Strength* pp xi-xii. Wpg: U of MB Press.

Flaherty, M. 1994. Inuit women: Equality and leadership. *Canadian Women's Studies 14*(4):6-9.

Indigenous Women's Network. 2000. Summary of Issues Affecting Indigenous Women: `Fourth World Conference on Women in Beijing, China, Available On-line, http://www.honorearth.com, April 10.

Jaimes, A. with T. Halsey. 1992. American Indian women: Indigenous resistance. In *The State of Native America* pp. 311-344.

Maracle, L. 1993. Racism, sexism and patriarchy. In H. Bannerji (Ed.) *Returning the Gaze* pp. 148-158. Toronto: Sister Vision.

Maracle, L. 1996. *I Am Woman.* Vancouver: Press Gang Publishing.

Miles, A.. 1996. *Integrative Feminisms: Building Global Visions 1960s-1990s.* New York: Routledge.

Osennontion and Skonaganleh:ra. 1989. Our world. *Canadian Women Studies 10*(2&3):7-19.

Royal Commission of Aboriginal Peoples. 1995. *Final Report*, Ottawa: Ministry of Supply and Services.

1   Shannon Simpson is of Anishinaabe and Scottish ancestry. She is the life skills counsellor at Nekenaan Second Stage Housing and is completing her masters in Women's Studies at York University in Toronto.

Sex, Fear, Women, Travel and Work: Five Triggers of Eurocentric Negativity

Sherry Farrell Racette[1]

Abstract

Consistent throughout colonial narratives is an unquestioning acceptance of the inherent superiority of the writer and the 'rightness' and inevitability of colonization. The purpose of this paper is to apply the post-colonial critique of such discourse as it describes the Métis, Saulteaux and other groups whose everyday lives intersected with the authors' colonial experiences.

Introduction

The emigrants arrived in safety . . . when an array of *armed men, of grotesque mold, painted, disfigured,* and dressed in the *savage costume of the country,* warned them that they were unwelcome visitors. . . . Indians agreed to carry their children and others not able to walk, but all the rest, both men and women had to trudge on foot. . . . The journey to Pembina exhibited a *strange perversion* of things: the *savage* in *aristocratic independence,* was completely equipped and mounted on a fine horse, while the *child of civilization, degraded and humbled,* was compelled to walk after him on foot. (Ross 1856:21-22)

Leshock (1995) examines mapping and travel narratives as colonial discourse which constructed "the colonized as a social reality" in acts of "imaginative geography" (Said 1978:54). Indigenous peoples were "rarely seen or looked at; they were seen through, analyzed not as citizens or even people, but as problems to be solved or confined, as the colonial powers openly coveted their territory" (Said 1994:145) and created empire through "image and fantasy" (Bhaba 1986:115). Ross's (1856) *The Red River Settlement: Its Rise, Progress and Present State* is among several travel and colonial narratives which have been selected for analysis using recent discussions on colonial discourse (Bhaba 1986, Said 1978, Young 1995). Consistent throughout these narratives is an unquestioning acceptance of the inherent superiority of the writer and the 'rightness' and inevitability of colonization. The purpose of this paper is to apply the post-colonial critique of narratives describing Métis, Saulteaux and other groups. The linguistic construction of the colonized subject is apparent; by isolating descriptive text, these images and the emotions they express and provoke become sharper. For example, the terms 'degenerate', 'degraded', 'debased' and 'disgust' occur frequently in the discourse on clothing, lifestyles, and people (see Keating 1825:110, Ross 1856: 79-80, 160, Hinde 1860:180). A comparative analysis of discourse reveals that although time periods, settings and authors vary, concentric circles of intense language are stimulated by the same triggers: sex, fear, women, travel and work.

Sex

> Modesty in the female sex appears to be a virtue unknown . . . they slip off [a kind of leather shift] . . . and deliberately walk into the water, entirely naked, in the presence of numbers of men, both old and young who pay no attention to them. (Henry 1897:326)

Henry's reaction and subsequent misinterpretation of the social context of nudity caused him to create in Fanon's (1994:37) words, "a kind of perverted logic" that "distorts, disfigures and destroys." The human body and sexuality created one trigger which stimulated intense language production in colonial discourse. According to Dunton-Downer (1995), the collective European conscience of the time was haunted by the very literal belief in their incestuous origins as descendants of Adam and Eve; compounded by a profound sense of their own vulnerability to sin. For Christians, nudity was a trigger for feelings of guilt and shame. When confronted by Indigenous nudity, Europeans such as Alexander Whitaker in 1613, described seeing the "naked slaves of the devil" (Berkhofer 1979:37). A complex and multifaceted response to the sexuality of Indigenous peoples was reflective of what Bhaba (1994:114) described as the "psychic trembling of Western sexuality".

While sex was a problematic area for Christianity, fraught with guilt and restrictions, Europeans were sexual beings. Colonial enterprise has been described by Hyam (1990:2) as the "export of surplus sexual energy". Young (1995:181) located the unfolding of nineteenth century scientific accounts of race within the "paranoid fantasy of the uncontrollable sexual desire of the non-white races and their limitless fertility". He identified this sexual fantasizing as "colonial desire: a covert but insistent obsession with transgressive, inter-racial sex, hybridity and miscegenation". Colonial desire was complicated by deeply rooted aversions towards sharing the European gene pool. In the Euro-Christian view, contact with 'the Other', the non-Christian, non-European presented a constant threat not only to Christian virtue and cleanliness; but sexual contact in particular threatened the very heart of European "social order and continuity" (Dunton-Downer 1995:2). Fear of miscegenation has been at the root of "much of the obscenity, fear, fascination, lust, scorn, degradation, and both real and pseudo-revulsion" expressed towards Indigenous sexuality (Zack 1995:26). Keating's (1825:166) narrative reflected his attitudes towards racial miscegenation. On entering Chicago, he wrote, "It consists of but few huts, inhabited by a *miserable race of men*, scarcely equal to the Indians from which they are descended". Later upon arriving at Red River, he continued:

> Their [Métis men] countenance is full of expression, which partakes of *cunning and malice*. When angry, it assumes all the force of the Indian features, and denotes perhaps *more of the demonic spirit* than is generally met with, even in the countenance of the aborigines. (41)

This horror of miscegenation coexisted with an attraction to the exotic, the female subjects of colonial "male power-fantasy" who expressed "unlimited sensuality are more or less stupid and above all willing" (Said 1994:145). European men were also keenly aware of the sexuality and masculine power of the men they came to dominate. They saw them as both sexual beings and sexual rivals. In 1823, Keating (1825:195) described a Winnebago man riding on horseback and acknowledged "man in a state of nature . . . unimpaired by the effeminating habits and vices of civilized life". His interviews with the men he encountered focused on speculated practices of cannibalism, incest and sexual promiscuity. He noted with some surprise that these practices, while not unknown to his informants, were not viewed in a favorable light. However, his description of Metea, a Potawatomi leader created both a physical picture and a speculated history:

> He has a *forbidding aspect*, by no means deficient in dignity, his features are *strongly marked*, and expressive of a *haughty* and *tyrannical disposition*. His complexion is *dark*. . . . We behold in him all the characteristics of the *Indian warrior* to perfection. If ever an expression of pity or kinder affections belonged to his countenance, it has been driven away by the scenes of *bloodshed and cruelty* through which he has passed. (85-86)

Some descriptions of men echo the "homoerotic phantasm" Porter (1994) found in other colonial texts. Keating's (1825) description of Wennega is full of detailed and sensual language:

> We could not help expressing our admiration for the *graceful and easy manner* in which this man rode across the plain, occasionally *allowing his blanket to drop . . . displaying the stout and symmetric shoulders and chest*. (195)

Ross (1856:160-161) similarly described the Dakota as "*light, slender men, quick as thought in their motions, expert runners, fine horsemen, shy as the wolf, wild as the buffalo*". These samples of colonial discourse create a fantastic image of First Nations and Métis men and associate them with imagined scenes of violence and unbridled sexuality. Words used to describe First nations and Métis men's appearance include: armed, grotesque mold, painted, disfigured, savage costume, fierce, miserable, and forbidding aspect. Men's faces were described as strongly marked, haughty, tyrannical, and dark; their qualities described as cunning malice, demonic spirit, aristocratic independence, matchless power, perfect knowledge, formidable, wild, heathen, loose and licentious, scoundrels, unnatural lusts, and beastly passions.

Fear

The drummers chanted, played tom-toms and cried

weird songs. . . . It was a spectacle. A dark night. *Weird, excited, terrifying* music and *yelling* issued from the great tent. . . . We were a *few white men* among a hundred . . . *frenzied almost naked Indians.* (King 1939:26)

King's 1939 description of the music he heard outside a Midewiwin healing lodge along the Bloodvein River in Manitoba expressed a fearful response which resonates through preceding generations of colonial discourse. This profound sense of danger, both spiritual and physical, took on visual form in medieval maps and persisted throughout the long history of departure from the safe confines of Europe (Leshock 1995:2-3). Smith and Uebel (1995:2) described the Christian image of the shepherd and the fold as "one of the dominant metaphors of ecclesiastical -- and cultural -- organization. . . . Outside the embracing domain of ecclesia everything is demonized". There was much to fear in colonial enterprise: dangerous voyages, the unknown, reprisal, resistance, and fear of new or repressed ideas. Situations which intensified a sense of dislocation and vulnerability often triggered fear and subsequent expressions of negativity. As Bhaba (1994:119-120) states, colonizers identify compulsively with a "persecutory They" always aware of those they are exploiting, seldom trusting, "caught in the ambivalence of paranoiac identification, alternating between fantasies of megalomania and persecution . . . haunted by the phantoms of racist fear and hate that stalk the colonial scene".

This is reflected in an order issued by the Hudson's Bay Company in 1688 "that you trust no Indians or Strangers within your Fort upon any pretense whatsoever" (Brown 1980:13). Every colonizer walked a knife edge between diplomacy, coercion and war. Henry's (1897) sense of insecurity during a trading exchange at a Hidatsa village in 1806, illustrates the linguistic negativity triggered by fear:

We were not so well received in this village . . . *they are proud and haughty*, and think there is no race upon earth equal to themselves. Were it not that they must have traders to bring them the arms and ammunition of which they stand in such great need . . . *a white man would stand a poor chance of his life.* (347)

In Ross's (1856) description of an incident where his party was threatened he expressed his sudden sense of vulnerability and fear rather than the appearance of Métis men:

> ... and almost at the same moment the war song and war
> dance were commenced in the fashion of the Indians. .
> .. On arriving at the place where the *hostile party* was
> assembled, we were struck by their *savage appearance*.
> They resembled more *a troop of furies, than human
> beings*, all occupied in the Indian dance. (168)

The combination of resistance, music and dance completely
stripped Métis men of all vestiges of humanity. Henry and Ross expressed
fear based on real tensions, but there were fears which were located
on a more subconscious level. Young (1992:2) describes a projective
space around the colonial subject into which the colonizer projects
"split off and disowned parts" of themselves. The European belief that
Indigenous peoples represented an earlier stage of human development
and subsequent fears of regression was a source of projected negativity.
"We are not only like savages . . . we also somehow psychically contain
them" (Dunton-Downer 1995:2). Ross (1856) expressed these fears of
European 'regression' when he commented on the perceived dangers of
interracial childhood friendships:

> Such habits . . . shed a *baneful influence* over European
> children, who grow up among them. So *degenerate* is
> our nature, and so powerful the force of example, that
> the amalgamation *deteriorates us* without improving
> them. (79-80)

Constructed lines of differentiation "served as defensive
fortifications -- between the Aboriginal and themselves, their past selves
and their current selves" (Dunton-Downer 1995:2). Indigenous existence
posed significant threats to European world view and political systems.
The colonies and the colonized presented an administrative challenge. The
survival of the system depended upon individuals maintaining their roles
and performing their duties while far beyond the reaches of government.
It was imperative that colonial agents view personal and systemic freedom
as a negative force, something to be feared (Falcon 1980:4-5). Ross
(1856:252) expressed his negative response to the freedoms cherished
by the Métis, calling their way of life *"wild and lawless"* and a
"barbarous state of society and self-will". The bodies which made up
each layer of the colonial system whether they were Indigenous or

150

European, were "directly invested in a political field" (Foucault 1975) and anything which posed a threat to the orderly management of the colonial project was a source of fear.

Women

Isham wrote "[The women] are very frisky when Young . . . well shap'd . . . Very Bewitchen." (Van Kirk 1980:23) during the mid-eighteenth century when the fur trade was an embryonic colonial project consisting of vulnerable men clinging to the shores of Hudson Bay. In contradiction to the fear and revulsion regarding interracial sexual relations, Indigenous women quickly became both the symbolic and physical site of the struggle for colonial dominance. As Rayna Green (1993) stated, "America is an Indigenous Woman". Post-colonial literature has focussed on interpretations of colonial sexuality as problematic and inherently violent.

> Women, as the biological 'carriers' of the 'race,' occupy a primary and complex role . . . women's exercise of their sexuality . . . and the construction of women within patriarchal discourse is inextricable from their construction as maternal, domestic and sexual laborers. (Williams and Chrisman 1994:17)

Land became the female object of male competition. A First Nations woman had become the symbolic visual representation of the Americas by 1571 (Green 1984, Dickason 1984). Acoose (1995:44) identified a fracturing of this constructed symbol into the "good and bad -- princess and squaw"; the one welcoming and assisting the colonizer and "the bad Indigenous woman or squaw (the shadowy lustful archetype which provided justification for imperialistic expansion." First Nations women became symbolically linked to territory, possession, domination and betrayal (Green 1984, Moya 1997). Descriptions of First Nations and Métis women found in colonial narratives reflect this ideology. They were admired when their appearance and conduct conformed to the standards of European beauty and feminine behaviors such as passivity and modesty:

> She possesses Indian features *softened* into the *more delicate contour of the Caucasian* and her figure is *tall,*

slender and *gracefully girlish*. Her eyes are *dark* and *deep*, a *sweet smile of innocence* plays on her *ruby lips* and *silky hair of glossy blackness* falls to her *drooping shoulders*. (Mayer 1986:168)

The women are *invariably fairer than the men* . . . I have indeed seen individuals as *fair* and the tint of the skin as *delicate, as any European lady* . . . *the half-breed women* are also slender . . . *exceedingly well-featured and comely* - many *even handsome*. (Ross 1856: 191-192)

Women who don't conform to these ideals are described as *"full painted squaws"* (Moberly 1938), but Hinde (1860:205) grants that "one *heathen girl, wild,* and *almost beautiful, triumphed* in a robe of scarlet cloth." Rundle (1977), a Wesleyan missionary was charmed in 1840-48 by:

The *penitents* this evening . . . six young females sitting together, their *long, flowing hair* was suffered to fall over their faces which were bent towards the ground and some of them were *weeping bitterly*. (31)

His words evoke Spivak's (1994:92-94) "white men saving brown women from brown men." Spivak sees women's role in the colonial project as key in maintaining the image of imperialism "as the establisher of the good society" and "the espousal of woman as object of protection from her own kind." Women are more desirable when they resemble European women and their persistence "in the habits and customs of their native country" was viewed negatively. Ross (1856:192) referred to the use of the blanket as "this invariable habit" which made women less attractive. Moberly (1922), invented a 'white' history for a woman that he admired:

The *belle of the ball* being a Blackfoot woman . . . She was *tall and very fair*, with a *splendid figure*. She was probably the offspring of an *unfortunate white woman captured* and brought up by Indians.(5)

Moberly wrote about Jasper post at the turn of the twentieth century, yet he conjured up the American dime novel image of Indians attacking wagon trains.

The decreasing need and subsequent replacement of First Nations and Métis women was reflected in colonial discourse as the language describing Indigenous women became increasingly negative (Van Kirk 1980). Moberly (1922) used the American term 'squaw' occasionally, King (1939), more often and Godsell (1938) consistently used the term as a subject-replacement for 'woman'. Having secured a colonial land base, Indigenous women could be devalued and replaced, their former symbolic value linguistically reconstructed by the late nineteenth century, into the dehumanized image of "easy squaws or whores whose only purpose is a sexual one" (Acoose 1995:45).

Travel

> . . . they are no better than *vagrant savages*. Wherever night overtakes them, they are at home. They camp in the open plains, in the woods, among the rocks, and along the rivers and lakes. Mr. and Mrs. Flammond . . . with a little girl about four years of age were *squatted gipsy-like* in one corner of the dwelling, which had neither table, chair, not stool to render it tolerable. (Ross 1856:94)

Travel was another trigger for negativity. Ross (1856) peppers his narrative with phrases such as "*wandering and degenerate*" (79), "*wild and lawless expeditions*" (252), and "*barbarous state of society*" (252) when he addresses movement. This negativity became more pronounced when compared to the language used to describe those who lived a more sedentary life. Hinde (1860) remarked positively on the Cree and Saulteaux living at St. Peter's mission at Red River and compared them to others he had observed living a more traditional lifestyle along the Winnipeg River:

> The sight of . . . the neat white houses of settlers at the Indian missionary village . . . aroused *such fair comparisons* between the humanising influence of civilization and the *degraded, brutal condition of a barbarous heathen race* . . . signs of *improvement in moral and social position*, rapidly create a healthy tone of feeling in passing from the cascades and rapids of

the Winnipeg, where *half-clad savages* fish and hunt for daily food, to the even flow of Red River where *Christian men and women once heathen and wild*, now live in hopeful security on its banks. (123-124)

Settling in one location humanized and altered one's status from '*barbarous heathen savage*' to '*Christian men and women*.' The relationship between civilization and stationary communities is rooted in "an ancient topas . . . that locates the source of all moral life within the civil or political community, the Ciceronian *civitas*, beyond which in Aristotle's metaphor, only beasts and gods can flourish" (Pagden 1995:132-133). Accordingly, people in motion left morality and social controls behind, carrying with them "a catalogue of human vices: tyranny, crime, ambition, misery, curiosity" (133). 'A person who lives away from society', 'without fixed abode', 'without regular habitation', in the European world was a savage (Dickason 1984:64-65). The counterpoint of 'savage' was 'civilised', 'orderly', 'cultivated', 'domesticated' and under control. There was little room for appreciating societies where the individual did not leave the civil and political community, but took it with them as a collective, mobile system. Movement became assimilated into the colonial rationale. "They roamed about and did not make proper use of their land" (Stevenson 1992:80). Indigenous movement became justification for invasion.

Ironically, while travel was presented as a threat to 'the good society', European aristocracy travelled without censure. The size of the carriage, and the breed and number of horses became status symbols. Those who could not travel freely could be better kept under control by those who benefited from their labor. When Ross (1856:21-22) saw independent Métis men mounted on buffalo runners bedecked with fine quilled and beaded saddles, while Scottish settlers walked, he perceived this as a "strange perversion of things". Any European could not possibly be on a lower social scale than the colonial subject.

The European preoccupation with civil control through restriction of movement was reflected in Ross's (1856) complaint that the Métis would "never become a thoroughly civilized people, nor orderly subjects in civilized communities" as long as they were free to travel on buffalo hunts and military expeditions. To value the colonial subject's right to pursue the aristocratic privileges of travel and hunting could potentially place the colonizer in a vulnerable position:

The half-breed hunters, with their *splendid organisation*

154

when on the prairies, their *matchless power* of providing themselves with all necessary wants for many months together . . . their *perfect knowledge* of the country . . . would render them a *formidable enemy* in the case of disturbance or open rebellion against constituted authorities. [They] could pass onto the open prairies at a day's notice . . . where men not accustomed to such a life would soon become powerless against them and exposed to continual peril. (Hinde 1860:181)

The rhythmic and systematic movement of First Nations and Métis communities fostered independence and placed them outside the control of the colonizer. Movement was an act of resistance.

Work

While the old men *saunter about in idleness*, the young are not slow to follow the example before them. The boy with bow and arrow, the girls with basket and berries, permitted to grow up in ignorance and *thoughtless levity* . . . a perfect model of savage life and manners, taught them by their *wandering and degenerate* parents. (Ross 1856:79)

They will do anything but farm, will drive ox-trains four hundred miles . . . go out in the Buffalo hunt, fish, do anything but farm. (Mair 1868:454)

Ross's use of the words 'idleness' and 'thoughtless levity' to describe the important work of hunting and berry-picking, is an illustration of the difficulty Europeans had in 'seeing work' in First Nations and Métis communities. Dickason (1984:14) proposed that this difficulty might have emerged from the absence of "individuals worn down by excessive labor" and the fact that in Europe "hunting was an aristocratic privilege". Europeans had class-based expectations regarding physical labor and a somewhat contradictory ideology that exempted upper classes from work while equating lack of industry with sin (Humphries 1988). In the hierarchy of Europe, Indigenous peoples had a role as slave or common laborer; leisure was the domain of the elite. Christianity equated the fulfillment of predetermined roles with doing one's duty as a means to reward in the next life.

> The regeneration of the inferior or degenerate races by the superior races is part of the providential order of things for humanity . . . Nature has made a race of workers, the Chinese race . . . a race of tillers of the soil, the Negro . . . a race of masters and soldiers, the European race . . . Let each do what he is made for, and all will be well. (Cesaire 1994:175)

The notion that certain classes and races of people were created for hard labor is expressed in Hargrave's (1977:167) descriptions of the back-breaking labor of the York Boat brigades. He described the Portage La Loche tripmen as "ranking very low", while simultaneously identifying the brigade as the "greatest and most important" link in the Hudson's Bay Company transportation network (160). Hargrave said "when efficiently performed, the work done, though of a healthy nature, is extremely severe" (165), but described the men performing this 'extremely severe' work as having "no regular mode of industry, but for hunting and fishing with longer interludes of total idleness" (166). Subservient work done under the supervision of the colonizer was key in advancing the colonial initiative. An Episcopalian missionary's statement in 1839 which stated that if Europeans could "induce them to become fixed and permanent, and more than all, let them be dependent on the produce of the ground for subsistence; then they are within our reach" (Berkhofer 1965:71). The reluctance of the colonial subject to farm, the only task valued as work, was a source of frustration. "Labor control and land ownership provided the context for the emergence of a strong white racial consciousness" as the language which diminished the work of Indigenous peoples became the language of dominance (Roediger 1991:8). "Colonial ideology held that improvident, sexually abandoned 'lazy Indians' were failing to subdue the resources God had provided and thus should forfeit those resources" (21). A perceived lack of work dispossessed one group, while asserting the God-given right of Europeans, through the virtue of their work to inherit the earth. Valuing the work done in Indigenous communities validated Aboriginal title to the land.

The Constructed Image and Maintenance of the Colonized

Eighteen similes and metaphors used as linguistic devices by nine authors writing across a century, reveal a pattern of constructed images which

156

sharply differentiated the colonial subject. With the exception of favorable comparisons to European women, the mental imagery produced is persistently non-human or sub-human and ascribed in Keating's (1959:41) words to a "low rank in the scale of civilisation".

Subject	Metaphor / Simile
Dakota men	quick as thought
	shy as the wolf
	wild as the buffalo
Métis people	like rabbits
	like freebooters
	gipsy-like
	like the American peasantry
Métis women	as fair as any white woman
	as delicate as European lady
	like a bird in the bush
	like most Indian women
	similar to the Formosans
Métis men	eagle eye
	like wild turkey cocks
	like a trader
	a troop of furies
	like the aborigines
Métis children	like a leech

The dehumanized state of the colonial subject was most emphatically constructed when the subject expressed resistance or asserted cultural tradition. Dance and music triggered fear and disorientation; subsequently stimulating some of the strongest language found in the narratives. The persistent image of 'frenzy' and 'fright' echoes from Ross's (1956:168) "troop of furies occupied in the Indian dance", King's (1939:26) "terrifying music and frenzied Indians", to Godsell's (1938) incredible linguistic distortion of a Cree round dance:

A hundred or more *wild, shadowy figures* moving in silhouette against the red glow of blazing fires. They seemed *strangely grotesque* and *unreal* as they swayed from side to side in time to the high-pitched quavering song of the drummers and the booming of the drums. Beyond, *bathed in the blood-red radiance* of the flames, were other *contorted figures* with *set faces and rolling white eyeballs, working* themselves into a *wild ecstasy* . . . somewhere in the distance, a lone wolf raised his snout and replied to the *howling* of the drummers with a long, unearthly wail. (195)

Through language, Ross, King, and Godsell constructed Cree, Saulteaux and Métis people into furies (the terrible goddesses of vengeance in Greek mythology), wolves, darkness and blood. The five triggers of eurocentric negativity continue to evoke what has become a form of symbolic shorthand. The concentrated language which both created the image of the colonial subject and reinforced the superior humanity and privilege of the colonizer speaks through one generation of authors after another. In 1993, the character 'Reggie' in the popular Archie comic series described himself at risk of 'going native'. The language used to construct his transformation is chillingly familiar.

> I would want to check my appearance constantly lest I go Native! Hair dank, dirty, unkempt. Cheeks sunken! Skin and nails filthy! Sunk to the depths of *degradation* and *despair*. *A sniveling, snarling animal!* No hope! No pride! No sense of decency! (Windspeaker 1993:3)

When confronted, the publisher stated that they were "not aware of the potential insult of the remarks"(3). This cyclical repetition of "imagery which has been indelibly engraved into the subconscious of all corners of society" actively maintains the dehumanized status of First Nations and Métis people (Hill 1996: 32). The image of Indigenous women as "debased, immoral . . . sexual commodity" (Francis 1992:121-122) has resulted in the brutal murders of women such as Helen Betty Osborne and Pamela George. The images evoked by media coverage of urban gang activity and their reappearance in the political vernacular of the 'New Right' attest to the continuing vitality of these constructed images. It is important not to dismiss this persistence as remnants of the past, but to recognize their active and continued construction. There is a profound 'tethering' of the image of the colonized to the identity of the colonizer, which should not be underestimated (Bhaba 1994, Young 1992). Canadians who wish to move beyond the language of colonialism must learn to define their identity outside notions of superiority and hereditary privilege and reject language which constructs spatial and linguistic differentiation. It remains the most fundamental task of the subject, First Nations and Métis people, to both challenge the construction of dehumanized images and actively assert our humanity at every opportunity.

Colonial Narratives

Godsell, P. 1938. *Red Hunters of the Snows: An account of thirty years experience*

158

with the primitive Indian and Eskimo tribes of the Canadian north-west and Arctic coast, with a brief history of the early contact between fur traders and aborigines.
Hargrave, J. 1871, 1977. *Red River.* Altona, MB: Friesen Printers.
Henry, A. 1897, 1965. *The Manuscript Journals of Alexander Henry (Fur Trader of the Northwest Company: 1799 - 1804.* Minn.: Ross and Haines.
Hinde, H. 1860, 1971. *Narrative of the Canadian Red River Exploring Expedition of 1857 and of the Assiniboine and Sask.* Ed: M.G. Hurtig.
Keating, W.1825,1959. *Narrative of an Expedition to the Source of St. Peter's River, Lake Winnepeek, Lake of the Woods, etc.1823.*Minn:Ross & Haines.
King, W. 1939. I become a Medicine Man. *The Beaver.* Dec., 1939.
Mair, C. 1868. Letters. In J.Hargrave (1871,1977). *Red River.* MB: Friesen.
Mayer, F. 1986. *With Pen and Pencil on the Frontier.* St.Paul, MN: Hist. Soc.
Moberly, H. 1922. Reminiscences of a HBC Factor: Sixty years of adventure and service in various sections of the far NW. *The Beaver.* March-April,
Ross, A. 1856, 1972. *The Red River Settlement: Its Rise, Progress and Present State with some account of native races and its general history to the present day.* Edmonton: Hurtig Publishers.

References

Acoose, J. 1995. *Iskwewak -- Kah' Ki Yaw Ni Wahkomakanak: Neither Indian Princesses nor Easy Squaws.* Toronto: Women's Press.
Berkhofer, R. 1965. *Salvation and the Savage:An Analysis of Protestant Missions and American Indian Response,1787-1862.* Wesport: Greenwood Press.
Berkhofer, R. 1979. The White Man's Indian: Images of the American Indian from Columbus to the Present. New York: Vintage Books.
Bhaba, H. 1986. *The Location of Culture.* London: Routledge.
Bhaba, H.1994.Self, psyche and the colonial condition.InP.Williams & L.Chrisman (Eds.)*Colonial Discourseand Post-colonial Theory.NY*: Columbia U
Brown, J. 1980. *Strangers in the Blood: Fur Trade Company Families in Indian Country.* Vancouver: University of British Columbia Press.
Cesaire, A.1994. From discourse on colonialism.In P. Williams & L. Chrisman (Eds.) *Colonial Discourse and Post-colonial Theory.* NY: Columbia U
Dickason, O. 1984. *The Myth of the Savage.* Edmonton: Univ. of Alberta Press.
Dunton-Downer, L. 1995. *The Horror of Culture. Cultural Frictions: Medieval Studies in Postmodern Contexts: Conference Proceedings.* Internet Site: www.georgetown.edu/labyrinth/conf/cs95/papers/dunton.
Falcon, L. 1980. The oppressive function of values, concepts and images in children's books. In R. Preisiverk (Ed.) *The Slant of the Pen: Racism in Children's Books.* Geneva: World Council of Churches.
Fanon, F. 1994. On national culture. In P. Williams and L. Chrisman (Eds.) *Colonial Discourse and Post-colonial Theory. NY:* Columbia Univ. Press.
Francis, D. 1992. *The Imaginary Indian: The Image of the Indian in Canadian Culture.* Vancouver: Arsenal Pulp Press.
Foucault, M. 1975. Power, knowledge and the body. *A Genealogy of Foucault.*

Internet Site: www.CSUN.Edu/" hfspc002foucB3.html/#

Green, R. 1984.Pocahontas perplex:Indian women in America. *Sweetgrass 1*(2).

Green, R. 1993. America is an Indigenous Woman. Audiotape No. 26-93. Austin, TX: WINGS: Women's International News Gathering Service.

Hill, R. 1996.The savage and the maiden:Hollywood's Indians. *Abor.Voice 3*(3).

Humphries, J. 1988. Protective law, the state and working class men.In R. Pahl(Ed.) *On Work:Historical and Theoretical Approach.*Oxford: Blackwell.

Hyam, R. 1990. *Empire and Sexuality*. Manchester: University Press.

Leschock, D. 1995. To conquer our right heritage: The medieval map and travel narrative as constructions of European identity. *Human Sciences Home Page.* Internet Site: www.gwu.edu/~humsci/inter/leshock.

Moya, P. 1997. Postmodernism, "realism", and the politics of identity. In J. Alexander and C. Mohanty (Eds.) *Feminist Genealogies, Colonial Legacies and Democratic Futures.* New York: Routledge.

Pagden, A. 1995. The effacement of difference: Colonialism and the origins of nationalism. In G. Prakash (Ed.) *After Colonialism: Imperial Histories and Postcolonial Displacements.* Princeton: Princeton University Press.

Porter, D. 1994. Orientalism. In P. Williams and L. Chrisman (Eds.) *Colonial Discourse and Post-colonial Theory.* New York: Columbia U. Press.

Roediger, D. 1991. *The Wages of Whiteness: Race and the Making of the American Working Class.* London: Verso.

Said, E. 1978. *Orientalism.* London: Routledge.

Said, E. 1994. From orientalism. In P. Williams and L. Chrisman (Eds). *Colonial Discourse and Post-colonial Theory.* NY: Columbia University Press.

Smith, D. and M. Uebell. 1996. Leaving the fold: Medieval cultural studies. *Cultural Frictions: Medieval Studies in Postmodern Contexts Conference Proceedings.* Internet Site: www.georgetown.edu/labyrinth/conf/cs94/papers.

Spivak, G. 1994. Can the subaltern speak? In P.Williams, L.Chrisman (Eds.) *Colonial Discourse and Post-colonial Theory.*NY:Columbia University

Stevenson, M. 1992. Columbus and the war on Indigenous People. In R. Bourgeault (Ed.) *1492 - 1992: Five Centuries of Imperialism and Resistance.* Winnipeg, Halifax: Society for Socialist Studies / Fernwood.

Van Kirk, S. 1980. *"Many Tender Ties": Women in Fur Trade Society 1670 - 1870.* Winnipeg: Watson and Dwyer Publishing.

Williams, P. and L. Chrisman. 1994. Colonial discourse and post-colonial theory: An introduction. In P. Williams and L. Chrisman (Eds.) *Colonial Discourse and Post-colonial Theory. NY:* Columbia University Press.

Windspeaker 1993. Racist remarks in comic ignite boycott.*Windspeaker 11*(12).

Young, R. 1992. Racism: Projective Id and Cultural Processes. U of E. London. Inte. Site: www.shef.ac.uk/uni/academic/N-Q/psysc/staff/ryoung/papers.

Young, R. 1995.*Colonial Desire: Hybridity in Theory and Race*London:Routledge.

Zack, N. 1993. *Race and Mixed Race*. Philadelphia: Temple University Press.

---

[1]   Sherry Farrell Racette is a Métis doctoral student at the University of Manitoba, lecturer at the University of Saskatchewan, and published artist.

The Long Road from Fort Simpson to Liidli Koe

Peter Kulchyski[1]

Abstract

This paper uses the change in the name of a Dené band to raise issues about community development and Aboriginal self-government. Statements by two elders around cultural difference and traditional justice provide entry and exit points on the 'long road' to local empowerment.

Introduction

In an interview for this study conducted by Elizabeth Fajber, Mary Louise Norwegian, an amiable, elderly woman who worked as community health representative in Fort Simpson, told the following story:

> Way back when they used to give glasses, the treaty glasses called. We'd get it once every two years, the free glasses. But when they check up for their eyes, we have interpreter there but they only hire interpreter to look up files, and she cannot be with a patient at the same time as being in the office, so yeah, we have interpreter there, but she's work in the office. So they bring this patient to the room and ask them -- because we have so many people in such a short days, just a few days we have to go through all those people -- so the first thing they ask them: 'do you read?' And those Native people say 'no'. So the kind of glass they give them is for distance, and they never stop to think, these Native women they do embroidery, and sew, and needlework. It's the same distance as reading a book. And then, so I went out of

my way and got a dish of beads and a beading needle and thread needle. So I just leave it there with the [unintelligible] sheets, and they take that and if they see a Native woman they give them that plate and they put thread needle around with needle and beads, and so it's working a bit better now. But it's still, you know, they get glasses and they have to wait two more years. They get distance glass, they cannot afford close range glass, they have to wait for two years. So, you know, that's, that was my biggest concern with eye care, for eye glasses for the Native people, while they have the chance to get it, they should get the right ones.

This story has all the force of a parable, involving as it does questions of 'seeing', of ways of seeing, and of the visibility of culture itself. Mary Louise Norwegian, the community health representative, notices that women coming for new glasses are being asked by the optometrist if they read, and if they answer negatively are given glasses for long distance. In a typically Dené fashion, instead of confronting the optometrist she leaves beads and needles lying around in this waiting room so he can *see* that some of the women clearly need glasses appropriate for the intricacies of bead work even though they do not read.

The story is a machine that layers the relationships between a non-Native medical specialist and Dené women. The doctor understands the mechanics of eye care; Dené women and men come to him for help. Although the doctor does not see exactly what kind of help they need, he thinks he does or thinks he can find out by asking questions. But an invisible cultural boundary separates him from them, his questions do not account for it, his medical practice is not as helpful as he believes it to be. Norwegian *sees* the disjuncture in the doctor-patient relation, and finds a way of making visible to the doctor his cultural blindness. This whole relation unfolds in the realm of sight, in the realm of what is visible, of what the elderly Dené women want to see and of what the doctor does not see. This is a story of how to make cultural difference visible and it stages the notion that culture itself is perhaps a way of seeing.

Susan Buck-Morss argues that "the 'trick' in Benjamin's fairy tale is to interpret out of the discarded dream images of mass culture a politically empowering knowledge of the collective's own unconscious past" (1990:273). This is certainly an important and viable program for those caught deeply within the web of late capitalist social relations. But what if the living memory of the collective was politically empowering, not as an unconscious past but as one aspect of the present? What images become politically empowering in such a context? The dialectical images that Michael Taussig (1987) rests so much interpretive power on? Or, perhaps, an image of an image, a story of a way of seeing, a story that reveals, makes visible, the limits of a way of seeing, a story that sees seeing itself and, as quietly and insistently as the needle, thread and beads placed on a plate in the physician's waiting room, implicitly asks us if we need a new pair of glasses.

'Moral Topography' and the Dehcho

Taussig is interested in "the way men [sic] interpret history and recruit landscape to that task" (1987:287). The landscape he is interested in, of Andean mountains and jungles, was suited to an imperialist moral vision of salvation and descent, good and evil.

> To imbue a landscape with moral and even redemptive significance is for most of us nothing more than romantic fantasy. But there are occasions when to travel through a landscape is to become empowered by raising its meaning. Carried along a line in space, the traveller travels a story, the line gathering the momentum of the power of fiction as the arrow of time moves across a motionless mosaic of space out of time, here primeval and divine. (Taussig 1987:335)

At the risk of decaying into 'romantic fantasy', it is nevertheless impossible not to say something about the landscape that situates each of the three communities of this study. The concept 'moral topography' at least has the benefit of constantly reminding us that these descriptions have nothing 'natural' about them, are imbued with the powers of narrative. The concept of moral topography invites reflection on the manner in which a community marks its relationship to the landscape. This is done using Fort Simpson as an example.

Fort Simpson is situated at the juncture of two powerful rivers, the *Naechag'ah* (Liard) and *Dehcho* (Mackenzie). Rivers are powerful metaphors, the coming together of rivers doubly powerful. The *Dehcho* is itself often characterized by Dené as the lifeblood, the heartbeat, of Dené culture. In the Slavey language, *deh* means river, *cho* means something more than great or large. Dené itself means people -- children, women, men, and elders -- or us people, or perhaps even people of the land.

Denendeh brings all these together, focused on the repeated 'de' vocable: land of the people of the river, people of the land of the river, river of the people of the land: the meanings circle each other, surround each other, repeat each other, reflect each other. Like the sound of a drum. Like the dance it inspires.

The river, in Dené history, ties people together. It provides a transportation link for the communities situated along its banks or the banks of rivers and lakes that run into it. The *Dehcho* carries everything away -- silt and water, life and dreams -- into a distant arctic ocean. The river is not bridged, a reminder of a force beyond human force, a reminder that human reality has not overcome all obstacles. Once a year, every spring, the river comes to life in a dramatic fashion, called 'break up', where enormous chunks of ice crash and thunder and split in the frenetic, explosive tearing apart that leads to renewal. This specific part of the Dehcho is one of its most important junctions. Other mighty rivers, the *Begade* (Keele), the *Sahtu de* (Bear), the *Teetl'it Gwinjik* (Peel), flow into the *Dehcho*. And the *Nahedeh* (Nahanni) flows into the *Naechag'ah* and the *Naechag'ah* flows into the *Dehcho*. *Nahe* meaning powerful in both a material and spiritual sense. Nahendeh is another name for the region, used by the territorial government as a voting district. A spiritually powerful land of rivers. *Naechag'ah* is one of the strongest rivers to be swept up in the path of the *Dehcho*.

Traditionally, even the tourists are told, this site was a gathering place for Dené. A coming together place: rivers and people. A sacred place, then. The site does not have the drama of cliffs and mountains; for that drama you have to go far up river, up Naechag'ah, up Nahedeh, to one of the mightiest waterfalls in the world: Virginia Falls, a suitable place to contemplate the mysterious power of the Kantian sublime. At Fort Simpson, the Dehcho does not inspire an instant sense of drama. When I first saw it I was not impressed and therefore disappointed: two big, sluggish, rivers coming together. Each so wide that the power is dispersed, too big to grasp. On Nahedeh, a much smaller river, you can feel the pulse that is its power, you can't forget it. Dehcho's pulse is so huge that it's muffled, like thunder in the distance.

Over the winding course of many years I have feelings of respect, of affection, of awe for this life force. Dené spiritual beliefs are intimately tied to, and are an enactment of, their close relationship to their land. Among the spiritual activities that I have seen Dené practice are separate ceremonies involving 'feeding' or 'paying' the land, the river, and the fire. The land needs to be fed or paid, particularly by strangers, who can make small bundles of twigs tied together with string or yarn or other small offerings to express their gratitude and ensure that they will not offer offense. Sacred fires will be lit during assemblies or other special occasions, and these will be fed with portions of feast food and tobacco. Feeding or paying the water is important for those who will undertake a journey by boat, where an offering of some tobacco or twigs or branches to the water, with prayers, helps to ensure safety and good travel.

I have my own stories of the Dehcho. Stories of travel, of camping, of fishing, of hunting moose, caribou, beaver, of picking mushrooms and berries, of sitting with friends beneath the high banks telling stories. I have travelled on the Dehcho in small boats with outboard motors, on ferries, in jet boats, by canoe and along its high banks on foot. The Dehcho has nourished me, brought me food and friendship, given me passage through great lands and strong vibrant Dené communities. I have my own stories of the Dehcho.

The Dehcho appears in many of the stories people in the area tell. One elder, Leo Norwegian, told us a tall tale as we chatted outside the band office in Fort Simpson on a hot, dry, summer day. We were talking about the last winter, which had been cold. He reminisced about the coldest winter he had experienced, in the late forties, when it reached seventy-eight below zero. He told several stories that stretched imagination, of crows that froze to death and moose with frozen ears. Then he said, that time, you could hear someone all the way across the river as if they were right next to you, "just like that", he said, gesturing a few feet away, his eyes twinkling. The image resonates, a peculiarly Dené image, of speech and of a river: to be able to talk across the mighty Dehcho.

After some time, after experiences and stories, after sitting on the banks and talking to Jonas Antoine and many others, after being drawn again and again to the point that overlooks the coming together of these rivers, after walking and running along the high banks, some of the power of the place, of its magnificence, pulsed in me. I have walked along the Dehcho in the early hours and watched the sunset blend into the dawn at this place where people and rivers come together. The moral topography here speaks simultaneously to coming together and being swept along; it speaks to underlying forces and currents of unimaginable strength and to the surface that belies those currents; it speaks to cycles and repetitions; it speaks to the everyday banality and to the moment of extraordinary explosive irruptive power.

Dené and Métis in Fort Simpson emphasized to me that they have to work together with non-Natives (called *Mola* by Dené). Like two rivers. A moral topography. The question is which river would be swept up and which would carry the other along.

Taking the Treaty

The difference between the official story and the people's story is most dramatically staged, and has its most important implications, in the story of the treaty. The difference between literal readings of treaty, involving interpretations of the treaties based on documents associated with treaty, and readings of treaty based on the 'spirit of the treaty' adduced from the oral accounts of elders, remains a key theme in Canadian Aboriginal politics generally. The treaty signing in Fort Simpson was a very specific event that did not follow the pattern of the other signing's of the same treaty, Treaty 11, along the Dehcho that summer of 1921.

Rene Fumoleau's *As Long As This Land Shall Last* (1973) reproduces both versions. Fumoleau quotes Treaty Commissioner Henry A. Conroy on the treaty negotiations. Conroy had been given a treaty prepared in Ottawa prior to meeting any of the Dené; it was his job to get the Dené to sign this treaty. Calling the meetings 'negotiations' in this context is a misnomer, except for the fact that the Dené viewed the process as one of negotiation, and attempted to secure conditions which were not dealt with in the written treaty. In Dené views, 'the treaty' consists of these oral promises as much as the written documents. Conroy and his treaty party, which included the Catholic Bishop Breynat, Royal Canadian Mounted Police Inspector Bruce, and translators, had already 'taken treaty' at Fort Providence, and reached Fort Simpson on July 8, 1921.

Conroy's account glosses over treaty negotiations. As quoted by Fumoleau, Conroy wrote of Fort Simpson in a letter to the Superintendent General of Indian Affairs:

> . . .we found nearly all the Indians awaiting our arrival. At first the Indians at this point were nearly unanimous in their decision to let 'well enough' alone and remain in the condition in which they had been heretofore, but after several talks and explanations, they all entered into Treaty, and elected their chief and headmen entirely to the satisfaction of myself, the Agent and all the white inhabitants, whose opinions count for anything. (1973:173)

Treaty negotiations lasted three days. Fumoleau writes: "there was a problem little discussed on Sunday, July 10. The chief who had been chosen for Treaty negotiations was Joseph Norwegian, but he 'wouldn't agree because he wasn't too sure what would be the outcome of the treaty.' When Joseph went away for lunch, Old Antoine was designated

as chief, signed the Treaty and received his Treaty money" (1973:174).
The Bishop, Breynat, noted many years later that "I may say that I am
responsible for the treaty having been signed at several places, especially
at Fort Simpson" (1973:173).

In 1973 the Indian Brotherhood of the Northwest Territories
filed a caveat with the land registrar arguing that their title had not
been extinguished by treaties 8 and 11, and therefore they still had a
claim to ownership. The land registrar turned their application over to
the courts, and Justice Morrow held a judicial inquiry into the legitimacy
of the caveat, ultimately ruling in favour of the Dené. Part of the
inquiry involved soliciting testimony from elders, who had been present
as adults or teenagers at treaty negotiations and could still remember
the events. One of these was Louis Norwegian from Jean Marie River,
for many years a sub-band of Fort Simpson. Norwegian's testimony
is worth quoting at length:

> Q: Were you present in Fort Simpson in 1921 at the
> time the Treaty was first paid to the Indian people
> of Fort Simpson?
> A: Yes, I was there at the time, and my grandfather,
> the Old Norwegian, was the leader at the time of the
> Fort Simpson band.
> Q: Would you describe what happened, to the best of
> your memory, and would you speak in short sentences
> so it can be interpreted.
> A: My grandfather, the old Norwegian, is the one who
> tried -- the Fort Simpson band tried to make a leader out
> of him or a chief out of him, and he was the one who was
> speaking for all the Indians at Fort Simpson. Every time
> they wanted to give money, the grandfather who was
> supposed to be chief, he did not want to take the money
> for no reason at all.[. . .] I remember that they have
> meetings to try to pay the treaty, and the Commissioner
> who paid the treaty tried to make the Indian leader take
> the treaty first, and they had a meeting for three days, so
> my grandfather did not want to take the money until he
> wants to be sure what it is all about, and my grandfather
> told me, 'I am not going to give any money for nothing,
> and five dollars means a lot, and we want to find out,
> and why do we take the treaty, so we did not want to
> take the treaty right away'. And they mentioned this to

my grandfather, that he knows the sun rises in the east and sets in the west, and the Mackenzie River flows, and what I will have to promise have been said by the treaty date [sic], and as long as the words exist, whatever the Commissioner told the Indians, the word would never be broken. My grandfather wants to know why they have to take that money from the people, and the Commissioner told him that the treaty is going to be developed in future years, that there would be lots of white people and if the Indians took the money they may be registered, and if there is enough white people in the country, the government will know wherever the individual Indian is going to be, and that is all the treaty amounts to...[. . .]

Q: I am reading from page 11 of Exhibit 4, and it indicates that Antoine signed as Chief. Do you have any recollection how that came about?

A: What happened is that they had a 3-day meeting and they have something to eat and when they went home and got supper there was one Indian Antoine was left behind, and they said there was no harm in taking the treaty, so the old man took the treaty. He was not elected, and that is what happened.

THE COURT: Perhaps you could ask him if Antoine was recognized as the chief at that time?

Q: Was Antoine recognized by the people of Fort Simpson as chief of the people?

A: As far as I know my grandfather was a leader at that time, but then this fellow Antoine was not a leader, but he was kind of greedy, and so he took the money while they [sic] people was away, and that is why everybody took the treaty and they made him a chief from then until he died.

EXAMINED BY MR. SLAVEN:

Q: I did not quite follow that. Was Antoine made a chief after he accepted the money and signed the treaty?

A: What is that?

Q: Was Antoine made a chief after he accepted the money and signed the treaty?

A: They say that once Antoine accepted the treaty the Indians did not make him the chief but the White men made him the chief. (347-49)

Conroy's account stresses that the Dené in Fort Simpson "elected their chief and headmen entirely to the satisfaction of myself, the Agent and all the white inhabitants, whose opinions count for anything" (Fumoleau 1973:349), significantly leaving out whether the election was 'entirely to the satisfaction' of the Dené who were to be represented.

Although the Dené accounts of treaty signing in Fort Simpson point to a certain 'illegitimacy' of the treaty -- specifically the fact that it was signed by an individual who was not the genuine representative of the people -- nevertheless the sanctity of the treaty and its status as a symbolic representation of solemn promises not to interfere with Dené life ways, guaranteeing the continuance of those ways for as long as the "sun rises in the east and sets in the west, and the Mackenzie River flows", remains a crucial basis of Dené politics in the Dehcho region. That is, Dené in Fort Simpson do not want to argue that the treaty was a fraud and should be torn up. Rather, they want their understanding of the treaty, a treaty of peace and co-existence, respected.

The Road to Fort Simpson

Fort Simpson's geopolitical status in the northwestern fur trade made it one of the early northern centres. It has a long history of comparatively long occupation by non-Natives. This occupation was given an enormous boost in the late sixties, when construction of the Mackenzie Highway connected Fort Simpson to southern Canada. Among the impacts traced to the highway were increased social problems associated with increased access to drugs and alcohol. The community had also had a large experimental garden and served as a food supplier to many communities along the river. The road made southern produce available more cheaply and ended the life of the garden. The road has had an extraordinary political importance to Fort Simpson, and has lead to a defining structure of the band's position in the years that followed. The population of Fort Simpson, about twelve hundred people, is mixed. Most of the community is Dené or Métis (mostly Dené, at about a five to one Dené to Métis ratio) but about forty-percent of the people are non-Native. Fort Simpson has to cope with 'the fact' of non-Native presence in a way few other small northern communities have had to. The physical structure of Fort Simpson reflects this fact.

The highway sweeps down a hill, crosses a bridge that connects the island Fort Simpson is on to the mainland, and promptly turns into the main street, on which are the main grocery stores, two hotels, gas station, other stores and offices, off which run neat streets of suburban style, row housing. Fort Simpson looks more like a suburb than any of the more isolated Dené communities, which have an architectural logic all their own. There is even something of a suburban grid, with '102nd Street' and so on. The highway that turns into a main street is a given in most prairie towns in Canada. You cannot see the river from the main street in Fort Simpson, at least, not until the road passes through town and meanders along the last few houses, merging with the street that runs along the banks of the Dehcho. Along that street are a few government buildings and a row of decidedly suburban homes, most of which are owned or lived in by prominent non-Natives in or from the community, and many government employees. The two streets merge and trickle along into the bush until they come to an abrupt halt, near the north end of the island.

In order to 'escape' the community, which was seen as rife with social problems, and to accommodate growth, two satellite communities emerged. One (Four Mile) is on the Naechag'ah, and looks like a more northerly community: less organized on a row housing model, opening up on to the river, constantly 'speaking' the river in its physical structure, only partly connected by service infrastructure. The other (Three Mile or 'Wild Rose Estates') is well off the river, in a fairly densely wooded area, but better serviced.

At the south end of the island, off to the right of the road just after the bridge that leads in to town, are the flats: a large field that now bears a huge wooden teepee, a concrete sculpture, a large cross, a partially enclosed meeting place, and a baseball diamond. This is the area where treaty days and where other important events marked by feasts or drum dances might be held in summer, and where Pope John Paul II delivered a papal address and blessing to the Aboriginal people of Canada in the summer of 1988.

A Conversation with Leo Norwegian

Leo Norwegian, an elderly man, could be found most afternoons around the trailer that serves as a band office in Fort Simpson, having a smoke outside, chatting with the staff, or the chief, or any number of non-Dené. He acts as an advisor to the chief, the band manager, the council, and some of the committees established by council. We talked a number of times, and it is always a great pleasure, whether he is telling tall tales about the coldness of winters gone by or talking more seriously about the community. He has lively eyes and a mischievous grin, I could see the child he had been as he told a story about playing a prank on his sisters, getting spanked by his mother to teach him a lesson, which he duly learned, saying of the spanking: "I still feel it!". I learned a great deal from him; two issues emerged as a strong theme in our conversations, overlapping with each other: that of Dené law and that of social assistance.

On the question of law, Leo was firm in his belief that Dené law "would [work today], if they let us". He expressed frustration with the dominant legal system, noting that "Dené, even if they don't know the [Dené] law, they don't recognize the European idea, don't want to recognize . . . government says 'well you don't recognize my law you go to jail'". This dissatisfaction was not with the local administration of justice, a point which he emphasized: "at the present law system the RCMP is doing a good job, I think, they're doing what they're told to do. They're going by the books. They don't bend the law. But I think we the people should be working with those people, meet them halfway." The dissatisfaction was rather on a deeper level, in part with the shape of law's structure, the boundaries of law: ". . . some places there shouldn't be a law and there's a law, and some places there should be a law and there's no law there!"

Leo Norwegian described how Dené law worked in the past, in comparison with the dominant legal system:

When I was a kid, they still used the law a lot, you know. Today if somebody commit a crime or broke the law, [they] bring [him] to the court house and they put him in front and they point a finger at him and the dirtiest thing they can find they throw it on there and work him down. Dené law, I seen a guy that, I wouldn't say what crime it was but he committed a crime, and so it was brought to the group and they put up a feast and he's in the crowd there, they didn't tell him why, he's in the crowd there, and everybody had a feast, everybody ate, and after everybody eat they set the fire, they pray, they set fire and then they start talking about different things but related to that guy. He's in the crowd but they make sure that he gets the message, by the time its finished, he gets the message. And then, they never mention his name or anything, they just will be already, we don't know who they're talking about, but finally he got up and said 'I promise I'm not going to do that no more'. He said, you know, 'I want to live with you people'. He says 'I don't want to be sent away and I don't want to be put to death or', you know. He just got up and say that. They never mentioned his name, nobody look at him, just talking and he got the message, and from then on he became a really, one of the leaders later on. That's the way they used to work.

The style of repetition seen in this story is important to Dené storytelling, and the particular repetitions here -- he's in the crowd, they had a feast, they set the fire, they never mention his name, he gets the message -- are all critical. This is a public event, food is shared, a fire is set (perhaps in the manner of the sacred fires used by Dené in 'feeding the fire' ceremonies which are an important aspect of their tradition) to signal the importance of the words spoken, the individual is never signalled out but recognizes himself in the talk that takes place, until finally he acknowledges receipt of this address. The focus is on rehabilitation, on achieving a voluntary acknowledgement by the law-breaker of his misdeed.

Norwegian's views contrast dramatically with the view Ryan (1995:57) attributes to Dogrib elders, where once placed in a 'justice' circle, "the offender was kept there until he or she admitted guilt, at which point the senior people and leadership would give the person 'harsh words'". Norwegian's description, emphasizes how the individual is not singled out, how whatever critical words are spoken they are not spoken directly at the individual, who can come to realize her or his misdeeds, voluntarily acknowledge them, at which point there is no longer a need for 'harsh words'.

Norwegian also had a great deal to say about social services, and was in general convinced that "social service, that's something that should be handled by band". He talked about how people drift into town from elsewhere and end up being supported, in an apartment, drinking away welfare money. It's the waste of human life that concerned him greatly, and he used the example of two elders who wanted money to help them get back on the land, but were refused, as a contrast, saying "that's deadly wrong". The system encourages people to stay in the community and do nothing, rather than supporting people who want to try to be independent and live more on the land. He also used a story from his own experience to elaborate on the problem:

A few years back I broke my leg and I ended up in hospital, and it just happened I was really low on money when it happened. So, I got a family, after two weeks in the hospital I went to social services. After I come out I need help and they said, 'you working?'. I said 'no, I can't work, my leg is broken'. 'Well who's truck you driving?' I said 'my truck'. 'Sell your truck and eat!' You know, I, if I had a, [making a rifle shooting gesture] ho, that's how mad I was . . . It wasn't me, if somebody, you could see it, eh, a person needs help, eh, and these people, they're working for social services, I don't think they, they're not all there, you know. If you ask them a question like that they don't answer you. You have to work through the book and find it, they can't even think for themselves. One old guy is coming out of there last winter, out of social service office? He was mad. He said I was trying to find something there they, . . . there's ten of them in there, some of them they don't even know their own dog's name! That's how mad he was. So that's how bad it is.

Yet he also had great respect for the basic idea of social support: "like the social service, it could be, it's a good program -- it's a good! -- if you do [it] the right way, you know". Leo's critiques are directed at the problem of form; in justice he has more respect for the local administrators than for those responsible for social services. It is not the existence of a program that is of concern, but the manner of its operation. In this context, his respect for Dené forms is noteworthy: "Dené way, a lot of ways its good you know. We survived for thousands of years. It's not written down but just passed down from generation to generation". This leads to the question of self-government, self-government as a mechanism to re-enact or re-inscribe Dené ways, not least in the areas of justice and social assistance. Through the long cold winter of 1993-94 another change was taking place in Fort Simpson; the Band searched for a new name, no longer wanting to be known as the Fort Simpson Dené Band. By spring it had arrived at or reclaimed a name that had been circulating and in use for a number of years. Fort Simpson Dené are now known as the Liidli Koe First Nation. Liidli Koe means 'people of the forks'. One part of the process of community development claiming its right to name itself, to give itself its 'proper name' had taken place. Although the substantive change was important, equally important was the move to reverse the deeply rooted nominalist power of colonialism, the move to establish that the Dené community can name itself, a critical decolonizing aspect of its right to determine its own mode of social being. That Liidli Koe is itself nearly unpronounceable to English language speakers marks the degree to which this other mode of social being may be distinct from the dominant order.

The distance between the Fort Simpson Dené Band and the Liidli

Koe First Nation may appear trivial to some, but it speaks to or opens the possibility for something vast. Liidli Koe is a place where people, having proclaimed and asserted their rights, do not allow outsiders to determine and control the community's agenda. Liidli Koe is internally focused at this historical juncture, on 'healing' the scars left by two centuries of colonial rule and on establishing the community as a foundation from which other values and ways of being can be re-established towards the "situational transcendence of the existing order", to borrow Dominick LaCapra's evocative phrase.

Leo Norwegian gave one of the strongest or clearest statements about what the project of Aboriginal self-government means, interestingly also illustrating a strong identification with the political project of self-government in his deployment of the 'we' form here: "self government, we're not trying to say we want to kick everybody out of office and take over. What we're saying is, what we did before, for thousands [of] years, if we did do it, we could do it again. But its not in a big way, you know. Slowly. Take over".

References

Buck-Morss, S. 1990. *The Dialectics of Seeing.* Cambridge: MIT Press.
Fumoleau, R. 1973. *As Long as this Land Shall Last.* TO: McClelland and Stewart.
LaCapra, D. 1994. *Representing the Holocaust.* Ithaca: Cornell University Press
Ryan, J. 1995. *Doing things the Right Way.* Calgary: University of Calgary Press.
Taussig, M. 1987. *Shamanism, Colonialism and the Wild Man.* Chicago: University of Chicago Press.

[1]   Peter Kulchyski (PhD) is the Head of the Department of Native Studies at the University of Manitoba. This text is excerpted from a chapter of the same title in Kulchyski, P. n.d. *Like The Sound of a Drum: Aboriginal Cultural Politics in Denendeh and Nunavut.* Unpublished.

The Spirit and Pain of Death

Nahanni Fontaine[1]

Dedicated to the Martin family and the community of Moose Lake.

An echo of wailing permeates this sacred land,
once so full of dignity, honour and joy.
The cries of generations past -
Our ancestors' blood lost for little if any return of promise and justice.

An Aboriginal community mourns and
silently screams the pain and anguish of death -
Our intimate sadistic lover.

One of the communities' youth is violently and
mercilessly pushed into the utter depths of -
Colonial despair, rage and helplessness.

And then eternal silence.

Oh the terror and disbelief at such a tragedy, surely never to occur again.
But wait, less than a week, and again the community shall be
thrown into the den of no return.
Another one of its youth, its future, is pulled into the realm of everlasting sleep.

Silence.

Watch as the community struggles to make sense of their loss.
What did we do? What didn't we do? What will we do?
Only examining the "we", never the "colonial them".
Watch as a mother sits in disbelieving tremor and desolation, waiting -
For the son she laboured for, to kiss and hug her just one last time.

Listen to the sibling sleep
in anguish and terror from dreams of return-
Return to the moment when she found him hanging in the closet.

Listen to the soft cries of hunger and thirst from a baby -
Who patiently attends his sixteen year old father's funeral.
The grandfathers and grandmothers can only watch and comfort-
The agony, anger and fear of their people;
While they guide the new ones into the sphere of eternal peace.

My pain runs so deep and
so profound for this community and its members at their loss.
I am so sorry for your hurt, your sorrow and your struggle.

What little strength I have is yours.
What little courage I have is yours.
What great love I have belongs only to you;
Take it and cloak it over your spirit and being on your path to healing.

For those of you who don't know, who have never experienced the perpetual
presence of death -
I resent you.
I resent that for the last hundreds of years -
Only a small portion of society has secured an intimate dance with death and its
timeless torture and misery.

[1]   Nahanni Fontaine is from Sagkeeng Anishinabe First Nation and completing
her Master's research in Native Studies, Women's Studies and Critical Theory at the
University of Manitoba.

Independent First Nations Child Welfare Law in Manitoba

Marlyn Bennett[1]

Abstract

The history of maltreatment of First Nations children has sparked the political motivations of First Nations people in Manitoba: Self Government. This paper explores historical factors that have precipitated the need for an independent First Nations Child and Family Law and to highlight the current legal and political environment. Given that discussions of 'laws' and 'legislation' are framed in a Western legal and political discourse, it must be reinforced that First Nations people must be the creators and enactors of this law on their own behalf.

Introduction

The most abysmal period in the history of Canada surrounds the maltreatment of First Nations children. This history has sparked the political motivations of First Nations people in Manitoba. The Assembly of Manitoba Chiefs (AMC) and the First Nations of Manitoba signed the Framework Agreement Initiative (FAI) to begin the process of creating self government. The magnitude of the task at hand for First Nations communities requires careful examination of past practices and laws, present political and legal climates, and future goals and aspirations. The following analysis explores historical factors that have precipitated the need for an independent First Nations Child and Family Law and highlights the current legal and political environment. Given that discussions of 'laws' and 'legislation' are framed in a Western legal and political discourse, it must be reinforced that First Nations people must be the creators and enactors of this law on their own behalf.

The administration and delivery of child and family services (CFS) to the citizens of Canada are activities considered within the jurisdiction of the Provinces by virtue of section 92(14) of the *British North America Act, 1867* (*Constitution Act, 1982,* Schedule B of the *Canada Act, 1982* (U.K.) 1982). The Federal government has the power to enact Federal laws with respect to the delivery and administration of CFS to First Nations on and off reserve, however, despite its ability to do so, it has chosen not to. Responsibility for services to First Nations communities is tossed back and forth between the Federal and Provincial governments, often it seems, without cognizance of the detrimental impacts it has inflicted on First Nations, on or off reserve. A brief background summary of the havoc created by policies based on European belief systems; carried out by the church, residential schools and child welfare system; and designed to assimilate and colonize First Nations peoples is provided in order to understand the current issues.

Traditional First Nations Families

First Nations peoples have always felt that their future depended upon the well being of their children and their laws were very clear about the welfare of their children (Young 1996b; First Nations Task Force on CFS 1993). Parents were the first lines of responsibility but the extended family is used extensively in parenting children. The term 'Family' has a much broader meaning for First Nations peoples that includes grandparents, aunts, uncles, cousins and other significant community members. The use of extended family is fundamental in First Nations child-rearing practices. Grandparents and Elders, in particular, have vital roles in child-rearing. It is the belief that the community as a whole has a legitimate role and assumes a primary responsibility to participate in the rearing and caring of all children (Young 1996b). If for any reason children were left without parents, an extended family member, or an interested citizen of the community would assume responsibility for those children. Those children then became members of that family but the original birth family was not forgotten nor ignored. This is in direct opposition to the practices of mainstream society, which today continues to uphold the norm of secrecy. Within the First Nations context, there was no secrecy in such family arrangements. Moreover, there was no word for 'adoption' in First Nations languages. With the coming of Europeans, this way of life changed forever the social fabric of First Nations communities (First Nations Task Force on CFS 1993, RCAP 1996). Many non-First Nations people today erroneously believe that the traditions, values and belief systems of First Nations cultures are no longer practised, or have simply disappeared. First Nations cultures have undergone fundamental changes to reflect contemporary times, their identity as separate and distinct peoples continues to be an important part of their existence as First Nations peoples.

The Residential School System

The changes and breakdown to First Nations families began with the colonization and the assimilation policies of the Canadian government, which were legalized through the *Indian Act* (McKenzie and Hudson 1985). The strength of these traditional families became fractured and weakened by a number of factors such as the involvement of the church and the educational process in the lives of First Nations peoples. The continued involvement of these institutions into the lives of First Nations peoples were in turn supported by a legal system that was alien to First Nations societies (Hamilton and Sinclair 1991, First Nations Task Force on CFS 1993). The removal of children from parental control was particularly devastating to the family system of First Nations. In the residential schools, funding by the Federal government, administered and operated by churches, parents had no control over what their children learned, and the critical skills needed for parenting were not handed down to the children. Young children were forced to abandon their Native languages to speak English, resulting in the severing of vital ties to their families and cultural environments. On a psychological level, First Nations children learned fear, self-hate and anger. Loss of their identity became acute. The damage caused indescribable pain. This suffering manifests itself throughout many First Nations communities and has a direct impact on alcohol and drug abuse, suicides, high incarceration rates, tragic deaths and the general disarray of First Nations communities (Hamilton and Sinclair 1991, First Nations Task Force on CFS 1993, RCAP 1996).

The Child Welfare System

The forced implementation of child welfare services administered by the Provincial government added another blow to the already devastating impacts on First Nations peoples from the residential school system. As a result of changes to the *Indian Act* in the 1950s, Provinces came equipped with the responsibility of administering CFS services over First Nations children. They had laws, rules, regulations, and standards. These laws, rules, regulations and standards were administered according to the way in which they were applied in non-First Nations communities. Young, inexperienced, non-First Nations social workers applied white values to the poverty stricken situations of First Nations families (McKenzie and Hudson 1985, Hudson 1987). Many poor First Nations children were placed in foster homes and never returned home. Those children who did find their way back home after prolonged absences: were alienated from their families and cultural environments (Hudson and McKenzie 1985), or found their families had been relocated or died (First Nations Task Force on CFS 1993). Many of these children were adopted to families in other countries and suffered identity problems, which contributed to an onslaught of personal problems and difficulty relating to their adoptive families and within mainstream society. There were many non-Aboriginal foster and adoptive parents who did their best to nurture, heal and raise First Nations children adopted into their care. Tragically, the outcome of adoption, even by conscientious non-Aboriginal parents has often been disastrous, as adoptees reached adolescence only to suffer the triply painful identity crisis of being Adolescent, Aboriginal and Adopted (Bennett 1998). The dysfunction experienced by First Nations children, families and communities are attributes left over from the colonial relationships, which First Nations have experienced under the continued tutelage of the Federal and Provincial governments (Hudson 1987). Instead of producing healthy First Nations citizens who can contribute to the social fabric of mainstream society, the government has created a people crippled by assimilative and colonial policies of the past and a dismal state of First Nations dependence upon Federal and Provincial governments. On the horizon, there appear to be no indication of financial relief in the social services sector for either levels of government.

Evolution of First Nations Child Welfare in Manitoba

To counteract the policies of the past, First Nations citizens within Manitoba have been instrumental in changing the reigns of control over child and family matters on reserve. There have been approximately four major changes in the delivery and administration of child welfare services on reserve to Manitoba First Nations citizens over the past 20 years.

The first embers of change imminently involving First Nations peoples began in the 1960's. There was no formal basis for the provision of child welfare services to registered Indian people on reserves prior to the 1960's (Hudson 1987, Hamilton and Sinclair 1991). There were three ways that children of First Nations ancestry could came into substitute care: Through the residential school system, in the name of education; When medical needs warranted apprehension of children based on the argument that medical needs could only be met in an urban centre; and when registered Indian children living off reserve were judged to be in need of care and protection (Hudson 1987).

During the 1960's provincial child welfare services were extended to First Nations communities through section 88 of the *Indian Act*. Section 88 of the *Indian Act* provides that a provincial law of general application, subject to certain restrictions, is applicable to First Nations living within any province. This section provided the provinces with the legal capacity to administer provincial CFS services to people outside their constitutional jurisdiction. As recalled at the beginning of this report, in Canada, sections 91 and 92 of the *Constitution Act, 1867-1982* allocates jurisdictional authority to the Federal government and the Provincial governments respectively. Matters related to Indians and Lands reserved for Indians remains an area exclusively assigned to the Federal government by virtue of section 91(24) of the *Constitution Act, 1867-1982*. Within the context of child welfare, section 88 abdicates the Federal government from legislatively occupying the field of child welfare as it relates to First Nations peoples on reserve, even though First Nations are a constitutional responsibility (Little Bear 1992). The Federal government asserted that the provinces had jurisdiction and responsibility in all matters not specifically mentioned in the *Indian Act*. As there was no explicit reference to child welfare in either the *Indian Act* or the Constitution, it followed that this area was the responsibility of the provinces (Little Bear 1992). Subsequent court decisions have confirmed the legal jurisdiction of the Province's ability to extend child welfare services onto reserves, regardless of the provincial incursion into a Federal sphere (*Natural Parents v. Superintendent of Child Welfare* 1976, 60 D.L.R. 3rd 148 S.C.C.). At present, the only First Nations community in Canada that can circumvent the application of provincial child welfare laws is the Spallumcheen First Nations in British Columbia. Spallumcheen First Nations operates a child welfare program pursuant to a band by-law passed under the provisions of the *Indian Act* (MacDonald 1983, 1987). Spallumcheen remains the only First Nations community to have achieved this degree of autonomy in child welfare administration. Subsequent attempts by other First Nations to enact child welfare laws similarly through the *Indian Act* have been unsuccessful (MacDonald 1985).

With the constitutional questions out of the way, there remained the problem of identifying which level of government had jurisdictional responsibility regarding the payment for, and the delivery of services to Indian families. A 1966 agreement was struck between the two levels of government to defray the costs of child welfare services for Indian peoples, which the province agreed to deliver (Canada 1987). However, this agreement only covered 14 reserves in the southern part of the province. In the northern and some southern parts of the province, there was no explicit agreement for the delivery of services except to the extent that the Department of Indian Affairs accepted billings for the cost put up by the provinces to maintain Indian children in substitute care. Intervention in First Nations affairs in the north were provided only in 'life or death' situations and service delivery was rarely carried out by persons of Aboriginal ancestry (Hudson 1987).

Once the provinces were in charge, and guaranteed payment for each Indian child they apprehended, the number of First Nations children made legal wards of the state quickly ballooned out of control. The typical form of Provincial intervention into the lives of First Nations peoples during the 1960s and 1970s focused on apprehension and removal of children rather than on preventive programming with the intention of keeping families united. As revealed in a major study by Johnston (1983) First Nations children became grossly over-represented in the child welfare system as a result of the Province's extended jurisdiction into First Nations communities. Johnston coined the phrase "sixties scoop" to describe this phenomenon. Johnston's study presented evidence that First Nations had good grounds for protesting against the massive involvement of provincial child welfare agencies in the removal of children from their families, communities and cultural environments. For example, in 1959, Johnston noted that Aboriginal children only represented 1% of children in care but by the end of the 1960s, 30 to 40% of all legal wards in the child welfare system were Aboriginal children, even though they formed less than 3% of the total national population in Canada at that time.

The 1966 bilateral agreement between the two governments has had a devastating impact on First Nations communities and families. Aboriginal children were taken away in hugely disproportionate numbers less for reasons of poverty, family dysfunction or rapid social change than to effect a continuation of the colonial argument. That is "the child welfare system was part of a deliberate assault on Native society designed to make changes in Native people". The white social worker, following hard on the heels of the missionary, the priest and the Indian agent, was convinced that the only hope for salvation of Indian people lay in the removal of their children (Fournier and Crey 1997). Hudson (1987) highlighted some reasons why the Province's intervention tactics were devastating to First Nations communities:

> • Intervention was based on removal of the child from family rather than on preventive programming and keeping family members together.

> • The values of young, inexperienced, non-Aboriginal, urban-trained social workers prevailed. These individuals had no knowledge of the colonial factors at play and no knowledge of the community's social or kinship networks and resources. Resolution of the problem resulted in children being removed from the community to unfamiliar environments.

> • The overwhelming tendency to use non-Indian substitute care for Indian children rather than utilizing the extended family systems of First Nations communities.

> • The practice of placing First Nations and other Aboriginal children for adoption within non-First Nations or non-Aboriginal people and outside of Canada. This practice was more common in Manitoba than any other province (257-262).

Increased intervention by the Provincial government into the lives of First Nations peoples climaxed with latent anger expressed by the First Nations peoples and their respective political organizations. They charged that the child welfare system imposed against them through s.88 of the *Indian Act* had "genocidal" affects on their culture, families and communities and that it had to stop (First Nations Task Force on CFS 1993). Later in 1982, the Minister of Manitoba Community Services (as it was then called) declared a moratorium on the international placement and adoption of Manitoba Indian and Métis children. The Minister in response to the protest of First Nations peoples, established a review committee to examine the child welfare system with respect to the adoption and foster home placements of children of Aboriginal ancestry (Kimelman 1985).

The child welfare system at that time gave little appreciation to the "values, lifestyles and laws" of First Nations peoples in Canada, and because the system imposed on them the "standards, cultural values, laws and systems" of the dominant society (Sinclair *et al* 1991). As a result of this anger, a new structure of delivery with respect to First Nations child welfare began to surface with surprising results. The push for a new mode of delivery started in 1979 with the Four Nations Confederation's (FNC)(which replaced the Manitoba Indian Brotherhood (MIB). FNC hired a child welfare consultant to develop a province-wide strategy and action plan for the devolution of child welfare services to Indian people (Hudson 1987). Prior to this move, there had been a few *ad hoc* local initiatives with First Nations bands entered into with DIAND to hire workers to provide non-statutory services (Canada 1987).

The FNC initiative culminated in the signing of the Canada-Manitoba-Indian Child Welfare Agreement in February 1982 (otherwise known as the "Master Agreement" or "Tripartite Agreement"). This agreement set out the general principles, process and financial arrangements for the provision of on-reserve child welfare and related family services. It was an enabling document, in that, for it to come into effect, subsidiary agreements had to be signed by "any band or group of bands" wishing to provide CFS services to community members. Through the Master and Subsidiary Agreements, the Government of Canada agreed to fund services, the Province agreed to empower them, and the Indian signatories agreed to design and deliver them (Hudson 1987).

Despite the perceived successes of these early endeavours, some First Nations agencies did experience growing pains under the Tripartite Agreements. An unforeseen issue surfaced that continues to be a thorn in the side of First Nations CFS agencies on reserve. Political interference comes from some elected chiefs and councillors who appear to have vested interests in obscuring child protection needs among their immediate family and friends. An example of this inference reared its head in the Dakota-Ojibway CFS (DOCFS) agency in Southern Manitoba. DOCFS was shaken to its core in 1992 by the death of Lester Desjarlias, a thirteen-year-old boy who had been tied to a tree and sodomized by a relative of the chief of his community. The perpetrator received more protection than Desjarlais, who committed suicide after he was repeatedly revictimized. Judge Brian Giesbrecht, who headed a 1993 inquiry into Desjarlais' death, delivered a scathing indictment of the DOCFS. But Giesbrecht was also equally and highly critical of the Federal and Provincial governments, which he said had off-loaded an enormous responsibility for Aboriginal social services onto First Nations but provided meagre financial resources and virtually no professional support (Giesbrecht 1993, Teichroeb 1997, Fournier and Crey 1997).

The signing of the 1982 Agreement had not pleased everyone. First Nations leaders were reluctant to accept Provincial law in their territories but feelings of ill will were put aside for the time being. The newly created First Nations CFS agencies and Chiefs were hopeful that the Tripartite process would eventually lead to the development of a Child and Family Act which reflected First Nations familial values and customs. The expectation was that five years after signing the 1982 Agreement this Act would be developed and implemented. To date, there has been little progress towards that goal but it is not for lack of trying but rather extends from the restrictions imposed upon the autonomy of First Nations agencies under the delegated model of Provincial authority. The reluctance of the provincial government to vacate the reigns over child and family matters to First Nations communities also plays a roll, which impedes upon that desire.

The Contentious Issue of Jurisdiction

Today, nine First Nations child and family agencies have emerged in Manitoba with mandates tied to the geographical reserve boundaries of the First Nations Tribal Councils, excluding registered First Nations living off reserve. The Chiefs and First Nations agencies emphatically state that the jurisdictional line must be properly drawn at membership, not residence, at least within provincial boundaries (Hudson 1987, First Nations Task Force on CFS 1993, Young 1996b). Although First Nations agencies have gained some autonomy over agency-specific policy development, the contentious issue of provincial jurisdiction remains. The jurisdictional void that First Nations peoples have experienced in the administration and delivery of CFS flows from the federal government's inability or unwillingness to occupy that particular field. The provincial government, under section 92(14) has jurisdiction over the administration of criminal justice and civil matters, which the courts have interpreted to include child welfare. One of the important features of these constitutional arrangements is that the province cannot legislate on matters that fall under the powers of the federal government. First Nations (Indians) and lands reserved for Indians, by virtue of the Constitution, fall within the scope of the federal government's power. However, the federal government has chosen to ignore its fiduciary responsibility to First Nations in this particular area and instead has surrendered responsibility for First Nations child welfare by passing it onto the provinces through section 88 of the *Indian Act* (Pellatt 1991). Today, all provincial laws related to CFS continue to apply as long as the federal government continues to vacate that particular area of jurisdiction (Young 1996b).

Models of Service Delivery

The existing model of service delivery of First Nations CFS agencies today does not represent anything close to full control over the delivery of CFS. There are four models of *control (assimilation, integrated, delegated authority and autonomous* models) that has been maintained by the provincial authorities over First Nations CFS agencies. This model gave way to a third model of control, which was relatively acceptable to First Nations.

The third model of control is the *delegated authority model.* This is the model, which is currently in place in Manitoba and in several other provinces. It authorizes First Nations agencies to administer the laws and procedures for the protection of children and the promotion of family well being on behalf of the provincial authority. The province retains ultimate authority over the provisions of the law, regulations and policies pursuant to it, and where required in law, the agencies are accountable to the provincial court system. This model provides that First Nations agencies are accountable to the province for the quality of service. If the province is not satisfied with the standards of service provided by the FN agency, it is empowered to rescind the mandate of that agency and either assume responsibility for delivery of service or delegate it to another agency. The funding source for this model resonates from the Federal government and not the province (Taylor-Henley and Hudson 1992).

The fourth model, *the autonomous model* lies outside the control of the Provincial governments. It does not exist anywhere in Canada. Its essential characteristic, as highlight by Taylor and Hudson (1992), entails the acknowledgement by the provinces that they have no jurisdiction over child welfare services insofar as First Nations children, families and communities are concerned. Whatever laws, policies, procedures, and standards in effect which define the relationships and respective rights and obligations of community, family and child, are created and executed by First Nations governments. When the well being of an Indian child is in question, provincial laws, courts or agencies have no more application than they would in any other sovereign state. In brief, Taylor and Hudson (1992) state that this model entails full recognition of Indian government jurisdiction over child welfare.

Limits on Autonomy of First Nations CFS Agencies

Under the existing provincial structure, there are a number of reasons, in addition to the models of provincial authority, as to why the autonomy of First Nations agencies is limited. The first of these reasons is related to the concept of self-government. There are two conflicting versions of what self-government for First Nations means. The First Nations view self-government as flowing from their existence since time immemorial on North America. The subsequent signing of Treaties did not rule out the First Nations right to continue to self-govern themselves. The Federal government's version is based on policy which recognizes the inherent right of self-government as being an existing right within s.35 of the *Constitution Act, 1982* (Canada 1995).

Self-government, in the full sense of the word requires a legislative, judicial and executive branch, which holds equally for all levels of the Federal and Provincial governments. Under the currently delegated authority model, the First Nations agencies have achieved only executive powers. The province continues to retain legislative powers and, through legislation, all powers over setting standards and licensing of substitute care and the like (Taylor and Henley 1992). And because there is no tribal court system, the First Nations agencies are obliged to continue to use non-First Nations courts. Add to this the fact that the Federal government controls the financial resources. The result is a tangled web of fragmented authority (Hudson 1987, First Nations Task Force on CFS 1993).

The second major reason for limitation lies in the jurisdictional denial to extend First Nations jurisdiction to registered First Nations children living off reserve. This jurisdictional constraint limits First Nations agencies ability to retard the loss of First Nations children and the separation of families to non-First Nations agencies in other provincial regions and urban centres. Despite the moratoriums placed on adoption of Aboriginal children to non-Aboriginal families outside the country, this trend has not diminished.

Hudson (1987) argued that First Nations agencies could not continue to rely exclusively on reserve-based foster homes to accommodate children requiring substitute care. Hudson notes that there are often medical, educational or social reasons for the use of off-reserve resources that First Nations agencies must be permitted to develop; but are prevented from developing because of the jurisdictional constraints set out in the *Indian Act* and the Agreements between the two levels of government with the First Nations child welfare agencies.

A third major issue is the conflicting views each party has with respect to the type of services that ought to be the major focus of First Nations agencies. The current act as it presently stands, even with the new provisions that come into effect later this year, favours the removal of children over the healing of and keeping families united. In early June of 1997 the Provincial government passed new legislative changes to the rights and safety of children. Amendments to the CFS Act resulted in Bill 47 *(The Adoption and Consequential Amendments Act* and Bill 48 *(The CFS Amendments and Consequential Amendments Act).* These amendments became law on March 15th, 1999. These amendments concern First Nations peoples as it has the potential to return the entire system back to an era reminiscent of the 'sixties scoop' where the human rights of First Nations peoples were ignored and children discriminately taken from homes and placed in cross-cultural adoptive placements.

The intent of the *CFS Act* is to protect children in need of protection. For First Nations CFS agencies the need to protect children is only one aspect out of a whole range of services that they provide. The emphasis must be on supporting communities, families and other significant care givers, such as extended families and grandparents. Therefore, protection of children is not enough. What is important is the protection and promotion of total family and community well being. If the family and community are equally healthy and self-sustaining, the child, in most circumstances, will also be healthy (Young 1996b).

First Nations peoples have always found the practice of separating children from families to be problematic. They have questioned why children are taken away and then resumed to the home, when the problems that existed in that family before the apprehension of the children, had not been resolved for the parents. Why not fix the home and the problems of the family rather than alienate the child from his/her family and cultural environment? Unfortunately, there is no funding allocated for services to families for early preventive measures to assist families experiencing difficulties. Placing children in care is a costly transaction, which is provided for through the provisions of the Act, and payment for such care does not include treatment, which many First Nations children require as a result of separation they experience when they come into care. Healing for families is a necessity because of the fallout from the colonial and assimilative practices of the past. Without the resources to heal the family, many children will continue to experience a revolving situation of living between home and being in care. The provincial legislation and its focus on apprehension rather than on holistic healing aspects result in more children in care, identity and emotional confusion, fractured family relations and prohibitive costs to child welfare agencies. Costs which are often absorbed by other institutions, such as corrections. One only has to look in homeless shelters, courtrooms, youth detention centres and prisons to find places full of Aboriginal people who grew up in non-Aboriginal substitute care. Over 90% of the Aboriginal inmates in prison come from either foster or adoption breakdowns (RCAP 1996). A person is an adult for many more years than s/he is a child. The consequences of the current Act's provision and the new amendments can tie up government funds for a longer period of time.

First Nations question why the government is willing to pay astronomical costs for someone else to give custodial care to their children while they stand by in helpless poverty because someone else controls the money and has the power to make decisions about their children. The First Nations agencies believe that the emphasis of service delivery should be on prevention and family services and not on apprehension of children from their families and communities (First Nations Task Force on CFS 1993). While protecting children from grave situations is a necessity, it unfortunately causes problems for children and family members. Children and their families are being damaged in the process and the government, by virtue of their legislative provisions, contributes to the continuing destruction of the social fabric of First Nations peoples.

Several core values guide and influence First Nations CFS agencies. Inherent in these values is the belief that First Nations individuals, children, families and communities have a distinct status and identity by virtue of their Indigenous origins, history, cultures and languages. This includes their Aboriginal rights and freedoms as identified by the Treaties and the *Constitution Acts* of 1867 and 1982. The core values are:

• First Nations children are best protected within their tribal communities. To protect these First Nations children one must also protect the families to ensure the survival of First Nations communities.

• First Nations children are the future of these Nations, and by virtue of this they are entitled to live in a healthy and prosperous environment.

• First Nations children are gifts from the Creator entrusted not only to the natural parents, but also to the extended family, clan and community. Therefore, the responsibility for raising a child does not rest only with the natural parents but also with the clan and the Nation.

• First Nations are entitled to services that respect and reflect the culture and traditions of their Nation. Their membership best determines the needs and priorities of the Nation, and thus all decisions and solutions must come from the community and its members.

• All social services must be community-based, culturally appropriate, reflecting the cultural and linguistic diversity of the First Nations.

• First Nations have a right to self-determination.

• First Nations self-determination means, but is not limited to, having exclusive jurisdiction over their children, no matter where these children may reside. This includes those children previously removed from their Nation and the generation before them.

• Provincial legislation has no place within First Nations communities; the use of provincial legislation is considered an interim measure until First Nations have developed their own codes and standards.

• First Nations have an inherent right of self-government. This includes the right to govern and implement CFS programs that address their distinctive rights and freedoms to First Nations communities, families and children.

• First Nations government involves but is not limited to: Jurisdiction over First Nations children despite residency; Legislation for all services; and Codes and standards for all services (Young 1996b).

This short but dramatic period of contact between the child welfare system and First Nations peoples has been well documented by others (Hudson and McKenzie 1985, Johnston 1983, Hamilton and Sinclair 1991, First Nations Task Force on CFS 1993, RCAP 1996, Fournier and Crey 1997). The agreements and developments referred to in this paper must be seen as part of the contemporary attempts by First Nations citizens to initiate a process of decolonization from the colonial forces and institutions that have played a significant role in their present subjugated states. The development of self-governing structures is itself a process of decolonization and CFS is identified as an area of expedited concern under self-government (RCAP 1996). It is no coincidence that First Nation peoples prioritize CFS, along with land claims, justice, economic development, health care and education as part of their self-government initiatives. [Cassidy and Bish (1989:10) note that "many Indian governments have selected education and the care of children in general as a major focus of their government activities."]

The 1994 Manitoba Framework Agreement Initiative

The First Nations communities within Manitoba have taken steps towards creating a future for themselves through the development of the FAI (AMC 1994). This historic agreement outlines the rules and framework for the transfer of Federal jurisdiction from Indian Affairs to First Nations governments. Under this initiative, First Nations will assume executive, legislative, judicial, and administrative powers over their communities (Brock 1996). FAI is based upon three primary objectives consistent with the Inherent Right to Self-Government (AMC 1994):

> To dismantle the existing departmental structures of the Department of Indian Affairs and Northern Development as they affect First Nations in Manitoba;

> To develop and recognize First Nations governments in Manitoba legally empowered to exercise the authorities required to meet the needs of the peoples of the First Nations; and

> To restore to First Nations governments the jurisdiction (including those of other Federal departments) to implement their own governing structures (Young 1996b, Fontaine 1996).

This controversial agreement is without precedent in the history of Canada and First Nations relations. Many believe that the agreement is a step backwards from the Charlottetown Agreement on Aboriginal self-government, which had promised constitutional entrenchment of the principle of self-government. Others have praised the FAI agreement as promising what Charlottetown failed to deliver - the achievement and recognition of First Nations' self-government in practice. Supporters of the FAI agreement maintain that it breaks new ground in establishing a process for terminating Federal government control over First Nations according to terms jointly defined by the Federal government and First Nations and at a pace determined by the First Nations. Supporters also acknowledge that this claim is controversial and rests as a theoretical proposition for the time being (Brock 1996). Under the Agreement, there three items were identified as expedited areas of development: Education Program; Fire Safety Program, and Capital Projects (Fontaine 1996). Child and Family Services was eventually identified as requiring immediate development (Southern First Nations CFS Project 1998).

Kathy Brock (1996) noted that there were two unresolved areas of concern that could have implications for the FAI process. Under FAI, the implications of the dismantling initiative for urban, non-status, Bill C-3 1, and off-reserve members of the First Nations are unclear. Secondly, prominent activists have questioned the wisdom of transferring powers to a male-dominated power structure such as exists within the First Nations communities without first securing guarantees for the rights and status of women and children. These activists cite examples of the abuse of women, the political interference of chiefs in women's shelters and child welfare agencies (160). While some of these concerns have been addressed by FAI hiring more women into the dismantling project at the decision making level, other questions remain unanswered. Even the potential protection provided by the application of the *Canadian Charter of Rights and Freedoms* to the new governments developed under FAI is uncertain since discussions on this matter have been deferred.

Another area of potential difficulty arises with the provincial government because it was not a party to the dismantling negotiations. The negotiations have been bilateral in accordance with the treaty and constitutional relationship between the Federal government and First Nations. As part of the process, the Government of Canada will ensure that Manitoba will participate in negotiations involving any matters of provincial jurisdiction and, that further, they will encourage the Province to pursue similar dismantling initiatives (Fontaine 1996). Extensive communications and consultations have been initiated and are in varying degrees of stages within First Nations communities. Consultation at every stage in the dismantling process was considered a necessity to ensure that the First Nations people are fully informed and have every opportunity to give their views on all aspects of the initiative (Young 1996a). In the meantime, DIAND's regional services and funding in all First Nations communities has been maintained until First Nations are able to take over administrative responsibility (Fontaine 1996, Brock 1996). This poses difficulties for implementing First Nations governments and negotiating specific arrangements affecting provincial areas of jurisdiction, such as provincial laws of general application that apply to: reserves, land transfers, resources, gambling, child welfare, citizenship (on and off reserve), and determining the capacity to assume full jurisdiction (Brock 1996).

Many First Nations grassroots members see FAI as an elite driven, top-down process that has ignored the input necessary from people at the community level. In addition, the FAI project has experienced a high turnover rate in both research staff and management. The most prominent change to FAI is the original signatories to the MOU and FAI Agreement (Ron Irwin, now the Canadian Ambassador to Ireland and Phil Fontaine, past Grand Chief of the Assembly of First Nations in Ottawa) are no longer parties to the process. The 62 FAI Community Co-ordinators, hired to disseminate the FAI process to the communities change frequently, are undereducated, and inadequately funded. Approximately 10 sector groups work under FAI, including: education, economic development, capital/infrastructure, child and family, fire and emergency measures, health, human resources, justice and the First Nations Government Representatives (FNGRs) (AMC 1998). Many of these sectors are developed in isolation and often operate with inadequate funding and staffing requirements. Funding requirements, fragmentation of sectors, and continuity in the overall progress are extremely important factors that could impede upon the success of FAI. These comments are based upon my observations and experiences as a "quasi-employee" of both FAI and the Southern First Nations CFS/FAI Research Project.

The Southern CFS/FAI Project

In response to the inadequacies of the present CFS system and its failure to meet the needs of First Nations children, the AMC made a decision to seek full legislative, administrative and executive control over CFS In September of 1995, they passed a resolution to expedite CFS under the FAI. The Chiefs Committee on CFS (CCCFS) and the Chiefs Committee on Dismantling (CCOD) met in November of 1995 passing a motion to secure funding for CFS to be developed in concert with FAI. Further discussions were held with the Chiefs in Assembly and with First Nations communities resulting in the emergence of two Manitoba CFS projects - the *MKO Child and Family Jurisdiction Project* (the Northern Project) and *the Southern First Nations Child and Family/FAI Research Project* (the Southern Project). The Northern project (carried out through Manitoba Keewatinowi Okimakanak Inc (MKO) in Thompson) compiled research on codes and standards regarding child welfare and completed a community consultation process with 26 northern communities. Both projects aim to restore full power and authority over CFS to First Nations, develop legislation, and involve communities in the development and decision making process. This paper focuses on the Southern project.

The Southern CFS Project is governed by a Task Group of agency directors from Anishinaabe CFS, Dakota Ojibway CFS,Intertribal CFS, Peguis Intertribal CFS, Southeast CFS, West Region CFS, and Sagkeeng CFS; with support and formal decisions from the CCCFS; and ex-officio advice from the Child & Family Advisor of the AMC. The Task Group provides direction and expertise to the Research Technicians hired to carry out the Workplan activities. West Region CFS administers the Southern CFS Project budget. The Southern CFS Project works co-operatively with FAI staff and management. FAI works in concert with the Southern CFS/FAI Workplan on jurisdiction and legislative development, provides liaison services and technical services to the Task Group and Research Technicians, and consults with the Southern CFS Project staff and Task Group members in matters related to CFS and research. The Research staff, although technically employees under both the FAI structure and West Region, work from the West Region CFS office in Winnipeg and meet with the Task Group members monthly to discuss and review the achievements of the Project's Workplan.

The Southern Research Project consists of five phases over a six- year period that complements the activities of the FAI and uses the community consultation function as identified by the FAI process. Phase I established a Task Group, project location and recruitment of employees to conduct the required research. The project is currently in Phase IV of its Workplan and is presently in the process of conducting community consultations on the development of a First Nations child welfare law. Ratification by the people of each First Nations in Phase VI will ensure the development of a community-based First Nations legislation for CFS that is culturally relevant and meets the needs of Southern First Nations communities.

Conclusions

Creating a future for First Nations permeates the goals and objectives of individuals and agency directors delivering CFS and this Project. While First Nations peoples do not know what the future will look like, they are adamant about taking steps towards the creation of that future through the development of a Child and Family Act. That Act will be the responsibility of and administered by First Nations peoples on behalf of their children, families and communities. Governments are ambivalent about offloading administration to the private sector, but First Nations embrace the idea of administering their own activities and no where is this more evident than in the child welfare field in Manitoba. The current child welfare legislation is considered to be operating on an interim basis. First Nations will take over this jurisdiction and enact their own legislation to restore authority, control, and responsibility over child welfare. Solutions and suggestions on how CFS will be delivered under FAI must come from both those who provide the services and those affected by the new law. In the meantime, the goal of distinct and culturally appropriate policies, standards and a First Nations CFS legislation and administrative structure remain important and vital priorities to the First Nations Peoples irrespective of its connection to the FAI process. First Nations peoples today know they face formidable challenges, but they also know that healthy, intact families will be the corner stone of their governments.

References

Assembly of Manitoba Chiefs. 1994. *The Dismantling of the Department of Indian Affairs and Northern Development, the Restoration of Jurisdiction to First Nations Peoples in Manitoba and Recognition of the First Nations Governments in Manitoba.* Framework Agree., Workplan,MU

Assembly of Manitoba Chiefs. *1998. Strategic Multi-Year Work Plan.* Wpg:MFA

Ayed, N. 1999. Native Boy returned to adoptive pair.*Globe and Mail,* Feb. 18.

Bennett, M. 1998. *Response to Third Year Law Student's Presentation on Adoption and Aboriginal Children.* Unpub. paper Law 45.399, U of M, Wpg.

Brock, C. 1995. Taking control: Dismantling Indian Affairs and recognizing First Nations Government in Manitoba.In D. Brown (Ed.)*Canada: The State of the Federation 1995.*(pp.145-170). Kingston: Inst. of Intergovl Rel.

Canada. 1987. *Indian CFS in Canada: Final Report.* CFS Task Force. TO:INAC.

Canada. 1995. *Aboriginal Self-Government: The Government of Canada's Approach to the Implementation of the Inherent Right and the Negotiation of Aboriginal Self-Government.* Published under the authority of the Honourable Ronald A. Irwin, P., M.P. Ottawa: INAC

Cassidy, F. and Bish, R. 1989. *Indian Government: Its Meaning in Practice.* Lantzville, BC: Oolichan Books and Inst. for Res. in Pub. Policy,

First Nations's CFS Task Force. 1993. *Children First, Our Responsibility.* Wpg.

Fontaine, P. 1996. Dismantling and Restoring Jurisdiction. In *J.* Oakes and R. Riewe (Eds.) *Issues in the North* pp.145-150. Edmonton: CCI.

Fournier, S. and Crey, E. 1997. *The Abduction of First Nations Children and the Restoration of Aboriginal Communities.* Van: Douglas & McIntyre.

Giesbrecht, B. 1992. *Fatalities Inquires Act into the Death of L. Desjarlais..* MB.

Halliday, B. 1999. 'Better life' adoption Slammed.*Wpg Sun.* February 27.

Hamilton, A. and Sinclair, C. 1991. *Report of the Aboriginal Justice Inquiry of MB, Volume 1: Child Welfare.* Minister of Justice.

Hudson, P. and McKenzie, B. 1985. Child welfare and Native People: The extension of colonialism. *The Social Worker* 49(2): 63-88.

Hudson, B. 1987. Manitoba's Indian Child Welfare services: In the balance. In J. Ismael and R. Thomlison (Eds.) *Perspectives on Social Services and Social Issues* pp.251-264. Ottawa: CCSD.

Johnston, P. 1983. *Native Children and the Child Welfare System.* Ottawa&TO: Can. Council on Soc.Dev.& James Lorimer.

Little Bear, L. 1992. Section 88 of the Indian Act and the application of Provincial laws to Indians. In J. Long and M. Boldt (Eds.) *Governments in Conflict? Prov. and Indian Nations in Can.* pp. 174-187. TO:Univ.Press.

MacDonald, J. 1983. The Spallumcheen Indian Band By-law and its potential impact on Native Indian Child Welfare policy in British Columbia. *Canadian Journal of Family Law 1(1):*75-95.

MacDonald, J. 1987. The programme of the Spallumcheen Indian Band in BC as a model of Indian Child Welfare. In J.Ismael and R.Thomlison (Eds.) *Perspectives on Social Services and Social Issues*pp.237-249 ON:CCSD

McKenzie, B. and Hudson, P. 1985. Native Children, Child Welfare and the Colonization of Native People. In B. Wharf and K. Levitt (Eds.) *Challenge of Child Welfare.* Vancouver: University of British Columbia

Patton, M. 1982. *In Practical Evaluation.* London: Sage Publications.

Pellatt, A. 199*1. An International Review of Child Welfare Policy and Practice in Relation to Aboriginal People.* AB: Can Res Inst for Law and Family.

Royal Commission on Aboriginal Peoples (RCAP). 1996. *For Seven Generations CDROM, 3 Gathering Strength, Chap 2: The Family.* Ottawa: Lebraxus.

Taylor-Henley, S. and Hudson, P. 1992. Aboriginal self-government and social services: First Nations - Provincial relationships. In *Canadian Public Policy Analyse de Politiques, XVIII:* 1: 13 -26.

Teichroeb, R. 1997. *Flowers on my Grave: How an Ojibwa Boy's Death Helped Break the Silence on Child Abuse.* Toronto: Harper Collin's Publishers.

Sinclair, M. Phillips, D and Bala, N. 1991. Aboriginal welfare in Canada. In N. Balla, J. Hornick and R.Vogl (Eds.) *Canadian Child Welfare Law: Children, Families and the State.* pp. 175. TO: Thompson Educ.Pub.

Southern First Nations CFS/FAI Research Project. *1998/1999. Southern First Nations CFSIFAI 199 8/99 Workplan.* Wpg: FAI

Young, D. 1996a. *Draft Briefing Book prepared for the AMC.* Wpg: AMC.

Young, D.1996b. *Manitoba First Nations CFS Agencies: Submission to the Prov. Government's Child and Family Review of the Services Act.* Wpg:AMC.

---

[1]   Marlyn Bennett is a member of Sandy Bay Ojibway Nation in Manitoba, a Masters of Native Studies student at the University of Manitoba, and consultant. This article is an edited report generated while she was project manager for the Southern First Nations Child and Family Research Project.

Role of Community Consultation in Self-Governance

Jeff Cyr[1]

Abstract

First Nation Peoples within Manitoba are of many different cultural backgrounds and can be found in equal numbers on and off-reserve. The socio-economic cultural complexity of this group cannot be ignored by those establishing self-government and evaluating its effectiveness over time. First Nations governance and laws requires adequate recognition of and support for the socio-economic and cultural reality of the communities' constituents.

Community Consultation and Self-Governance

At the heart of the self-governance process is a culturally diverse population of First Nations found in equal numbers on and off-reserve. The socio-economic cultural complexity of this group cannot be ignored by those *conducting* the process, nor by those *evaluating* its effectiveness over time. To establish truly representative First Nations governance and its subsequent laws requires adequate recognition of and support for the socio-economic and cultural reality of the communities' constituents, including the colonial experience. A long history of colonialization has engendered distrust, fear and anxiety in the communities of First Nations peoples as any involvement with the European laws was purposely destructive to the people and their culture (RCAP 1997). Suggestions of a "top-down" approach typical of the federal constitutional structure, imposed time frames, and resource restrictions increase the apprehension of First Nations people.

The following passages reflect an understanding by the Canadian government of the principle elements of creating good governance. However, it is the complex *process* of addressing cultural diversity, of building human and physical resources, of creating laws and governing principles that are directed and inspired by the people that will ensure the creation of long-lasting, culturally responsive governing institutions.

> *Outcomes must grow out of a consensus of the people of the First Nations and out of their history, culture, and institutions. Outcomes cannot be imposed (AMC 1994:1). It means recognizing traditional customs, including their role in governance; celebrating Aboriginal languages, heritage, and culture; assisting to build the capacity of Aboriginal institutions to handle new responsibilities; and working to establish mechanisms to recognize sustainable and accountable Aboriginal governments and institutions. (Indian and Northern Affairs [INAC] 1997:7)*

First Nations must have opportunities to participate, control and own the progress toward self-determination. It is imperative that the process be respectful of cultural diversity and that diversity be entrenched in its documentation and institutions. The only effective way of ensuring this is to utilize a comprehensive community consultation approach at every phase. Originally, the mandate for this process in Manitoba was handed to a project managed by the Assembly of Manitoba Chiefs (AMC) entitled the Framework Agreement Initiative (FAI). FAI was created to conduct research and create the institutions of self-governance for the 60 First Nations who signed the Agreement. Due to changes in priorities at INAC, internal pressure to show budgetary responsibility in the wake of the HRDC funding fiascos, and an internal lacklustre performance by some FAI sub projects and FAI management overall, FAI is quickly fading into non-existence, threatening the grass roots connection. Warry further discusses the necessity of community participation in self-governance at a grassroots level:

> The goal of Native self-determination, in concert with its political counterpart, self-government, involves recognition of inherent and sovereign rights. It encompasses political control, rather than simple administrative authority over community affairs. The control and ownership of intellectual property, as well as natural

resources, is intrinsic to this process. The ability of Native communities to determine their future is quite naturally related, in part, to their ability to generate meaningful research. . . . Native leaders have rejected this latter approach [consultation with only leaders or policy makers] as a strategy which governments use to rationalize Indian policy or to make policy more digestible to the public at large. (Warry 1990:62)

The issues surrounding self-governance are so extremely important that they deserve the time and attention involved with community consultation. Furthermore, such consultation is vital because it is the conceptualization and adoption of new policy, not simply the evaluation or modification of past policies. Community consultation and the development of self-government is in keeping with the preexisting inherent right and the constitutional right to self-government. The goal of self-government is unquestionably clear "the right of First Nations to exercise authority and to legislate in areas such as social and cultural development, resource use, family laws, revenue raising and economic development" (Warry 1990:62); the process is remarkably unclear.

Historically, the federal government has demonstrated their inability to successfully legislate and create programs on behalf of First Nations children and families; it has explicitly tried to extinguish First Nations culture, or implicitly tried to assimilate it into mainstream society. Outlining this history is part of reaffirming the role of the people in determining the content and structure of a new First Nations system of governance. Secondly, it is important to outline where community consultation has occurred in the past and present. To this end we look at judicial decisions and the governments own policy statements. Thirdly, it is crucial to highlight the difference between traditional forms of knowledge and First Nations views on attaining knowledge. This aspect of attaining knowledge lies at the heart of the research and consultation process of any new governing initiative.

Colonialism, the Word from the Courts, and Community Consultation

The colonial and federal governments of Canada have, respectively, passed extensive amounts of legislation over the last 150 years that governs the lives of First Nations peoples (Armitage 1995). Every report from the infamous *1966 Hawthorne Report* to the recent *Royal Commission on Aboriginal Peoples* (RCAP 1997) has unabashedly stated that both the federal and provincial governments have failed in their attempts to legislate and govern on behalf of First Nations Peoples. From the time after the original treaties were signed, through the Indian Act and onto modern day legislation, federal government legislation has focused on control and "containment" of First Nations people. While the initial catalyst of legislation was removal of the First Nations people from certain areas of land for economic appropriation, the character of legislation changed to focus on absorbing First Nations peoples into the dominant European cultural base. Assimilation and domination through forcible adoption and removal, through the residential school system, or through the social welfare systems of the provinces were the legislative norm up until the late twentieth century (RCAP 1997, Armitage 1999). In the view of First Nations peoples, the approach that Canadian governmental legislation has taken has been removed and disconnected from the population it seeks to govern and highly paternalistic in its outcomes. As an early RCAP report on traditional First Nations governance explains: "The European system of governing, reflected in the *Indian Act,* is based upon levels and a hierarchy of power. This hierarchy suggests that people are not capable of knowing what is in their best interests and therefore removes them from the decision making process" (RCAP 1997:22). The FAI has moved beyond the ineffective top-down authoritative structures typical of federal government, to involving the maximum number of people in the process of self-government. The fear, anxiety and mistrust resultant from colonialism will not quickly, if ever, disappear. In reality, it is illogical for First Nations people to accept any limitations on the self-governance process placed by the same government that has for years sought to marginalise their place in society by every means possible.

Although the historical injustice of past legislation and the demands of creating a new representative government that emanates from the communities should be sufficient to substantiate the community consultation research process, further necessity has been generated by the Canadian legal system. The 1969 federal governments' White Paper and the early 1970's court decisions signalled a move from the paternalistic fallacy of thinking of First Nations peoples as "wards of the state" to an understanding that First Nations peoples have a special relationship with Canada. Recent court decisions have clearly stated that disputes between the First Nations people and the federal government are resolved via negotiation rather than through the courts (Bell 1998). In *Donald J. Marshall v Her Majesty the Queen,* Binnie stated on the nature of the appeal that "I would allow this appeal because nothing less would uphold the honour and integrity of the Crown in its dealings with the Mi'kmaq people to secure their peace and friendship" (1999:168). In terms of community consultation, the courts were even more insistent in the cases of *Delgamuukw v. Queen (1998)* and in *Corbriere v. Canada (1999)* about the nature and depth of the negotiation process. The conclusions reached by the Supreme court regarding Delgamuukw were specifically about Aboriginal title to lands and spoke to the crowns responsibility to First Nations:

> This aspect of Aboriginal title [future use of land] suggests that the Crown's fiduciary obligation may be satisfied by involving Aboriginal peoples in decisions concerning their lands. In most cases, the standard will be significantly deeper than mere consultation. Some cases may even require the full consent of an Aboriginal nation, particularly when provinces enact hunting and fishing regulations in relation to Aboriginal lands. (1998:18)

The passage suggests that the court has an idea, a negative one, of how a consultation process usually operates in the federal government. The notion that full consent would be required in order to enact legislation regarding hunting appears to be a sound basic requirement, given the integral cultural connection between the people and the land. As in the case of the *Halfway River (1997)* land rights, the appeal judge, Huddart, stated that the Crown is "required to initiate a process of adequate and meaningful consultation to ascertain the nature and scope of the treaty right at issue" (1997:45). Although these do not speak to the goals of community consultation, it can be easily inferred that full consent and pre-negotiation community consultation may be a minimal requirement for creating self-governing legislation. It becomes increasingly clear from the legal decisions alone, if not the practice of government, that there are two different visions of the consultation process being used. The federal government, for time and financial constraints, practices consultation at the group level, often drawing erroneous conclusions about individual actions and needs. Consultation as understood by First Nations people is a process that seeks to bridge the individual and group level of analysis issues by first informing and then building consensus at several levels.

Delgamuukw also explicitly validates oral tradition as equivalent to European methods of attaining evidence, suggesting that oral tradition is the key to gaining and transmitting knowledge regarding First Nations principles, values and community practices such as customary adoption. Consultation thus serves the many aims of informing the public, attaining consensus, building resources and accessing the traditional knowledge base of the community. Further in *Delgamuukw* is the explicit direction that in dealing with Aboriginal people the federal government must "bargain" or "negotiate" and that these must occur in good faith. In the judgement Chief Justice Lamer was very clear on this point when he said:

> Finally, this litigation has been both long and expensive, not only in economic but in human terms as well. By ordering a new trial, I do not necessarily encourage the parties to proceed to litigation and to settle their dispute through the courts. As was said in *Sparrow*, at para. 1105, s.35(1) "provides a solid constitutional base upon which subsequent negotiations can take place". Those negotiations should also include other Aboriginal nations which have a stake in the territory claimed. **Moreover, the Crown is under a moral, if not legal, duty to enter into and conduct those negotiations in good faith. Ultimately, it is through negotiated settlements, with good faith and give and take on all sides, reinforced by the decisions of this Court,** that we will achieve what I stated in *Van Der Peet. (1998:para 186)*

Corbriere (1999) is also clear-cut in its treatment of the 'negotiation in good faith' principle and the need for in-depth consultation. As stated in the decision, the length of time, administrative difficulties and expense associated with change is not justification for the federal government to ignore court decisions or other sections of their own stated policy. The duty towards consultation contains three basic requirements; (a) full information, not only about the nature of the project but also in regards to its impact on First Nations; (b) the Crown must inform itself of the practices and views of First Nations; and (c) consultations must be both meaningful and reasonable (Lawrence and Macklem 2000). However, the duty is not limited to these actions but contains a second level of obligation to consult. The 'good faith' component suggests that the government show sensitivity to Aboriginal values, recognize different communication styles and build relationships rather than merely fulfilling a bureaucratic requirement (Lawrence and Macklem 2000).

How We Know, How You Know

The desire to pursue in-depth community consultation is more than policies and agreements, judicial decisions and cultural differences. It is how modern First Nations people gain knowledge of their past and connect that past to the present and future. The relentless subjugation of Aboriginal peoples since the 1500's has left many scars on First Nations and nearly caused the loss of much of the wisdom, knowledge and secrets of the ancestors. The process of rebuilding that knowledge has met stiff resistance by the dominant European epistemology. The Western world makes knowledge objective and tries to stand outside the process so that it is not contaminated by human 'experience' (Ermine 1992). First Nations peoples have long sought knowledge through subjective experience (Ermine 1992). The people and community form the base of any knowledge experience. Modern Canadian society and government relies heavily on scientific knowledge and its technologies to control and maintain societies (Franklin 1992). The technological methods of gaining knowledge have politically marginalised, disenfranchised, and made irrelevant the experiences of people. For example government speaks of 'deliverables', 'timelines', and 'efficiency' rather than people and implications. The self-governance process seeks to gain knowledge of community traditions, practices, values, beliefs and behavioural norms and enshrine them in the legislation. Consultation is self-governance, not a step in a bureaucratic program, but a path to knowledge from which emanates new governing structure.

Conclusion

Self-governance must proceed at the pace of the people and their communities. The following teaching should be taken into account by researchers, leaders and governments alike:

> Their [the White Man] gift is movement, they move very fast and we move a slower path. It's like the Original Man, he was the last one to leave the Creator's side, and the White man was the first one to leave, he didn't even look back to the gifts he was given and look at them now, he's lost all his gifts, he doesn't know who he is and he moves very fast . . . Anishinaabe was the last one to leave the Creator's side . . . We walk very slow and examine what's there and we don't jump into things

right away. . . . The White man has to understand that and not push us, he's always pushing, trying to make things happen right away. (Elder Liza Mosher in Kulchyski *et al*. 1998)

Moving slowly towards important moments in First Nations history highlights the diversity and uniqueness of Aboriginal peoples and reflect that each community is at a different stage of social, economic and political development. All communities are at different levels of readiness to move forward on self-governance, this must be respected by federal and Aboriginal leadership.

References

Armitage, A. 1999. Comparing Aboriginal policies: The colonial legacy. In J. Hylton (Ed.) *Aboriginal Self-Government in Canada*. Sask: Purich.

Armitage, A. 1995. *Comparing the Policy of Aboriginal Assimilation: Australia, Canada and New Zealand*. Vancouver: UBC.

Assembly of Manitoba Chiefs. 1994. *The Dismantling of the Department of Indian Affairs and Northern Development, the Restoration of Jurisdiction to First Nations Peoples in Manitoba and Recognition of the First Nations Governments in Manitoba*. Framework Agree, Workplan & MU.

Bell, C. 1998. New directions in the law of Aboriginal rights. *Can Bar Rev*.

Delgamuukw v. Her Majesty the Queen. 1998. 1 C.N.L.R., pp.14-97

Donald J. Marshall v. Her Majesty the Queen. 1999. 4 C.N.L.R pp. 161-212.

Ermine, W. 1992. Aboriginal epistemology. In M. Battiste and J. Barman (Eds.) *First Nations Education in Canada: The Circle Unfolds*.Van: UBC.

Franklin, U. 1992. *The Real World of Technology*. CBC Massey Lect. TO: Under Anansi.

Halfway River v. British Columbia. 1997. 4 C.N.L.R., pp. 1-64

Her Majesty the Queen v. Corbriere. 1999. 1 C.N.L.R., pp. 19-71

Indian and Northern Affairs Canada. *1997. First Nation Community Profiles*

INAC. 1997. *Gathering Strength: Canada's Aboriginal Action Plan*. INAC.

Kulchyski, P., McCaskill, D., and Newhouse D. (Eds.) 1998. *In the Words of Elders: Aboriginal Cultures in Transition*. TO: University Press.

Lawrence, S. and Macklem, P. 2000. From consultation to reconciliation: Aboriginal rights and the Crown's duty to consult. *Can Bar Rev*. 79(Feb.).

Royal Commission on Aboriginal Peoples. 1997. New era for the Anishinabek.

Warry, W. 1990. Doing unto others: Applied anthropology, collaborative research and Native self-determination. *Culture* X (1).

---

[1]   Jeff Cyr (MA) is a Métis consultant and worked as a Research Analyst for the Southern First Nations Child and Family Research Project.

Ma Mawi Wi Chi Itata
Family Violence Program

Jocelyn Proulx and Sharon Perrault[1]

Abstract

Aboriginal teachings and traditions are blended with mainstream content and theory to formulate the Ma Mawi Wi Chi Itata Family Violence Program. This program offers services to children, women, and men within the community and at Stony Mountain Federal Correctional Facility. This article describes the services offered, the philosophy of the program, and the constant efforts to expand services to fit the changing needs of the community, including research partnerships.

Introduction

Aboriginal teachings and traditions are blended with mainstream content and theory to formulate the Ma Mawi Wi Chi Itata Family Violence Program (FVP). This program offers open and closed group services as well as individual and Elder counselling. Their services extend to children, women, and men within the community and at Stony Mountain Federal Correctional Facility. This article describes the services offered, the philosophy of the program, the constant efforts to expand and modify services to fit the changing needs of the community, a summary of program evaluations, the benefits of community or academic research partnerships, and the importance of community perspectives in providing solutions to family violence.

Community and Colonization

Colonization has left Aboriginal people exposed to racism, exploitation, and institutional abuse. A significant proportion of Aboriginal children were raised in residential schools. These schools created a psychological as well as physical distance between parents and children; individuals report experiences of neglect, psychological, physical, and sexual abuse (York 1990). Efforts were made towards the eradication of traditional ways, spiritualism, and languages which were considered barbaric, and replacement with mainstream Christian beliefs and the English language (Lee 1992, McGillivray 1997, Palmer and Cooke 1996). In the 1960s and 70s, the child welfare policy removed many Canadian Aboriginal children from their homes and adopted them into predominantly Caucasian urban homes. In the United States, Aboriginal children were advertised for adoption in local newspapers. These children suffered the loss of their family, their way of life, their culture, and their country of origin (McGillivray 1997, York 1990).

In Canada there is an over representation of Aboriginal children in the child welfare system and numerous placements are common (Gil 1982, Palmer and Cooke 1996, Zylberberg 1991). Although many foster homes offer care and comfort to children, some are characterized by abuse, neglect, and racism (McFadden and Ryan 1991). Children placed in group homes or youth care facilities also face potential abuse from staff and other children (Tomkiewicz 1984).

Colonization and Family Violence

Most children in residential schooling, foster care, and other institutional care, incurred damage to their physical, behavioral, affective, cognitive, and social developments. Their opportunities for secure attachments and cultural identity has been impaired resulting in problems relating to others, caring for others, trusting others, poor self-image, an incomplete sense of identity, and low self-esteem (Hirschbach 1982, Shkilnyk 1985, York 1990, Zylberberg 1991). The loss of positive parenting models adversely affected their parenting skills, leaving the subsequent generation vulnerable to child welfare placements (Lee 1992, Palmer and Cooke 1996).

Although many of the institutional abuses experienced by Aboriginal people are no longer part of social policy, the cycle of violence and the intergenerational impact of violence continues. Spousal abuse in Aboriginal families is approximately seven times the national average and the incidence of sexual abuse is very high (Timpson 1995). Individuals experiencing multiple forms of abuse have learned to interact in violent ways. Witnessing of violence between parents and other family members only strengthens this lesson and normalizes the experience of violence in their lives. They have learned to live with aggression within the context of love, affection, and intimate relationships. Violence increases the risk that their children will be placed in institutional care. Thus, the abuse incurred by Aboriginal people through Canadian social policy is perpetuated through multiple generations. The shared experience as a First Nation cannot be separated from the abuse they experience or perpetrate; therefore family violence programming must recognize this history of abuse, help the participants to identify it in their own lives and come to the realization of how it has affected their own behaviour and their relationships.

Community Perspective

Traditionally Aboriginal people's sense of family was based on an extended community network (Lee 1992). Clan mothers were the life givers; teaching respect for self, the creator, and for all others, and sharing, kindness, honesty, trust, and humility. Parents passed these teachings on to their children. These beliefs and attitudes of general respect for all living things negated feelings of low self-esteem, negative emotions towards others, and violent behaviour. Thus the Aboriginal community was itself a family system that had a reciprocally supportive relationship with the individual families residing within its bounds. It is this sense of family, this sense of community, that must be nurtured in order to bring healing to Aboriginal people. A healthy community can empower its people through education, and by taking a strong position on violence and support services. Only in ensuring healthy community living can we begin to heal and restore families to live free from family violence.

Blended Programming

There has been a recent increase in the number of blended programs available to Aboriginal people. These programs combine mainstream programming content with an Aboriginal specific process. Much of mainstream program content is based on well documented theory and research. The blended programs present information in such a way that traditional teachings, cultural values, and Aboriginal experiences are respected and incorporated into the program process and content. Theoretically programs will be better accepted and attended by the Aboriginal population when they can identify with the program philosophy and ideology. In support of this type of programming, the program evaluations that have been completed at the FVP have found that the cultural and traditional teachings are the most favoured aspects of the program and there is an appreciation for reintroducing this path of healing into their lives (Proactive 1994, Proulx and Perrault 1996). The Ma Mawi Wi Chi Itata FVP has delivered community based Aboriginal specific family violence programming since 1987. The FVP has responded to community needs and expanded programming to all segments of the Aboriginal population. Services initially were available to women and children and now include men. Blended programming that follows family violence theory and the Medicine Wheel teachings of: truthfulness and new beginnings; emotional expression; personal development and power; and dwelling in the centre of things and healing, are offered. Group and individual counselling is available to all individuals who access our community or institutional services. In addition, talks with an Elder are arranged as part of the programs, and can be arranged on an individual basis. The general program goals are to heal broken spirits, renew a sense of cultural identity, and help individuals live violence free lives, thereby creating the basis for a healthy community.

The services offered include a flexible and unstructured open support group for children whose parents are attending adult programs. The group is designed to provide children with a safe environment in which to deal with family violence issues. The group counsellor acts as the advocate and source of support for children who may be living in a violent home situation. A dating violence prevention program for youth is planned to encourage the formation and maintenance of healthy intimate relationships.

For women, there are both open and closed group programs. Open groups present informal sessions on specified topics. Attendance is voluntary and therefore the composition of the group changes from one session to the next as women access support according to their needs. Closed groups are formally structured and attendance is compulsory, group composition is stable. The open group sessions impart information about family violence, provide information about other community resources, allow for sharing and emotional support, and help women establish safety plans. The closed support group educates women on family violence issues and establishes an environment where knowledge, skills, and personal strength can be achieved and used to help women heal from family violence. Recently a Healing Women's Spirit Group has been established for sexual abuse survivors. Survivors need to understand and heal from early sexual abuse before they can completely heal from family violence. Women learn to cope with the residual emotional, cognitive, physical, and psychological effects of abuse. Information and skills are taught that allow compulsive coping mechanisms to be replaced with more adaptive coping strategies.

Services for men also consist of open and closed group programs. The open group works towards helping men understand issues related to self confidence; providing strategies for dealing with anger; and furnishing the support required to change their lives. The closed group educates men about violence issues, provides them with the skills for dealing with anger, and decreases their sense of isolation and dependence on the victim is decreased. Through the principles of kindness, honesty, caring, sharing, and faith, the men learn to take responsibility for their behaviour, and learn to contribute to a safe and violent free family environment. Men may be self-referred, referred from collateral agencies, halfway houses and/or crisis services, and court mandated referrals. The FVP is one of the few programs that will provide services to men with charges pending. Many of the men who attend the community based program have been referred through Parole and Probation Services. This, combined with the fact that approximately 49% of the federally incarcerated inmates in Manitoba are Aboriginal (Griffiths and Verdun-Jones 1994), many of whom are either incarcerated for violent offenses or have a history of violent behaviour, indicated a need for family violence programming within federal correctional facilities. Beginning in 1993, the FVP contracted with Correctional Service Canada for the delivery of the men's closed support group within Stony Mountain Federal Correctional Facility. The format of the group was modified to better address institutional logistics and experiences. The skills learned may be applied in the institution, with their families, and within the community upon release.

Program Evaluations

Evaluations of the community based programs have been conducted. Interviews with children, women, and men attending group programming were completed by Proactive in 1994. Comments from participants of the children's group and the women's open and closed groups have indicated a satisfaction with group processes. Respondents reported a decreased sense of isolation, increase sense of hope, and an improvement in their family life. The cultural components of the program were greatly appreciated by these women. Participants in the mens' open groups reported an appreciation for the openness and honesty of the groups and facilitators, and increased self-knowledge. In the closed group, men indicated an improvement in family relationships and a decrease in violence perpetration.

In an evaluation of the Family Violence Program Stony Mountain

Project was completed by the authors in 1996. Interviews were conducted with 46 inmates who were past program participants, 16 current program participants, 10 case management officers, and 6 guards. All interviewers were Aboriginal; all were trained in interviewing techniques and guidelines for the institution. Informed consent was obtained and confidentiality assured. Protocols involved both closed and open ended questions. Responses to open-ended questions were tape recorded; responses to closed-ended questions were recorded on the protocol itself.

Inmates reported a general satisfaction with the content and process of the program. The majority of participants felt that the program had provided them with the means to control their anger and violent behaviour and had given self-insight. They expressed a liking and respect for the program and a belief in its effectiveness in helping them deal with their violence. Most felt the information assisted in communication with others, in dealing with emotions, particularly anger, and in easing the tension encountered in the prison system. Most of the service providers interviewed corroborated these reports, observing changes in inmates behaviour that included increased understanding of violence and its impact on others, a tendency to find alternative solutions to problems, and improved relationships between inmates and staff. The most favoured aspects of the program were the cultural teachings and ceremonies. Many inmates found comfort in the fact that there would be a familiar resource, in the form of the FVP in the community which they could access upon release from prison.

This component of our services that clearly exemplifies the full potential of community care. The men at Stony Mountain Correctional Facility who have accessed the program within the institution are encouraged and often mandated to attend the community based program. These men are already familiar with the program and with the facilitators, which increases their degree of comfort in going to the community agency and attending the open or closed support groups. The healing that begins in the institution can then be continued and/or maintained in the community. These men can, and often do bring their partners and children for programming. Thus, the entire family works toward spiritual healing and a healthier, violence free life. The family and community come together in pursuing their path of healing. As in traditional times, it is the community that will heal its people from the violence they have experienced. This community perspective can impact healing in both programming and research.

Research and Community or Academic Partnerships

The dedication to quality programming and responsiveness to community needs has contributed to an interest in research. The evaluation of the community based programs revealed a need in the community for services for youth and provided the impetus for the youth dating violence prevention program that is now being structured. A study of the Stony Mountain Family Violence Program indicated the necessity of additional sessions to allow the men to process difficult and painful material. Further, two sessions on parenting and three new sessions on sexual abuse have been added and are in the process of being evaluated and modified. Literature reviews supporting the information and theoretical applications of the programs will soon be documented in the manuals for each program. The improved quality of programs and the recognition and substantiation of these programs has been accomplished through the research process.

Family Violence Program research is the result of a community-academic partnership with RESOLVE, a family violence research centre at the University of Manitoba. The blending of community and academic expertise generates a product that is theoretically and methodologically sound as well as socially relevant. This partnership has provided systematic evaluation and improvement of the program, and opened the potential for national accreditation of the program delivered at Stony Mountain Federal Correctional Facility. This type of accomplishment requires much work and a variety of skills. Collaborative endeavours ensure the efficient achievement of these tasks, and serves as an example of a more global community of concerned and dedicated individuals coming together to heal its members.

Conclusion

The community approach is evidenced in the programs offered by the Ma Mawi Wi Chi Itata Family Violence Program and in the research conducted with academic partners. The problem of family violence is extensive and requires the utilization of all of the efforts and skills available within the community. Finding solutions concerning the complexities and intricacies of family violence cannot be found working in isolation. Strategies for the elimination of family violence need to be discussed by a variety of community members, policy makers, and people who are facing similar challenges in other regions of the country or the world. In so doing, opportunities become available towards the eradication of violence in families and in society as a whole. Learning becomes enhanced when sharing information and working collaboratively across areas of expertise and across nations and countries.

There are a number of areas where these collaborative efforts can be applied. A myriad of treatment and healing methods need to be developed and implemented. Creating a diversity of family violence programming ensures that families have options when accessing services. Extensive literature in the area of family violence still needs to be documented and augmented. Much work remains to be completed in order to gain a more comprehensive perspective of this important issue. Thus, maintaining healthy families must be a focus for members of the immediate community as well as members of the more global community. Innovative approaches to programming and research maximize the opportunity of finding effective solutions to family violence.

References

Gil, E. 1982. Institutional abuse of children in out-of-home. *C&YS 4* (1-2): 7-13.

Griffiths, C. and S. Verdun-Jones. 1994. *Canadian Crim. Justice.* Harcourt-Brace.

Hirschbach, E. 1982. Children beyond reach? *Child &Youth S4* (1-2): 99-107.

Lee, B. 1992. Colonization and community. *Com. Dev. J. 27* (3): 211-219.

McFadden, E. and P. Ryan. 1991. Maltreatment in family foster homes: Dynamics and dimensions. *Child and Youth Services 15* (2): 209-231.

McGillivray, A. 1997. Therapies of freedom: The colonization of Aboriginal childhood. In A. McGillivray (Ed.) *Governing Childhood.* Dartmouth.

Palmer, S. and W. Cooke. 1996. Understanding and countering racism with First Nations children in out-of-home care. *Child Welf. 75* (6): 709-725.

Proactive Information Services 1994. *Ma Mawi Wi Chi Itata Family Violence Program: Final Report.* Unpublished. 338 Broadway, Wpg, MB.

Proulx, J. and S. Perrault. 1996. *An Evaluation of the Ma Mawi Wi Chi Itata Family Violence Program Stony Mountain Project.* Unpub. Wpg, MB.

Shkilnyk, A. 1985. *A Poison Stronger Than Love: The Destruction of an Ojibway Community.* New Haven, CT: Yale University Press.

Timpson, J. 1995. Four decades of literature on Native Canadian child welfare: Changing themes. *Child Welfare 74* (3): 525-546.

Tomkiewicz, S. 1984. Violence and negligence towards children and adolescents in institutions. *Child Abuse and Neglect 8* (3): 319-335.

York, G. 1990. *The Dispossessed.* Toronto: Little, Brown, & CO.

Zylberberg, P. 1991. Who should make child protection decisions for the Native community? *Windsor Yearbook to Access to Justice 11*: 74-103.

[1]   Jocelyn Proulx (PhD) is a Research Associate with RESOLVE, a family violence research centre at the University of Manitoba. Sharon Perrault, is Métis, the Central Site Manager, and Team Leader of the Ma Mawi Wi Chi Itata Family Violence Program, as well as the Associate Community Director for RESOLVE.

Aboriginal Women and Violence: Standpoint Analysis

Lisa Murdock[1]

Abstract

While much attention has been devoted to the issue of violence against women, feminist writers have neglected the issue of violence by women. Consequently, there has been a negative impact on theory development, research, and the provision of services to women who engage in violent behaviour. This paper argues the need to redirect our attention to women's intimate violence from the standpoint of Aboriginal women who engage in violent behaviour.

Violence Against Women and Women's Use of Violence

Feminists have transformed the issue of men's violence against women from a private to a public problem, exploring theory development, research, and the provision of services for both female victims of violence and male batterers. They have created rape crisis centres and battered-women's shelters which provide a safe environment for abused women and their children. They have ensured the enforcement of laws which extend the rights of protection to abused women and guided the federal and provincial governments in the implementation of domestic violence initiatives designed to assist abused women and their children (Ursel 1993). Sociologists and other researchers are now paying particular attention to the various types of abuse that women experience, particularly within intimate relationships (Schwartz and DeKeseredy 1993). As a result of the myriad of surveys and qualitative studies with abused women and violent men, we now acknowledge the types and seriousness of the violence, its effects on the lives of abused women and their children, the dynamics of violent relationships, and the widespread and pervasive nature of the issue. In Canada alone, it is estimated that 5.38 million women 18 years and over have experienced at least one incident of physical or sexual assault since the age of 16 years (Johnson 1996).

Several researchers have argued that violence claims victims of both sexes (Cook 1997, Pearson 1997, Straus *et al* 1980) as "violence between husband and wife is far from a one way street" (Straus 1978: 447-8). Straus (1978) found only a slightly higher incidence of violent acts for husbands than for wives (12.1 % versus 11.6 %, respectively), and that wives who engaged in violent acts did so somewhat more frequently than husbands (with median figures of 3.0 and 2.5%, respectively) (Gelles 1974, Steinmetz 1977). Some writers are now claiming that within the context of intimate relationships, "men and women are equals in violence" (Laframboise 1999, Pearson 1997). Feminist writers either deny women's violence altogether or to assert that women are violent only in the context of self-defense or provocation (Berk *et al.* 1981, Dobash and Dobash 1979, McLeod 1984, Saunders 1980). Nevertheless, Canadian crime statistics 1996 reveal that of 126,294 adults and youths charged with committing some form of assault, 15 percent (18,669) were female (Canadian Centre for Justice Statistics 1996). Data available for 1997 on female inmates convicted of committing crimes against the person reveal that the victim was most often known to the offender as a boyfriend/girlfriend, acquaintance (26%), spouse or ex-spouse (21%) (Finn *et al.*1999). While the proportion of females charged with crimes against the person is much smaller than males, these figures do suggest that women are capable of violence, and a good portion of their violent behaviour involves intimate partners.

Because their numbers are small and their crimes are generally considered to be less serious in comparison to men's, women who come into conflict with the law for violent offences have been marginalized or made invisible (Glick and Neto 1982). This invisibility has had a negative impact on theory development, research, and service provision for women who engage in violence (Bonta *et al.*1995). Theories of criminal behaviour have been largely based on observations of male offenders and men's criminality (Naffine 1987). Theorists either attempt to explain women's crime by the same constructs used to explain men's crime or they create fundamentally different explanations based on gender stereotypes of appropriate femininity. In this case, women who engage in violent behaviour are often pathologized or seen as "abnormal" (Bonta *et al.* 1995). Violent women have been the subject of relatively few empirical studies and are typically discussed in terms of such infrequent phenomena as female serial killers or spousal murderers (Bonta *et al.* 1995). Of the relatively few studies of violence by women other than killing, most have applied conventional research methods and theoretical approaches to "measure" the violent acts themselves and see how these acts "measure up" to violent acts by men (Shaw 1995). The neglect of women's violence has been especially evident in terms of the provision of services to women who engage in violent behaviour. From her study of women in Canadian correctional institutions, Shaw (1991) concluded that although the women in her study reported that the majority of programs were helpful, they were frustrated by the lack of access to some programs and the inability to choose when and which programs they preferred. So long as the issue of women's violence is neglected, the provision of adequate support and resources with which to respond to the needs of these women will remain unmet.

Although the simplistic notion that "men are violent and women are not" contains a grain of truth, this image misses the complexity and texture of the lives of women who might use violence against their intimate partners (Shaw and Dubois 1995), particularly within the context of less extreme circumstances than spousal killing. By neglecting to adequately address women's violent behaviour, women are denied agency and their capacity for violence tends to be ignored. Certainly, it is invidious to treat women who engage in intimate violence as a "special case". By asserting that women are solely victims of violence and that if we do engage in intimate violence it is for self-defense or provocation, feminists undermine many of the aims of the Canadian women's movement. By failing to acknowledge women's use of violence, society's polarized dichotomy of masculine and feminine gender role expectations is reinforced; all women become "passive victims" and all men become "aggressive villains" (Tong 1989). To hold to this view merely reproduces an essentialist and uni-dimensional understanding of women's and men's inherent "natures". By this account, women cannot be held fully accountable for their actions (Kirsta 1997).

Developing a Standpoint Analysis

To address the issue of women's intimate violence, it is first necessary to locate a standpoint from which to analyze or explore the issue. According to Cain (1990), this involves a number of considerations: choosing a site from which to work; theoretically reflecting upon one's own experiences and connections with the issue under study; and being accountable to those individuals from whose standpoint one chooses to work. Developing a standpoint analysis, then, involves implementing a collaborative approach to the research which engages both the researcher and the researched in a joint enterprise, yet it does not mean that the researcher and the researched share the same views. We all think, speak, write, create, and distribute knowledge from a specific location in society, from a particular standpoint or site. While our views and opinions may change over time, so too will our sites. Since these relationships are historical and ever-changing, they condition and contour the way we think about the world; they also inform our identity. Recognizing these differences in opinion and the connections with and between a particular standpoint is essential. If I want to know *about* women who engage in intimate violence, then I must move into a site that is connected *with* women who engage in violence. Moving into a specific site involves much more than simply connecting with individuals who share this same site. It involves theoretical reflexivity; "thinking about oneself in terms of a theory and understanding theoretically the site in which one finds oneself." It means making connections, both historically and culturally, with those whose site I occupy and to theoretically reflect upon my personal experiences and relationships that have historically and culturally brought me to this particular site. Only then I will be able to make knowledgeable statements and claims about women who engage in intimate violence (Cain 1990).

Accountability is another critical component of standpoint analysis. In the case of women's intimate violence, this means giving the women the space they need in which to express their own understanding (their standpoint) of their violent behaviour and the social contexts in which it occurs. This involves listening to and hearing what the women have to say (Comack 1999) and producing knowledge useful to these individuals. While my own personal experiences shape my values and beliefs, the subjectivity of the women studied will be taken into account. It is to these women who engage in intimate violence that I, as a researcher, remain primarily accountable (Cain 1990).

Making the Case for a Standpoint Analysis

In the case of women's intimate violence, the main objective of a standpoint analysis is to gain a better understanding of the issue and circumstances. Nowhere is the need for an analysis of women's violent behaviour more pressing than in the case of Aboriginal women. While violence is not an "Aboriginal problem", it certainly is a prevalent problem among Aboriginal people. People of Aboriginal descent are clearly over-represented in the Canadian criminal justice system. Although Aboriginal people comprised a mere two percent of the Canadian adult population, they accounted for 15 percent of admissions to provincial/territorial institutions, 17 percent of admissions to federal facilities (Finn *et al.* 1999), 52 percent of women charged with violent offences are Aboriginal and 48 percent of women charged with violence against their partners or ex-partners were of Aboriginal descent (Comack In Press). By listening to women's own accounts of their experiences with violence, it may be possible to situate women's violent behaviour within their own social contexts and locations; their race, class, age, and gender and to identify the problems, conflicts, dilemmas (Comack 1996), nature and source of the issue. I am well aware of the reality of women's intimate violence through personal observation and experienced. At one point in my life, I struggled to cope with my own use of violence and my own inability to discuss and seek assistance. Even today, intimate violence on my part is not an issue that I care to admit. By approaching the issue of women's intimate violence from the standpoint of women who engage in violent behaviour, we offer the potential to meet the needs of women facing domestic violence issues in their lives and in their homes. By listening to what women themselves have to say about their own experiences with violence, we may provide a map for understanding women's intimate violence in terms of how it develops and what the issues are for those involved. Above all, by taking a standpoint approach to women's intimate violence, we offer the potential to highlight some of the general principles related to appropriate interventions for women's use of violence and, thus, assist in the re-construction of healthier, safer communities in which to live.

References

Berk, R., Berk, S., Loseke, D. and Rauma, D. 1981. Mutual combat and other family violence myths. In D. Finkelhor, R. Gelles, G. Hotaling and M. Straus (Eds.) *The Dark Side of Families*. Newbury Park, CA: Sage.

Bonta, J., Pang, B. and Wallace-Capretta, S. 1995. Predictors of recidivism among incarcerated female offenders. *The Prison Journal* 75(3): 277-294.

Cain, M. 1990. Realist philosophy and standpoint epistemologies or feminist criminology as a successor science. In L. Gelsthorpe and A. Morris (Eds.) *Feminist Perspectives in Criminology*. Milton Keynes: Open U

Canadian Centre for Justice Statistics 1996. *Adult Correctional Services in Canada*. Ottawa: Minister of Industry.

Comack, E. 1996. *Women in Trouble: Connecting Women's Law Violations to Their Histories of Abuse*. Halifax: Fernwood Publishing.

Comack, E. 1999. Producing feminist knowledge: Lessons from women in trouble.

Theoretical Criminology: An International Journal 3(3): 287-306.

Comack, E. (In Press). *Gendered Violence: Are Women "Men's Equals in Violence?"*. Report for Canadian Centre for Policy Alternatives (Manitoba).

Cook, P. 1997. *Abused Men: The Hidden Side of Domestic Violence*. CT: Praeger.

Dobash, R. and Dobash, R. 1979. *Violence Against Wives*. New York: Free Press.

Finn, A., Trevethan, S., Carriere, G. and Kowalski, M. 1999. Female inmates, Aboriginal inmates, and inmates serving life sentences. *Juristat* 19(5).

Gelles, R. 1974.*The Violent Home: A Study of Physical Aggression Between Husbands and Wives*. Beverly Hills, CA: Sage.

Glick, R. and Neto, V. 1982. National study of women's correctional programs. In B. Price and N. Sokoloff (Eds.). *The Criminal Justice System and Women: Women Offenders, Victims, Workers*. NY: Clark Boardman.

Johnson, H. 1996. *Dangerous Domains: Violence Against Women in Canada*. Toronto: Nelson.

Kirsta, A. 1997. *Deadlier Than the Male: Violence in Women*. NY: Harper Collins.

LaFramboise, D. 1999. Men and women are equals in violence *NatPost*Jul10th: A1.

McLeod, M. 1984. Women against men:examination of domestic violence based on an analysis of official data and victimization. *Just. Quar.*: 70-193.

Naffine, N. 1987. *Female Crime: The Construction of Women in Criminology*. Australia: Allen and Unwin.

Pearson, P. 1997. *When She Was Bad: Violent Women*. New York: Viking.

Saunders, D. 1980. The Police Response to Battered Women: Predictors of Officers' Use of Arrest, Counseling, and Minimal Action. (Doctoral Dissertation, University of Wisconsin-Madison, 1979). *DAI*40: 6446-A.

Schwartz, M. and DeKeseredy, W. 1993. The return of the 'battered husband syndrome', typification of women as violent. *Cr,Law&SocChge*20:249-265.

Shaw, M. 1991. *Survey of Federally Sentenced Women: Report to the Task Force on Fed. Sentenced Women on the Prison Survey*. No. 1991-4. Ottawa

Shaw, M. 1995. Conceptualizing violence by women. In R. Dobash, R. Dobash and L. Noaks (Eds.). *Gender and Crime*. Cardiff: University of Wales

Shaw, M. and Dubois,S. 1995. *Understanding Violence by Women: A Review of the Literature*. Ottawa: Federally Sentenced Women Program.

Steinmetz, S. 1977. *The Cycle of Violence: Assertive, Aggressive and Abusive Family Interaction*. New York: Praeger.

Straus, M. 1978. Wife beating:How common and why?*Victimology*2(3/4):443-458.

Straus, M., Gelles, R. and Steinmetz,S. 1980. *Behind Closed Doors: Violence in the American Family*. Garden City, NY: Anchor Press/Doubleday.

Tong, R.1989. *Feminist Thought:A ComprehensiveIntroduction.*Boulder:Westview

Ursel, E. 1993. Family and social policies. In G. Ramu (Ed.) *Marriage and the Family in Canada Today*. 2nd Edition. Scarborough, ON: Prentice Hall

[1]   Lisa Murdock an Aboriginal MA (Sociology) student at the U of MB. She acknowledges the ongoing support and guidance from her thesis advisor, Elizabeth Comack, and from Sharon Perrault, the Family Violence Program Team Leader and Central Site Manager at Ma Mawi Wi Chi Itata Centre.

Intellectual Disability and Aboriginal People

Cheryl Martin[1]

Abstract

Aboriginal individuals with intellectual disabilities are more highly represented in the provinces institutions than non-Aboriginal individuals. Advocacy movements are demanding that citizens with intellectual disabilities take their rightful place as full participants in society, yet, it appears that the institutional experience continues to be the norm for people who are Aboriginal. The purpose of this paper is to explore reasons for this trend, using perspectives from professionals and Aboriginal people who have intellectual disabilities.

Defining the Problem

Currently, in Manitoba, Aboriginal individuals with intellectual disabilities are more highly represented in the provinces' large, hospital-like settings than in community agencies or services. A source in one institution estimates that between 20% and 25% of its' population is Aboriginal yet only 10% of the province's population is Aboriginal (RCAP 1997). At a time when advocacy movements are demanding that citizens with intellectual disabilities take their rightful place as full participants in society, institutional care is most commonly experienced by Aboriginal peoples manifesting such disabilities (Evans *et al.*1985).

There were two components to the study. I explored the possible reasons for high rates of institutionalization of people who are Aboriginal and have intellectual disabilities. This was done through the use of key informant interviews, where people with professional expertise were asked to give their perspective. The second component involved ensuring that the story of individuals was heard. Through interviews with Aboriginal people who have intellectual disabilities, or their families, there was an opportunity to understand the struggles and problems that led to institutionalization.

Methods

This was a qualitative research study based in Manitoba. Interviews were conducted during two periods: a preliminary study in the spring of 1997 and the thesis study during the summer and fall of 1998. The data are comprised almost entirely of the transcriptions of eighteen taped interviews. Another portion of data is made up of the contextual notes and notes from debriefing sessions after each interview. A third part of the data collection occurred in February of 1999 when administrators who provided direct services for people with intellectual disabilities were contacted. In the thesis study four Aboriginal research assistants were involved (I am a non-Aboriginal person, who does not at this point in life have a disability) and provided valuable insights into perspectives, history and on-going issues of Aboriginal people. Research assistants identified potential participants in the study, made participants feel comfortable during interviews, translated information, and participated in a debriefing session following each interview.

Four family interviews with Aboriginal people and their families provided personal accounts of their experience of having an intellectual disability and being Aboriginal. Two administrators from institutional settings provided their perspectives. Three provincial departments and one federal department representatives provided insights related to the jurisdictional issues. Five representatives from organizations run by or for Aboriginal people were interviewed for insights on a desirable future for Aboriginal people with intellectual disabilities as well as ideas about over-representation in institutional settings.

Who is Responsible for Funding and Delivering Services?

The lines of responsibility for funding and delivering services from each branch of the government to people with disabilities are unclear. One government employee said that if you walked into a group of people from all branches of government and asked who is responsible for making life good for Aboriginal people with disabilities, "No one would put up their hand" (Transcript 1: 8). Federally, the Department of Indian and Northern Affairs, has primary responsibility for Aboriginal people living in reserve communities and Health and Welfare Canada funds medical services to reserve communities (Transcript 5). Although these departments do not ensure services for people with intellectual disabilities they do take responsibilities for providing services to children and families. For example, if a child was in need of protection, an agency run by Aboriginal people could receive funding from the federal government because the government must uphold provincial child protection legislation on the reserve. This is not the case for people with intellectual disabilities, one participant stated: "right now, I can tell you truthfully, there is nothing there for them at this point" (Transcript 3:7). The provincial government is the funding source for services to people with intellectual disabilities, providing a "continuum of services" (Transcript 4:3) ranging from institutional care to highly integrated community residential and day programs. The provincial government is not mandated, nor is there a legal obligation, to provide services for Aboriginal or non-Aboriginal adults with intellectual disabilities. The Vulnerable Persons Act (1996), which is provincial legislation related to people with intellectual disabilities, outlines various rights related to decision making, abuse, and protection for people with intellectual disabilities; it does not entitle citizens to services. Although the province does not provide funding to reserve communities, some participants felt this was inappropriate because the block funding provided to the province from the federal government is meant to provide health, education, and community services to all Manitobans including people living in reserve communities (Transcript 2:7). The federal and provincial governments are in a period of fiscal restraint and are in the process of dismantling the Department of Indian and Northern Affairs with First Nations taking over these functions, including medical services (Transcript 7). Generally the Aboriginal participants felt these changes were positive, and somewhat unpredictable.

Over one third of the reserves in Manitoba, "have no ready access to a service centre" (Royal Commission on Aboriginal Peoples 1997:133). To access medical and social services, many Aboriginal people are flown out to an urban centre (Fricke 1998, Halliday 1993). For people with intellectual disabilities, institutionalized services are most frequently accessed. Medical and social service training is a significant issue (Social Planning Council of Winnipeg 1996). In remote communities, "there is nobody trained" (Transcript 7:18) to work with people with intellectual disabilities so they must go off reserve for support. Aboriginal organizations have recently begun training so that the expertise stays within Aboriginal organizations (Transcript 2:18). Off-reserve services "are not the kinds of systems, I don't think, that we would set up for our families or for our children" (Transcript 6:7) and these 'community based' services are not used as readily by Aboriginal peoples as other citizens. An informal phone survey (conducted as part of this study) of community based services for people with intellectual disabilities in Winnipeg, indicated that about 5% of participants were Aboriginal, yet they comprise of about 10% of the Winnipeg population (RCAP 1997). Whether or not this under-representation is an issue depends on individual families' level of satisfaction with institutionalization. No services incorporate Aboriginal perspectives or are deliberately culturally sensitive to Aboriginal participants.

What are the Effects of Poverty?

Participants stated that financial poverty was the primary reason for institutionalizing Aboriginal people with disabilities. When living in communities with high levels of personal financial poverty, energy and resources are focussed on basic survival. People feel disempowered, unable to bring about change, and unable to develop alternate ways of providing care. They take the most conservative option in care provision, namely institutionalization. If government or agency funds were available to develop services based in Aboriginal paradigms these services may be the preferred choice for Aboriginal peoples with intellectual disabilities.

In reserve communities poverty leads to no resources to obtain the basic essentials such as housing, heating, electricity, running water, food and clothing and other supplies. High transportation costs, unemployment, reliance on welfare, and under-employment in reserve communities result in higher rates of poverty than in non-Aboriginal urban and rural settings. For Aboriginal people with intellectual disabilities living on reserves, poverty leads to no resource base for developing support services and disempowerment. Even for people living off-reserve, poverty and disempowerment inhibits service development and advocacy for Aboriginal peoples with intellectual disabilities.

Effects of Racism and Past Institutionalization

The issue of racism is very complicated. One participant said "I think racism, today, when it does happen, is so much more subtle" (Transcript 8:15). Generally, participants stated that overt racism was not a primary problem leading to institutionalization. Comments included: "The jurisdiction is more heavier than the racial thing" (Transcript 3:24); "I don't know, if it really had to do with racism, than it is bureaucracy and what is [money] saving tactics" (Transcript 2:12); and "I don't know how much of it is racism and how much of it is classism and how much of it is just cultural difference" (Transcript 6:11). Due to the complexity of poverty, health care, and related issues, racism, as we traditionally think of it, may not be the predominant factor according to those who were interviewed; however, less obvious forms of racism still exist. For example, "It seems that the kids that are born with severe disabilities are whisked way very quickly" (Transcript 1:5). This pattern of being taken away for services (education, health, and training) has a long history and it is not surprising that the same practice is used for children with intellectual disabilities. Often community placement is difficult to arrange; for example, an individual might visit three or four potential residential service providers and day programs to identify the best combination. Social workers or advocates are involved at each of these visits. Institutional options are easier because all services are provided in one location, the process can be completed in one trip. This kind of easy access may have contributed to the increased use of the institutional model in the past (Child and Family Services 1994).

Participants felt that institutionalization would never have been what Aboriginal people accepted for people with intellectual disabilities. Aboriginal world views perceive people with intellectual disabilities as having gifts, making contributions, and carrying important roles within society; concepts new to the non-Aboriginal disability service system. These deep cultural values are also reflected in the families that have pushed for community, versus institutional, services over the last thirty or forty years (Dybwad 1990). It is primarily because of advocacy that institutionalization is no longer the sole option for most parents in the mainstream culture, however there has been little opportunity for urban or rural Aboriginal families to form or join similar advocacy groups (Bluehardt *et al.*1999).

Individual Stories

The institutional experience of Aboriginal people was best explained by individuals who have disabilities or their family members. The points raised above are confirmed in their stories. The personal stories of these individuals (pseudonyms are used) are recorded in their own voices (Martin 2000) and summarized below.

Donald Morgan was born in 1963. When he was two he experienced seizures that left him with physical and intellectual restrictions. For most of his life he has been involved with various kinds of service including foster care, group homes, sanatoriums, hospitals, and sheltered workshops. He has experienced physical abuse, lied to by services providers, separated from his family, and never been paid for his labour. Currently, he is very content living with his mother and members of his extended family.

Joanne Simpson has a brother and sister living in an institutional setting. Her sister, Colleen, has lived in this setting for about twenty years and is currently in her late thirties, and her brother, Jim, has been there all of his life. Colleen was not born with a mental disability but when she was about three months old she fell off the bed. This seems to have caused some damage, which down the road, lead to epilepsy, inappropriate medication and finally the development of behavioural and intellectual problems which resulted in institutionalization. Joanne's brother was born with a mental disability, possibly the result of a medical prescription taken by his mother before he was born.

Kelly has an adopted son, Darrel, who she adopted when he was five days old and is now twelve. Darrel contracted herpes from his birth mother which resulted in brain damage and fairly extensive physical disabilities. He stayed home until he was about eighteen months old. At that time Kelly became pregnant and was no longer physically able to handle him because of his need for twenty-four hour care so he was institutionalized.

Cassandra is a nursing student and has a brother, Tom, who has been in an institutional setting for about eighteen years. She and her family came from a northern reserve community. In recalling how her brother was institutionalized Cassandra said, "I was still pretty young when he did leave, so I didn't really know very much that was happening, but I think he was diagnosed as mild retardation due to solvent abuse" (p. 3). She said that Tom's behaviour started to change, his school marks dropped, he began getting into trouble and finally he ran away from home. She feels at this point that the solvent abuse has caused brain damage and the result is that "his total personality is different . . . his speech is pretty well gone" (p. 4).

The family stories confirm many of the themes mentioned by other participants who did not have a family member with a disability.

All families report a lack of resources in reserve communities and for Colleen, Jim, and Tom the remoteness of their communities compounded the problem. Their institutionalization resulted in a loss of connection with family, a loss of advocacy, and a loss of language. All family participants described how institutionalization was the only option that parents felt they had available. Poverty was another problem cited in all of the family interviews. In some instances participants referred to personal poverty and in others to the overall material poverty of the reserve community. Three of the four families indicated that racism was a factor that in some way affected the institutionalization of Aboriginal people with intellectual disabilities. They also said that decisions were being made that were out of their hands and in some instances they were not informed about decisions. This feeling of not being in control was identified most clearly in the family interviews.

Recommendations and Conclusions

One of the questions that participants were asked was what they would 'like to see' for Aboriginal people with intellectual disabilities. Naturally, a fundamental issue that must be noted before thinking about supports is the complicated issue of the legal, jurisdictional, and policy conundrums related to funding. Without some focus on funding by the federal, provincial, or band governments, it seems unlikely that there will be any change. In terms of service design and delivery, people gave an over-riding response stating they would be best supported within the context of family and community. Participants stated the importance of language, of viewing disability from a holistic perspective, and the value of developing the giftedness of all community members. It was important that people receive services in their home communities and that services be individualized to the specific needs of families. A related suggestion was that the funding used for support be attached to the individual rather than to a particular service or agency. The importance of hiring Aboriginal staff to work with Aboriginal people who have intellectual disabilities was mentioned in several instances.

Several themes have been identified that help to explain why Aboriginal people with intellectual disabilities have been institutionalized. These include: jurisdictional issues, problems related to being in a remote community, problems associated with poverty, a history of having been exported from home communities in order to get services, problems related to racism, a lack of training about disability issues, problems related to services and resources, lack of clear legislation, and finally, a lack of advocacy for change. These conclusions were drawn from the words of people in government, in service delivery, in advocacy groups, and from people with intellectual disabilities and their families.

References

Bluehardt, M., Durst, D., Morin, G. and Rezanoff, M. 1999. Urban First Nations persons with disabilities: Triple jeopardy! Paper presented at the conference, *Research to Action*, sponsored by the Atlantic Health Promotion Research Centre, Dalhousie University & Canadian Paraplegic Association, Halifax, Nova Scotia.

Child and Family Services Program Centre 1994. On policy and research with respect to First Nations Child and Family Services of Northern Manitoba. *Understanding the Health Care System and It's Impact on First Nations Child and Family Services.* Presented to the Board of Directors of Awasis Agency.

Dybwad, R. 1990. *Perspectives on a Parent Movement: The Revolt of Parents of Children with Intellectual Limitations.* Cambridge: Brookline Books.

Evans, J., Hunter, A., Thompson, D. and Ramsey, S. 1985. A study of institutionalized mentally retarded patients in Manitoba: Over-representation by Canadian Indian children. *Journal of Mental Deficiency Research 29* (2):153-164.

Fricke, M. 1998. First Nations people with disabilities: An analysis of service delivery in Manitoba. (University of Manitoba, 1999). *Masters Abstracts International 37/02:* 604.

Government of Manitoba 1996. *The Vulnerable Persons Living with a Mental Disability and Consequential Amendments Act.*

Halliday, B. 1993. Completing the Circle: A report on Aboriginal people with disabilities. The standing Committee on Human Rights and the Status of Disabled Persons. Available: http://www.schoolnet.ca/aboriginal/disable3/3-e.html

Martin, C. 2000. *Intellectual Disability and Aboriginal People.* Unpublished MEd thesis. Faculty of Education, University of Manitoba.

Royal Commission on Aboriginal Peoples. 1997. *For Seven Generations: An Information Legacy of the Royal Commission on Aboriginal peoples.* [CD-ROM]. Ottawa: Libraxus.

Social Planning Council of Winnipeg, (1996). *Aboriginal Persons with a Disability: Training and Employment Challenges.* Winnipeg: Social Planning Council of Winnipeg.

---

[1]   Cheryl Martin's (MEd) is an instructor at the Developmental Services Worker Training Program at Red River College and continues her research on issues influencing Aboriginal people with intellectual disability.

A Birth Mother's Perspective on Fetal Alcohol Syndrome

Chris Loewen[1]

Abstract

Fetal Alcohol Syndrome (FAS) is a birth defect caused by heavy prenatal alcohol exposure and manifested by a cluster of specific features. The FAS diagnosis is employed when children whose mothers abused alcohol during pregnancy have some features in each of three categories craniofacial anomalies; growth deficiency; and Central Nervous System (CNS) effects (Stratton et al, 1996). It is critical to understand this issue from the birth mother's perspective.

Introduction

Fetal Alcohol Syndrome or Fetal Alcohol Effects (FAS/E) and their relationship to Aboriginal peoples is attracting much attention as studies indicate a higher prevalence of FAS/E among Aboriginal populations. Children with some of the physical, cognitive, or behavioural characteristics of FAS were labelled FAE to capture a child's educational and/or social needs without a definitive medical diagnosis (Aase 1994). An FAE label fails to specify issues or to identify the level and extent of need in affected children. In 1996, the American Institute of Medicine redefined FAE into two categories, Alcohol-Related Birth Defects (ARBD)(congenital anomalies) and Alcohol-Related Neuro-developmental Disorders (ARND)(central nervous system damage)(Stratton *et al.* 1996). Much has been written by the experts about FAS/E from the medical perspective: epidemiology, physical and behavioural characteristics and prevalence over the past 30 years; little has been written about FAS/E from a sociological perspective. Much of the literature points a finger squarely at the Aboriginal birth mother. Yet, her voice remains silent.

What causes her to drink when she is aware of the risks? And if she is unaware, why was she not made aware? Through a series of in-depth interviews with an Aboriginal birth mother, Susan, (a pseudonym) shares her perspectives in this paper.

Methods

Through my work as an FAS/E consultant for an Aboriginal Child & Family Services agency, I met Susan who was interested in being involved with this research and conducted in-depth interviews four times over a period of 10 months. I combined an historical analysis of the relationship between alcohol and Aboriginal Peoples with Susan's case study. Susan's chronology was collected to determine the factors which contributed to her life experiences, including her personal history, a family tree, and events which she felt were significant. Information gathered during this "oral history" phase was used to help formulate the second set of questions. These included questions about other family members and friends relevant to the study. The purpose was to determine how family members were affected, and what effect friends and family had on the informants. The third set of questions dealt specifically with the Susan's experience with and attitude toward alcohol, pregnancy; and FAS/E. Susan read the transcribed notes after each interview in case she felt she had said something that she did not want published, nothing was removed from the original prose text.

Exceptionally High Rates of FAS in Aboriginal Populations

In a survey requested by Foggy Creek First Nation in Manitoba, 178 students aged 5 - 15 were studied. Of these, 46% had some alcohol exposure before birth, 30% were exposed to high levels of alcohol in uteri. Ten percent had physical evidence of being adversely affected by prenatal alcohol exposure: eleven were identified as FAS and seven as Partial FAS. Prevalence of FAS ranged from 31 to 62 per 1000 children; the prevalence of alcohol related birth defects (FAS plus Partial FAS) ranged from 51 to 101 per 1000 children (Kowlessar 1997). Depending on the studies used, these FAS rates are 15 to 180 times higher than the estimated worldwide incidence. In another study conducted by West Region Child and Family Services, of 216 children in care in October of 1994: 67% (145 of

216) had behavioural or learning disabilities characteristic of FAS/FAE children; 91% (196 of 216) were in care because of alcohol abuse within their family; and between February 1993 and June 1994 the birth mothers of 17 permanent wards died as a result of alcoholism (WRCFS Report).

Literature and clinical observations support that FAS and FAE affect Aboriginal children disproportionately compared with all other groups. The highest prevalence of FAS/E was reported in Aboriginal communities in British Columbia (18.5%) (Robinson *et al.* 1987) and the Yukon (42.5%) (Asante 1985). However, critics argue that other factors, including socio-economic status, myths about drinking patterns and race, need to be explored before any results are confirmed (National Health/ Education Consortium 1994). Although alcohol abuse is not specific to low income populations, socio-economic status may influence the relationship between maternal drinking and FAS/E (Sparks 1993, Stratton *et al.* 1996). According to Streissguth and LaDue "poor women appear to have a higher risk of fetal alcohol effects than middle-class women" (in Sparks 1993:83). Also, convenience and myths about alcohol use have encouraged many funded studies to be done with American and Canadian Indian reserve populations, giving the impression that FAS is more common among aboriginal peoples when in fact the belief that FAS is a 'Native' issue may be based more on research methodology than fact (Jones 1997).

Why People Drink

"Several theories accounting for alcohol addiction suggest that in many cases alcohol is used primarily to escape or forget painful emotional experiences rather than primarily for its euphoric-inducing quality" (Richards 1993:47). The disease concept of alcoholism offers invaluable heuristic utility in clinical situations on both individual and systemic levels. The effectiveness of this model stems from its ability, in part, to remove the moral stigma of alcoholism and its attendant guilt (Wallace 1977). The disease model also acknowledges that the addicted individual requires treatment rather than punishment (Sparks 1993). It is "the nature of alcoholism . . . that its victims are rendered by the disease itself less and less capable of spontaneous recognition of the severity of their symptoms" (Johnson in Weiner *et al.*1991:15). In addition the use of alcohol increases animosities between spouses (Lithman 1979), increases jealousies and promiscuity (Hamer 1965), confirms "Indianness" and other identity issues (Lemert 1958, Lurie 1971), provides imagined status (Morse in Hamer

1965), serves to resolve interpersonal conflict (Robbins 1975), and for some the 'high' generated by alcohol is the prime reason for its over consumption (Lemert 1958, Lithman 1979, Mancall 1995, Hamer 1965). This displacement of responsibility and justification for the use and abuse of alcohol is also seen in those who blame the biophysiological makeup of the Indian for their inability to 'hold their liquor'. According to May (1992, 1994), the notion that Indians metabolize alcohol more slowly than non-Indians is a myth, metabolism is an individual trait with more variation found within ethnic groups than between them, and that socio-cultural variables are major factors in alcohol related behaviours.

This leads to the more specific question, why would a woman drink throughout her pregnancy? How could this woman care about, let alone, love her child? What factors have contributed to the stigma currently attached to the Aboriginal Community at large vis-à-vis FAS/E? These are difficult questions that need to be asked and answered. It was crucial for me, as an employee of an Aboriginal child welfare agency to understand this issue from the perspectives of an Aboriginal mother who drank during her pregnancies.

Susan's Story

Susan was born in 1959, just outside a small community in the southwestern region of Manitoba. She is Aboriginal and one of nine children: seven biological siblings and two step-siblings, all but one is a current or recovering alcoholic. The one non-alcoholic in the family is her eldest sister, who was born mentally handicapped. Her father, mother and two stepfathers were all alcoholics. Both her biological father and first stepfather died in their early 50s of kidney disease associated with their drinking. Her mother lives with her second stepfather and currently neither drink. Susan's grandfather on her mother's side was also an alcoholic, her grandmother did not drink. No information was available about Susan's grandparents on her father's side. Susan lived on the Foggy Creek reserve for many years. She started drinking at the age of 12 and quit drinking at the age of 26. She gave birth to three children and drank throughout all three pregnancies. Her first child, Brenda, died in 1988 at the age of 12, due to complications associated with Cystic Fibrosis. Her second child, Debra, is 21 and has two children of her own. Her third child, Jeffrey, is 17.

[My earliest recollections] I could just remember, like when I was probably about four or five . . . that's about the only time I could remember,

but I was sexually abused at that age. That didn't come to me until I was older. Like it was an older person and never knew growing up. Every time I seen an old person I would just cringe or I would really pull back. Like I never really knew I was doing that until after I sobered up and then I noticed . . . that's when I started noticing what was going on and that's when I started remembering little bits and pieces. He's dead now. But my mom recently told me he also sexually abused my little sister. And I think he did it worse to her. Not saying that mine was any, you know, easier or better or anything, but she was telling me a little bit more about my sister and it really hurt. Like I had no idea that happened to her too.

Susan's family moved around a lot. By the time she was nine, her biological father had left her mother for another woman, Susan and her six siblings had moved to Brandon where Susan's mother met another man and began drinking: *She was still drinking. Cause I remember when we moved [to Brandon], I went to see my sister in Winnipeg and then I came back. I went to where we used to live, and I remember coming in, walking into that house and it was empty, but I heard someone upstairs. So I went up the stairs. It was my oldest brother and my stepfather. They were both drunk. And they were just sitting up in the room talking and drinking. And I asked where mom was and they said she already went to the new house. So I knew she'd be drinking because they were drinking. So I walked down to the new house. Sure enough, mom was there and she was drunk. She wanted to go to the grocery story and I thought, "oh shit!" It was so embarrassing. To have her and then walking into the store with this drunk . . . it was really, ugh! I remember I called her a bitch. I got really mad at her for something and then she grabbed the belt and she hit me with it. And that's the first time, I think, and then I cut my wrists. I don't know if it was because here was this woman that, you know, hit me for the first time and it really did something . . . I don't know. But that's the first time I tried to commit suicide. Already then I can already see something was wrong.*

Beginning to Drink

It was at age 12 that Susan started drinking and smoking. Her family was still extremely transient. I asked her where she was living at this time: *All over. Kind of all over. Staying with a sister. Staying with mom. Kind of all over. Wherever I went. Stayed with an auntie. Winnipeg, Brandon. There was an auntie too. When I was younger I stayed at her place a lot. And she was the one that talked to me. She did the talking. I probably at that time cared more for her than I did for my own mother because I was . . .*

*there was a person that was talking to me and acknowledged my existence.
She was everything. But she was never . . . my uncle stabbed her to death.
She had 11 kids - my cousins - and they were all adopted, everywhere. The
States, everywhere. But she played a very important role in my life at that
time. So her death was just another, you know, being in the violent way, it
just got me more angry. And I never knew how to deal with that. Like even
when I heard that she was stabbed, I just ended up getting really sick, like
really sick, fever, sick, sick, I remember getting sick.*

Susan was 15 when her auntie was murdered. Susan tried school,
but as she puts it "it didn't work out. There was no support. No one to
take it home to. Nobody to give me encouragement." She remembers that
"pretty well my entire family" was put into those "simple classrooms".
This simply added to "the already low self-esteem" she had of herself.
It was at about the age of 12 or 13 that Susan "pretty well gave up on
school": *Then I ended up drinking, like lots. But I remember pretty well
the first time, like that I did start drinking, I blacked out. All I knew was
that I really enjoyed it because blacking out meant I wouldn't remember. It
took me away . . . And then I ended up getting pregnant and I had my first
child when I was 16. I drank lots with her. I drank lots. Probably weekly.
Like every weekend for sure, if not more. Cause I wasn't just a person that
would drink for a day or two. Like I'd drink longer than that. Like I could
remember being pregnant with her drinking so much that you know you
try to drink and you take a sip of the beer and all it does it foam up all
inside you. . . . So I learned that I all I've got to do is drink whiskey and
that'll calm it down, and then you can drink more beer. So that's what my
oldest daughter was basically swimming in, a lot of that. And even like
my fighting and that, was still going on when I was pregnant with her. So
I could have lost her in many ways. Not just with the drinking, but with
the fighting and the carelessness and . . . I remember driving pregnant
with her and passing out and, you know, stuff like that and waking up just
before I hit the ditch and things like that.*

Giving Birth and Parenting

Brenda, Susan's first child was born in 1976 in Brandon, Manitoba. Susan
remembers waking up after giving birth and asking about her baby. She
was told that her child was sick, had been rushed to a hospital in Winnipeg
and that she (the baby) might die: *So, there I was, you know, just 16 at the
time, and my mom . . . my mom at the time was not around. She was going
to try to recover somewhere I think at a dryout centre somewhere at that
time. So I just . . . all I knew is that I had to go find this baby. So the day*

after, I think it was, when they still couldn't tell me, you know, if she was dead or alive. I remember, like I was all stitched up and I was in a lot of pain and I could barely sit but I was determined to go find that baby. It's kind of sad, you know, thinking about it, you know this kid going out to find this baby. But maybe I was looking for something at that time too, something, I don't know. Brenda had been sent to the Intensive Care Unit at the Health Sciences Centre in Winnipeg. She just had all these tubes. I couldn't even carry her for the first while. And then after a while they were able to get her out of there but she was still hooked up to a bunch of stuff. But I'd sit there from probably 8 in the morning till it was dark. And I stayed sober for a while that time. Then after probably, you know, coming, I can't even remember, maybe a month after going every day, every day to the hospital, the nurses advised me to take a break and, you know, just go home for a while, which I did. But I started back drinking again and just carried on with my drinking.

Brenda was eventually diagnosed with Cystic Fibrosis. She experienced countless operations in the ensuing years. For the next 2 ½ years she moved back and forth between hospitals in Brandon and Winnipeg: *So I think with her being born and the way she was and all what was going on, added to more confusion in my life. And like I said, I never did have my mother to talk to about it, to cry with, to talk with. So I was really alone, like really alone with this baby now, this sick baby. But I ended up in another relationship and I got pregnant again . . . [Debra was born on October 4th, 1978. When she was 1 ½ Susan decided, for the sake of Brenda's health, to move to Alberta.] With this one I drank, but not as much, but I tried everything to drink. I couldn't even hold the whiskey down with this one. That's terrible to say, but the whiskey wouldn't even stay down. Like I tried like all kinds of different things. Like just to drink. It was bad. So I experimented throughout my pregnancy to try and see if I could drink. I did a little bit but . . . well, I don't know what a little bit is though. But I did drink with this second one. But whether there's some damage done, I don't know, I really don't know with my second one. My first one I really think there, there, you know . . . some damage through my drinking was done to the first one. To the second one, I don't know. Like she's struggling today. She is struggling in many ways. But here the second one really got it bad because not only was she being neglected through my drinking, but all my time went to the other one, whatever time she got. So the second one I think really got it really bad.*

Susan admits that she didn't do a lot of the parenting at this stage in her children's lives. Her sister and mother helped out. I asked her if Child & Family Services ever got involved: *I remember once they came to my house. And a lady came from welfare. She said something. I says "Ah" this is my attitude back then. Like she said she was going to take them and I said "just fuckin' take them" and I slammed the door and after she never came back. But I don't know. I don't know what I would have done if she did. I don't know. Maybe I would have just let her too, I don't know. Like those days were just . . . Basically I just lived moment to moment. Whatever happened, happened sort of thing . . . But during all this time I lived believing that I was like our sis.* [She is speaking of her eldest sister who was born with a mental handicap.] *Because my mother was told at one time that all Native kids were simple. My mother still looked at the non-Aboriginal person as the "know-it-all". Like they know everything and whatever they said was the gospel truth. She said, "Oh what can I do? I thought that was the truth back then?" And that basically she didn't push us in anything because she knew she would be expecting too much if she did try. And all through this time, from the time I was 11 till the time I gave birth to my second child, there was a lot of suicide attempts in between. I can't even tell you how many now. I don't know.*

By the time [Brenda] was four, her doctors pretty well gave up on her. They said, "This child's going to die." She was a skeleton. Like she was a walking bag of bones and coughing. She couldn't breath and she barely ate and she was a mess, and so I decided to take her somewhere else. So I brought her to Alberta, and that's where they pretty well took her in, put her on all kinds of medication, everything. In fact the doctors said she was the worst case of Cystic Fibrosis to live. I got her to Calgary, and they gave her lots of medicine and kept her alive for eight more years after that.

I met my dad [for the first time when I was 20, in a bar in Calgary]. Am I ever glad I didn't meet him before because . . . like I said, I'm going in to meet this person, but nobody's ever told me anything about him. So, you know, I guess growing up I still had probably a belief that I had a dad out there who's wonderful. He knew my sister-in-law but he didn't know who I was, or my other sister. But he looked up and he said "which one is my daughter?" And I said "me". You know, that's basically how it was. We sat down and drank, got stoned. That was my encounter with my dad. He was a drug dealer and probably a pimp. Useless, useless, useless man. But again, I have to come to terms with all that. Then [1983] I ended up with my third child, and I drank with this one. I think there is some, definitely some effect from my drinking with him. This one hurt because I just started realizing what the damage alcohol could do to a child. That's just been recently. But it hurt. Dammit, it hurt when I started realizing what I actually was doing. I don't know if even back then, I don't know if you could have reached me anyway, because there was so much pain and very little contact as far as my mother goes. Knowing her, she might have been telling me to quit drinking too. But nobody could get to me, you know, get through to me at that time.

Drinking and Hospitals

Susan spent a lot of time in hospitals as a result of drinking over the years, but she related the following experience as one that stands out most in her mind: *We were drinking. Oh my, we were drinking lots. We were drunk and I guess this guy tried to stop me and I cut him up too. I don't remember going to the hospital. There were other times I woke up in the hospital after drunks and then I knew I did something, but half the time I didn't know what the heck it was I did, if I took pills or did something, or . . . The same old life. Like it wasn't going nowhere. It wasn't changing. Nothing was changing. It was just pure hell. So when I came to, I opened my eyes and I seen the hospital again and I went "shit". You know, nothing's changing, nothing . . . It was like I was numb by this time. I just didn't care. I just didn't. I remember closing my eyes, but I felt something on my neck. Something thick on my neck and I was trying to think, what the heck happened, and then I heard somebody . . . people talking and I kind of opened my eyes. There was two police officers right at the foot of my bed. Then I heard them talking about there might be attempted murder charges laid against me. I don't know. I just . . . I didn't really care at that time. I didn't know if they were going to put me in jail. I don't know who it was that I hurt. I didn't even know I hurt anybody at that time, really, to tell you the truth. But I knew they were talking about me. I remember it was a man and a woman cop. And so when they finally realized I was starting to wake up they . . . I remember the male saying "Make sure you handcuff her" and the female cop said "Well, look at her. Look at her, she's not going nowhere". And she was right because I didn't care what they did with me . . . I didn't care if I was going to jail or if I actually killed somebody. I didn't care because I felt I deserved to be locked up anyways. I don't know, I just didn't care where they were taking me. And then, cause that's when they told me, when they were taking me out of the hospital, that they were taking me to an institution, a mental institution. If I tried to run there would be a warrant out for my arrest.*

Looking back on it I must have looked like a little puppy dog, you know, just walking. I just didn't care. I didn't even ask questions. They wouldn't even say what for, what you have to do or who I hurt. I didn't care. I don't even know how long I was locked up now. Probably two, three months, I don't know. I remember going in and the doctor would come and check me out. Check out my stitches and stuff. I had about 50 some on this arm. But there were stitches on the inside too. Same with my neck, on the inside. But I don't remember doing it. But that's the time I was, just really concerned I was crazy. This really did it so I . . . at that time this is proving that there is something wrong with me, that all those simple classrooms that I had, had to be there because there was something wrong with me. The way I was treated, like it's through my whole life, us being Native and stuff like that, but it really, really screwed me up bad. So it confirmed it like I said, so when I came out of the hospital, I didn't even go home to see my kids. I went straight to the bar and just got drunk.

Quitting

Susan quit drinking on July 12th, 1985. Although she does not point to any one singular event as the seminal point in her healing process, she does talk about a number of significant occasions that played a role in this process: *I remember I was sitting at a booze can in Calgary. And that's where you can, like drink all the time. And this one guy came up to me and, he was a friend of my brother's, and he was just looking at me, and then he said to me, "You don't belong here". And of course I got angry, you know like, "Who the hell are you?" and, but what he said, you know, somehow it affected me because I just got up and I just smacked him. I slugged him pretty hard. But what he had said really did something to me. And then after that, like I was no where near on any safe ground, mind you. I did go back drinking. I don't even know how many recovery centres I went through, lots. Like I'd only get a few days sobriety and end up drinking again. But that was when I started to try to do something.*

And then the final one [booze can], the final one I remember. I had been out drinking and I ended up back in a booze can. And I got a lickin', a bad lickin'. I don't remember. My sister-in-law tells me, she tells me, she told me she remembered what happened. I must have blacked out because I don't even remember this. She said this guy made an advance at me and she said you got up and told him, you know, told him off and you swung at him and then he swung at you and she said the next thing she knew was three great big women came from upstairs from this place we were at. And she said they all jumped on you, they choked you so bad she said. They knocked you right out and they were kicking you and things like that. But again, I don't remember nothing. But I do remember coming to. And I just looked over. I seen they were all after her, all on her this time, and then I got up and I just started swinging again.

So after that I went home, and then the person I was living with at that time made me go to the hospital because I was all beat up and stuff like that and in pretty rough shape. So I went to the hospital and they wanted to keep me. They did some X-rays on my face because I had a lot of blows to my head, like big bumps on my head and stuff, and it showed that I had three breaks in my jaw. So they told me that they wanted me to stay in of course, and that they were going to call in a plastic surgeon before they would do anything - to help with the wiring and stuff. So that night they asked me if I wanted painkillers, something for the pain and I said, and just motioned my head "no". And I didn't feel anything. I really didn't feel any pain. And that's what I find really sad, is when a person, you can be beaten up so bad, and there is just no more physical pain left in that person. And that's where it went to with me. And I was just laying there. Then all of a sudden, I don't know what happened. It's like for the first time in my life my eyes were opened [and] I saw all my kids around me - my three kids - and I was just looking at them and I was wondering, "I know these kids are mine but who are they?" Like, you know, because my life has been so, so mixed up, and the drinking made my life so hazy and . . . And so for the first time I seen my children and they were crying and it's like my eyes were opened for the very first time in my life. And then I realized, you know, that I had three beautiful children but I didn't know who they were. You know I really didn't.

And then it hurt me because I saw them crying, but all of a sudden I felt pain. I just felt pain all over . . . and it felt good. It really felt good because I hadn't felt pain in so long. Like inner pain, but not that physical part. So I said, ya, I finally said I need something, so they gave me something for the pain. But that night when they wheeled me to my room and stuff, and I was in the hospital room and that's when I said "Okay God, I'm throwing the towel in now and I can promise you I'll try to stay sober one day at a time now." Just, that's all I can do, and I knew that. Like I couldn't take it any further than that. And to this day I still can't. I can't tell you if I'm going to be drunk tomorrow, because I might be. But if I can work on just for today I can handle that, so that's what I was doing for myself with God in my own room that time. And I really meant it. I can literally feel myself, you know, when I think back on it, feeling complete defeat against alcohol, and admitting, you know, just totally admitting 100% that I was beaten by it and that there was no way out: that I knew it would kill me at a very early age if I continued. So anyway, I said "Okay, if the price for what I've done, you know, how badly I've screwed up is to suffer to be wired up and suffering for six months, however long it's going to take to be wired up, so be *it, I'll go through that pain." But that's nothing compared to what I was, you know, the inner pain I talked about. Almost feeling like a zombie most of the time and stuff.*

I kind of looked at the operation as being second, and you know, I'd just have to go through. So the next day the plastic surgeon was there and they sent me down for more X-rays and they couldn't find any breaks in my jaw. So they just said it was probably just due to the X-ray machine or whatever, or faulty whatever. But whatever it was, it didn't really matter because I was ready to go through whatever I had to. I like to think it was kind of like a little miracle, and now I realize there's so many of those little miracles that we don't even pay attention to. But that was my last time I drank. It was a really difficult, I think, cause none of them [detox centres] were Aboriginal, none of them. But I'm not blaming them for my drinking. Like I'm not saying that, but I think a lot of it was the same old, same old thing for me. I don't know. Maybe if I had something to relate to, it would have been better or easier, I don't know. Like the more that I think about it. Like I was so disconnected from society, like really disconnected and not growing up with my people. I wasn't even connected there . . . and not having an identity to start off with, like it was just, it was hard, it was difficult.

I think not knowing nothing about yourself. Imagine growing up with a life not knowing nothing. Not knowing where you came from. Not knowing your background. Not knowing your grandparents and then being put down for who you are, but you don't understand why. You know, being called "You're a dirty Indian", things like that, you know. Not fully understanding what it was all about. Like for me it was more confusing because I didn't grow up with them. You know, I didn't grow up on the reserves. I think knowing the history of my people [would have helped], knowing what I was up against, knowing that I wasn't just this defect walking around confused. Like I was so confused about everything. But I couldn't connect it to anything, cause I didn't do any research. I never knew anything. My mother never let me in on any of the history or anything. And it was like I was just there.

Susan talks about the importance of disconnecting with certain people and activities. She completely disassociated herself from her father who "wanted nothing to do with me after I sobered up." She quit hanging around booze cans and the people that drank: *I did a lot [to stay occupied while trying to sober up]. I did, like, I realized that my daughter was going to die. And I knew that if I didn't start working on some of the guilt I was feeling that I wouldn't be able to live with myself. So I really threw myself into, like I continued with a lot of AA meetings and things and I worked at building our relationship. Cause I look at our relationship before and it was like, you know, just so silent. I'd go to the hospital and she'd sit on my lap: there was never no talking, never no nothing, and it was how we, the only way I knew. I remember having her on my lap one time. I was looking at her and I seen some tears in her eyes and I finally asked her, like, "what's the matter" type thing, and we started talking. And so I kinda had to start from learning how to talk. But I had three years to work with her. And I asked God at that time, just give me two things, that's all I'm asking for. Like I know you're going to take her in the end. Like I knew that. But the thing was, is don't take her before I'm ready - give me that time. And the other one was, don't let her die without me there. So that's the two things I focussed on and worked at.*

. . . [S]obering into a life I did not know. So it was hard and like, when I sobered up, I kind of sobered up into that kind of identity. And that's who I became to know me as for the first time basically. I guess as a caregiver. As someone who, who was, how can I say it, someone's life relied on me. That's how important I became. In my world I needed to be sober to help this child. I needed to keep learning what I could. I think, working with her, you know, with all that I did with her, keeping her alive, really taught me a lot about how powerful and strong I really am as an individual. Like with her I did things that . . . she brought out a lot in me. She brought out a lot of strengths that I didn't think I had. She helped me to fight the system. Because I knew that if I was passive, or whatever, none of what I did would have happened. Like, there's time when, I remember I went into the hospital and she was laying in the crib and I couldn't recognize her. Her face, I couldn't recognize. Her little legs were just going steady. You know, kicking steady and she was a purple, bluish colour. And the only way I recognized her was she had a birthmark on her leg, and that's the only thing. And they had, like I said, they had her two arms tied down. You could tell she had cried so much. Just little sounds were coming out of her, so I just got really mad and untied her and wrapped her in a blanket and I says, "I'm taking her out of the hospital". And the nurse tried to stop me and I says, "Stay the fuck away from me", I told her. "What's the matter with you?" The nurse said can you wait and we'll call the doctor right away. So I thought for a second and I says okay, but if he's not here right away, I says, I'm going to leave with my baby, and I'm taking her home. So anyway, the doctor came, and he was there quite quickly and I told him, I says, "I don't know what you guys are doing to her, but look at her." I said, "I don't even recognize her." So he checked her over, and he yelled at that nurse and he was really mad because she had dehydrated so bad that I don't know what would have happened if I

*didn't show up. But I was mad and was able to voice myself in the right way,
in the right time to make things happen, you know, for her.*

Drinking, Children, and Parental Relationships

Susan had three sober years with Brenda. Her wish of having Brenda die at
home was granted. Susan called her mother to come out to Calgary when
it looked like Brenda wouldn't live much longer. Brenda had been in and
out of a coma for quite some time when her mother called from Medicine
Hat: *And then that's when I told her, I said, "Mom the doctors were here,
they stopped all of her medicine. You better get out here." Brenda had
been out of it for quite a while already, like not coming to. She was just
completely, you would think comatose by this time. But really, really, like
just your faith or whatever you want to think, but mom just walked into
the room and Brenda opened her eyes and she looked at her arm and put
it around my mom and just said "I don't want to sleep any more." And
she closed her eyes and she died.*

*Just because I quit drinking didn't mean they [Susan's other two
children] had me as a mother, because like I said, my entire time went to
her [Brenda] pretty well. I mean, they were fed, kind of like I was I guess.
But a lot of my energy went into my daughter. [My relationship with them]
wasn't good. It's like I went into shock. Like I said, my identity, what I had
sobered up into was this, like I said this important person, but I lost it all
again. And I think that was the toughest for me. Like what do I do, where
do I go, who am I now that . . . it was hard. And my other kids, again, like
they not only suffered through my drinking. When I did sober up, I spent
more time with her of course, and after she died, I kind of went into that
own world. And then by the time I realized, like for instance, my daughter
needed me, it was already too late, cause she was in her teens, and now
I'm trying to play mother role. She thought "like, right". You know there's
this person that cares all of a sudden and wants to be a part of my life,
like, get out of my face, you know. But I understood that, so that's what
kind of helped. So she kind of went on her little ways for a while, like
drinking and doing her own experimenting. So they suffered a lot, a lot
along the way. Like my daughter just went wild with the drinking and
running around and I couldn't hold her down. At that time I had gotten
into another relationship and he tried to sexually assault her. And again,
because we had gotten a trailer, like we were buying a trailer, our life
was kind of, I thought, going somewhere. And then that happened and
I knew right there my whole life was cut again and I went through the
motions and again I went into shock. I went through the motions of taking*

her to the police station and doing a statement and things like that. And then she had to live with that.

[My daughter went through that wild drinking stage because]... she has a lot of potential of full-blown alcoholic too I believe. It's there. But I keep talking to her. And I think with her maturing up and having somebody to talk to. Like I keep telling her you know, you've got me to talk to. I says, I look back and I have nobody, like nobody to talk to, nobody to tell me what was right and what was wrong. I think she still needs lots of work, mind you, but I think she's on the right path. Like getting to love herself as a Native person, and that's where it all has to begin.

[To continue on my road of healing] I think the biggest, biggest thing that helped me was going back to university and learning about my people, and not feeling that I was 100% a total defect. After I realized what I was up against - not just me but my people, like a lot of Aboriginal people - with my past history and what's going on today, and not taking all that blame upon myself and kind of putting some of that blame back to society. Saying, "Here you take it." You know, talking about the residential schools, what they did, everything like that - you take that part and just give me my part I need to work on: that chunk that I need to work on. And so that's what I'm doing now. I can live with that, that part of me. But I just couldn't live with ... feeling 100% to blame for everything. [I needed to learn about my history] Like, when my mom had me, I was born into a woman that was raised in residential schools. It helped me to understand why my mother raised us the way she did. It helped me to understand so much about my life. And in the end, I'm not crazy, and I'm not, like I said, a dirty soulless Indian here. You know it helped me to understand that and where that all came from, and why I felt that way. I did a paper on my mom at the university. And I'm telling you, I must have cried for two weeks straight it hurt so bad. But mind you, by the time I did this paper I had done my own journey. I had already gone into my own childhood and dealt with a lot of my own issues of my own childhood.

So by the time I was looking at my mom, I think it helped me to be able to focus on her rather than on myself, because I did a lot of my own kind of healing in that part. So when I did this paper on my mom, and I actually went to the residential school she went in, like where she spent her childhood in, I could actually see her standing there, the little girl, alone, scared and oh, it was so awful. And I couldn't help it because everywhere I looked I can see this little girl and I just wanted to grab her and protect her from what was done to her. [My relationship with my mom now] it's beautiful. It's wonderful. I still have to overlook a lot of things in her. But isn't that what really means true friends, when we can do that?

Like there's things she does that get me angry, that I have to let it go and know that in her heart, I know she really, really loves all of us. Like, it hurts sometimes, because now she's raising foster children and she can hug those kids and hold those kids and do everything, kind of like what I can do now for my child. But my younger siblings, even my older ones, they're wondering how come she's doing that to them and she still can't even tell us that she loves us today or hug us. You know, when you do hug, you can feel the tension. I understand what's happening here, but for the ones that haven't done any healing, I understand their anger and their confusion even though they're adults.

I think a lot of it [the evolution of my relationship with my mother] had to do with me, with my own healing. Like I had to go back into my own childhood and then not only did that, I took it further and went back into her life: what it would have been like and then I even took it as far back as my grandmother. And then through my healing, when I started to heal, I then really hated her when I was looking at my past for what she did: or rather, what she didn't do. What she neglected to do as caring for us as kids and things. And so I made a complete circle. And then I hated her and now today I just love her unconditionally.

[Debra's relationship with her child, Felicity, is helping to break the cycle of dysfunction] . . . it's going to take more generations. It's becoming more aware of what we're doing. It's educating Felicity now. We can work with Felicity at a very young age and now start, you know what I mean, so it's going to take more than just now. Because I think it's just really starting for us because Felicity's dad is an alcoholic and a druggie. [Debra has also started to break the cycle.] Maybe [she drank] in her earlier part before she knew she was pregnant, she could have possibly drank then. But once she found out she was pregnant, that was it. She quit completely.

My healing is going to be forever. There's been so much damage done each time that it's not over in a lot of ways. It's not like something I can say, well this is my past, I've dealt with it, door's shut, carry on, because like I said, a lot of siblings are still drinking and they are where I was at.

Conclusion

Several weeks ago I got together with Susan. She asked if we could go outside and talk. After some time, she said she had begun drinking again. She said that it seemed that for her, her purpose for living was in some way, over. She knew her children were "going to make it". She didn't feel needed in the same way any more. She was so needed by her dying daughter. She had a purpose, a reason for being. Her son and daughter both needed her to ensure they didn't go on the same path she followed as a child. But now, with the confidence that they would be okay, Susan felt she was no longer important, and so she went on a drinking binge. She said, "Chris, I always told you this was not going to be easy, and that I could start again at any time." Susan is scared of the future. What has happened to Susan only reinforces all she had to say about the importance of her identity. She feels that her identity is now in jeopardy. She is no longer engaged with society in the same way. In her mind, her raison d'etre has ceased to exists.

There are no easy answers or quick fixes for a woman who has been through what Susan has. Over the years she has built up a network of strong people; strong people she has helped and who have helped her. These are now the people who will give Susan her raison d'etre. She has contributed much in her life. She has shared her stories so many will not have to endure what she did. She has given much of herself so her children and grandchildren will not have to suffer the same pain she endured for so many years. As Susan says, "My healing is going to be forever".

References

Aase, J. 1994. Clinical recognition of FAS: difficulties in diagnosis. *Alcohol: Health and Research World 18* (1): 5-9.

Asante, K. 1985. *Survey of Children with Chronic Handicaps and Fetal Alcohol Syndrome in the Yukon and British Columbia*. Ottawa: Health & Welfare

Hamer, J. 1965. Acculturation stress and the functions of alcohol among the Forest Potawatomi. In J. Hamer and J. Steinbring (Eds.) *Alcohol and Native Peoples of the North* pp. 107-153. Lanham, MD: University Press of America.

Jones, K. 1997. *Using an Ecological Model to Support Children with Fetal Alcohol Syndrome in the Community*. Winnipeg, Manitoba (unpublished).

Kowlessar, D. 1997. *An Examination of the Effects of Prenatal Alcohol Exposure on School-age Children in a Manitoba First Nation Community: A Study of Fetal Alcohol Syndrome Prevalence and Dysmorphology.* Unpublished master's thesis, University of Manitoba, Winnipeg,

Lemert, E. 1958. The use of alcohol in three Salish Indian tribes. In J. Hamer and J. Steinbring (Eds.) *Alcohol and Native Peoples of the North* pp. 49-71. Lanham, MD: U. Pr. Am.

Lithman, Y. 1979. Feeling good and getting smashed. *Ethnos 44*(1-2):119-133.

Lurie, N. 1971. The world's oldest on-going protest demonstration: North American Indian drinking patterns. *Pacific Historical Review 40* (3):311-332.

Mancall, P.1995. *Deadly Medicine: Indians and Alcohol in Early America.* London: Cornell University Press.

May, P. 1992. Alcohol policy considerations for Indian reservations and border-town communities. *J of Nat Cntr 4* (3):5-59.

May, P. 1994. The epidemiology of alcohol abuse among American Indians. *Am. Indian Cult. and Res J. 18* (2):121-143.

National Health/Educ. Consortium 1994. *Fetal Alcohol Syndrome: Impact on Children's Ability to Learn.* Occasi Paper #10.

Richards, H. 1993. *Therapy of the Substance Abuse Syndromes.* London: Jason Aronson.

Robbins, R. 1975. Alcohol and the identity struggle: economic change on interpersonal relations. *Am. Anthro.75:*99-122.

Robinson C., Conroy, J. and Conroy, R. 1987. Prevalence of fetal alcohol syndrome in an isolated community in British Columbia. *Canadian Medical Association J 137:*203-207.

Sparks, S. 1993. *Children of Prenatal Substance Abuse: School Age Children Series.* California: Singular.

Stratton K., Howe, C. and Battaglia, C. (Eds.) 1996. *Fetal Alcohol Syndrome: Diagnosis, Epistemology, Prevention and Treatment.* Washington: Inst. of Med., Nat Academy Press.

Wallace, J. 1977. Issues in alcoholism therapy. *Alc. H. Res. W.* June.

Weiner L., Morse, B. and Garrido, P. 1991. FAS/FAE: Focusing prevention on women at risk. *Moderation Rdr May/June.*

West Region Child and Family Services. 1994. October. *West Region Internal Survey.* Winnipeg, Manitoba: Author.

[1]   Chris Loewen (MA) recently graduated from the Native Studies Masters Program at the University of Manitoba.

Monsoni and the Smallpox Epidemic of 1737-39

Paul Hackett[1]

Abstract

The human landscape of Canada changed remarkably during the centuries following contact between the Old World and the New. Some Aboriginal groups disappeared as separate entities or relocated to new territories. Helping to drive these changes was the importation of Old World diseases causing exceptionally high rates of mortality in and extremely unbalanced manner where some groups escaped while others were devastated. The purpose of this paper is to explore the impact of disease on the Monsoni.

Introduction

The human landscape of Canada changed remarkably during the centuries following contact between the Old World and the New. Within a short period of time some Aboriginal groups that encountered early European observers disappeared as separate entities or relocated to new territories. New identities emerged as groups coalesced to form multi-ethnic political units. By the second half of the seventeenth century the patterns of Aboriginal settlement and alliances in the eastern half of Canada had changed almost completely from a century before and continued to change into the eighteenth and nineteenth centuries with increasing frequency. Recreating landscapes of identity and territory of Aboriginal peoples in the Central Subarctic and adjacent territories has been especially problematic, owing to the fragmented nature of the historical record (Bishop 1981, Pettipas 1994). Helping to drive these changes was the importation of Old

World diseases. Smallpox, measles and influenza exhibited great virulence among the Native people of the Americas and caused exceptionally high rates of mortality. Equally important, these epidemics often had an uneven impact; and some groups escaped for a time while others were devastated. For both these reasons, disease played a critical role in effecting political and territorial changes, throughout the Americas (Dobyns 1983, Ewers 1972, 1973, Taylor 1977, Trimble 1985, Decker 1989, Denevan 1992, Verano and Ubelaker 1992, Cook and Lovell 1992, Boyd 1985, Hackett 1999, Milner 1992).

Several basic responses to massive epidemic-induced depopulation have been documented among diverse Aboriginal peoples since the first epidemics struck the New World during the early sixteenth century. Among the more common were settlement shifts and territorial abandonment, the consolidation of surviving groups and the creation of complex societies formed by the amalgamation of survivors from different ethnic or cultural groups (Dobyns 1983).

This paper explores the fate of one such Native group, the Monsoni. While figuring prominently in the historic record of the early eighteenth century, the Monsoni have remained elusive in their origin and identity, and their disappearance from the record following the mid-point of the century has long been cause for speculation. This research examines the matter in the context of a little known, but crucial, smallpox epidemic that passed through northwestern Ontario and part of Manitoba during the period 1737-38. It argues that the once independent Monsoni were so reduced by the epidemic that they were forced to open their territory to other allied groups, losing their identity in the process. This paper sheds light on the fate of this small but important Aboriginal group, and also provides additional evidence of a process by which other formerly autonomous groups disappeared from the human landscape of the New World.

Early History of the Monsoni

Little is known of the history of the Monsoni prior to the eighteenth century. What evidence exists has led to confusion in the historical literature over their home territory and their tribal and linguistic affiliations. Some early testimony supplied by the Jesuit priests has caused several researchers to conclude that they were a Cree band, originally from the James Bay area or from the adjacent country to the north of Lake Superior. For instance, in the 1670s, Father Charles Albanel placed the "Monsounik" along a great river emptying into James Bay (Thwaites 1959). Father Antoine Silvy, considered the Monsoni to be a wandering tribe living to the north of Lake Superior, as far as Hudson Bay (Dickson 1980). The Jesuit historian Pierre Charlevoix (1866 III: 168) later stated that the Monsoni dwelled "at the head of Hudson's Bay".

Modern scholars have extended these early reports forward in time to encompass the Monsoni met by La Vérendrye around Rainy Lake, whom, they argued, were Cree who had migrated from their original homes about Lake Superior or James Bay. For instance, Bishop and Smith (1975), concluded that the Monsoni were Cree and placed them near the mouth of the Moose River and that the Ojibway were confined to the country east of Michipicoten Bay on the north shore of Lake Superior until after 1700. By 1700, Bishop (1974) stated the Monsoni had moved inland towards Lake Nipigon. Bishop (1981) was not convinced that there was only a single Monsoni group, however. Hickerson's (1967) influential conclusion that the Monsoni formed a branch of the Cree led him to insist that Ojibway occupation of the Rainy Lake area by the Ojibway did not begin until 1736. More recently, Heidenreich and Noel (1987) represented this surmised movement by the Monsoni "Cree" from Moose River to Rainy Lake in their map of Native locations. Conversely, Hlady (1960-61), following Morton (1939), considered them to be an Ojibway group in control of the Boundary Waters at an early date. Greenberg and Morrison (1982) suggested that the Ojibway, among them the Monsoni of Rainy Lake, had lived in the Boundary Waters area prior to contact, and that the name Ojibway was later applied to them by fur traders who were unfamiliar with their true identities. Although this testimony seems to support that conclusion, other evidence makes it clear that this was not the case (Figure 1).

Instead, it would appear that the Monsoni were Ojibway and that they had occupied the territory wherein La Vérendrye found them long before the 1730s. Critical evidence on this subject came to light in 1982, with the publication by Greenberg and Morrison (1982) of a previously unknown document, credited to La Vérendrye, which clearly identifies the Monsoni as being Ojibway-speakers living in the Rainy Lake area as of the early 1740s. Moreover, other evidence suggests that they had been living there, or nearby, since at least the late seventeenth century. In 1684, the Sieur Duluth established a post at Lake Nipigon, designed to intercept the Monsoni before they traded with the English on James Bay (Margry 1876-86). This would have been illogical and ineffective had the Monsoni been settled along the Moose River, only a short distance from an English post (Figure 1). Instead, it was an ideal location from which to meet

Native people from the western part of the Boundary Waters who were intending to trade with the English on James Bay. La Potherie, who was at Fort Bourbon (York Fort) late in the seventeenth century, identified the Monsoni as a group who lived in that post's hinterland and who sought the role of middleman in the fur trade with the Hudson's Bay Company (Tyrrell 1968, Bishop 1981). Both of these conditions would have been met by a location in the Rainy Lake-Rainy River area, which lay alongside important travelling routes connecting Lake Superior, James Bay and Lake Winnipeg. However, La Potherie implied that the Monsoni occupied a region between the Hudson Bay Lowland Cree and the people of the swamps, or savannahs (Tyrrell 1968). According to Tyrrell, this would have placed the Monsoni in the Trout Lake area, along the Severn River, or far to the north of Rainy Lake. In this, La Potherie may have been mistaken, since he no doubt had an imperfect knowledge of the geography of the York hinterland. If, as La Potherie implied, the Monsoni did seek the middleman role, this might explain their appearance in the area of Lake Superior and James Bay. Prior to the eighteenth century, acting as an intermediate fur trader generally required taking long journeys to reach the French or English posts.

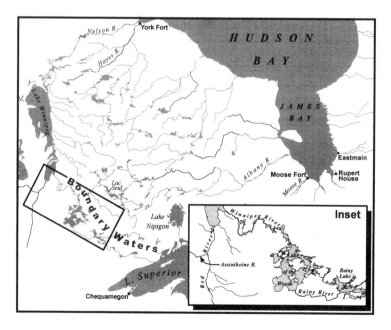

Figure 1. Map of Boundary Waters area inhabited by Monsoni.

The summer-time presence of the Monsoni on the Moose River or at Sault Ste. Marie, where they were found in 1671 (Thwaites 1959), was most likely a temporary sojourn, part of a much larger pattern of trade-related travel. Had the Monsoni been located in the vicinity of James Bay at this time then it is very unlikely that they would have been trading at York, or attempting to cultivate the role of middleman.

The Monsoni During the Eighteenth Century

Composed of members of the Moose clan, the Monsoni seem to have been one of the Northern Ojibway bands. According to Dobbs (1744) and Chauvignerie (O'Callaghan 1853-61:IX) the Monsoni totem was a moose. Thus, they were similar to the many clan-based, proto-Ojibway bands that resided around Sault Ste. Marie during the seventeenth century (Hickerson 1988). Based on Native testimony and traditions, the nineteenth-century Ojibway historian, William Warren (1984: 84), wrote that "a large band [of the northern division of the Ojibway] early occupied and formed a village at Rainy Lake." There can be little doubt that he was referring to the Monsoni.

More is known of the Monsoni during the 1730s when the French, under La Vérendrye, began to settle permanent trading posts among them. By this time they were residing at Rainy Lake and along the Rainy River, perhaps as far as Lake of the Woods (Jones 1893, Burpee 1927, O'Callaghan 1853-61). Bishop (1981) had other Monsoni living along the Nipigon River in the 1730s, but it is clear from a reading of the primary documents that these Monsoni merely traded at the local post, and did not reside along the river (O'Callaghan 1853-61). This area provided an exceptionally diverse resource base that could support large numbers of people, with wild rice, large game, fish, and other foodstuffs (Waisberg 1984, Holzkamm et al. 1988). It was also a critical location in the approach to the Canadian Northwest, for those who were settled there controlled access to the main canoe routes leading to the valuable fur lands to the north and west (Figure 1). Consequently, the Monsoni were a numerous and powerful people, playing a leading role in the economic and military affairs of the day.

By the 1730s the Monsoni were allied with the Cree and Assiniboine who lived nearby, as well as with other Northern Ojibway bands, in waging frequent war on the Dakota Sioux and Southwestern Ojibway who lived to the south. They could easily raise several hundred warriors for a war party, and carried great influence with both the French and neighboring Indian bands (Lovisek 1993). At this time they had several village and war chiefs, but their principal war chief was named La Colle, a leader whose weight in military issues extended to the Cree and Assiniboine (Loc. Cit.). In times of war, and perhaps even in civil matters, La Colle seems to have exercised authority over all of the assembled Monsoni (Ibid.: 287). During this era, the Monsoni were perhaps the pre-eminent group in the western Boundary Waters, and they figured prominently in the records of the day.

The 1737-38 Smallpox Epidemic and the Monsoni

The decline of the Monsoni as a dominant force in the region began with an epidemic. In 1737 smallpox reached the west from eastern North America, having made its way slowly from the American ports of the eastern seaboard. The progress and effects of this smallpox epidemic are traced in Hackett (1999). Like many other Old World afflictions before it, this disease had been introduced by a ship from Europe, in this case a vessel from Ireland that sailed to Boston. After spreading through the American colonies and to Canada, it proceeded westward into the interior of the continent, moving to the south of the Great Lakes. The disease eventually surfaced among several Cree bands that had attended a meeting with the French at the Forks of the Assiniboine and Red Rivers in May of 1737. This epidemic resulted in an unknown but apparently significant number of deaths among groups living on the Winnipeg and Saskatchewan Rivers (Burpee 1927). In April of 1738 it broke out among the Monsoni and some Cree who were preparing to go to war with their long-time enemies, the Dakota Sioux. According to La Vérendrye's son, the Monsoni and Cree were prevented from continuing on their intended trip, having been "obliged to stop with the loss of a considerable number of their people carried off by that disease" (Ibid.: 282). This affliction was to have considerable long-term implications for the Monsoni, and for the human geography of the Rainy Lake region.

The impact of this disease was tremendous, especially to the Monsoni. Estimates of pre and post epidemic Monsoni warrior counts suggest a marked decline in their population immediately following the epidemic. The aforementioned La Vérendrye document, which provides a crucial snapshot of the Aboriginal populations of the region during the period immediately following the epidemic is not given and has never been firmly established in the secondary record, but instead has been vaguely dated by researchers. Thus, for instance, Greenberg and Morrison (1982) suggested a date of circa 1730-40. Obviously, the date is crucial for the purposes of assessing the impact of the epidemic, in that there would be markedly different implications depending on whether it had been written before or after smallpox had visited the Monsoni. It is possible to provide a much tighter time frame than that which has heretofore been suggested, based on internal logic. For example the document refers to Fort Bourbon, on the Saskatchewan River near Lake Winnipeg, which was constructed in 1742 (Wilson 1952). As well, La Vérendrye is identified as a Lieutenant, but was promoted to Captain in 1745. In all probability, then, it was written between 1742 and 1745, or immediately following the epidemic. In this document it states that the Monsoni could muster only 140 men among the three bands at Rainy Lake, with a few more residing on the Winnipeg River (Greenberg and Morrison 1982). This would appear to be all that remained of the adult male portion of the group's population. Conversely, La Vérendrye's pre-epidemic estimates of Monsoni warriors greatly exceed his estimate from the post-epidemic period. For example, on May 7, 1734, nearly 400 Monsoni warriors gathered in order to go to war against the Dakota Sioux (Burpee 1927). Given perhaps four persons per warrior, the Monsoni population may have declined from about 1,600 to just over 560 in a very short span of time. The use of four individuals per warrior is merely an estimate and probably a conservative one at that. Charles McKenzie, who traded with the Mandan and who later resided at Lac Seul for a considerable period of time, employed an estimate of six individuals per warrior to calculate Indian populations (NAC MG 19, C4 Volume 38). This evidence is especially significant in that the Monsoni, although forming several bands living in the region of Rainy Lake, comprised a distinct and readily identifiable people living in a relatively confined area, without the many subdivisions that were characteristic of the Cree and Assiniboine. Thus, there is not the same problem of identifying which subgroup living in what region was afflicted that is experienced when studying the latter two groups. It is fairly certain that such estimates include all Monsoni bands. Such a population decline fits the pattern of post-contact epidemic depopulation observed on countless occasions among the Aboriginal peoples of the Americas.

Circumstantial evidence tends to confirm that the Monsoni experienced a high degree of mortality at this time. Three years after the epidemic, in 1741, the Monsoni chief La Colle and his people again went to war against the Sioux, returning with large numbers of their enemy as slaves (Burpee 1927). Prior to that time, the capture of "slaves" does not appear to have been a motive for Monsoni war excursions. This represents a significant change in motivation on their part. In other contexts, epidemic depopulation induced some Indian groups to wage war for the same purpose. Thus, following devastating epidemics the Iroquois of the Northeast and the Piegan of the Canadian Plains went on military expeditions against their enemies in order to capture enemy females and children to replace those lost in the epidemic. In some instances, Huron warriors were even kept alive by the Iroquois following their capture, to be adopted into their tribe (Johnston 1987, Trigger 1987, 1989). Given the heavy losses experienced by the Monsoni only a few years earlier, it is likely that this attempt to obtain "slaves" was actually a similar means of trying to replenish a population recently depleted by smallpox.

The Monsoni may have resorted to another common strategy for group survival following the epidemic, that of amalgamation with other surviving groups. A well-documented response to severe mortality among Aboriginal groups in North America has been the coalescence of the remnants of formerly autonomous peoples into a combined social group in order to surpass a population threshold, either for defensive or subsistence purposes. While in many cases this would involve survivors from the same linguistic and tribal divisions reforming into new arrangements, it could also lead to the emergence of "poly-ethnic" villages; villages comprised of people from different cultural or linguistic groups (Dobyns 1983, Taylor 1982). Perhaps the best example is that of the Mandan who, following the 1779-83 and 1837-38 smallpox epidemics, merged with the surviving Arikara to produce new villages (Wood and Thiessen 1985, Lehmer 1977). As well, the diaspora following the epidemics of the early seventeenth century in eastern North America and the warfare accompanying the fall of Huronia in 1649 saw the creation of major refugee communities crossing linguistic boundaries, such as the Ottawa-Huron settlement of Chequamegon on Lake Superior (White 1995, Trigger 1987). This may explain the presence of a small number of Monsoni living with the Barrier Cree along the Winnipeg River immediately after the epidemic (Greenberg and Morrison 1982). Prior to 1738, every indication in the historical record pictured the Monsoni as an independent people, living in a contiguous territory in the Rainy Lake-Rainy River area, territorial coherence that was reflected in the maps of the period. Simultaneously, observers described the Winnipeg River as solely the domain of the Cristinaux, or Cree (Jones 1893). It may be that these few Monsoni were attempting to preserve their existence by joining with a nearby Cree band.

In a similar vein, many Aboriginal groups replenished depleted populations by inviting others to join them. William Warren noted that following the almost complete decline of the Sandy Lake (Minnesota) Ojibway due to the 1779-83 smallpox epidemic their numbers were greatly augmented by additions from Lake Superior (Warren 1984). Likewise, in 1671 Father Charles Albanel said of the Montagnais of the Lac Ste. Jean (Quebec) area that in the wake of population decline due to war and smallpox they were regaining their former population levels "by additions from the outside Nations" (Thwaites 1959: LVI: 155-157). A similar process seems to have occurred among the Monsoni subsequent to the 1737-38 epidemic. During the decades that followed, they were increasingly joined at Rainy Lake by other Ojibway-speaking peoples from the vicinity of Lake Superior, people who had once been their enemies (Hickerson 1967). This began in December of 1736, when numbers of Saulteux from the south of Lake Superior sought refuge with the French at nearby Vermilion River for fear of the Dakota Sioux (Burpee 1927). Although this occurred prior to the appearance of the disease at Rainy Lake, every indication suggests that the process accelerated following the devastation of the Monsoni, as other peoples increasingly joined them. While acknowledging the appearance of the Southwestern Ojibway in Rainy Lake area, Hickerson's insistence that the Monsoni were Cree caused him to misinterpret this migration as one of Ojibway replacement of the former Cree inhabitants.

For the Southwestern Ojibway, the opportunity to move to Rainy Lake provided them with some separation from the Sioux, with whom they had just broken their alliance, as well as with access to the rich local resources and a strategic location in terms of controlling the fur trade. For the Monsoni, the additions bolstered their numbers and provided necessary security against Sioux incursions. As time passed, the Bear clan joined the Moose clan (the Monsoni) as the predominant totems of the people living in the region (Hickerson 1974, Lovisek 1993). As a result of the epidemic, there emerged a new and much more heterogeneous regional population than had been the case when the Monsoni alone lived in the area.

Aftermath

Despite the evident mortality caused by the smallpox, the Monsoni did not disappear immediately following the epidemic, for there remained substantial numbers of survivors. Nor, in fact, do they seem to have abandoned the region [although researchers such as Hlady (1960-61) have surmised that they left the region], as has been the case with the remnants of other Native groups who have survived severe epidemics. Including the

Cree, for example, who were said to have abandoned the Red River valley following the devastating 1779-83 smallpox epidemic, enabling Ojibway to expand into the territory (Ray 1988, Peers 1994). Members of the Moose clan, presumably descendants of the original Monsoni, continued to reside at Rainy Lake at least into the nineteenth century (Lovisek, 1993), and probably much later. Nevertheless, as time passed the Monsoni, as an independent and dominant corporate entity, disappeared from the scene and from the historical record. This loss of group identity was a consequence of the epidemic as surely as had they been completely annihilated by the disease itself.

For a brief time after the epidemic the Monsoni continued to exist in a semblance of their previous form. For example, La Vérendrye continued to refer to them as Monsoni, as did Joseph La France, a renegade *Coureur de Bois*, who spent over a month with Monsoni at both Rainy River and Lake of the Woods while on his way from Sault Ste. Marie to York Factory in 1741 (Dobbs 1744). Their principal chief, La Colle, remained active, and continued to lead war parties against the Sioux during the early 1740s (Burpee 1927). Shortly thereafter, the Monsoni ceased to appear in the records of the non-Native explorers and traders. When La Vérendrye's successor, St. Pierre, passed through Rainy Lake in 1753, instead of calling the inhabitants Monsoni, he called them Oueschekgagamiouilimy (Margry 1876-86: VI: 649). Meaning "people of the ridge" (Mooney and Cyrus 1971: 372). The use of a name related to local topography is significant because it identifies the entire regional rather than a specific totemic group. Two decades later, Alexander Henry, the Elder, met a village of Chipeways, or Ojibway, on the Rainy River (Bain 1901). Even as the fur trade became increasingly intense in the Rainy Lake area thereafter, the Monsoni were nowhere to be found in the historical documents.

The disappearance of the Monsoni can be attributed to the losses that resulted from the epidemic and to their attempts to maintain their numbers following that devastation. As other Ojibway people moved into the Rainy Lake-Lake of the Woods area, the Monsoni seem to have lost their separate identity and their dominant position in the eyes of non-Native observers, instead merging with the new arrivals. Rather than remaining a single identifiable totemic group as they were when La Vérendrye was in the area, they became part of a larger, undifferentiated, regional Ojibway population comprised of members of multiple clans. This process is significant, in that it seems to be analogous to the breaking down of several proto-Ojibway, corporate clan villages (or nations) beginning around Sault Ste. Marie in the seventeenth century. Hickerson (1988) believed that this process formed the basis for the emergence of the larger Ojibway tribe. In the case of the Monsoni, the primary impetus was not related to the fur trade or military needs, but was more the result of a devastating smallpox epidemic.

In turn, these political and territorial changes may have led to a shift in the cultural practices of the region's people. In all likelihood, the Monsoni were of the Northern Ojibway (Warren 1984). However, based on the descriptions of later observers, modern researchers have tied the Ojibway of the Rainy Lake area to the Southwestern Ojibway, who resided to the south and west of Lake Superior and who had much more elaborate customs and practices (Waisberg 1984). Even the political leadership of the Boundary Waters region was, in a way, lost by the Monsoni. Following the death of the powerful Monsoni War Chief, La Colle, that role was subsequently assumed by another Ojibway, Nittum, who was a member of the Bear clan. Nittum (or the *Premier*) was among (and perhaps the first) of a series of hereditary Grand Chiefs in the Rainy Lake region, each having that same totemic association (Lovisek 1993). Monsoni were marginalized by the influx of post-epidemic arrivals that was necessary for their survival in the region.

Conclusions

The apparent disappearance of the Monsoni provides a glimpse into the fate of other Aboriginal peoples in the Americas during an earlier era. From the first epidemics, countless Native groups were devastated by disease, in many cases before European observers arrived on the scene. Many disappeared from the human landscape. Although it may be that some were so depleted in numbers that they ceased to exist, others would have suffered a fate that was comparable to the Monsoni. Weakened by their losses, they were forced to join other groups or to invite others to join them, losing their separate identity in the process.

References

Bain, J. (Ed.). 1901 [1809]. *Travels and Adventures in Canada and the Indian Territories between the Years 1760 and 1776 [Alexander Henry, the Elder]*. Boston: Little, Brown.

Bishop, C. 1974. Ojibwa, Cree, and the Hudson's Bay Company in northern Ontario: Culture and conflict in the eighteenth century. In A. Rasporich (Ed.) *Western Canada Past and Present*. pp. 150-162. Calgary: McClelland and Stewart West.

Bishop, C. 1981. Territorial groups before 1821: Cree and Ojibwa. In J. Helm (Ed.) *Subarctic*. Handbook of North American Indians, vol 6. Washington: Smithsonian Institution.

Bishop, C. and Smith, M. 1975. Early historic populations in northwestern Ontario: Archaeological and ethnohistorical implications. *American Antiquity 40*: 54-63.

Boyd, R. 1985. *The Introduction of Infectious Diseases among the Indians of the Pacific Northwest, 1774-1874*. Unpublished Doctoral Dissertation. University of Washington.

Burpee, L. (Ed.) 1927. *Journals and Letters of Pierre Gaultier De Varennes De La Verendrye and his Sons, with Correspondence between the Governors of Canada and the French Court, Touching the Search for the Western Sea*. The Publications of the Champlain Society, vol. 16. Toronto: The Champlain Society.

Charlevoix, P. 1866. *History and General Description of New France*. New York City: John Gilmary Shea.

Cook, N. and Lovell, W. (Eds.). 1992. *Secret Judgements of God: Old World Disease in Colonial Spanish America*. The Civilization of the American Indian Series, 205. Norman and London: University of Oklahoma Press.

Decker, J. 1989. *'We Should Never Be Again the Same People' The Diffusion and Cumulative Impact of Acute Infectious Diseases Affecting the Natives on the Northern Plains of the Western Interior of Canada 1774-1839*. Unpublished Ph.D. Dissertation. York University.

Denevan, W. (Ed.). 1992 [1976]. *The Native Population of the Americas in 1492* (2nd edition). Madison: University of Wisconsin Press.

Dickson, I. (Ed. and Trans.). 1980. *Letters from North America [Silvy, Antoine]*. Belleville, Ontario: Mika Publishing.

Dobbs, A. 1744. *An Account of the Country Adjoining to Hudson's Bay, in the North-West Part of America*. London: J. Robinson.

Dobyns, H. 1983. *Their Number Become Thinned: Native American Population Dynamics in Eastern North America*. Knoxville: University of Tennessee Press.

Ewers, J. 1972. Influence of the fur trade on Indians of the Northern Plains. In M. Bolus (Ed.) *People and Pelts: Selected Papers of the Second North American Fur Trade Conference*. Winnipeg: Peguis Publishers.

Ewers, J. 1973. The influence of epidemics on the Indian populations and cultures of Texas. *Plains Anthropologist 18:* 104-115.

Greenberg, A. and Morrison, J. 1982. Group identities in the boreal forest: The origins of the Northern Ojibwa. *Ethnohistory 29*(2):75-102.

Hackett, P. 1999. *'A Very Remarkable Sickness': The Diffusion of Directly Transmitted, Acute Infectious Diseases in the Petit Nord, 1670-1846*. Unpublished Ph.D. Dissertation, Winnipeg: University of Manitoba.

Heidenreich, C. and Noel, F. 1987. Trade and empire, 1697-1739. In R. Harris (Ed.) *Historical Atlas of Canada, Volume 1: From the Beginning to 1800*

(Plate 39). Toronto: University of Toronto Press.

Hickerson, H. 1967. Land Tenure of the Rainy Lake Chippewa at the beginning of the 19th Century. *Smithsonian Contributions to Anthropology* 2(4):41-63.

Hickerson, H. 1974. *Ethnohistory of Chippewa of Lake Superior. Chippewa Indians III.* New York: Garland Publishing.

Hickerson, H. 1988 [1970]. *The Chippewa and Their Neighbours: A Study in Ethnohistory* [Revised and expanded edition]. Studies in Anthropological Method. Prospect Heights, Illinois: Waveland Press.

Hlady, W. 1960-61. Indian migrations in Manitoba and the west. *Papers Read before the Historical and Scientific Society of Manitoba, Series III* (17 and 18):24-53.

Holzkamm, T., Lytwyn, V. and Waisberg, L. 1988. Rainy River sturgeon: An Ojibway resource in the fur trade economy. *The Canadian Geographer* 32(3):194-205.

Johnston, S. 1987. Epidemics: The forgotten factor in seventeenth century Native warfare in the St. Lawrence region. In B. Cox (Ed.) *Native People Native Lands: Canadian Indians, Inuit and Métis.* Ottawa: Carleton University Press.

Jones, A. (Ed.). 1893. *The Aulneau Collection, 1735-1745.* Montreal: Archives of St. Mary's College.

Lehmer, D. 1977. The other side of the fur trade. In W. Wood (Ed.) *Selected Writings of Donald J. Lehmer.* pp. 91-104. Lincoln, NE: J+L Reprints.

Lovisek, J. 1993. The political evolution of the Boundary Waters Ojibwa. In W. Cowan (Ed.) *Papers of the Twenty-fourth Algonquian Conference.* pp. 280-305. Ottawa: Carleton University.

Margry, P. (Ed.). 1876-86. *Decouvertes et Etablissementes des Francais dans L'Ouest et dans le Sud de L'Amerique Septentrionale, 1614-1754.* Paris: D. Jouaust.

Milner, G. 1992. Disease and sociopolitical systems in late prehistoric Illinois. In J. Verano and D. Ubelaker (Eds.) *Disease and Demography in the Americas.* pp. 103-116. Washington and London: Smithsonian Institution Press.

Mooney, J. and Cyrus, T. 1971 [1913]. Monsoni. In *Handbook of Indians of Canada.* p 372. Toronto: Coles.

Morton, A. 1939. *A History of the Canadian West to 1870-71 Being a History of Rupert's Land (the Hudson's Bay Company) and of the North-West Territory (including the Pacific Slope).* Toronto: University of Toronto Press.

NAC (National Archives of Canada) MG 19, C4 Masson Collection

O'Callaghan, E. 1853-61. *Documents Relative to the Colonial History of the State of New York; Procured in Holland, England and France edited by J. Brodhead.* Albany, New York: Weed, Parsons.

Peers, L. 1994. *The Ojibwa of Western Canada.* Manitoba Studies in Native History. Winnipeg: The University of Manitoba Press.

Pettipas, L. 1994. Who were the "Snakes?". *Manitoba Archaeological Journal* 4(1-2):33-42.

Taylor, J. 1977. Sociocultural effects of epidemics on the northern plains: 1734-1850. *The Western Canadian Journal of Anthropology VII*(4)55-81.

Taylor, J. 1982. *Sociocultural Effects of Epidemics on the Northern Plains: 1735-1870.* Unpublished M.A. Thesis, Missoula: University of Montana.

Thwaites, R. (Ed.). 1959 [1896-1901]. *The Jesuit Relations and Allied Documents: Travels and Explorations of the Jesuit Missionaries in New France 1610-1791*(Reprint Edition). New York City: Pageant Book.

Trigger, B. 1987 [1976]. *The Children of Aataentsic: A History of the Huron People to 1660.* Kingston and Montreal: McGill-Queens University Press.

Trigger, B. 1989 [1985]. *Natives and Newcomers: Canada's "Heroic Age" Reconsidered.* Kingston and Montreal: McGill-Queen's University Press.

Trimble, M. 1985. *Epidemiology on the Northern Plains: A Cultural Perspective.* Unpublished Ph.D. Dissertation. University of Missouri-Columbia.

Tyrrell, J. (Ed.). 1968 [1931]. *Documents Relating to the Early History of Hudson Bay.* New York: Greenwood Press.

Verano, J. and Ubelaker, D. 1992. *Disease and Demography in the Americas.* Washington and London: Smithsonian Institution Press.

Waisberg, L. 1984. An ethnographic and historical outline of the Rainy River Ojibway. In W. Noble (Ed.) *An Historical Synthesis of the Manitou Mounds Site on the Rainy River, Ontario.* Manuscript in National Historic Sites Branch: Parks Canada.

Warren, W. 1984 [1885]. *History of the Ojibways, Based on Traditions and Oral Statements.* Minneapolis: Minnesota Historical Society Press.

White, R. 1995. *The Middle Ground: Indians, Empires, and Republics in the Great Lakes Region, 1650-1815.* Cambridge Studies in North American Indian History. Cambridge: Cambridge University Press.

Wilson, C. 1952. La Verendrye reaches the Saskatchewan. *Canadian Historical Review 33*(1): 39-49.

Wood, W. and Thiessen, T. (Eds.). 1985. *Early Fur Trade on the Northern Plains: Canadian Traders among the Mandan and Hidatsa Indians, 1738-1818.* The American Exploration and Travel Series. Norman: University of Oklahoma Press.

---

[1]   Paul Hackett (Ph.D History) is the recipient of the University of Manitoba Distinguished Dissertation Award for Arts, Humanities and Social Sciences (2000) presented by the Faculty of Graduate Studies and the Alumni Association.

Cultural Value of Food Among the Naskapi

Treena Orchard[1]

Abstract

Food is a powerful symbol of cultural values and identity, especially for Aboriginal people who no longer practice their traditional food harvesting methods on a full-time basis, yet consume and appreciate "country" or "bush" foods. This paper explores the use of food among a group of former hunter-gatherers living in the interior region of northern Quebec, the Naskapi from Kawawachikamach.

Introduction

For the Naskapi, "bush" or "country" food is collected by hunting and gathering caribou, geese, ducks, lake trout, ptarmigan, beaver, fox, muskrat, hare, marten, Labrador tea, and a variety of other plants and berries (Armitage 1991). Since involvement in the fur-trade during the mid-nineteenth century, tea, sugar, and bannock are also included. Naskapi of all ages and researchers consider wild plants and animals healthier than store-bought items (Borre 1991, Kuhnlein 1984, Wein et al. 1989, Shepard and Rode 1996). Such foods are also valued through their connections to the past and with the meaning of being Naskapi. The nutritional benefits of these foods is easily determined, it is more difficult to measure the qualitative value. Literature dealing with the socio-cultural value of food focuses on the positive aspects including the symbolic connection to a previous time and a more idyllic way of life. In addition to describing the meaning and value of food, it also illustrates the usefulness of looking at food and the values surrounding it as sites of potential conflict, especially with reference to the issue of cultural identity.

The Field Site and Methods

Field research was conducted in the Naskapi community of Kawawachikamach, Quebec from May through September 1997. The Naskapi are Northern Algonquin-speaking peoples living in the eastern and northern parts of the Quebec-Labrador peninsula, historically referred to as the 'Montagnais-Naskapi'. 'Naskapi' was used in a broader sense (Mailhot 1986), it is now only used for this local grouping. The groups living in Labrador, and in some parts of Quebec, refer to themselves as 'Innu'. Kawawachikamach (600 population) is one of 13 Innu communities (15,000 people) in Quebec and Labrador. It was constructed between 1981-1984 with funds from the North Eastern Quebec Agreement (1978), a sister agreement of the larger James Bay and Northern Quebec Agreement (1975). From 1956, when they moved from the Ungava Bay region to the town of Schefferville, the Naskapi lived with the Montagnais, a neighbouring group of Innu. Inter-marriages occurred between the two groups, Naskapi women generally marrying Montagnais men, resulting in Montagnais spouses living in Kawawachikamach and Naskapi spouses living in the Montagnais community (Matemekosh) located 10 km to the south of Kawawa.

Kawawachikamach is situated at the juncture of Lakes Peter and Matemace in the Labrador Hills. It operates on a small infrastructure and offers basic services and employment, including: Band Office, radio station, school, dispensary, police station, Naskapi Development Corporation, day-care centre, garage, pump house, gas bar, post office, grocery store, and café. Wage employment supplemented with social assistance and/or monetary returns from hunting trips and outfitting ventures form the basis of the Naskapi economy. An all season gravel road links the community to the former iron-ore mining town of Schefferville (population 3000) located 15 km to the south. Schefferville offers air and train routes on daily and weekly schedules respectively, and many goods and entertainment services such as craft stores, a Northern food and hunting supply store, hotels, and an arena used for such social events as feasts and weddings.

Initially, I assumed the role of research subject, answering their many inquiries about my family, place of origin, purpose for being there, marital status; and observed and interacted with community members by participating in local events. I helped organize a six week Summer Youth Program; supervised the evening activities at the school gym; went on a number of fishing trips; and attended community feasts, weddings, a funeral, and the high school graduation. This involvement enabled me to observe a variety of social situations in the community and allowed me to show my genuine concern for life in Kawawachikamach as a member of the community, not just as "the anthropologist".

I conducted a number of semi-structured interviews during my four months in the community, 15 with teenagers, 11 with adults, and 3 with Elders. Although the subject of my research was the social life and experiences of adolescents, the topic of food arose often and was encouraged by my interest in hunting and fishing. All ages talked to me about food and other subjects surrounding eating, the act of hunting, and the cultural value of these pursuits. I was often associated with teenagers because of my research interests; because of my volunteer work adults associated me with contributing something of value, in terms of my time and tangible "work", to the village. I became friends with teenagers, parents, young adults, and Elders. Move between a range of social, age, gender, and occupational groups made my circle of informants, friends, and acquaintances a representative spread of the community population.

Food and Spirituality

When the Naskapi were nomadic hunter-gatherers their life centered around the caribou and the animals' yearly migrations to the interior of the Quebec-Labrador peninsula (Robbins 1988). The meat, bones, and skin of the caribou provided their spiritual, physical, and nutritional sustenance. Animals gave themselves to the hunter, which obligated the hunter to respect the animal spirits (Speck 1935). Thanks was shown by performing various ceremonies, following strict rules regarding the consumption of the animals, and by dreaming and drumming to communicate to the animal worlds. The most significant ceremony, the *mokoshon*, includes the ritualistic eating of caribou marrow, fat, and bones (Henriksen 1973). Care was taken to avoid contaminating caribou; for example, all fat (*pimin*) and marrow was consumed in the tent where it was made, no food was spilled, utensils were kept clean, and alcohol [including home made spruce beer (Robbins 1973, Degnen 1996, Wadden 1991)] was not consumed.

Parts of the *mokoshon* ceremony were seen at the high school graduation feast and dance where everyone was given a plate of bush and store-bought food (chicken, caribou, bannock, salad, and vegetables). As people were finishing their meals a man distributed bits of food from large silver tray to those who requested it. I was told it was caribou so I asked for a piece and as I was about to bite into what looked like a very fatty chunk of meat coated in sand or breading my "field mother" (head of the household I lived with) took it and put it with hers in a container. She said we were not allowed to eat it because we were going to be drinking alcohol that night. Later I realized this was the central ingredient of the *mokoshon* ceremony. This incident reveals how intact traditional ideology is pertaining to the sacredness of bush food. Although the *mokoshon* ceremony is no longer central to their survival, the special food, along with the culturally prescribed rules is still an important part of social gatherings like weddings, funerals, baptisms, and the graduation feast; a testimony to their long standing spiritual traditions and the flexibility of these traditions. This is significant because it was generally observed during the 1960s and 1970s that the performance of this ritual was declining along with widespread neglect of animal bones, especially among the youth (Armitage 1985, 1991; Fouillard 1995).

Sharing Food

The sharing of food has always played a very functional and complex role within Naskapi social organization. As hunter-gatherers it was in everybody's best interest to share; sharing one's catch one day meant the assurance of receiving part of someone else's catch another day (Leacock 1986). Due to the egalitarian nature of Naskapi society an accumulation of food could lead to social conflict, and thus people were morally obligated to share (Robbins 1988). The act of sharing also established prestige, temporary political power, and reinforced supernatural sanctions surrounding the act of sharing, especially of caribou (Henriksen 1973).

In Kawawachikamach sharing is cyclical; it ensures that everyone receives a similar amount of food and that everyone is treated fairly. On a fishing trip that I took with seven Naskapi men and three male teenagers approximately 300 speckled trout were caught, of which I contributed five. At the end of the week-end our catch was distributed evenly. After we received our fish the largest one was given to me. Initially I felt foolish, then I realized that I could finally participate in the familial and communal sharing patterns that I had benefited from during my stay.

The sharing of bush food holds nutritional and spiritual significance for elders because they were raised on them, many dislike store-bought food (Degnen 1996), they are knowledgeable about living in the bush, and they know the significance of respecting the animal spirits (Armitage 1985). I was aware of these cultural beliefs and the grandparents of my host family supplied most of the bush food I ate during my time in Kawawachikamach, so I shared the fish with them. Although we were unable to communicate in each other's language, when I presented them with the fish we 'spoke' on a level much deeper than talking.

Food and Identity

Food and subsistence practices are used to assert political presence, as with the James Bay Cree (Feit 1986, Adelson 1992, Richardson 1976), it symbolically represents who they are as a distinct cultural group (Degnen 1996, Fouillard 1995), and reflects ambivalence about cultural identity. I witnessed many instances where people's involvement with food (both store-bought and country) symbolized difficulties in the transition to a life that blends traditional and modern cultural influences. The ensuing paragraphs briefly discuss a few examples of identity ambivalence.

The concept of identity is multi-vocal, meaning different things at different times or places. In Kawawachikamach one of my closest friends was Sara (pseudonym), a young single mother in her early 20s. In a conversation about our favorite foods she mentioned recently learning how to process bush food. Before she learned this skill her grandmother embarrassed her about her inability; once she learned the skill her grandmother was very proud and so was she. On the other hand, Sara disliked the smell of the fish I received on the fishing trip which surprised me seeing as she liked to prepare and eat bush food. The issue of identity ambivalence made more sense when I remembered that Sara had not been raised in the village and had only moved there with her son a few months before I arrived. Sara had told me it was to fit into life in Kawawachikamach, interactions with her peers made her feel like she was not a "true" Naskapi. Not knowing how to prepare bush foods may have compounded her feelings of isolation as she repeatedly told me that knowing how to do so was part of being Naskapi. The bush food preparation, initially caused Sara to feel insecure about her identity and then helped her to express herself as an authentic member of the community.

In the next example the issue of identity ambivalence is related to store-bought food. On several occasions my field mother (Louise) purchased food she did not know how to prepare so she either read the directions over several times, asked me to prepare the food, said that she forgot how to prepare the food, or put it away without asking for advice. Often she and her 19 year-old daughter argued about the proper way to prepare the food. Her daughter usually criticized Louise for not knowing what to do and for being so "traditional", whereas Louise saw her daughter as bossy. This situation shows the effects of different life experiences across the generations, with the younger woman appearing more knowledgeable about store-bought food. However, I also observed instances of the daughter's ambivalence about these kinds of food. For example, once the daughter had a large amount of money to spend on food, yet she appeared uncertain about what to buy, settling in the end for some junk food and fruit. This example indicated that people of all ages are adjusting to new products and that their unfamiliarity with store foods is a potential identity conflict.

These examples have indicated that knowing how to prepare bush food and eating them is an important part of what it means to be Naskapi. Country foods are not eaten or prepared daily so knowing how to prepare store-bought foods has become integral to their eating habits, survival and identity. However, store food has not yet been imbued with any identifiable cultural meaning. The preparation of store foods are sites of potential conflict, not just between generations about food, but about Naskapi cultural identity. Naskapi relationships to food, spirituality, sharing, and cultural identity illustrate the tenacity of traditional values in the contemporary setting. Food preparation is a powerful medium of expression used by individuals to mark their sense of achieved identity or to symbolize identity ambivalence.

Comparison with other Groups

The ritualistic eating of food, especially sacred foods, and the development of practices to avoid contamination of such foods, is a common feature of many subarctic and arctic peoples (Riddington 1983). Tanner 's (1979) account of the Mistassini Cree of northern Quebec's treatment of bush food and animals, especially those of the caribou, is very similar to that of the Naskapi. While the mokoshon ceremony was not a central component of Cree religion, they used scapulamancy and the drum to divine hunting spots and to communicate with animal spirits. As with the Naskapi, they regarded contamination of bush foods, in particular animal bones, as spiritually dangerous and a sign of disrespect to the animal spirits that provided them with food. To avoid contamination of animal bones (either by dogs eating them or careless placement of the remains by other people) they were placed high in tree tops or atop special scaffolds created specifically for this purpose. Avoidance of bush food and animal contamination is also an integral part of Inuit spirituality. Their intimate relationship between human-animal-environment, which directly affects their patterns of and ideas about food consumption, is currently in flux (Purich 1992, Nuttall 1992). High levels of contaminants in arctic animals and plants pose serious health threats if eaten in large quantities over a long period of time, the issue of food contamination is a particularly important part of Inuit decision-making processes regarding food (O'Neil et al. 1997). As they decide which animals to hunt and eat, scientific "facts" about the level of contaminants in their traditional food source are weighed against their indigenous beliefs about the spiritual ties between humans and animals. The spiritual connection between humans and animals is celebrated and consecrated in the act of consuming foods like seal meat and blood, so decisions the Inuit make about eating traditional foods are often very emotionally and spiritually charged and difficult to resolve Borre (1991). Consumption, treatment and protection of animals and the food they provide, continues to be invested with significant spiritual meaning. Naskapi use of food supports this continued respect that many First Nations people have for the sacred relationship between humans, animals, and the spirit world.

The link between traditional foods and elders is noted by scholars working with Aboriginal peoples from many areas (Ross 1992, Richardson 1976, Riddington 1988). Like Naskapi Elders, Elders from other areas have a special affinity for these foods because they were usually raised solely on traditional food, prefer them over store-bought varieties, and are the most knowledgeable about the rules that need to be followed to properly respect animals and the spirit world. Providing Elders with these foods and respecting them helps to ensure the survival of the group (Armitage 1985,1991).

Along with the spiritual sanctions regarding food sharing, there are many social and political functions of sharing. Among Aboriginal hunter-gatherers in the Canadian subarctic and arctic, many of whom traveled in small, mobile, and highly interdependent groups, cohesion was necessary for survival. Sharing acted as a form of social control, ensuring harmony among the group (Briggs 1970, 1995). People's awareness of the negative social and emotional ramifications of not sharing food with other members of the group (i.e. ostracizing, gossip, and exclusion from the group) was such that stinginess about food was a very uncommon form of behaviour. Henriksen (1973) showed how the sharing of food also functions as ideology and a form of temporary and small scale political leadership. Sharing practices among a group of Innu in Labrador were such that the hunter who shot a caribou was obliged to give the animal to his hunting partner. If a hunter transgressed this culturally sanctioned rule he would risk serious social disruption within the group, which could endanger the lives of everyone in the hunting camp. He also observed differences between sharing practices in the bush and in their coastal village of Davis Inlet. In the bush, refusal to share could lead to death and serious social disharmony, it was rarely observed. In the community, the socio-cultural context of life was not yet infused with the same kind of deep spiritual and historical meaning, which led to many instances of people behaving in a stingy manner about food, even bush food. During my field research Naskapi used similar food sharing practices in the bush and community. This is most likely a result of the frequent movements the Naskapi make between the bush and the settlement, a system of living that was not well established among the people of Davis Inlet at the time of Henriksen's research.

Hunting practices and the assertion of Aboriginal hunter's rights are used politically to resist the encroachment of Euro-Canadian institutions and powers for a variety of Aboriginal peoples (Richardson 1976, Feit 1986, Adelson 1992). Such efforts on behalf of Aboriginal people are powerful expressions of the strong links between hunting, bush foods, and cultural identity and their desire to continue such practices and consumption patterns in the contemporary context. Another connection commonly made with respect to identity and food pertains to the health and nutritional properties of bush foods.

Degnen (1996) argues that eating bush foods is a way to become healthier and stronger, and it is also part of the larger process of community healing. In this instance bush foods are understood within the context of psycho-social suffering and are viewed as the tie that binds people together as they collectively reconstruct their lives and sense of themselves as a people.

These analyses allow us to understand how contemporary food treatment and harvesting practices reflect the different ways in which Aboriginal people construct and assert their cultural identity. However, the emphasis that is placed on bush or traditional foods seems somewhat misplaced for two reasons. First, in most Aboriginal communities people do not subsist solely on traditional foods but rely on a combination of bush and store-bought foods, with the latter making up the bulk of their diet (Wein *et al.*1989, Kuhnlein 1984). As the Naskapi vignette featuring Louise and her daughter illustrated, although store-bought foods have little cultural meaning when compared to bush foods, this does not mean that they play a neutral role in their lives. On the contrary, store-bought foods and the preparation of them were shown to be very rich sites from which to observe how people negotiated their identities and express feelings of doubt or ambivalence about their relationship to these foods.

The second point is that store-bought foods and their preparation can be very useful tools to gain insight into not only how individuals construct their notions of who they are, but how this process and kind of identity expression differs across the generations. This was illustrated in the two vignettes involving members of Louise's family. Many writers have commented on such differential food preferences, how elders display an affinity for traditional foods and younger age groups generally subsist on a combination of the two kinds of food, usually more on the store-bought varieties (Wein *et al.* 1989). This dichotomy between food types is often explained in relation to different lifestyles, hunting practices, and varying levels of interaction with Euro-Canadian society among age groups in a given population (O'Neil 1983, 1986, Berkes and Farkas 1978). Although this is an accurate reflection of how food is consumed and regarded in most Aboriginal communities, these studies also tend to ignore the role of store-bought foods as a medium of expressing people's cultural identity.

These points enhance our understanding of Aboriginal people's treatment of food in the modern setting, and are directly linked with larger issues that influence how individuals and communities construct their notions of cultural identity. It has been acknowledged that the decrease in hunting and trapping among Aboriginal peoples since their move to settled life, and the concurrent decline in eating bush foods, has had devastating psycho-social and cultural effects on their way of life and their sense of who they are as a people or nation (Ross 1992, Wadden 1991, Scott 1986). The situation becomes problematic when Aboriginal people's identities are treated as homogenous, fixed entities, as only having meaning when linked with a past way of life that has been reconstructed in the modern context as being ideal and superior to that of the present day. The cultural values and ideologies that dictated people's lives in the past continue to define and shape how individuals organize their lives and think of themselves today. However, in their day to day living Aboriginal people draw upon a complex blend of cultural influences, Aboriginal and non-Aboriginal, as they construct their identities. That First Nations people themselves do not rely solely on the past to define who they are supports my contention that in our analyses of the link between food and identity bush foods should not be favoured over the store-bought varieties.

Conclusion

In summary, Naskapi attitudes toward food reflects the persistence of traditional values and beliefs, and how changes in this sphere of cultural activity affect people's ideas about food and themselves. Bush foods and store-bought varieties are powerful symbols of people's sense of pride in, or ambivalence about, their cultural identity. The role of non-traditional foods in the process of identity construction are particularly important. Although store-bought foods and their preparation are not yet invested with any significant cultural values, they are very useful indicators of the process of identity expression and negotiation. These data call attention to the complex roles played by different kinds of food in the lives of contemporary Aboriginal people. The critical analysis of the cultural expression of food is extremely useful as a means to gain insight into the changing nature of identity construction and negotiation among Aboriginal people.

Acknowledgments

Contributions from the Northern Science Training Program, Institute of Social and Economic Research at Memorial University of

Newfoundland, and my friends and informants are gratefully acknowledged. Their contributions made this research possible. My field mother is thanked for assuming the role of my mother during my field research, introducing me to people in the village, including me in family and community celebrations, and becoming a very close friend.

References Cited

Adelson, N. 1992. *Being Alive Well: Indigenous Beliefs as Opposition Among The Whapmagoostui Cree.* Unpublished Doctoral Dissertation. Anthropology, McGill University.

Armitage, P. 1985. *Domestic Production Among the Innu of La Romain: Persistence or Transformation?* Unpublished M.A. Thesis. Anthropology, Memorial Univ. of Newfoundland.

Armitage, P. 1991. *The Innu (Montagnais-Naskapi).* NY: Chelsea Hs.

Berkes, F. and Farkas, C.1978. Eastern James Bay Cree Indians: wild food use and nutrition. *Ecol Fd &Nut* 7:155-172.

Borre, K. 1991. Seal blood, Inuit blood, and diet: a biocultural model of physiology, cultural identity. *Med Anthr Qrtly*5(1):48-62.

Briggs, J. 1970. *Never in Anger.* Massachusetts: Harvard University

Briggs, J. 1995. Vicissitudes of attachment: Nurturance and dependence in Canadian Inuit family relationships, old and new. *Arctic Medical Research.* 54(1):24-32.

Degnen, C. 1996. *Healing Sheshatshit: Innu Identity and Community Healing.* Unpub. M.A. Thesis. Anthropology, McGill Univ.

Feit, H. 1986. Hunting and the quest for power: The James Bay Cree and the whiteman in the 20th C. In B.Morrison & C. Wilson (Eds.) *Native Peoples-The Canadian Experience.*(181-223). Toronto: McClelland & Stewart.

Fouillard, C. (Ed.) 1995. *Gathering Voices.* Vanc:Douglas&McIntyre.

Henriksen, G. 1973. *Hunters in the Barrens. The Naskapi on the Edge of the White Man's World.* St. John's: ISER Books.

Kuhnlein, H. 1984. Traditional and contemporary Nuxalk Foods. *Nutrition Research* (4): 780-809.

Leacock, E. 1986. The Montagnais-Naskapi of the Labrador Peninsula. In R. Morrison & C. Wilson (Eds).*Native Peoples Canadian Experience* (pp.140-170). TO: McClelland and Stewart.

Mailhot, J. 1986. Behind everyone's horizon stands the Naskapi. *Ethnohistory* 33:384-418.

Nuttall, M. 1992. *Arctic Homeland.* Toronto: University of Toronto

O'Neil, J. 1983. *Is It Cool To Be An Eskimo?: A Study of Stress, Identity, Coping, and Health Among Canadian Inuit Young Men.* Unpub. Doctoral Dissertation. Dept of Anthro. Uof CA (San Fran-Berk).

O'Neil, J. 1986. Colonial stress in the Canadian Arctic: An ethnography of young adults changing.In C. Janes, R. Stall and S. Gifford (Eds.) *Anthropology and Epidemiology* (pp. 249-274). Dordrecht: D. Reidel Pub.

O'Neil, J., Elias, B. and Yassi, A. 1997. Poisoned food: Cultural resistance to the contaminants discourse in Nunavik. *Arctic Anthropology.* 34(1):29-40.

Orchard, T. 1998. *Teenagers of the Tundra: The Teenage Experience Among The Naskapi of Kawawachikamach, Quebec.* Unpublished M.A. Thesis. Dept of Anthropology. Memorial U of Nfld.

Purich, D. 1992. *The Inuit and Their Land.* Toronto: James Lorimer

Richardson, B. 1976. *Strangers Devour The Land.* NY: A.A. Knopf.

Riddington, R. 1983. From artifice to artifact: Stages in the industrialization of a northern hunting people. *Journal of Canadian Studies.* 18(3):55-66.

Riddington, R. 1988. *Trail To Heaven-Knowledge and Narrative in a Northern Native Community.* Van: Douglas & McIntyre.

Robbins, R.1973. Alcohol and identity struggles. *Am. Anthro* 75:99-122.

Robbins, R. 1988. *Modernization and Social Change Among the Schefferville Naskapi.* Unpub.State U of NY at Plattsburgh.

Ross, R. 1992. *Dancing With a Ghost-Exploring Indian Reality.* Markham: Reed Books

Scott, C. 1986. Hunting territories, hunting bosses and communal production coastal James Bay Cree. *Anthro* 28(1-2):163-173.

Shepard, R. and Rode, A. 1996. *The Health Consequences of 'Modernization'. Circumpolar Peoples.* Cambridge Univ P.

Speck, F. 1935. *Naskapi. Savage Hunters of the Labrador Peninsula.* Norman: University of Oklahoma .

Tanner, A. 1979. *Bringing Home Animals. Religious Ideology, Mode of Production, Mistassini Cree Hunters.* St. John's: ISER

Wadden, M. 1991. *Nitassinan.* Vancouver: Douglas & McIntyre.

Wein, E., Sabry, J., and Evers, F. 1989. Food health beliefs of Northern Native Canadians. *Ecology, Food and Nutr.* (23):177-188.

---

[1] Treena Orchard, recipient of numerous awards including the J.G. Fletcher Award and University of Manitoba Graduate Fellowship, is a doctoral student in medical anthropology.

The Omushkego Oral History Project

Louis Bird and George Fulford[1]

Abstract

> In this paper, Fulford describes and contextualizes
> the Omushkego Oral History Project within scholarly
> research paradigms pertaining to First Nations peoples.
> This is followed by Bird's dialogic text using the
> Omushkego story telling tradition. Bird and Fulford
> discuss their work together and in so doing provide
> a model for ethnohistoric research incorporating both
> Aboriginal and academic perspectives. Issues regarding
> the translation and transcription of oral texts are
> also identified.

Introduction and Methods

The Omushkego Oral History Project began in June 1999, when an interdisciplinary team at the University of Winnipeg commenced to research and write a history of the Omushkegowak ("Swampy Cree") people living on the southwest coast of Hudson and James Bay. The team's work revolves around Omushkego storyteller and elder Louis Bird who has collected more than 300 hours of audiotapes recording his people's legends and oral history. Bird, a member of the Winisk First Nation, spent the last 35 years amassing this remarkable collection of interviews, stories and personal reflections. About 75 per cent of the material is recorded in the Omushkego language, with the remainder being in English. The Omushkego Oral History Project is coordinated by George Fulford; other members of the team include: Jennifer Brown, Doug Hamm, Maureen Matthews, Carolyn Podruchny, Mark Ruml, Donna Sutherland, and Kimberley Wilde. The team is headquartered in the Centre for Rupert's Land Studies at the University of Winnipeg. The Social Sciences and Humanities Research Council has provided funding to transcribe and translate thirty of Louis Bird's tapes, these funds are gratefully acknowledged and additional funds are being solicited.

The process used to conduct this research is as follows: In phase one CBC Radio journalist Maureen Matthews assist Louis Bird with the selecting and re-recording of stories from Bird's collection onto digital audiotape. In phase two the stories are translated and transcribed by replaying the digital master tape so Louis Bird can record a simultaneous English translation on a second digital audiotape. At times Louis Bird also provides an interpretive commentary in English. The second tape, which contains the original story in the Omushkego language, Bird's English translation and his commentary, is then used for transcription. Bird transcribes the story into the Omushkego language using a syllabic font on his laptop computer. Other team members assist transcribing the English translation and commentary. The first draft or preliminary format of the transcription is laid out onto a page divided into three columns. The original version in the Omushkego language occupies the central column, the English translation is to the left and the commentary is to the right. The text is then checked for typographical errors. In the final format Louise Bird will likely provide an Omushkego translation of his English commentary, and both versions will either be annotated to the text or presented in a separate interpretive section. We envision two volumes to be published under the aegis of the Centre for Rupert's Land Studies. The first will be authored by Bird and will contain three sections. Section one will comprise the Omushkego and English versions of the stories laid out on facing pages with annotations presented as endnotes. Section two will consist of Louis Bird's commentary in the Omushkego language and English. Section three will consist of a glossary of Omushkego words. The second volume we envision will be an edited collection of interpretive essays written by members of the Omushkego Oral History Project and outlining their own research contributions.

Phase three of the project involves ethnohistoric and linguistic research. Once a story has been translated and transcribed, copies are provided to team members who are assigned the task of combing journals, post records and other manuscripts from the Hudson's Bay Company Archives. The goal is to provide supporting documentation and additional provenience for Bird's stories. Other members assist Bird in analyzing and interpreting the stories to determine what they reveal about pre- and post-contact Omushkego life. Still others are involved in compiling a glossary of key Omushkego terms to help readers understand those subtleties of the Omushkego language which may elude translation.

These findings will be annotated to the final Cree and English versions of the manuscript. Dauenhauer and Dauenhauer (1999) provide an excellent description of the process of editing, transcribing, and annotating Native-language texts which serves as a model for our own work.

Other Related Oral History Research

The Omushkego Oral History Project is the first known attempt to link a traditional Omushkego storyteller with a team of academic researchers in order to create a history combining "indigenous" and "academic" perspectives in both the Omushkego and English languages. It is also the first known project in which the storyteller exercises complete editorial control in all phases of the work. This is entirely appropriate, given Bird's considerable expertise and extraordinary investment of time in creating his collection of stories. There are, nevertheless, a significant number of scholarly books and articles pertaining to Omushkego language and culture that have been compiled by other academic researchers. Foremost is Ellis' (1995) extensive collection of Moose and Swampy Cree stories. Gleaned from an extensive residence in Kashechewan, Ontario during the early 1960s, these stories have particular value to linguists and folklorists. Ellis includes an informative introduction and detailed notes to each of the narratives and an exhaustive glossary of Swampy and Moose Cree stems. Unfortunately it includes almost no oral history; cultural and historical contexts, including information on traditional Mushkego spiritual beliefs and practices and on the fur trade, are also lacking.

The Algonquian Text Society at the University of Manitoba, has produced a number of other fine collections of narratives in the Plains Cree and Ojibwe languages, with English translations (Bear *et al.* 1992, Vandall and Douquette 1987, Williams 1991, Whitecalf 1993). The University of Alberta Press has also published a number of such texts (Kegg 1991, Minde 1997). These texts are produced as sources of linguistic data and as curriculum materials in Native-language classes. They are compiled with a keen eye for formal accuracy and detail, and the life histories of the Native contributors to these books are of considerable interest. With the exception of Whitecalf, these stories are generally of limited ethnographic and historical interest. This also applies to Bloomfield's (1930) classic collection of Plains Cree texts.

Hallowell (1955, 1976, 1992) and Preston (1975, 1982) produced excellent ethnographies of Algonquian peoples focused on documenting and exploring traditional worldviews and values. Unfortunately, these researchers' limited recording of and fluency in Algonquian languages and consequent reliance on translators, restricted the corpus of material, particularly in the realm of ethnohistory. A more historical orientation by Flannery (1995) and Beardy and Coutts (1996) are rich in stories and in glimpses of Cree culture and lifeways of 60-100 years ago. They also pay little attention to language and deeper issues of world view and philosophy.

Moving beyond the area of Algonquian ethnohistory, projects of similar scope to that of the Omushkego Oral History Project have been undertaken by Parks and DeMallie (1992) and Cruikshank (1990, 1996, and 1998). Appreciating the critical importance of historical texts in Native languages, Parks and DeMallie have collaborated with fluent Native scholars to work towards a new level of understanding the experiences of First Nations peoples. Members of the Omushkego Oral History Project share their goal of documenting authentic Native voices, but have the good fortune of working with living texts spoken by living voices. Like Parks and DeMallie (1992: 106), we seek to combine approaches from history, anthropology, religious studies and linguistics with authentic voices to "situate native language texts in the fullest possible historical and cultural context".

Cruikshank has devoted her career to documenting the oral histories of Yukon elders. As in our own project, she presented her most significant work in two volumes: unedited stories (1990) and her own reflections and interpretations (1998). Looking at how different kinds of narrative influence our understanding of the past and citing Turner's (1988) distinction between history and myth, Cruikshank (1996: 451) makes the important statement that "both [history and myth] can be understood as representing particular kinds of historical consciousness." Nabokov (1996: 24) makes a similar observation, stating that myths and legends "fall into that time zone which collective memories almost touch." But there is yet another factor which links the Omushkego sense of mythic and historic time: a sense of place. As Fulford and Bird (1998: 2) have observed, "legend and history merge with the Omushkegowak landscape as a kind of personal and collective storehouse of dreams and memories." Brody (1981) and Chatwin (1987) made similar insights into the merging of legend, history and landscape in Aboriginal cultures.

In addition to the scholarly works already mentioned, members of the Omushkego Oral History Project are guided by the recommendations of the Royal Commission on Aboriginal Peoples (RCAP). In its report the Royal Commission emphasized that "language is one of the main instruments for transmitting culture from one generation to the other and for communicating meaning and making sense of collective experience" (Government of Canada 1996: 91). It also highlighted the need for educational institutions at all levels to help develop Aboriginal language programs and culturally sensitive curriculum. The RCAP report also emphasized (Ibid. 88) that "records and recollections of [Aboriginal] history should be collected, preserved and made more accessible to all Canadians before it is too late." Furthermore, "positive action is needed to help those seeking ways to express, conserve, restore and document their cultures in all their richness and diversity" (Ibid.: 89). Moreover, the Royal Commission acknowledged the importance of Elders as "living embodiments of aboriginal traditions and cultures" and declared that "new institutions must build on the core teachings and aboriginal traditions and the contemporary insight of the elders" (1996: 103).

In the spirit of the RCAP recommendations, members of the Omushkego Oral History Project seek to promote the fullest possible understanding of Bird's stories. In so doing, we are ultimately guided by Bird's own rich knowledge and life experience as an Omushkego storyteller.

Discussing the Omushkego Oral History Project

The ideas in the following dialogue were first discussed during an open-ended, unscripted presentation on December 3rd, 1999 at the University of Manitoba. When we were invited to submit our presentation for inclusion in this volume we agreed that Loius Bird would make a 90-minute tape-recording about his reflections on the process of collecting legends and oral history, which George Fulford would transcribe. Working together, the authors selected portions of the resulting transcript to be included in this paper. Fulford then inserted his own words into appropriate sections of the text, commenting on many of the issues raised by Bird. In addition, he inserted a quotation from F. X. Fafard's *Catechism de Persévérance* (1924), about which he invited Bird to comment. Louis Bird's commentary was inserted and the authors reviewed the complete text. In response to an anonymous reviewer's requests, George Fulford added an introduction and clarification.

The dialogue between Bird and Fulford is a hybrid, neither a purely oral nor a purely written form of discourse. The reviewer astutely noted this, commenting that the dialogic text felt less like a dialogue than "two voices in parallel, simultaneously 'talking on the page'". The phrase "talking on the page" refers to Murray and Rice's (1999) seminal collection of essays on editing Aboriginal oral texts. This stylistic difference reflects the fact that the authors are "talking" in two different registers: Louis Bird in an oral monologue transcribed from audiotape and George Fulford in a written monologue, to be inserted between selected portions of Bird's monologue. This parallelism also reflects differences in the authors' personal styles of presentation. But a careful reading shows that these differences are amplified as a result of the techniques used to create this textual artifice.

Exigencies of time forced us to present our ideas in the way that we have. While neither author would recommend this model of writing to others, or necessarily use it again ourselves, it has permitted us to situate our original dialogue in the context of what we are doing in the Omushkego Oral History Project and to present our words in a way which captures some of the feel of what we originally said. In addition, the process of creating this dialogic text highlights some of the vexing problems that beset all who endeavor to transcribe oral discourse.

L.B. (Louis Bird)

I began collecting stories in 1965. The very simple reason that got me thinking about collecting stories - our elders who have seen the actual traditional cultural activities. The way we used to do things. These guys were dying. [Throughout the dialogic text Bird tends to refer to his teachers as male even though the earliest and most profound influences on his storytelling were his Mother and maternal Grandmother. Gender-specific references in the text is the consequence of Bird expressing himself in his second language rather than evidence of sexism or bias (also see Brown 1992). Gender-specific pronouns and nouns referring to an individual's sex do not exist in the Omushkego language, which defines gender in terms of animacy.] 1965 was the time the last two elders like that died. That's what made me awake. These people used to tell us stories. They know all about the old culture - living in the bush. That's what got me to think we are losing them and we're not going to hear them any more. And I thought maybe we should start collecting stories. But how to save them? It was not possible to write them. So the easiest thing to do was to record the things as one could remember. In that way they could be kept somewhere. A kind of rough draft. That's what I thought. Because they were dying off. The real ones. You see, the ones that died in 1965 - they were the last people who were born in the 1800s. So they were the ones who actually lived in the bush, being skillful and self-sufficient. They did not rely on anyone. They lived in the wilderness very masterfully. They know the life. And they're the ones who told the stories about what they saw when they were young. And they were the ones who heard their grandfathers [and grandmothers] telling them how the life was before [contact with Europeans]. So that's the reason I wanted to record their stories. From 1965 I began to do that. I just recorded any elder that I can meet - from Moosonee to Kashechewan and Albany, Attawapiskat, Winisk, Fort Severn, and people originally from York Factory that I met in Churchill and those later on that I met in Gillam, where they moved after they abandoned the old community of York Factory. So that's how I began to collect stories.

G.F. (George Fulford)
Doug Ellis has also collected Omushkegowak elders' stories on audiotape. His book and accompanying audiotapes comprise a substantial work of scholarship on the Omushkegowak people. Ellis shows great respect for his Native informants, whose voices comprise the vast majority of the pages of his book. There is a good sample of Cree legends and narratives, an insightful introduction which traces some of the major genres of Omushkego storytelling, and a really useful glossary of Omushkego words at the end of the book. What makes your collection of stories different from that of Ellis?

L.B.
That book doesn't talk much about our original culture. The shamanistic part is missing. It's not total. In order to understand the legends he wrote, one has to understand what makes the story interesting [from an Omushkego point of view]. And what makes the story interesting is shamanism. Because he left that out, the stories are very weak not as powerful as they used to be. And Ellis does not interpret the legends. He does not show the reader how to apply them to real life.

G.F.
Perhaps that blind spot in the book is there because Ellis is an Anglican priest. But really, it could be said about practically any book about Omushkegowak people that was written by an outsider. Where Ellis' book is strong is in his attempt to understand the Omushkego language. For instance, he makes an important distinction between the Omushkego words *aatanoohkana* 'legends or sacred stories' and *tipaachimowina* 'news, gossip, stories (including oral history)'. As I understand it, *tipaachimowina* can be historically contextualized whereas *aatanoohkana* take place in a mystical place and time. The two kinds of stories seem to be situated on a time continuum. Legends are historical accounts of events that took place

at a time nobody can remember; events in more recent stories can be more or less situated at a particular place and time. But, as you have told me before, legends and stories are equally real accounts of historical events. The old stories *kete tipaachimowina* are what in English we call "oral history". Some of these old stories in your collection go back to the very first contact between Omushkegowak and European peoples more than 400 years ago. Beyond this horizon lies the mythic world of *aatanoohkana*.

L.B.
Aatanoohkana are real stories that happened a long time ago. They actually happened. Take Wisaakechahk. What happened in his stories happened to a real person. We remember the story, but we forget that guy's name. So we insert that name "Wisaakechahk". It's the same with Chahkaapiish. His real name has been forgotten. Same thing with Wemishoosh. These people existed way before the time of Europeans, maybe 10,000 years ago. So actually the legends are real happenings from way past.

G.F.
So much is lost when a story is translated from *ininiimowin* ['the Omushkego language'] into English. I never cease to be amazed about the way in which Omushkego words are put together. Omushkego words resemble entire phrases and even sentences in English. The way your language works reveals so much about traditional Omushkego culture. For example, the word *tipaachimoowin* is composed of the initial morpheme *tipaa-* 'to measure or judge', the medial stem *aachimo* 'to tell a story' and the abstract final *-win* which changes verbs into nouns. [Morphemes are the smallest word-like units to convey meaning. In most Omushkego words they consist of initials (roots), medials and finals (stems) (Ahenakew 1987, Goddard 1990, Wolfart 1996).] A variety of inflections conveying complex grammatical information are added to roots and stems. My analysis of these and other Omushkego words focusses on the relationship of linguistic form and meaning and thus departs somewhat from more formalistic approaches. *Tipaachimoowin* is thus literally "a measured telling". On the other hand, *aatanoohkaan* begins with the initial *aata*, which is likely an abbreviated variant of *aachimo*. Next comes the medial *noohko*, which seems to be a variant of *nohko* meaning 'to become visible or manifest'. The abstract final *-kaan* (a variant of *kan*) conveys the idea of something manufactured or created by humans. Both Omushkego words for "story" thus share the root *aachi* (and its variant *aata*) which may be derived from *itwe* 'to speak or say'. Alternately, these words may be

derived from the root *aachi* (and its variant *aata*) which conveys the idea of impeded movement. *Aatanoohkaan* might thus be conceptualized as "a manifestation of something stuck or caught". Language does this when it is harnessed in the aid of memory. It captures images of ideas and events. This idea of a legend being a tool to catch images from the distant past makes me think of the "dream catchers" that were traditionally hung on Omushkego cradle boards to attract good dreams and spirit helpers. Legends and dream catchers may work in similar ways.

The Omushkego word for legend conveys a lot of information. But there is more. In *ininiimowin* words are distinguished on the basis of whether they are animate or inanimate. Sometimes the same word can be both. In such cases, animacy is used to convey a particular nuance or shade of meaning. You can tell whether an Omushkego word is animate or inanimate on the basis of its plural suffix. So the word *aatanohkana* means legends. The inanimate plural marker *-a* tells you that legends are inanimate. But the word *aatanohkanak* means the characters in legends. The animate plural marker *-ak* tells you that the characters in legends are animate. The distinction between legends and the characters in legends is not merely a simple matter of grammatical convention. We find a similar pattern in the Cree words for "dreams" (*pwaamowina*, which are inanimate) and "dream spirits" (*pwaamowinak*, which are animate). Dream spirits, like the characters in legends, inhabit their own separate worlds. These worlds are animated by the beings which inhabit them. Without such beings - without a life force or energy - these world are inert. Dead. They come to life through the agency of the beings which inhabit them. In his essays about the Saulteaux people along the Berens River, the anthropologist A. Hallowell used the term "other-than-human persons" to describe the beings inhabiting dreams and legends. He also states that the Saulteux people (whose language is very close to that of their Omushkegowak neighbours to the north) called such spirits "grandfathers". The Saulteaux and Omushkegowak people use the same term - *nimooshominaanak* 'our grandfathers' - to describe such beings.

L.B.

What you have said is true. But it is said in the way that an anthropologist speaks. When an Omushkego uses his language he knows what it means. It doesn't have to be explained or analyzed. It is usually an outsider, someone who doesn't fully understand, who wants to ask "Why?" Now I will tell you how my elders used to teach. Legends and dreams were our guides. I was aware of this when I was recording the legends and stories. I didn't want to impose an order on them. I wanted to have the stories just as I heard them. So I just recorded everything. As much as I can remember what they say. And I just record it. Mostly it was culture. Traditional activities. And *mitewiwin* ['shamanism']. I asked the elders about *mitewiwin* because I knew they were the ones who knew it. How it was before Christianity. How the people connect themselves with the spiritual things and the material things. So they tell me all those things. But some of them didn't want to tell me because they had been instructed not to tell the young children about those things, because they were considered "devil's work". So they were reluctant to tell me exactly how it's done. But persistently I tried to convince them that I would not play with the things they gave me, I would not make fun of it. I was just doing it for the purpose of recording our Omushkegowak history and that in the future this information will be very useful for the next generation - those who will want to know how their ancestors used to live. And that's why I did that.

So I did collect stories - all kinds of them. At first I just put them in randomly. I didn't organize anything. Just the way I hear it. I didn't mind doing that because I was only collecting. Just as if I collect a bundle of things and pile them there. That's what I did in my mind as I collect the stories. I didn't organize them. I just put them in a tape recording. I was thinking that after they had been written down they could be organized according to different subjects. Is it possible to divide different subjects? Will it be any better if it was divided into each subject? That is what I planned to do at that time. I thought the subjects could be separated from the total. One subject like *mitewiwin* could be separated from the culture, just to talk about it. But that doesn't work. When you want to hear about the total First Nation culture you have to include the spiritual practice. That's the only way to understand totally what the First Nations culture is. If you separate spirituality from the rest there is nothing complete. There's always something questionable when you do that. Only after you have heard all of that do you begin to see the whole picture - what the First Nation culture was. And that's what I wanted to capture. And that's what I have.

G.F.
I have always been interested in the derivation of that word *mitewiwin*. Anthropologists have tended to translate it as "shamanism". But the word itself says so much. There's that *win* ending again, making *mitewi-* (the doing of *mitewiwin*) into a noun. Then there's the rest of the word. In the Omushkego language the heart is *mitehi*, a hand drum is *tewihikan* and a

camp or village is *otenaw*. The idea of intense feeling or throbbing pain is conveyed by the root *tew*. It seems as if the heart, the drum, the centre of the camp and an intense throbbing feeling are somehow all connected in the word *mitewiwin*. How do you understand it?

L.B.

Well, *mitewiwin* is the name of a method of doing something that you believe. *Mitewiwin* means the same as what we mean with the English word "Christianity". Practicing Christianity is what has been taught a long time ago and been carried on and institutionalized and used in one culture of many different nations. So *mitewiwin* is just like naming that action - the way our ancestors have begin to form their ideas connecting the material world and the spiritual life. This is what *mitewiwin* means. But there are certain actions to be done before one can actually wholly practice *mitewiwin*. It's just like any other spirituality. They have to want it. They have to believe it. They have to sacrifice themselves. They have to purify themselves. They have to fast. They have to deny themselves luxuries when they want to train themselves. And that's what *mitewiwin* is beginning to do. If you don't do that, you don't have it.

G.F.

The French sociologist Emile Durkheim (1965)wrote that "religion is something essentially social." What he meant by that was that the sacred is really only the everyday world of people, elevated onto a higher plane. You could say that Durkheim turned the Genesis creation story on its head. Rather than God creating man in his own image, Durkheim suggests that Man makes god in his own image. Now one may dispute Durkheim's scientific understanding of spirituality, since it seems to be based on a concept of disbelief rather than belief. But the idea that a people's spirituality is rooted in their way of life has always fascinated me. Here's an example of what I mean. I grew up in a big old rambling house surrounded by pastures and woodlots. The St. Lawrence River was my back yard. I can't tell you how many hours I spent sprawled out by the water's edge, listening to the lapping of the waves on the rocky shoreline and watching the changing patterns of the clouds in the sky. That way of life remains with me, even though I've spent most of my adult years in cities. I'm not religious in any conventional meaning of the term. But I do have a concept of spirituality which is based largely on my experience with Nature. I'd say that my concept of spirituality is based largely on my childhood experiences, with the way I was socialized to interact with and understand my environment. I've only spent three years living in the North, but based on my limited experience of living and travelling in the bush I imagine that growing up in that environment must have had a profound influence on you and others of your generation, that you still carry the bush in your heart. So now I'm getting to the big question. Do you think young people who have grown up in cities can learn to successfully practice spiritual traditions such as *mitewiwin* that originated in the bush?

L.B.

That is truly a very good question. I'm always trying to compare *mitewiwin* with Christianity when I'm asked this question. How does the Christian become a holy person if he lives in the city or he lives in the bush? It's the same question. So, this *mitewiwin* began in the wilderness. That's where it originates. That's where the elders acquire it. They grew up in the wilderness and they practice it there. And it supposedly comes easy to them in the wilderness, where it's pure and there's no pollution, no noise, no other attraction but pure mind when they are going into what they can seek. That's called *nataawepawaamowin* "dream quest". So they have to be very pure. *Nataawepowaamowin* - you can do that only once. It just means "to search for a dream". But there's another kind of dream quest too. *Shiishikwanipowaamowin* means you do it again and again and again. You can dream what you want to dream. But with *nataawepowaamowin* you only want to dream about this one thing. That's what *nataawepowaamowin* means.

The old people prefer to do *shiishikwanipowaamowin* in the fall. In the fall when there's nothing else to bother them. There are less flies at this time. So you can lay down without bugs. The only thing that bothers them at this time is the cold. The cold makes them sort of half-asleep. You know the way it is when you get cold - you sort of get sleepy. And that's what makes them into that state. They keep themselves in that state and nothing else bothers them. So they really concentrate. They forget they have a body. They begin to see things in their mind. So in the fall - we usually recommend it. If the young people want to do it, we advise the early spring, just before when the flies are. Just when it's mild enough to spend a night out without freezing to death. They're not supposed to take a comfortable bed or blanket. They are told to take very little. Do you know how the bear hibernates? He slows down his metabolism. A Native person can do that too by laying there without eating so much. Just laying there. And he begin to get half-asleep and his mind is all that works. And that's when he begins to see things that he wants to see in his mind. *Shiishikwanipowaamowin*. Now I'm going to tell you one word - the only word - that is connected to this *shiishikwanipowaamowin*. *Shiikaawepanihchikan* is a sieve or strainer. When you have flour - you take the flour from the sack and strain out the impurities. *Shiikawepanihchikan* - that's what they call that. So, in your dream that's what you're doing. Specifying the dream that you want to remember and straining out the rest of the junk. *Shiikaawepanihchikan* - that's what it means.

G.F.

So the roots of *shiishikwanipowaamowin* 'dream quest' and *shiikawepani-hchikan* 'flour strainer' are the same. The root *shiikawe* means to strain out or sift. It seems to suggest a shaking movement. And repeating the first syllable suggests repetitive action. So *shiishikwanipwaamowin* is literally "repeatedly sifting out a dream". It seems to me that *powaa*, which is the root for "dreaming" also has a connection with the action of shaking or drawing out. So when one pours out salt from a salt shaker one says *powinam* 'he shakes it out.' Threshing wild rice is *powaham* and threshing wheat is *powawew*. The suffixes of these words show a distinction between wild rice and wheat that is based on animacy, but in both cases the root *powa* signifies the act of threshing, which involves shaking. That root also appears in the word *powinesiiw* 'he draws infection out of a wound'. And finally, it seems to appear in *ospowaakan* 'a pipe'. The initial syllable of the Omushegowak word for pipe is problematic it may be derived from *osii* 'to create,' from *spakw* 'to have a certain taste,' or from *soopaht* 'to suck'. It's really hard to tell. But the medial is almost certainly *powa* and is related to the act of drawing out smoke. Thus the acts of shaking out impurities and dreaming seem really closely related. Perhaps they are also related to so-called "rapid eye movement" during the dreaming phases of sleep and the process of drifting in an out of consciousness during the dream quest. Maybe even the movement of a shaking tent. Does what I say make sense?

L.B.

Dreams and legends are teaching tools. And the language is part of it. It all connects. Now, back to the legends. There are five major [Omushkego] legends. They are used for education. Like Wiisaakechahk - it's a legend used to introduce young people to what life is going to be. The teenagers question about many things. So the Wiisaakechahk there is showing them what can happen. The old people don't speak to the teenagers. They let the Wiisaakechahk show their youngsters. For example, most teenagers want to know about sex. How? Why? When? They cannot ask their parents directly and the parents do not have the answers. It's not proper to talk about these things as a parent. But it's possible through the elders. That's why the elders are the ones to tell the legends. They're the ones who know how to put the legends to inform the young person. To see the way it is. The elders know exactly what the young people think. What they want to do, when they want to try something. They know the young people. So they created the legends which will explain things about life to the young people. So that's what those legends are used to do - to inform the young people. Not only the young people. Also the grownups. All five legends are like that. They are interpretable. They can be enjoyed. You can laugh where it's funny. But when it comes to interpreting them - then you get to be serious. So that's what it means. People from different age groups can be entertained. They can laugh together.

Legends are "icebreakers". You know - when strangers come together and don't quite feel right. A legend will just melt that and open up their friendship. So they are very flexible. They are useful that way. But once they are written down they may become rigid. They were good the way they were because they were not rigid. But once you write them down one way, they will stay that way. Many elders have said this to me. But if you write at least five different versions of each legend, then they might still remain flexible. So there are many explanations of these things if you listen to the elders. The legends are used that way. They were the basis of education - especially of the mind. The mind of a person. Wonders are answered in there. And questions that cannot be answered can be expressed in legends very easily. So that's how good they are.

G.F.

As you know, I have lived in both Kashechewan and Peawanuck. During my three years in those communities I was struck by the impact television was having on Omushkegowak children. It seemed the kids spent more time glued to TV than they did talking to their parents and grandparents. The traditional stories seemed to have been completely replaced by the stories on television. And to understand most of the programs on TV the children must speak English. So more and more children in Omushkegowak communities are growing up learning English from TV and speaking English to their parents. This is reinforced in the schools, where English is the medium of instruction. Many children are no longer able to communicate directly with their grandparents because the grandparents speak only their Native language and the children speak only English. That doesn't bode well for the continuing use of stories as traditional teaching tools. That's why it's so important to develop culturally sensitive texts for use in Omushkegowak schools. If these texts are written in both *iniimowin* and English then they might serve both to teach reading skills in the Native language as well as to teach Omushkegowak history and culture.

L.B.

The transition to the European way of life has happened so fast. The First Nations had to understand the nature of the Whiteman's culture that came upon them. First they have to learn how to survive and how to understand the new way of life. It's not possible for us to put our traditions in a form that will be readily understood by other cultures. And the culture that is coming upon us is so quickly changing. The project we are undertaking now could have been done 35 years ago if my people were not so rapidly influenced by modernization. But we were so busy trying to understand the Whiteman [new term for non-Native newcomers to the Americas] - we never even thought about writing about our own culture. We didn't do that. We forgot our own education system to put our children into the Whiteman's system.

Some of my people even forgot they had a form of writing. When they begin to understand what they were losing - now they want to write something. But the computer has replaced the pencil and typewriter. That's what the holdup is today. No elders can be found in the First Nations communities who can use a computer to write syllabics. That is why we cannot do these things now. We will have to catch up with those things first. We'll have to learn how to use computers and also retain the knowledge from the old cultural traditions. We have to train our young people how to read and write syllabics again, with the computer. Then it might come easy.

G.F.

I remember sitting with you during the spring of 1996 and translating excerpts from a catechism book which you used as a boy in St. Anne's Residential School in Fort Albany. The book had a black cover and was entitled *Catechisme de Persévérance*. It was written in syllabics under the direction of Oblate Father F. X. Fafard (1924). I'd like you to look at a section entitled *kishemanito otoonashwewina* 'Gods Law'. It refers to the Ten Commandments in the Bible. The following extract [originally written in syllabics, transcribed into Roman orthography using the system developed by Nichols and Nyholm (1979)] is from a homily given in answer to the question *awena ka wanitotak animeniiw nistam wanashwewina* 'who is breaking the First Commandment?':

Ekwana kaa manitokatat machimanitowa awesisam kiisiko piismwa, wachaakoosha
He who worships the Devil, animals, the sun, stars,

nesta oshichikana. Kaa paachitat itwehikaniniiw, koosaapatamowininiiw,
and creations (i.e. false idols). He who does drumming, shaking tent,

machinikamowininiw, nesta machimakoswininiw, machip-itwawininiw nesta
evil singing, and evil feasting, evil smoking and

shishikwanipowamowininiw wesa ekwanihi machimanito otishitwawin.
dream quests because these are the Devil's creations.

L.B.
Bishop Vincent - he's the Bishop of Moosonee. He's only about 60 years old. He's younger than me. He used a ceremonial pipe and sweetgrass. He also does smudging. A few years ago I said to him: "You know, Father, that was supposed to be a great sin". He asked: "Why do you say that?" I told him it was written down in the Roman Catholic catechism book. "I never saw it", he said. "I never saw it". So I showed it to him. What you just quoted. I read it. I even translated it for him. He never mentioned anything after that. So I heard that he burned those books - the catechism books. He burned them. In Fort Albany they sank them in the middle of the river with stones. Out in the middle of the river. *Chiistaapatamowak* - it means they took out their anger - stoned them. Maybe it's my fault. They did that so that people wouldn't criticize them for what was said in the past. Now they can drum, do smudging and burn sweetgrass if they want to pray. But the books said don't do it. So now they have burned them. They don't want the Native people who can read [syllabics] to read those things. In the European culture there were many times that books were burned when ideas changed. Burn the books so nobody will be able to read them. But it will not solve the problem for the people who have lived through these things. It might solve the problem for the young generation. It might ease the tension. Material life may be more acceptable after that. The Great Spirit may wonder himself.

G.F.

What is to be done for elders like yourself, who lived through the experience of attending residential schools and reciting the lessons from the catechism books?

L.B.

We have to tell our elders who have accepted Christianity that it is alright to go back to their traditional spiritual activities. But there are many elders in my culture who believe that their own spiritual traditions are evil. They don't even want to see anyone go to the sweatlodge. That has to be overcome. Either these people will have to die off, or they will have to learn to be flexible and go along with the Christian religious authorities who have apologized for what the missionaries did in the past. Then our elders will have restored their cultural dignity. But not yet. Not today. There's still resistance amongst our people. The Christian leaders are ready to apologize. Now we can go back and use the drums. We can burn the sweetgrass if we wish. But these things were condemned in the past.

G.F.

Are you angry about what happened to Omushkegowak people?

L.B.

I'm not angry with those priests. They thought they were doing the right thing. You can't blame them. It was only that period of time. Sometimes I think the priests were sometimes right. When you study the First Nations spiritual activities. How dangerous it could be. Two *mitewak* [shamans] could kill each other when they didn't like each other. There was no protection. There was no power beyond those *mitewak*. Except the Great Spirit. That's the only power above those *mitewak*. So they actually had control over everything. The priests saw that. That's why they condemned it. Two *mitewak* could find an excuse to fight each other and as they fight each other they became madder and madder until one dies. You've seen that many times in European culture too. Sword fights and duels - just to show how quick they are. So they kill. And it was legal because they were defending their honour. The shamans were like that too. But the priests didn't condemn European gentlemanly honour the same way they condemned the *mitewiwin*. They didn't do that to the Whiteman's activities. The Europeans were able to ignore the sins of their own people who were religious. The Church did not condemn them. But the Church condemned First Nations cultural practices. That's why the First Nations submitted. The threat was so great and so powerful. The Bible was very impressive to people who never wrote. They were beaten there. They just couldn't resist. That's why *mitewiwin* went underground. It went underground for many years until the 1930s. The last Omushkegowak people who practiced *mitewiwin* died in the 1930s. I've looked back many times in my mind. Why did my people lay down thousands of years of beliefs because some other person came around and said it was wrong? And the Great Spirit himself did not punish them before. Ten thousand years they existed. If the Great Spirit thought they were bad he would have destroyed them a long time ago. Wouldn't he? That's what I think.

G.F.
I'd like to return to the Omushkego Oral History Project. You once envisioned it as being like putting up a tipi. Do you remember?

L.B.
Yes. Putting up a tipi requires three poles that are firmly driven into the ground to hold the rest. To make it rigid. You put three poles together. You tie them at the top. And then after you tie them firmly, you stand these three poles and spread them evenly until they firmly stand by themselves. After that you begin to put the rest of the pieces. So you need 17 sticks around, plus those three. Then you need four extra poles to move the canvas covering the smoke hole at the top. There's two pieces of canvas on top, so you need two poles for each piece to shift them around. That's the way the Omushkego does it. That's what *taastahowaakan* means - the beginning of making the tipi. Well, this project of transcribing and translating some of my stories is like putting up a tipi. We have put up the tripod already. We have the materials we can use. We have the stories. The real stories that come from the elders. I have brought them in here - in this place where we are going to make this thing.

And then there are the others who are joining us in this project. All our skills will help us to put up the tipi together. The stories which were formerly only in the mind will be put in writing. In syllabics. After that - after we have put this invisible thing of the mind onto paper - it's like having the canvas for the tipi. Then what we will have to do is to explain what it means. So others can understand what kinds of things we used to make this thing. That means that we will translate it into other languages. Then speakers of other languages will have also shared the knowledge of how this thing is created. And the last thing we will need to do is place the covering over the tipi frame. And that will be when we have transcribed all the tapes. When we have transcribed and translated it all we will have finished putting up the tipi. Everything then will be visible. Ready for our grandchildren. That's the idea.

References

Ahenakew, F. 1987. *Cree Language Structures.* Winnipeg: Pemmican.

Bear, G. *et al.* 1992. *Our Grandmother's Lives As Told in Their Own Words.* F. Ahenakew and H. Wolfart (Eds. and Trans.). Saskatoon: Fifth House.

Beardy, F. and Coutts, R. 1996. *Voices from Hudson Bay.* Montreal: McGill-Queen's University Press.

Brody, H. 1981. *Maps and Dreams.* Toronto: Douglas & McIntyre.

Brown, J. 1992. Afterword. In A. Hallowell (Ed.) *The Ojibwa of Berens River, Manitoba* pp 111-115. Toronto: Harcourt Brace Jovanovich College

Chatwin, B. 1987. *The Songlines.* London: Jonathan Cape.

Cruikshank, J. 1990. *Life Lived Like a Story.* Vancouver: UBC Press.

Cruikshank, J. 1996. Discovery of gold on the Klondike: Perspectives from oral tradition. In J. Brown and E. Vibert (Eds.) *Reading Beyond Words: Contexts for Native History* pp 433-459. Peterborough: Broadview

Cruikshank, J. 1998. *The Social Life of Stories.* Vancouver:UBC Press.

Dauenhauer, N. and Dauenhauer, R. 1999. The paradox of talking on the page: Some aspects of the Tlingit and Haida experience. In L. Murray and K. Rice (Eds.) *Talking on the Page* pp3-41. Toronto: UniversityPress.

Durkheim, E. 1965 [1912]. *The Elementary Forms of the Religious Life.* J. Swain (Trans.). New York: The Free Press.

Ellis, C. 1995. *Cree Legends and Narratives.* Publications of the Algonquian Text Society. Winnipeg: University of Manitoba Press.

Fafard, P. (O.M.I.) 1924. *Catechisme de Persévérance.* Quebec: Action Sociale

Flannery, R. 1995. *Ellen Smallboy: Glimpses of a Cree Woman's Life.* Montreal and Kingston: McGill-Queen's University Press.

Fulford, G. and Bird, L. 1998. Louis Pennishish, Mushkego Storyteller. Paper presented at the "Perspectives on Native American Oral Literature" Conference held at the University of British Columbia.

Goddard, I. 1990. Primary and secondary stem derivation in Algonquian. *International Journal of American Linguistics* 56(4): 449-483.

Government of Canada. 1996. *People to People, Nation to Nation: Highlights from the Report of the Royal Commission on Aboriginal Peoples.* Ottawa: Minister of Supply and Services.

Hallowell, A. 1955. *Culture and Experience.* Philadelphia: U of Pennsylvania

Hallowell, A. 1962. Ojibwa ontology, behavior and world view. In S. Diamond (Ed.) *Culture in History: Essays in Honor of Paul Radin* pp 19-52. New York: Columbia University Press.

Hallowell, A. 1966. The role of dreams in Ojibwa culture. In P. von Grunenbaum and R. Caillois (Eds.) *The Dream and Human Societies* pp 267-292. Berkeley: University of California Press.

Hallowell, A. 1976. *Contributions to Anthropology.* Chicago: University of Chicago Press.

Hallowell, A. 1992. *The Ojibwa of Berens River, Manitoba.* J. Brown (Ed.) New York: Harcourt Brace Jovanovich.

Kegg, M. 1991. *Portage Lake Memories of an Ojibwe Childhood.* J. Nichols (Ed. and Trans.) Edmonton: University of Alberta Press.

Minde, E. 1997. *Kwayask- e-kii-pe-kiskinowaapahtihicik 'Their Example Showed the Way'.* F. Ahenakew and H. Wolfart (Eds. and Trans.). Edmonton: University of Alberta Press.

Murray, L. and Rice, K. (Eds.). 1999. *Talking on the Page: Editing Aboriginal Oral Texts.* Toronto: University of Toronto Press.

Nabokov, P. 1996. Native views of history. In B. Trigger and W. Washburn (Eds.) *The Cambridge History of Native Peoples of the Americas* 1(1):1-59. Cambridge: Cambridge University Press.

Nichols, J. and Nyholm, E. 1979. *An Ojibwe Word Resource Book.* Saint Paul: Minnesota Archaeological Society.

Parks, D. and DeMallie, R.. 1992. Plains Indian Native literatures. *Boundary 2*(19):105-47.

Preston, R. 1975. *Cree Narrative: Expressing the Personal Meanings of Events.* National Museum of Man Mercury Series. Can Ethno Serv Paper 30.

Preston, R. 1982. Towards a general statement on the Eastern Cree structure of knowledge. *Papers and Proceedings of the Thirteenth Algonquian Conference.* W. Cowan (Ed.). Ottawa: Carleton University.

Turner, T. 1988. Ethno-ethnohistory: Myth and history in Native South American representations of contact with western society. In J. Hill (Ed.) *Rethinking History and Myth: Indigenous South American Perspectives on the Past* pp 235-281. Urbana: University of Illinois Press.

Vandall, P. and Douquette, J. 1987. *Stories of the House People.* F. Ahenakew (Ed. and Trans.). Publications of the Algonquian Text Society. Winnipeg: University of Manitoba Press.

Williams, A. 1991. *The Dog's Children.* L. Bloomfield (Trans.) and J. Nichols (Ed.). Publications of the Algonquian Text Society. Winnipeg: University of Manitoba Press.

Whitecalf, S. 1993. *The Cree Language is Our Identity.* H.Wolfart and F. Ahenakew (Eds.). Publications of the Algonquian Text Society. Winnipeg: University of Manitoba Press.

Wolfart, H. 1996. Sketch of Cree, an Algonquian language. *Handbook of North American Indians* 17: 390-439.

[1]   Louis Bird (Elder) is an Omushkego storyteller from Winisk First Nation. George Fulford (PhD) is a professor of Anthropology at the University of Winnipeg and coordinates the Omushkego Oral History Project.

Champagne-Aishihik Enterprises
Haines Junction, Yukon

Wanda Wuttunee[1]

Abstract

Chief Paul Birckel heads the Champagne Aishihik band and oversees all social programs and economic development initiatives including one of their successful business ventures, a construction company called Champagne-Aishihik Enterprises Limited. The company employs a number of band members on a permanent basis and provides training opportunities for other band members on a seasonal basis. The purpose of this paper is to outlines the history and development of this construction company.

Introduction

Chief Paul Birckel heads the Champagne Aishihik band and oversees all social programs and economic development initiatives including one of their successful business ventures, a construction company called Champagne-Aishihik Enterprises Ltd. Based in Haines Junction, the company employs a number of band members on a permanent basis and provides training opportunities for other band members on a seasonal basis. The company is successful with revenues growing steadily under Paul's stewardship. It has been a successful venue for training and has provided employment opportunities for many band members thus fulfilling its original mandate. The company's reputation has developed in the community and its client base has expanded beyond the Territorial government. Despite the pressures of running a band-owned business, Champagne-Aishihik Enterprises has survived. Critics have scrutinized the company's performance and have sometimes made it a political issue. These pressures will likely shape the future of the company but Paul and his employees are pleased with the company and its potential to have a positive impact on the lives of band members. The following section outlines the history of the construction company.

History

Champagne-Aishihik band is made up of over 700 members who are descendants of two Aboriginal groups: the Southern Tutchone and the Coastal Tlingit. A merger occurred between two bands and now there are close to 300 members living in Haines Junction with the majority of the remaining members residing in Whitehorse. Band members also reside in communities throughout the southwestern section of the Yukon including Champagne, Aishihik, Canyon Creek, Kloo Lake and Klukshu. The band conducts its economic development initiatives under two main companies: Dakwakada Development Corporation and Champagne-Aishihik Enterprises Limited

Champagne-Aishihik Enterprises Ltd. began operations in the summer of 1976. Unemployment among band members was high and Harold Kane, the company's general manager recalls, *One of the principal reasons the construction company was started was to create employment for our people.* Paul was elected chief of the band and has been re-elected every term since 1980. He has taken steps to expand the company in his role as company president. Paul recalls: *In 1980 when I started, all we were doing was hauling garbage, wood, water and sewage. Since then we've expanded quite a bit. We bought some heavy equipment including a grader and a loader and started doing our own roads. Construction of band members' houses was contracted out at that time. We started doing most of that ourselves although we contracted some of the houses out, depending on our manpower.*

Paul is a driving force behind many of the changes that are addressing the social and economic problems faced by his people. Prior to becoming chief, he worked for a utility company for fifteen years as a self-taught mechanic. Then he went to work for the Council of Yukon Indians, a political organization for six years. At the same time, he took night courses on book-keeping and general management courses. Paul notes, *Whatever I learned I picked up on my own. I've been through a lot of courses at night school but basically I've done it on my own.* He is a successful entrepreneur in his own right and operates a business services company. Paul recalls some of the activities undertaken by the band since he became chief. *One of the first things that we did was to reorganize the band. We developed a new band constitution and we were the first band to set a membership code. We were also the first band to sign an Alternate Funding Arrangement (AFA) with Department of Indian Affairs. An AFA is almost like block funding. We handle our own child welfare program, which is a first again for the Yukon and almost first across Canada. We've developed our own operations manual and it's fairly successful. We place some of the kids that were in the territorial child welfare system back with their parents. Finally those parents are beginning to look after their kids. This contrasts with the way the Yukon Government handled our kids. They were taken completely away from the band and were institutionalized.* Most band funds are channeled into social programs. Paul comments on the status of social problems for his band as compared to other *bands: In a way, our band is probably better off than other bands although we feel our problems are horrible. In some places I have visited, young kids were drunk in the middle of the day. I go to some bands and I see members sleeping under a table or passed out somewhere . . . It's unusual to see somebody in our band staggering around in the middle of the day. We have a couple of guys that don't have any skills or tools and they get drunk once in awhile but not like that. We're trying to find ways to solve our problems but we sometimes don't realize how lucky we are until we visit somewhere else.*

Unemployment is another major problem. However, more young people are wanting to work because they see what their friends can buy when they are employed. Paul states: *They're buying cars and skidoos and getting into debt and they have to service those debts. They're more mobile and they buy good clothes and good houses. It all builds up their self-confidence and they want to stay sober. . . . We still have a few young guys who haven't found their way, but they're just being young and I'm not sure how you're going to change that. I'm not going to preach to them. They've got to get that energy out of their system before they settle down. One of the things that we've tried in the past that has worked fairly well, is that we've hired students right out of school in the summer with funds from the government. We put them to work in the construction company and they have to work so many hours a day . . . It was a bit of a failure in the summer of 1989 because some of the kids were just too lazy to work but I think it's worked in the past and will work in the future. It's tough. Things happen all around here which makes it tough on everybody. For example, sometimes street drugs come in from somewhere and everybody gets high on them. It's something that I'm not sure we can get away from.*

Operations

Champagne-Aishihik Enterprises Ltd. generated total revenues of $1.7 million in 1989. Paul states: *We build houses and roof trusses and do road construction. We're putting in water and sewer right now in Haines Junction. We put in a chip boiler last year, so we'll be selling heat mainly to the band. We do much of the mechanical work on the water and sewer system but we do bring in people for specific jobs on our projects, such as on the chip boiler. . . . We've built houses and done road construction all over the Yukon for the Territorial government. The majority of our revenue comes from contracts for housing, roof work, preparation of construction sites and for hauling water and sewage. In the winter, we build roof trusses. Our biggest customer is Beaver Lumber. We also run the boiler system for the band. With the revenue we employ people to cut wood as a job creation project. Ninety percent of our employees are band members.*

      The organization is headed by Harold Kane the general manager and a band member. The housing superintendent, Phil Zaitsoff is a non-band member who handles the housing and truss plant. He handles all design work for the trusses. Paul notes, *We build roof trusses that support the roof covering. The design is quite technical because the truss handles different stresses. Since they are used in the north, the truss has to be higher up than normal so we can get proper air function. We work with an engineering firm who puts their engineer's stamp on our truss plate designs.* Harold Kane has been general manager for the past eight years. He came to the position with extensive experience in the road building industry in the Yukon and British Columbia. When he started, Harold recalls, *We had only two permanent employees and now we have about five. My job is not really clearly or perfectly defined. I do what needs to be done. Sometimes, I'll run equipment, do mechanical work or welding. I'll even cook in camp if necessary.* The band and the government are the major customers of the company. Bids are submitted for government projects, as well as to private corporations. As Harold notes: *Notice of project bids are watched for by people in the band office and we rely on the mailing list from the government. Bonding has been a major problem because operational dollars were a long time coming. We couldn't bid on the bigger jobs because we didn't have the money to meet the bonding requirements. We only owned one or two trucks to start with but now we must have a million dollars in trucks and tools.*

      In the construction industry, a general contractor such as Champagne-Aishihik Enterprises must put up a certain sum of money called a bond when submitting a bid for large contracts. This bond shows the client that the company will not fold before completion of the project and acts as a guarantee that the successful bidder is financially capable of carrying on the project. It is usually a percentage of the total value of the project. It can be very difficult for new companies with little operating capital to meet the bond requirements. Another non-band member prepares all the bids and designs software to handle the company's computer needs. Paul notes: *We're computerized to some extent. Accounting and payroll are on computer and Larry Jacobson uses it to prepare all the estimates and bids. We're working on developing a software job costing program because we can't find a programme that will fit our needs. There are some programs on the market but they're expensive. We would have to buy their hardware and not use ours. We're still looking for something but we don't have the money to go ahead. If we did have, then we would hire our own people to design the program for us.*

Staff

There are five permanent staff in addition to the managerial staff. There are approximately fifty or sixty seasonal positions including trainee positions in the peak summer period. The hiring policy is to offer jobs to qualified band members first and then seek non-band members for any vacant positions. Training positions are only for band members. If employees want to take time to hunt or fish, then it is taken as regular vacation time any time other than during the peak summer months. Paul says: *We do have five or six guys who stay on almost all winter. We try to find projects to involve the rest of the employees in the winter but houses are taking so long to build that we're either into December and January anyway. In the 1989/90 season we're going to try to make it year round, so that we can keep the good employees working. We'll do the majority of the houses and hopefully be ready to start the last house around January or February. By the time that's finished, we'll be starting a new year again.* As Harold notes, *Most of the good workers do stay but everything is governed by the contracts that are in the public sector. It is all seasonal work which means that you can't plan your life around it.* The company faces some staffing problems including high turnover among trainees, shortage of skilled manpower, absenteeism and few management trainees. Policies have been undertaken in order to address some of these issues while other issues are accepted as unavoidable for band-operated businesses. The following discussion addresses these issues. As mentioned earlier, the mandate of the company is to provide training opportunities for their band members. However, there are downsides to the training program initiative. Paul explains: *We've been doing training programs but that is our downfall right now. The people we've trained have moved somewhere else so we're continually having to pay for new training programs. We've applied for training dollars and we've received a little bit here and there but not enough to meet our needs. The biggest obstacle that is stalling the expansion of our operation is mainly lack of skilled manpower. [Other problems arise with trainees] . . . The abuse of the equipment is high and the cost of maintaining that equipment is very expensive. Some of our trainees are very careless with the equipment. A truck was burned up once and it adds up. There are a lot of little things that happen and we can't keep track of it all. Lately we're bringing a number of young guys who are coming along well so this problem should be minimized.*

In the summer of 1989 there were ten to fifteen trainees working on construction projects. Paul states: *We've got a few seasoned operators who are very good. At our carpentry site, most of the guys who were running equipment want to be carpenters now so we're lining up their training. We did manage to build our band hall extension with almost all trainees except for a couple of journeymen carpenters. The training programs are an investment for us in the long run but it's still kind of painful.* Planning for new projects is difficult with the seasonality of the work and the employee turnover. Paul states: *It's a hard thing to get a handle on because you never know if the skilled people are going to be available for work. Then some people only work for a week or two weeks and then they're gone. They've decided to quit, go work somewhere else or they have problems with their girlfriends and they decide to give it up for awhile. However, I do find that people are willing to work more and we're finding that more and more people in the community are willing to stay on longer all the time . . . I think attitudes are changing because everybody is working. There are people with drinking problems still but it's not as bad because it's only on the weekend. In the summer, the majority of guys worked seven days a week so any drinking problems were at a minimum. One technique that has worked well in the past is if someone didn't come in until Monday or Tuesday because they got drunk on the weekend, we would tell him to take the rest of the week off. He can come back the week after and work . . . It's worked to a certain extent with some people because they've sobered up or run out of money and they want to get back to work. However some guys only work for a month or two months every year then they fall off the wagon and they don't come back until the next year. Sometimes we might give too many chances to people but we're under a lot of pressure from the community to do that.*

It can be difficult to take disciplinary action due to these community pressures. Paul states, *Those are some of the teething problems that we have. It seems to make a big difference if it's a non-band member that is the boss and fired them. If it is Harold who fires somebody then a lot of people are after him so he feels the pressures quite a bit more than I do. Sometimes he hurts and last year he quit for awhile because of the conflict. We got him back finally.* From Harold's perspective there are pros and cons to being the general manager and a band member. He says, *On one hand their loyalty is there. On the other hand, it's hard to discipline some of the people that you grew up with. You end up left out in the cold in the community for awhile. It's a chain reaction that spreads through families. However, it's probably going to be common in just about any band-owned corporation.* Some difficulties have been encountered with attracting employees who can handle middle or upper management responsibilities from within the band. Paul recalls: *When Harold left last year we couldn't find anyone else to take his place. It's hard attracting people when other employers can offer a better salary. We've tried promoting people in the past but it didn't work out. One person decided being boss meant sitting in the truck and doing nothing. Last winter, we put on management courses but it was hard for people to do it. We either get people whose heads get bigger and they float two feet off the ground but don't get anything done or people are just scared of doing it. . . . We do have a couple of guys that have developed and are happy. One fellow worked one summer but he got drunk and never came back that year. Then the next year we got him back and tried him out as the foreman. He changed totally. He comes to work early in the morning until late at night working at keeping all the guys busy. Where we're lacking trainees is in the middle and top management area. We do have some good people, unfortunately they work with other organizations.*

Reasons for Success

As discussed, Champagne-Aishihik Enterprises is successfully fulfilling its mandate as a training and employment center for band members. The growth in sales and profits can be attributed to various factors including Paul's continuing influence and his philosophy on decision-making. Promoting a team spirit and cultivating a good reputation in the business community have also contributed to the company's growth. An important influence on any company's operations is the vision held by the management team for the way to guide company operations. When that vision is working satisfactorily for the company and its shareholders then the continuing influence of the management team can be critical to the company's success. Bringing in new management or a board of directors, as commonly happens with band elections, can be very disruptive to a company. Champagne-Aishihik Enterprises has very likely benefited from Paul's re-election as band chief since 1980, as reflected by the growth in permanent employees and company revenues. Paul equates the pressures of running a band-operated business with that of running a family business, he states: *Everybody wants to make sure that they are hired or that you hire this person or that person. It's hard to work sometimes because there is a lot of conflict and you're caught in the middle. It's a real juggling act although we do fairly well. I know other bands have a real struggle. It can be very difficult if a new chief gets elected and he brings all his family and his people with him. Current employees are pushed out. . . . I don't operate that way. We want to act consistently and we try to promote a team spirit. A key element for that team attitude is that they have to respect the people that they work for. I also promote working together so that there is no conflict between Aishihik members and Champagne members. The two bands have been working together for quite a few years so it's not a big problem. It's just that once in a while a conflict occurs between personalities so that issue crops up every now and then.*

Paul's management philosophy for all of the band's operations is to move forward decisively. He says: *I've had meetings where it is hard to deal with anything because people are so scared to take a step. The way I look at it if I make a decision then I'll be right at least 50% of the time. . . . There are going to be mistakes but at least we're moving forwards and not going backwards. Some bands take a wait and see attitude while others want to fight the system. It slows everything down. Some guys just raise hell at every meeting. Then everybody gets jittery and upset so it's hard to work in that type of environment. I like to get things done.* A growing source of revenue is from the private sector because of the company's successful bidding and developing reputation in the industry. In the beginning, it was difficult as a new company with no track record.

According to Paul, another obstacle to overcome was the negative perception by some of the industry regarding a native-owned business. Paul states: *Most times being a native business closes doors. We have to work twice as hard for contracts. For that reason, people don't give us work like a regular company or phone us regularly for jobs to bid on. . . . The government has been good for us because we can bid in the open market and outbid anybody else. We outbid the competition rather consistently. But I think we don't get as many private contracts as we would if we were a white business. We're building our reputation and credibility but there's still that prejudice out there. It's going to take a long time for people to get over that but it will come.*

Areas for Improvement

Several areas which could be improved are further computerization of the company's operations, a better apprenticeship program and lower bonding costs. Completing computerization of the company operations depends on funding for regular or customized computer programs and computer-training for employees. Generally band members who receive technical training at a college, plan to apprentice and then become journeymen. In order to pass through the apprenticeship phase, the apprentice has to receive guidance from an accredited journeyman. Harold states: *Since the local college opened, I think it's making quite a difference for us. Students get the post-secondary training in the college rather than trying to get on-the-job training with us. . . . It is good but the only trouble we have is, we don't have very many journeymen who can supplement the apprenticeship programs because journeymen are very expensive. We don't turn people away but I give them the option. One of the mechanics just graduated and he can't get his ticket from here but he still prefers to work here. He's not going to be certified which is a shame.*

The bonding problem which was alluded to earlier is a situation that Champagne-Aishihik Enterprises has faced for most of its operating history. Since they have had more losses than profits, bonding companies and banks are very cautious in any financial dealings. Paul hopes that several more profitable years will ease this situation. Paul explains the way they currently meet bonding requirements. *We have a new company called Denendeh Ventures. We buy bonding insurance from them. This year it cost us $4,000 to have a sum of money that we can use whenever we want to bid on a job. That's expensive. Once we get a job and we need the money, we have to pay the regular interest rate on it.*

Environmental Friendliness

Paul is proud of the company's record for minimizing the impact of their operations on the environment. He states: *It is part of our tradition as native people that Mother Earth be protected. For example, we try to eliminate any unnecessary tree cutting and if we are building a road then we will try to get gravel from gravel pits that have already been created. This philosophy is hard to put into words because it is an integral part of our way of life.* Harold adds, *We are the guardians of the land and if we ruin it then that is our heritage that is affected.* Environmentally safe practices are followed by all successful contract bidders.

Future Development

The short-term plan for the construction company is to maintain the current level of revenue, hire a president, continue funding education and promote development of a practical component in the college training programs. There may be a move to sub-contracting more work out to band members or privatizing the company. Once a positive cash flow is established from the construction company and other band investments then additional economic development is planned. Given the number of investments and programs that the band is currently involved in, Paul does not want to stretch his resources by expanding the construction company at this time. He says, *I don't want the company to get any bigger right now because the bigger you get the more headaches that come. The next step is to hire someone to oversee all our operations.* This person would relieve Paul from some of his duties and allow him to concentrate on planning the band's future development. The training of band members remains a major objective. Paul plans to encourage Yukon College to incorporate actual work experience into the training programs. He states, *We need to develop a good training program with on-the-job training. It's okay for somebody to go to school and train to be a mechanic but it's very different when you put them on the job. They learn the theory but they need to learn the practical side also.* This program improvement would ease the supervisory burden that is placed on the construction company when a new graduate begins work. Paul states: *If we were as big as the Yukon Territorial Government Maintenance Yard where they have their equipment and lots of mechanics then new guys could work along with other mechanics. They would learn faster and learn the right way to do things. But we're not that big and we don't have as many people with the experience to supervise the new fellows.*

In order to get around this problem, they plan to encourage graduates to get experience elsewhere and then come back and work for the band. It will be difficult because they need all their manpower for current projects. There is the risk that these band members will choose to stay where they are rather than return to the band. The band plans to continue to encourage band members to take training to alleviate the shortage of skilled labor. The band does not offer scholarships but according to Paul, *We tell them to go to school. We can't provide everything but we'll help them. We only fund short programs even though some of our people want to go for a longer term. We can't afford to let them go because we need them. We can't bid on projects if we don't have skilled people to hire.* One of Harold's major objectives for the construction company is to increase the level of sub-contracts let to band member companies and investigate the implications of privatizing the company. He says: *I try as much as possible to use as many band members as sub-contractors that are available. However, the general feeling I get from people is that there should be more privatization of the company. People want to increase personal benefits. This could mean that band members contribute equipment to the company which continues as the principal contractor. Then all the band members have their own incentive to bring projects in and they contribute and benefit from operations. The band won't be the principal source of economic development in the community. The down side of privatization is, if there is a certain amount of money to be made, they're not going to waste time to train anybody.*

Any further economic development must be financed through the land claims settlement or through increased revenues from current band investments and operations. Harold sees his biggest challenge as making the construction company more profitable: *We can't train people at our current level, compete in the private sector and expect to show large profit margins. Private contractors just hire the best people and get the job done. Eventually we'll have enough trained people that will decrease our training expenses and contribute to our profits. We'll still be training but on a smaller scale.* Once more capital is available then current joint venture projects will be expanded and more economic development investments will be made.

Profile in the Community

Alleviating the unemployment problem among band members remains a priority for Paul. The employment opportunities provided by Champagne-Aishihik Enterprises have been augmented by other development initiatives. Putting people to work on the land working for Parks Canada or conducting tours has been successful. Paul explains, *It's surprising that even people with drinking problems, who are sent out in the bush to do slashing work for Parks Canada, are doing well. They are in their environment and have some responsibility. I think we're winning some of the battles that way. But it's hard and painful and sometimes it wears me down.* For people who follow a more traditional lifestyle, Paul states: *We set up a tour company so that we can get our band members who have horses to take tours out. It's gradually working since it's more of a traditional style where they feel comfortable in the bush anyway. They know horses and there's not too much else to do. We help them with their books or do their book-keeping for them and just pay them for their time. It cuts down on their paperwork and they don't have to look at the marketing side which we can look after.*

Advice to New Business

A band-owned business can be the best choice to accomplish the objectives of chief, council and the band membership. It can serve as a vehicle for acquiring funding that individuals might not be able to access. It can provide a means to deliver training programs that individual businesses can not afford. Spin-off benefits occur for local small business owners who are subcontracted for work with band businesses. Opportunities can be provided to band members that they might otherwise not receive. For example, if an employee is consistently late or unreliable due to a drinking problem, a band-owned business is flexible enough to make a difference in that person's life by encouraging better work habits. Many times small businesses would terminate the employee because they could not afford to provide a second chance. The quality of work on band projects could be better because the employees care that fellow band members receive their best efforts. Paul and Harold have a number of insights into the pitfalls of running a band-owned company. Besides the issue of trained band members moving to other companies, it is difficult to juggle the training priority with any type of profit objective. In addition, political pressures exist from the community because the board of directors and the chief executive officer are elected band representatives as well as company officials. Many times there are political ramifications to a business decision that is taken and these repercussions have to be accounted for by management. These are problems that individuals in private businesses do not face with similar regularity, if at all. With regards to worker migration, Paul laments, *One large construction company has half our people working there. They're all good carpenters and some have their journeymen papers. It's all we've been doing for the last eight years is training all these bloody carpenters and then they're gone. Many young men want to work in the city because it's more exciting.* With the high costs associated with training employees, it is very difficult to make competitive bids and earn a profit. The training costs increase operating expenses which means fewer profits or breakeven. Paul states: *We bid on some of these jobs and we might break even or make a little bit of a profit. Most of our competitors can go to Canada Manpower and get all the skilled people they want. Then they do the job and lay the guys off because they've got no further responsibility. Whereas, we have a responsibility not only to get the projects but house and feed them and find work for them.*

      While it makes sense to have a policy of hiring qualified band members to run band-owned businesses, sometimes it is difficult to find a band member who can also handle the political pressure. One option is to consider hiring non-band members for management positions. A band member who is manager is on the front lines when hiring or firing a fellow member. It is a hard position to be in which Harold acknowledges: *If I look at the long-term, then I figure I'm doing something but sometimes it gets pretty rocky. The biggest thing to handle are the family conflicts. Actually it shouldn't be but in any band operation there is always a high degree of politics. It's probably the hardest part of being the general manager in a band-owned company because everybody's got their fingers in the pie so to speak.*

It's hard to give advice to other people on how to handle it because Harold says: *After eight years, I haven't even learned to handle it. I don't have a problem so much with my employees but certain factions in the membership make a political issue of a specific decision then it becomes very hard to be in my position. A few young people come and give me encouragement when I feel little bit down. It's nice to see that they see what I'm trying to do and it is appreciated.* Harold has advice before starting a band-operated business: *I think other bands should do an in-depth feasibility study. Band-owned businesses are very hard to get off the ground and keep running. The political issues are a large part of the problem. It's really hard and there are going to be a lot of downfalls.*

Summary and Conclusion

Champagne-Aishihik Enterprises Ltd. is a company that is successfully providing employment and training opportunities for band members. It is becoming more profitable under the guidance of Chief Paul Birckel and general manager, Harold Kane. Despite the political pressures that appear to be integral to a band-owned operation, business continues and is beginning to thrive. The number of trainees that have worked on projects over the years continues to grow as do the number of permanent employees. Paul has filled the role of leading strategist for the band's economic and social initiatives since he was first elected chief in 1980. In this period of time he has been able to implement a number of major projects and set the stage for additional programs to meet the need for further education, more employment opportunities and address the addiction problems faced by some of his constituents. He recognizes that there are no instant cures or miracles but knows that problems can be overcome and gains made over time. Paul takes an aggressive but well-reasoned approach to decision-making. Paul promotes a team atmosphere among construction company employees with Harold's assistance. Employment opportunities are given to young people that are going to school or who are recent graduates. Some assistance is provided to apprentices but they have limited resources for those employees seeking their journeymen papers. Attitudes seem to be changing in the community in favor of employment. More people want to work as they see what other employed band members can afford to purchase or gain the self-assurance to stay sober and employed. Harold's main challenge is to keep the projects coming in so that these people are steadily employed. As general manager, Harold is on the front lines if any conflicts arise in the community due to his decisions. Those pressures are not easy to handle but the appreciation that he receives from young people encourages him to continue. He is a skilled general manager who takes pride in the company's accomplishments. He tries to solve problems such as employee turnover and absenteeism, by working closely with his employees. It is difficult to match wages and benefits that are offered by larger companies but there is a sense of pride and loyalty that is fostered in band member employees by the company's accomplishments. Revenues have grown dramatically over the last ten years. The next challenge facing the company is to continue their profitability so that further investments can be made in economic development projects. As more band members are trained and join Champagne-Aishihik Enterprises, training costs will decrease and this should be reflected in greater profit margins. Increased profitability will mean that the company can qualify for bonding insurance and bid on larger projects. This will promote the company's growing reputation and credibility in the industry which should lead to more projects and a continuing cycle of growth and profitability will be set into motion. Operations will continue to reflect a respect for Mother Earth that matches the beliefs of their band members. Champagne-Aishihik band has a reputation of being progressive and achieving many of its goals due to the success of a number of their undertakings and the birthplace of leaders in territorial and national native political organizations.

[1]   Wanda Wuttunee (PhD) is a member of the Red Pheasant First Nation in Saskatchewan and a professor in the Department of Native Studies. This is an edited version of a paper reprinted with permission from Wuttunee, W. 1992. *In Business for Ourselves: Northern Entrepreneurs.* Arctic Institute of North America and Faculty of Management, University of Calgary, Montreal: McGill-Queen's.

Foreign Robe of Tradition and the Right to 'Aboriginal-Self'

Catherine Glass[1]

Abstract

This paper examines the discourses surrounding Traditional Environmental Knowledge (TEK). It redefines the emerging neo 'TEK' as the invented construct and manipulation of a non-Aboriginal institution which attempts to codify, reify, acculturate and control the customary practices and knowledge of the community and individual Aboriginal person.

The Foreign Robe of Tradition

Shall we be able to put on, like a new suit of clothes, ready-made symbols grown on foreign soil, saturated with foreign blood, spoken in a foreign tongue, nourished by a foreign culture, interwoven with a foreign history, and so resemble a beggar who wraps himself in kingly raiment, a king who disguises himself as a beggar? (Jung 1968:14)

Traditional Environmental Knowledge (TEK) encircles valuable teachings pertaining to the maintenance of balance, harmony and spiritual respect between individuals, and nature. This paper questions the role of non-Aboriginal traditions that attempt to codify and secularize TEK, and the difficulty of institutions to fully incorporate the spiritual and cultural Aboriginal traditions of TEK.

TEK literature attempts to define, protect and record TEK within a written format. This format usually removes TEK from its esoteric, oral traditions into a non-Aboriginal, written, open-access usable format. TEK can then be accessed for the purpose of research or to create government laws, policies and regulations pertaining to a variety of issues such as environmental management. Non-Aboriginal recognition of TEK can be traced back to *Our Common Future* or the *World Commission on the Environment and Development* (WCED), where it was coined for the empowerment of vulnerable groups (WCED 1987). The 'packaging' and codification of TEK contradicts the purpose of empowerment, because TEK is redefined into an emerging 'neo-TEK' that is invented, constructed and manipulated by non-Aboriginal institutions which codify, reify, acculturate and control the customary practices and knowledge of the Aboriginal communities and individuals. The more recent trend in selecting the use of Participatory Action Research (PAR) and collaborative research methodologies is an important step for mitigating these problems. PAR ensures which communities define, conduct and analyze research projects, minimizing the possibility of exploitation and manipulation of knowledge, and providing the impetus for empowerment and self-determination (Ristock and Pennell 1996: 115).

Institutions do not capture the whole of TEK because they do not include all members of the community and individuals comprise the pieces to the whole of the traditions. Institutions, like Co-Management Boards, negate the traditional customs and culture of the community by assuming that one individual can represent the community. Unawareness of customary traditions, like consensus-style decision making, inadvertently develops 'neo-traditions' or inverted traditions through non-Aboriginal hierarchical institutions governed by foreign laws. Hobsbawm (1983) defines an invented tradition as:

> Invented tradition is taken to mean a set of practices, normally governed by overtly or tacitly accepted rules and of a ritual or symbolic nature, which seek to inculcate certain values and norms of behavior. In repetition, which automatically implies continuity with the past. In fact, where possible they normally attempt to establish continuity with a suitable historic past. (2)

Hobsbawm delineates between invented and customary traditions where custom "is to give any desired change (or resistance to innovation) the sanction of precedent, social continuity and natural law as expressed in history" (1983:2). TEK is gathered from customary traditions then recorded, defined and codified creating invented or neo-traditions (Ranger 1983). In Canada results are an invented tradition controlled by government institutions with a vested interest in securing rights to land and resources. Co-Management Boards have also been established for solving disputes between different resource users and have been useful in this respect. They have also been developed for the input of traditional environmental knowledge. But they are non-Aboriginal institutions governed by non-Aboriginal regulations and policies. The term "management" exemplifies this statement as it is not even an Aboriginal term (RCAP 1996):

> The purpose of the Aboriginal management systems, based on traditional ecological knowledge, was to counteract resource depletion and ensure the survival of the group. Aboriginal people have not abandoned their traditional tenure and management systems either in concept and practice. (524)

There is a difference between management and TEK. Empowerment is not gained through the imputing of knowledge into an institution that is completely irreconcilable with the traditions of that knowledge. What is gained is a new form of hierarchical dominant power whereby:

> [I]n this system the place of the First Nations peoples is at the bottom. This is alien to the fundamental elements of our society, where we are accountable only to the Creator, our own consciences and to the maintenance of harmony. (RCAP 1996:435)

Traditions are altered and prevented from changing when an institution attempts to govern what is customary. For instance Morrow and Hensel (1992) discuss the clashing of cultures and customary practices in Alaska:

> A young man from the same village where this incident occurred expressed considerable psychological distress in the face of contradictions between the systems. Wherever endangered or out of season birds are within range, he said, "I feel guilty when I shoot and I feel guilty when I don't shoot". The one violates Western Law, the other Yup'ik morality. (51)

This dichotomy within the individual inhibits what is customary because of the codification of a new tradition where, "any legal recognition of 'custom and tradition' inevitably restricts future action by its effort to define custom in ever more restrictive terms as precedents are tested in court" (Morrow and Hensel 1992:46). Shils (1981) asserts that traditions eventually dissolute and pass away or amalgamate with other traditions as they lose adherence through syncretisms. If non-Aboriginal institutions are concerned with the protection of TEK the oral, esoteric and gnostic content of TEK must be respected and trusted along with traditional Aboriginal forms of governance, law, rules and codes of behavior.

The Right to 'Aboriginal-Self'

'Selves' are derived from unconscious contents that become altered by becoming conscious (Jung 1968). The 'Self' is like a child who one day saw his or her image in water (the unconscious). Being unable to show people the picture in the water, the child built something from items in the playroom to show this image to others. Essentially, 'Self', is the built image constructed by the individual. If another child decided to re-build the items; he or she would have prevented the first child from returning to the 'stream' to see the original 'Self,' and hinder the right to 'Self.' Aboriginal traditions are the pool from where the 'Aboriginal-self'' finds the reflection. Traditions and teachings are altered by non-Aboriginal institutions when the personal, spiritual, and the individual relationship between the Creator(s) and the spirit world is disregarded. When individuals in academia and government utilize TEK they must collaborate with a belief in, a trust of, and a respect for all the traditions that encircle Aboriginal epistemologies and philosophies.

Spiritual traditions, are especially powerful tools for the actualization of First Nation individuals and communities. Adherence to non-Aboriginal institutions, laws, policies and regulations hinders 'Self' by undermining confidence in the spiritual traditions, customs and community culture surrounding individuals. Jung (1968:7) discusses how images and knowledge is transformed, muted and the meaning lost through formulation and codification, "We can just feel our way into it and sense something of it, but the original experience has been lost." TEK is derived from a personal spiritual relationship of respect with nature that is lost in the written word. This personal sacred experience is altered and fragmented when oral Aboriginal traditions of interaction with and respect for nature are transformed into a non-Aboriginal relationship of management or control over nature when recorded in a written form. The transformation of personal spiritual relationships into invented neo-traditions affects the individuals and communities by imposing non-Aboriginal ideologies and by influencing how individuals and communities accumulate or interact with their cultural, spiritual and natural 'world'. The spiritual component of TEK is a valuable tool for 'self-actualization' because it is a personal and communal experience. Law or policies cannot destroy or erase the spirit, however altering aspects of how an individual interacts and learns about their spiritual traditions can alter those traditions. The creation of neo-traditions in written format affects the teachings by creating a pool of words that loses its dynamic esoteric illustrative content.

Alfred (1999:80) acknowledges a need for the decolonization of thought in order for the individuals to reclaim the collectivity of the soul and adopt patterns of thought and action, "that reject the colonial premises" and create or adhere to self-conscious traditionalism. The right to 'Aboriginal-Self' becomes injured when the individual is faced with dichotomies of traditions that are incongruous. The non-Aboriginal written tradition of management and control of nature is an impediment to the return to traditionalism. It impedes the manifestation of the 'Aboriginal-Self' and thus impedes the collective will of the 'Aboriginal-collective'. Foucault, discusses his views of the collective will pertaining to the Iranian revolution where he claims that for, "the revolution to be politically operative had to entail a radical transformation in the subjectivity of the people" (Foucault 1988:211). The collective will of Aboriginal communities begins with the subjectivity of the individual to resist foreign ideologies and institutions that define, oppress, and repress Aboriginal individuals from defining themselves according to their own traditions.

Conclusion - The Sewing of the New Robe

> I will tell you this story because you have been good to me. You must learn it well and tell it to the children where you live. The songs I have sung, too, can be used whenever you want to give thanks, or if you really want to pray for something. The drum I made for you can be used wherever you go, but you cannot give it away, because it was made for you alone. (Moore and Wheelock 1990:xxv)

Knowledge is a personal and sometimes spiritual experience. Knowledge is derived from the image of the 'Self' it is accumulated by individuals within a society and community. It is rooted in the sacred traditions encased by the culture and customs of that society. These customs can be altered and invented by foreign dominant institutions and ideologies which negate certain traditions and practices through a subjective and objective filter. The written invented traditions are then utilized to regulate the individual within that society. Governing and managing, by foreign rules, impedes the individual from defining the image of 'Self' because it is only fragments of the original whole. The 'Aboriginal-Self' and the 'Aboriginal collective' must shed the foreign robe of tradition. And sew a new robe based on Aboriginal traditions that is fitting to the customary cultures that it enfolds.

References

Alfred, T. 1999. *Peace, Power, Righteousness: and Indigenous Manifesto*. Oxford.

Foucault, M. 1988. Iran: The spirit of a world without spirit. In L. Kritzman (Ed.) *Foucault: Politics, Philosophy, Culture interviews and other writings 1977-1984*, pp. 211-224. New York: Routledge.

Gamble, J. 1986.Western applied science in northern societies. *Arctic* 39(1):20-23.

Graveline, J. 1998. Resistance retheorized: The Native perspective. In *Circle Works: Transforming Eurocentric Consciousness* pp 38-48. NS: Fernwood

Hobsbawm, E. 1983. Inventing traditions. In E. Hobsbawm and T. Ranger (Eds.), *The Invention of Tradition* (pp 1-14). Cambridge:e University Press.

Irwin, C. 1988. *Lords of the Arctic: Wards of the State*. Halifax: Dalhousie.

Jung C. 1968. *The Collected Works of C.G Jung Volume 9 Part I: The Archetype and the Collective Unconscious*. London: Routledge.

Kruse J. 1998. Co-management of natural resources: A comparison of two caribou management systems. *Human Organization 57*(4):447-458.

Moore P. and Wheelock, W. 1990. *Wolverine Myths and Visions, Dené Traditions from Northern Alberta* Edmonton: University of Alberta Press.

Morrow, P. and Hensel, C. 1992. Hidden dissension: minority-majority relationships and the use of contested terminology. *Arctic Anthropology* 29(1):38-53.

Ranger, T. 1983. The invention of traditions in colonial Africa. In E. Hobsbawm and T. Ranger (Eds.) *The Invention of Tradition*, pp 211-263. Cambridge.

RCAP 1996. *Restructuring the Relationship*. Ottawa: RCAP.

Ristock, J. and Pennell, J. 1996. *Community Research as Empowerment: Feminist Links, Postmodern Interruptions.* Toronto: Oxford University Press.

Sadler, B. and Boothroyd, P. 1994. *Traditional Ecological Knowledge and Modern Environmental Assessment.* Vancouver:UBC Centre for Human Settlements.

Sawchuk, J. 1991. State Structures and Imposed Identities: The Invention of "Indian". In J. Sawchuk (Ed.) *Readings in Aboriginal Studies, Volume 2: Identities and State Structures.* pp 1-8. Brandon: Bearpaw Publishing.

Shils, E. 1981. *Tradition*. University of Chicago Press.

World Commission on the Environment and Development. 1987. *Our Common Future.* Oxford: Oxford University Press.

[1]   Catherine Glass is a graduate student in the Department of Native Studies at the University of Manitoba.

Understanding Lakota Sioux Healing

Jonathan Ellerby[1]

Abstract

Unlike the biomedical therapies common to Western culture, for the Lakota, healing is an intrinsic element of their world view, their community ceremonial life, and the life process of each individual. Most Lakota people understand their healing holistically: in terms of world view, practitioner characteristics, spiritual relationship, processes, techniques and practices. This paper addresses the multivalent nature of Lakota healing practices.

Lakol Wicoh'an: Healing and the Lakota World view

This paper examines the role of healing in the Lakota world view; identifies the basic communal sacred rites; provides a brief overview of the basic types of Lakota healers; and discusses the role of the individual in the overall procurement and maintenance of health. *Lakol wicoh'an* refers to "the Lakota way of life" and includes the entire world view and lived experience of the Lakota people (St. Pierre and Long Soldier 1995). Of all the communities within Aboriginal North America, the Lakota Sioux, who reside primarily in South Dakota and peripherally in surrounding areas, with some communities as far north as Canada, have been one of the most heavily studied (Lewis 1990, Rice 1998, Walker 1980). The majority of the literature on the Lakota focuses on the nature of their world view and ceremonial practice (DeMallie 1983, 1984, DeMallie and Lavenda 1977, Densmore 1920, 1992, Dorsey 1894, Erdoes and Lame Deer 1992, Feraca 1961, 1962, 1963, Lynd 1864, Mails 1979, 1991, 1997, 1998, G. Pond 1889a, 1889b, S. Pond 1986, Powers 1975, 1982, 1986, Stolzman 1986a, 1986b, Steinmentz 1970, 1984, 1990, Rice 1989, 1991, 1994, 1998, Riggs 1872, 1880, 1893, Walker 1917, 1980, 1982, 1983, Wallis 1947, Wissler

1905, 1907, 1912.) Much of the historical ethnographic study of the Lakota examines their beliefs and ritual; recent popular work has centered on the narratives of Lakota healers and spiritual leaders (Erdoes and Lame Deer 1992, Mails 1979).

Though the literature is full of discrepancies due to poor scholarship, ethnocentrism, reductionism, and the ignorance of Sioux pluralism and regionalism, a few emergent and common themes are consistent (Meyer and Ramirez 1996, Rice 1998). These common themes, or elements, do not comprise a universal Lakota world view, but universally contribute to Lakota world views. Some of the essential elements of Lakota Sioux world views, may be summarized as follows (Powers 1975: Rice 1998).

The Spirit World. The Spirit World is real and as complex as the visible world. Spirits provide both instruction in healing and the capacity and ability to heal for most healers. Spiritual beings, including *wanagi* (ghosts) and *taku wakan* (Sacred Beings), effect the health and well-being of people. Illness is often understood as an expression of a spiritual condition or incident (Brown 1992, DeMallie 1983, DeMallie and Parks 1987, Powers 1975, St. Pierre and Long Soldier 1995, Walker 1980).

Symbiosis. All sentient beings are interrelated and interdependent. The making and maintenance of good relationships with all forms of beings, especially spiritual beings, is essential for a good and healthy life. Relationships of all kinds have an effect on health and play a role in healing. Healthy relationships, human and spiritual, are a primary health determinant (DeMallie and Lavenda 1977, DeMallie 1984).

Individuality. Individuals are shaped by their specific, personal relationships to human and spiritual worlds and thus are understood to have, and are respected for their unique views and experiences (Amiotte 1989, Brown 1992). Illnesses take on unique qualities in each person, regardless of common symptoms. Similar illnesses and symptoms may have different spiritual causes and/or sources. No two patients are treated identically. Some variation based on individual nature and need (mental, emotional, physical or spiritual) is always intentional and understood as necessary in healing practices.

Vision. Closely related to the preceding principles is the centrality of vision. Vision is a general term used to describe direct human experiences with the Spiritual World. Vision related ceremonies and experiences are primary vehicles of communication with non-human beings. Vision is central to the training of healers, the diagnosis of individuals, the identification of remedy, and at times may itself be a healing experience which may affect direct and immediate change on all or any level of an ailing person (Brown 1992, Dugan, 1985, Irwin 1994, Mails 1997).

Pluralism. Individual Sioux world views vary and need not be reconciled. Each individual experientially develops their spiritual life based on vision, ceremonial participation and a unique process of healing. No single articulation of world view, healing practice, ritual process or belief can be identified as universally, unequivocally Lakota (Rice 1998). Different healers have different healing gifts, medicines, spirit helpers and approaches; two healers may treat identical symptoms differently. Healing practices exist within an ever-changing spectrum of possibilities (Mails 1997, Powers 1975). Meyer and Ramirez (1996:103) note: "Unlike the world view of modern philosophical thought, the traditional Lakota/Dakota world view does not engage in the deliberate establishment and maintenance of consciously articulated propositions or beliefs."

Process Centered. Sioux world views and healing are process centered. Formal systematization and institutionalization are contrary to the unfolding nature of Lakota people's life experiences and healing practice. The nature of reality is unfolding, human experience is in process and the Spirit World can never be entirely known. As such, healing practices are also in a constant state of change, addition, and adaptation. Lakota medical beliefs and practices are not reducible to a static, repeatable range of procedures (Deloria 1973). Healing experiences are a part of a lifelong journey and not isolated events.

Spiritual Holism. Every aspect of Sioux life and experience are inextricably interrelated in a spiritual system that cannot be fully understood in part. Meaning and functionality both depend on a holistic frame of reference that affirms a spiritual nature to the context, source, material, patterns and process of reality (Meyers and Ramirez 1996).

These principles, or dynamics, of interrelated epistemology and ontology are intrinsic to every aspect of Sioux life, and are especially evident and active in their healing practices and understanding of health. A recognition of each is necessary to understand the natural role of healing in the life process and the centrality of healing in all Sioux ceremonial life.

Sacred Rites: Healing and Community Ceremony

Among the Sioux there were, historically, seven central community ceremonial rites (Catches and Catches 1999, Powers 1975): *Chanunpa*: The Sacred Pipe Ceremony; *Inipi*: The Sweat Lodge; *Hanblecheya*: The Vision Quest; *Wiwanyag Wacipi*: The Sun Dance; *Hunkapi*: The Making of Relatives; The Keeping of the Soul; and *Ishna Ta Awi Cha Lowan:* Preparing a Girl for Womanhood. These ceremonies, occur during different stages of human life, and seasonal change. Though different in nature, the common focus among all of them was the health and healing of individuals and the community. Preventative health practices were central to the Lakota way of life (Mails 1997). Proper, regular involvement in the essential community ceremonies was, and still is, seen as fundamental to this health concept (Bucko 1998, Duran and Duran 1995, Lewis 1990).

The prohibition of Sioux ceremonies and gatherings during the 1800s and 1900s resulted in the loss of cultural continuity, knowledge and reduced the importance and frequency of these ceremonies (Erdoes and Crow Dog 1995, Lewis 1990, Pettipas 1994). Today, these ceremonies are practiced in varying degrees depending on the region and the community. The most common of these community ceremonies today are the Sweat Lodge, the Pipe Ceremony, the Vision Quest and the Sun Dance (Erdoes and Lame Deer 1973, Powers 1975, Lewis 1990, St. Pierre and Long Soldier 1995). Each of these four ceremonies are used to bring psychological, physical, spiritual and emotional healing to individuals and communities (Erdoes and Lame Deer 1973, 1992, Lewis 1990, Lyon and Black Elk 1990, Mails 1979).

Chanunpa: The Sacred Pipe Ceremony. Any use of the Lakota Sacred Pipe is considered both a ceremony and a healing event. One of the most sacred and central objects of the Lakota, the *Chanunpa* embodies everything holy and is intrinsic as a component to virtually every major ceremony, especially the seven sacred rites (Brown 1953, Lyon and Black Elk 1990, Powers 1975). The *Chanunpa* is a powerful intercessor and serves to connect human beings to spiritual beings and realities in a way otherwise only common to visions. Maintaining and bringing about health and healing are fundamental to the use and function of the *Chanunpa*, "When you have that *Chanunpa* [Sacred Pipe], you have to be humble and sincere. You ask for *health* and *help*. These are the two key words that the *Chanunpa* carries" (Lyons and Black Elk 1990:54).

Inipi: The Sweat Lodge Ceremony. The *Inipi*, which may be translated as "to make live" or "to make the soul strong", is a ceremony unto itself and a component element of other ceremonies like the *Yuwipi*, the Sun Dance and the Vision Quest (Bucko 1998, Walker 1980). The *Inipi* is used in preparation for other ceremonies and events, for specific "doctoring" or healing treatments, and commonly as a regular preventative health care practice. The *Inipi* "strengthens the life [vitality] and purifies the body" (Walker 1980:83); "*Inipi* makes clean everything inside the body to put out of [a person's] body all that makes him [or her] tired, or all that causes disease, or all that causes him [or her] to think wrong" (Walker 1980: 83, 84).

Hanbleceya: The Vision Quest Ceremony. While it is possible, *Hanbleceya* is not known for its capacity to bring about immediate physical healing (Dugan 1985, Irwin 1994). Mental, emotional, and spiritual wellbeing, however, are commonly remedied and maintained through this rite (Lewis 1990, Powers 1975). *Hanbleceya* plays a variety of roles in healing among the Lakota. For healers and spiritual leaders, *Hanbleceya* is a fundamental means by which they acquire, develop and expand their healing gifts and abilities (Erdoes and Lame Deer 1973, 1992, Powers 1975, Walker 1980). Among the non-ritual specialists, the "lay" community, *Hanbleceya* also serves many purposes, such as to help in the understanding of a spontaneous vision experience; to prepare for another ceremony like the Sun Dance or *Yuwipi*; to gain insight into personal issues and vocation; or to entreat spiritual forces for healing. Black Elk notes that *Hanbleceya* is an important experiential conduit that "give[s] strength and health to our nation" (Brown 1953: 44).

Wiwanyag Wacipi: The Sun Dance Ceremony. Finally, the Sun Dance is known as the great annual Lakota ceremony of renewal, thanksgiving and healing (Amiotte 1987, Brown 1953, Holler 1995, Mails 1979, 1991, 1997). This summer ceremony incorporates all the various rituals described in this section. Since communal health and individual health are inextricably interrelated, this community ceremony is vital to the health of Lakota communities and individuals. Most Sun Dance participants pledge to dance without food or water for one to four days, with the intention of invoking healing in their lives and the lives of those they love (Mails 1998). Additionally, within the Sun Dance, there is often one or more specific rounds devoted to the direct healing of people attending. Lakota people attest to the incredible power of the Sun Dance to heal diseases and conditions untreatable by Western medicine. Cancer, paralysis, psychiatric disorders, and emotional traumas are only a few examples of some of the illnesses and conditions that may be healed during a Sun Dance (Lewis 1990, Mails 1998, Walker 1917).

Wapi'yekiya: Lakota Healers

While health and healing is an inseparable aspect of virtually all Lakota experience, it is possible to identify individuals who specialize in healing work. More definitive than categories of healing practice, there are many types of healers among the Lakota *wapi'yekiya* (Lakota medical practitioners) (St. Pierre and Long Soldier 1995). Unlike other aspects of health and healing, Lakota *wapi'yekiya* fit models of classification and specialization similar to those found in the Western medical system (Mails 1997). Terms and categories like pharmacology, physical therapist, psychiatrist, surgeon, internist, psychologist, chaplain and even highly specialized fields like nephrology and neurology all find reasonable correlates in the Lakota system.

Lakota healers can be categorized on two levels: in terms of their physiological and disease specializations; or, in terms of the source and nature of their healing practices. At present, it is difficult to rely on the literature to provide a detailed discussion of the disease and system specific specializations of the Lakota. This is an area of study that has historically been lacking (Lewis 1987). On the other hand, approach based categorizations are possible. Though not exhaustive, it is possible to identify six main categories of healers based on their practices and the means by which they attain and use those practices (this section draws heavily from (Powers 1986: 164-195): *Wicasa Wakan*: The Holy Ones; *Pejuta Wicasa*: Medicine People; *Wapiye*: Shamans; *Wakan Kaga*: Sacred Performers; *Wicahmunga*: Wizards and Witches; and *Winkte*: The Third Gender. Of these six groups, the first three listed are the most common today, whereas the last three categories have decreased in use, endorsement and prevalence since historical records (Powers 1975, Wissler 1912).

Wicasa Wakan. The *Wicasa Wakan* always composed a small segment of the Lakota population. These men and women are a combination of mystic and healer. Having trained in various healing arts and having been given many healing gifts and abilities, the *Wicasa Wakan*, lead a rigorous life of the highest moral and ethical calibre and generally do not fully become acknowledged until post-menopausal in age. A *Wicasa Wakan* may practice within any of the following categories of healers; however, counselling, spiritual leadership, metaphysical insight and an exemplary lifestyle set the *Wicasa Wakan* apart (Erodes and Lame Deer 1973).

Pejuta Wicasa. The *Pejuta Wicasa* are most commonly referred to in English as "Medicine Men and Medicine Women". These terms come from the literal meaning of "*pejuta*", which refers to medicinal plants. *Pejuta Wicasa* receive spiritual guidance and use ceremony just like the other healers of the Lakota, however, they specialize in pharmacological remedies (Erdoes and Lame Deer 1973, Lewis 1990, Power 1975, 1986). These healers treat as wide a range of illnesses and conditions as any healer, but specialize in the treatment of day to day ailments, like wounds, tooth aches, sprains, gastroenteritis and broken bones. Material (plant, mineral or animal) based treatment, contextualized by ceremony and spiritual interaction is characteristic of the Medicine Person. A wide age range is represented among these healers, though younger adepts are less common. Men and women are equally represented (St. Pierre and Long Soldier 1995).

Wapiye. The *Wapiye* were known for their ability to heal primarily through direct interactions with spirits and travel in the spiritual world. In this type of healing the healer is seen as a conduit or intercessor for spiritual powers and Spirit Beings. *Wapiye* may work in a variety of settings or ceremonies, however, they traditionally focus on the use of *Yuwipi*, *Lowanpi*, and *Inipi* ceremonies. The *Yuwipi* and *Lowanpi* are similar ceremonies, most often held at night in a pitch black room, and involve the loud presence of singing, drumming, and an intricate arrangement of ceremonial items and community supporters. In these ceremonies supernatural feats and unexplainable experiences (such as the entrance of a buffalo into the ceremonial room) often occur while the shaman is in contact with the spiritual world (Erdoes and Crow Dog 1995, 1973, Kemnitzer 1969, 1970, Lewis 1987, 1990, Lyon and Black Elk 1990, St. Pierre and Long Soldier 1995). Among the main types or classes of *Wapiye* (shamans) were the *Yuwipi*, the bone doctors, and those who had specific powers related to specific Spirit helpers (such as Eagle Medicine Catches and Catches 1999). The ceremonies used by each of these are similar in organization and principle, yet they differ in detail. *Yuwipi* shamans are tied up at the beginning of their ceremony and during it are released by spirits. These ceremonies frequently involve the physical presence of spirits evidenced by flashing lights in the blackened room. Bone doctors use a hollow bone to suck the illness out of the patient. The ceremonies of spirit specific shamans would be similar to the *Yuwipi* but unique in the sensory experience of the shaman's spirit guide/helper. These helpers may be animal or human spirits and require highly specialized songs and ceremonial equipment (Erdoes and Lame Deer 1973, Powers 1982). Most *Wapiye* tend to men and, like other healers, are more commonly older.

Wakan Kaga. The *Wakan Kaga*, are sacred performers who perform sacred and superhuman feats based on gifts and abilities given through vision experiences. These people were historically organized into societies or "cults" and, though healing is not their central role, many have exceptional abilities to heal. Depending on the society, both men and women can be sacred performers. Some societies, like the

Double-Woman Society, are all women, some are mixed gender and some are for only men. The *Heyoka* Society, Wolf Society and Buffalo Society are examples of societies of sacred performers (Dorsey 1894, Lowie 1913, Powers 1975, Wissler 1912).

Wicahmunga. *Wicahmunga* are Lakota men and women with spiritual knowledge and power that operate outside the standard Lakota societies that govern people's roles and relationships. Uncommon in recent literature, the English terms for these people are "wizards and witches". Approached with caution, *Wicahmunga* were powerful people and employed a range of abilities and practices to heal and treat the sick. They are consulted based on their individual strengths for treating a particular illness or condition.

Winkte. The Lakota *Winkte* is a third gender among the Sioux. Male in body, *Winktes* identify themselves in varying degrees as women. Some *Winktes* take on the full dress, deportment and social role of women. *Winktes* were known to have a variety of unique healing abilities and sacred gifts to cure or ensure health. *Winkte* practices were highly individual. While there is vast evidence for the existence of *Winktes*, there is little detailed information in the literature on their healing practices and procedures (Lang 1998, Powers 1986 Rosco 1998, Williams 1986).

Canku Luta: Walking the Red Road

The most critical aspect of Lakota healing lies in the role of the individual. It could be said that "choice" and "commitment" are two of the most powerful and fundamental healing practices among the Lakota (Arbogast 1995, Duran and Duran 1995, Mails 1991, Rice 1998). Healing is highly dependent on a person's conscious decision to engage the various levels and areas of healing available. For example, participation in community ceremony is always based on choice and commitment; the work of Lakota healers is patient-centered and heavily dependant on the relationship between healer and patient; and spiritual relationships demand individual responsibility. Healing begins and ends with the individual and their relationship to *Taku Wakan*, the sacred powers of life, spirits, and *Tunkashila, Wakantanka*, the Creator. The *Canku Luta*, or Red Road, refers to a lifestyle which is based on following and honouring the *Lakol'wicohan*, the Lakota way of life. Health and healing emerge naturally from leading a life based on the inherently healing Lakota beliefs and ceremonies: today this is known as "walking the Red Road" (Arbogast 1995, Brown 1953, DeMallie 1984, Neihardt 1971).

Each Lakota person may draw from a wide range of self, healer, and community based healing practices. As well, today, Lakota people draw from other systems of medicine such as the Western biomedical system, and, increasingly, systems from other cultures (Arbogast 1995, Lewis 1990, Lyon and Black Elk 1990). Though some Lakota practices have become uncommon, their pluralistic approach to healing allows them to engage an every widening range of healing practices based on their own history and tradition. The following list provides a brief summary and overview of the self-directed and selected practices common to Lakota people today: self-medication and prevention (herbal remedies, exercise, diet, sacred objects, sobriety); spiritual practice (smudging, prayer, *Chanunpa, Hanbleceya, Inipi*); healing specific ceremonies (*Yuwipi* and *Lowanpi)*; communal ceremonies (sun dance and *Inipi*); western medicine and treatment; and alternative therapies (acupuncture, massage, Chinese herbalism).

Conclusions

When examining the literature on the Lakota it becomes clear that healing is not reducible to common practices, procedures or institutions. Healing is understood as a natural and ongoing aspect of the human life process. Healing is central to the Lakota world view and may occur on many levels in a variety of contexts. Through a holistic view of life and the cosmos, Lakota people understand that every aspect of a person's life effects their health and may be a source of disease. In particular, malicious Spirit Beings and spiritual transgressions may result in illness. As such, maintaining good relationships to human and spiritual communities is both a prerequisite of health and a powerful remedy. Relationships are maintained, fostered and incurred through the participation in regular community ceremonies such as the *Chanunpa* (Sacred Pipe Ceremony), *Inipi* (Sweat Lodge), *Hanbleceya* (Vision Quest) and the *Wiwanyag Wacipi* (Sun Dance). These ceremonies are, in a true sense, practices that sustain and repair health. Individuals with specific forms of illness and disease attend these ceremonies specifically for the healing that can occur within each. In some cases, specific "doctoring" components are added or emphasized. For example, a "doctoring round" may be integrated as one of the rounds in an *Inipi*. Whether the specific healing of acute and/or chronic illness is required or not, community ceremonies are always healing in nature.

The healers of the Lakota span a wide range of specializations and techniques. Among the most common are the *Wicasa Wakan* (The Holy Ones), *Pejuta Wicasa* (Medicine People) and *Wapiye* (Shamans). Each of these healing specialists excels in healing ceremonies and remedies that are common to their individual healing class/type and distinctly specific to their own life experience, personality and relationship with the Spirit World. For example, all *Pejuta Wicasa* specialize in herbal treatments; each, however, will specialize in the use of specific herbs and will also specialize in the healing of specific illnesses and diseases. The management of healing practices and rituals in Lakota communities is largely done by the spiritual leaders and healers of each community. Their power and ability is derived from spiritual realities and sources which, in turn, govern and manage the healers and spiritual leaders. Healing is a force that is a part of every level of Lakota life. The intensification of healing in the experience of a community or individual is ultimately subject to the intent and commitment of individuals. Whether through self-care, healing treatments, communal ceremonies or the direct intervention of spirits, healing is based on the conscious desires and efforts of each Lakota person and inextricably involves the health of other individuals, communities and the Spirit World.

References

Amiotte, A. 1987. The Lakota Sun Dance: Historical and contemporary perspectives. In R. DeMallie and D. Parks (Eds.). *Sioux Indian Religion*. Norman: University of Oklahoma Press.

Amiotte, A. 1989. Our other selves. In D. Dooling and P. Jodran-Smith (Eds.), *I Become Part of It.* pp. 161-172. New York: Harper Collins.

Arbogast, D. 1995. *Wounded Warriors: A Time for Healing.* Omaha: Little Turtle

Brown, J. (Ed.) 1953. *The Sacred Pipe: Black Elk's Account of the Seven Rites of the Oglala Sioux.* Norman: U. of Oklahoma.

Brown, J. 1992. *Animals of the Soul.* Rockport, MA: Element.

Bucko, R. 1998. *The Lakota Ritual of the Sweat Lodge: History and Contemporary Practice.* Lincoln: U. of Nebraska Press.

Catches, P. and Catches P. 1999. *Sacred Fireplace Oceti Wakan: Life and Teachings of a Lakota Medicine Man.* Santa Fe, NM: Clear Light.

Deloria, V. 1973. *God is Red.* New York: Delta Books.

DeMallie, R. 1983. Male and female in traditional Lakota culture. In P. Albers and B. Medicine (Eds.). *The Hidden Half.* Lanham, MD: University Press

DeMallie, R. 1984. *The Sixth Grandfather*. Lincoln: University of Nebraska.

DeMallie, R. and Lavenda, J. 1977. *Wakan:* Plains Siouan concepts of power. In Fogelson and Adams (Eds.). *The Anthropology of Power*. NY: Academic

DeMallie, R. and Parks, D. (Eds.). 1987. *Sioux Indian Religion.* Norman: UofO.

Densmore, F. 1920. The Sun Dance of the Teton Sioux. *Nature* 104:437-440.

Densmore, F. 1992. *Teton Sioux Music and Culture.* Lincoln: U of Nebraska.

Dorsey, J. 1894. A study of Siouan cults. *B. of American Ethnology* 11: 351-544.

320

Dugan, K. 1985. *The Vision Quest of the Plains Indians.* Lewiston: Edwin Mellen

Duran, E. and Duran, B. 1995. *Native Am. Postcolonial Psychology.* NY: Univ.

Erdoes, R. and Crow Dog, L. 1995. *Crow Dog: Four Generations of Sioux Medicine Men.* New York: Harper- Collins.

Erdoes, R. and Lame Deer, J. 1992. *Gift of Power: The Life and Teachings of a Lakota Medicine Man.* Santa Fe: Bear and Co.

Erdoes, R. and Lame Deer, J. 1973. *Lame Deer: Seeker of Visions.*NY: Simon.

Feraca, S. 1961. The Yuwipi cult of the Oglala and Sicangu Teton Sioux. *Plains Anthropologist* 6: 155-163.

Feraca, S. 1962. The Teton Sioux Medicine cult. *Am. Indian Tradition* 8:195-196.

Feraca, S. 1963. *Wakinyan: Contemporary Teton Dakota Religion.* (2). Browing, MT: Museum of Plains Indians.

Holler, C. 1995. *Black Elk's Religion: The Sun Dance and Lakota Catholicism.* New York: Syracuse University Press.

Irwin, L. 1994. *Dream Seekers.* Norman: University of Oklahoma.

Kemnitzer, L. 1969. Yuwipi. *Pine Ridge Research Bulletin 10: 26-33.*

Kemnitzer, L. 1970. Cultural providence of objects used in Yuwipi: A modern Teton Dakota healing ritual. *Ethnos* 35: 40-75.

Lang, S. 1998. *Men as Women, Women as Men: Changing Gender in Native American Cultures.* Austin: U.of Texas Press.

Lewis, T. 1987. The contemporary Yuwipi. In R. DeMallie and D. Parks (Eds.) *Sioux Religion.* Norman: U. of Oklahoma.

Lewis, T. 1990. *Medicine Men.* Lincoln: University of Nebraska Press.

Lowie, R. 1913. Dance associations of the eastern Dakota. *Anthropological Papers of the Amer.Mus.of Natural History* 11 (2).

Lynd, J. 1864. The religion of the Dakotas. *Coll.ofMinnesota Hist. Soc* 2: 150-174.

Lyon, W. and Black Elk, W. 1990. *Black Elk: The Sacred Ways of a Lakota.* San Francisco: Harper and Row.

Mails, T. 1979. *Fools Crow.* Lincoln: University of Nebraska Press.

Mails, T. 1991. *Fools Crow: Wisdom and Power.* Tulsa: Council Oaks Books.

Mails, T. 1997. *Spirits of the Plains.* Tulsa: Council Oaks Books.

Mails, T. 1998. *Sundancing: The Great Sioux Piercing Ritual.* Tulsa: Council Oaks Books

Meyer, L. and Ramirez, T. 1996. *Wakinyan hotan*: The inscrutability of Lakota/ Dakota metaphysics. In S. O'Meara and D. West. *From Our Eyes: Learning from Indigenous Peoples.* pp. 89-105. Toronto: Garamond

Neihardt, J. 1971. *Black Elk Speaks.* Lincoln: University of Nebraska Press.

Pettipas, K. 1994. *Severing the Ties that Bind: Government Repression of Indigenous Religious Ceremonies on the Prairies.* Winnipeg: U of MB Press.

Pond, G. 1889a. Dakota superstitions. *Coll.of the Minnesota Hist. Society* 2:215.

Pond, G. 1889b. Dakota Gods. *Coll. of the Minnesota Hist. Society* 2: 219.

Pond, S. 1986. *The Dakota Sioux in Minnesota, as They Were in 1834.* St. Paul, MN

Powers, M. 1986. *Oglala Women: Myth, Ritual and Reality.* Chicago: University Press.

Powers, W. 1975. *Oglala Religion*. Lincoln: University of Nebraska Press.

Powers, W. 1982. *Yuwipi: Vision and Experience in Oglala Ritual*. Lincoln: Univ.

Powers, W. 1986. *Sacred Language: The Nature of Supernatural Discourse in Lakota*. Norman, OK:University Press.

Rice, J. 1989 *Lakota Storytelling: Black Elk, Ella Deloria, and Frank Fools Crow*. New York: Peter Lang.

Rice, J. 1991. *Black Elk's Story: Distinguishing its Lakota Purpose*. Albuquerque: University of New Mexico Press.

Rice, J. 1994. *Ella Deloria's the Buffalo People*. Albuqerque: U of New Mexico

Rice, J. 1998. *Before the Great Spirit: The Many Faces of Sioux Spirituality*. Albuquerque: University of New Mexico Press.

Riggs. S. 1872. Concerning Dakota beliefs. *American Philological Association, Proceedings of the Third Session*.

Riggs, S. 1880. The theogony of the Sioux. *American Antiquarian* (2) 4.

Riggs, S. 1893. Dakota grammar, texts and ethnography. In J. Dorsey (Ed.) *Contributions to North American Ethnology* (9). Washington, DC: Gov't.

Rosco, W. 1998. *Changing Ones: Third and Fourth Genders in Native North America*. New York: St.Matin's

Steinmentz, P. 1970. The relationship between Plains Indian religion and Christianity: A priest's viewpoint. *Plains Anthropologist* 15: 83-86.

Steinmentz, P. 1984. *Meditations with Native Americans: Lakota Spirituality*. Santa Fe, NM: Bear and Co.

Steinmentz, P. 1990. *Pipe, Bible and Peyote Among the Oglala Lakota: A Study in Religious Identity*. Knoxville: U.of Tenn.

St. Pierre, M. and Long Soldier, T. 1995. *Walking in the Sacred Manner*. New York: Simon and Schuster.

Stolzman, W. 1986a. *The Pipe and Christ: A Christian-Sioux Dialogue*.SD:Tipi.

Stolzman, W. 1986b. *How to Participate in Lakota Ceremonies*. SD: Tipi Press.

Walker, J. 1917. *The Sun Dance and Other Ceremonies of the Oglala Division of the Teton Dakota*. New York: AMS Press.

Walker, J. 1980. *Lakota Belief and Ritual*. Lincoln: Nebraska Press.

Walker, J. 1982. *Lakota Society*. Lincoln: University of Nebraska Press.

Walker, J. 1983. *Lakota Myth*. Lincoln: University of Nebraska Press.

Wallis, W. 1947. The Canadian Dakota. *Anthro Papers of the Am MNH* (41).

Williams, W. 1986. *The Spirit and the Flesh: Sexual Diversity in American Indian Culture*. Boston: Beacon Press.

Wissler, C. 1905. The whirlwind and the elk in the mythology of the Dakota. *JAm Folk-Lore* 18:257-268.

Wissler, C. 1907. Some Dakota myths. *J Am Folk-Lore* 20: 121-131, 195-206.

Wissler, C. 1912. Societies and ceremonial associations in the Oglala Division of Teton Dakota. *Anthro Papers of the Am Mus of Nat History* (11) Part 1.

---

[1]   Jonathan Ellerby (Reverend, MA), a recent graduate from the Department of Native Studies, focuses his research on Aboriginal world views and spirituality.

Testimony of a Once Homeless Aboriginal Woman: *I Can Only Start From My Own Story*

Rae Bridgman[1]

Abstract

This life history of a formerly homeless Aboriginal woman provides an opportunity for one story to be told. The article experiments with a form in which narrative and commentary are split to help us listen to this story without interruption. Within a moral framework, we hear a story that attests to ill health, abuse, neglect, alcoholism, violence, deep friendship, and an abiding sense of reason. Two questions underlie the article: "How does she name herself in her own narratives?" and "How does she find meaning in her own experiences?"

Stanza I. How Do You Know This Isn't Your Mother?

I'm finding that about 15 years ago, I had started dealing with the bag ladies on the street and helping them whenever I saw one. It was just something that I did. It was just more of a moral thing. I just happened to see them, and whenever I saw them, they always looked like they were struggling with their stuff, so I would just automatically go out of my way and ask them if they need any help. Whatever it may be, even if it's crossing the street. And I helped a number of people, a number of the older women across the street, and I got to know them. I never knew their names or anything, that wasn't why I wanted to help them. I just wanted to - I saw them. And if I saw people, there was many a times I'd walk some of these women across the street and I got to know them and these business men started cracking rude remarks to them and I would turn to them and say:

How do you know
this isn't your mother?
This could be your mother.
This is obviously
someone's mother.
How dare you.

    I used to get really upset
at the people in their fine, fancy
suits and you know, lovely hairdos
making cracks about people they
knew nothing about. It was more,
I guess I did it because it was
something I didn't want to become.
So I think it was a combination of
two things. One, because I didn't
pity them, but I felt something
for them, and I needed to do
something in order to make them
feel like they were still wanted. As
well as the fact, as it was a lesson
for me, that this is something I
could become if I don't really
watch what's happening.
    It was because, for me,
I'd see them and I had so many
different things going though my
mind. At one point, I guess I almost
felt like I didn't care for anyone.
I didn't want to deal with society
anymore. And I felt myself sort
of slipping into a sort of doing
exactly that sort of not caring for
society just living from my bags,
going from place to place, using
a cart, and carrying, I was, at
one point, actually carrying bags.
It sort of brought reality back to
me saying that, if I'm not going
to do this.
    I'm too young, for one

Subtext

1.

Many words.
Amazing words.
Cultivated words....
The issue is not that Native
peoples were ever wordless
...their words were literally
and politically negated.
(Perreault and Vance
1999:xv)

How does she name herself
in her own narratives?
How does she find meaning
in her own experiences...?
(Lionnet 1995:3)

I am an anthropologist who
has documented four innovative
demonstration housing projects for
chronically homeless women and
men in Toronto since 1994--Street-
City (Bridgman 1998a, 1999a);
Strachan House (Bridgman 1998b,
1999c); Savard's (Bridgman n.d.[b]
n.d.[c], 1999b); and Eva's Phoenix
for homeless youth (Bridgman
n.d.[a]). Sarah and I had many
informal conversations over two
years. I remember the day she told
me it was her son's birthday. I
didn't know she has a son. He
was a rape baby, she said. She has
not seen him since his birth. She
gave him up after he was born and
keeps his small photograph beside
her bed. She never showed me this
picture. Yet why do I see it so
clearly in my mind?

thing, to really start worrying about where I'm going and what I'm doing, I've got places to go, there's lots of things that I'd like to do, and the only way I can do this is if I start working on these things. And if I didn't know, and I'd kept getting barricades, you know walls put up in front of me saying you can't do this, you can't do that. So I ended up slowly reverting back into being something that I never wanted to become. And it took me a long time to finally get out of that. And of course I was an alcoholic as well. That didn't help. Whenever I was being pushed back even, I would go automatically, go and hit the booze, and I would try again. After a while I'd get sick of that and I'd try it again, and it just seemed to go back and forth for about 15 years. It started out, it all basically started when I left Children's Aid. I was 17 when I left Children's Aid.

Stanza II. And I was Considered Un-Adoptable

I was born, well, there's actually a varied dispute about where I was born. My birth certificate says I was born here in Toronto. Department of Indian Affairs says I was born up on Manitoulin Island. However, I was very ill, and I was brought down to Sick Kids [Hospital for Sick Children in Toronto]. So for the first three years of my life were basically in and out of the hospital. Actually first nine years of my life were in and out of the hospital.

I had nephritis. Nephritis is a kidney disease. I had no control of my kidneys, very weak kidneys. I only have one functioning kidney and the other one is just sort of there. It doesn't function well, so I still have to really worry about that. It's mostly a childhood disease, but back then, when I was born, they didn't have OHIP [Ontario Health Insurance Plan], so people were still paying for medical treatment and they just couldn't afford it.

My parents - I only know one. My mother, I don't know who my father is, I don't know where she is now. She gave me up when I was born. She gave me up basically when I was ten months old. So I don't even know. At one point she was living in Toronto. I don't know if she's still there or not. Well, I knew her name and later when I turned 19, I actually got a chance to meet her by coincidence, but that's an altogether different story.

When I was given up at ten months, I was still in and out of the hospital, I was put in an orphanage which is still, that building actually is still standing, even today. And I was there until I was three. During those times, before I turned three, I had I guess my foster sister Patricia, who was the eldest of the Curry's, was a volunteer, and she used to come in and I really took to her, and then I moved in. My sister would

come and take me out all the
time and then I was introduced to
her parents which turned into my
foster parents, and they took me
in. Children's Aid at the time (it
wasn't doctors at Children's Aid),
it was doctors at the time who
had to say who could be adopted
and who couldn't be. And I was
considered un-adoptable. Because
of my medical condition. So I was
never allowed to be adopted. So
I spent from the time I was three
until the time I was 17, almost 18, I
was with Children's Aid.

Stanza III. That's Part of My Survival

I had an interesting life. How I
managed to be - a lot of people,
that's part of my survival, after
being told I would never amount
to anything. I was never doing
anything right, I mean when I
wasn't doing anything I would get
in trouble. How I managed to be
able to come out of this, and not
be more severely damaged, I don't
know. But I've always managed to
maintain that, obviously no one's
out there for me, and the only
one who's going to do anything
for me, is me.

So I've managed to be
able to keep myself sane, and
keep myself from going - I could
have served you know. Who knows
where I could have been? I could
have been damaged for life and
been under psychiatric care for
the rest of my life, or I could be

Today, a day in November, we sit
together for four and half hours.
She tells me about her life. She is
my age, just past forty. The tape
recorder whirs imperceptibly. The
smoke from her cigarette idles
about us. She fingers the necklace
she wears. There is a bear's claw
on this necklace. I feel its smooth
sharpness for a moment.

2.

One party may write a story, but
one party's story is no more the
whole story than a cup of water
is the river. While this may
seem obvious, it underscores
what it is we do when we tell,
transcribe, or write about oral
texts. (Sarris 1999:xi)

This subtext was written after
Sarah's testimony. Verb tenses
were changed to express the
intimacy and immediacy of Sarah's
and my memories. The subtext
establishes a context for Sarah's
narrative and is subsidiary to
her words. Sarah's narrative is
ordered as it was told, transcribed,
edited, and identifying details
were changed for confidentiality.
Stanzas were inspired by events,
voice tone, or pauses as Sarah
thought through different eras
of her life. I took an active
role through my presence, facial
cues, questions or encouraging
responses. Finnegan (1998)
outlines with care and rigour
her editorial decision-making

dead, or I could be serving years of jail time. Everybody says that I have every right to be angry. And I've sat back and said, "Why?" It would have been a complete waste. For some odd reason, something always kept saying to me, "Sarah, you're here for a reason." You may not know what it is. You may know years later. It took me years, and I still don't even know why I'm really here and how I got though all this. But, still ticking. People didn't start believing me until I turned nineteen. People started saying to me, "Sarah, you are somebody." Then it took me another year for me to be convinced.

From the age of nineteen on, I - my mother, actually my foster mother was the one that introduced me to the hotel system. I was kicked out when I was seventeen. When I turned seventeen, I was actually kicked out. There were two years that nobody knows about yet. From the ages of seventeen to nineteen, I was sort of in what they call an independent program in Children's Aid. Within that period in time, I was supposed to have learned how to take care of myself, getting a job or going to school, however by the time I turned eighteen, I was literally cut off from Children's Aid. Literally, no if, and no money, no nothing, no place to stay. Nothing. I was kicked out. I was told to move within two weeks. It was what they called an independent program. And that was what they called a stepping stone for wards of Children's Aid to help them be independent. And then two weeks later before I turned eighteen they said, "In two weeks time you have to be out of this house." They gave me the impression that they were going to help me continue my schooling. 'Cause I planned to go on to university, or college, one of the two, and they said they would help and then they changed their mind, and said no. No particular person, just "They." Children's Aid, that's all I can say, because they're the ones that turned around and gave the decisions. It wasn't my worker, it was "Them."

Stanza IV. The Only Person I Could Turn to Was My Mother

So I had two weeks to find a place. "What? Please?" You know, I had no money coming in, and what money I did have coming in was what the Children's Aid was giving me to survive on, which was very little, and of course there wasn't enough to pay the first and last month's rent, let alone get anywhere. So when I left, the only person I could turn to was my mother. And my mother was actually the one that called the first hostel I ever stayed at.

My parents were hitting into their late fifties. My mother had just had open heart - mother had been seriously ill, and was having a lot of surgery. I don't know what Children's Aid had told them, but they must have told some pretty bad stories about me, because I never moved back. I mean I would visit them, but I would never stay more than a few days, before they would literally ask me to leave. And it's not like I would ever, they would try to correct me, they put me down even more. It was like every time my mother turned around, I'd be offering, I was constantly offering help, and between what I was doing and what they were saying to me, there was an awful lot of - mother was going though menopause at the time, too. So my mother was going through a really hard time, though her menopause. I mean they disowned me then. My father was the one that brought me back and said, "Your mother's really going though a hard time. She doesn't know what she's doing." And I said, "OK, no problem." And my mother really got me upset because I didn't know what was going on with her. And had it not been for my father, I would have disowned them when I was 14.

And so it was my mother that helped me get through. And I didn't want to go there. I didn't want to go home. I didn't want to go back to their place 'cause I knew my mother was still going through - and it wouldn't have helped me in the least. So she suggested I go to this hostel, and so I went. It was pretty intimidating, the first hostel. I was, the very first

processes. These processes are not explicitly acknowledged enough in many accounts.

To give primacy to Sarah's story, I presented my thoughts as subtext. You too will "'listen with your eyes' and compare Sarah's story to your own experience and study" (Murray and Rice 1999:xviii).

3.
To have the right to remember the past and to have the right to imagine a future. (Fawcett 1986:207)

These voices from the borderlands belong to people who dwell in cultures of displacement, transplantation, or oppression. They challenge notions of ethnicity and identity by speaking from unresolved historical dialogues between continuity and disruption, essence and positionality, home and journeying, old roots and new... telling us...that this place of unease and discomfort, can be a place of strength.... (adapted from Sandercock 1995:84)

Literature on homelessness focuses on housing conditions, socioeconomic issues, urban street youth, health issues, skid row lifestyle, endemic homelessness in the rural and urban Aboriginal population. The issues are summarized *thought when I walked in was, "Why the hell am I in here? What is this place?" It made it even worse because someone had stolen my glasses, so I couldn't see. I have 80/20 vision. Well, 20/20 is perfect. 80/20 is, well, I'm almost blind. It takes me, for me to take off my glasses, this is how close I have to be in order to see anything. Everything else is a complete blur. In fact, just look at you. You look like a round ball. So I couldn't see, but all I could hear every once in a while, was this woman growling at me once in a while. I just wanted to hide. I was very intimidated. So it took me a couple days before I could actually feel comfortable.*

Also, at that time I was becoming an activist, because of being a Native, I didn't know anything about being a Native, up until that point. I started being on activist when I turned eighteen. I started hanging out with the Native population, going to various types of meetings. So I started dressing Native, and I learned to do beadwork and wearing my hair in ties, and having feathers in my hair, and just being - don't know, Native activism. Like AIM, I was part of the American Indian Movement as well. It was a conscious decision, though I didn't know why, 'cause I didn't know. Well, I didn't know the culture, so I wanted to learn about the culture. So I was wearing my hair in ties, I had leather entwined in my hair. So I was wearing that and of course, walking into this hotel and having this woman glowering at me, intimidating me. I guess it must have been a week later I got my glasses.

So I walked in, the very first staff member that I remember, her name was Claudie. She was sitting at the dining room table. There was about 15 women sitting around there, and there was one woman sitting beside her, and her name was Catherine. Claudie said, "Sarah, why don't you come and join us, and I'll introduce you to everybody".

Stanza V. We Were Street Sisters

No sooner had I walked by the woman that was sitting beside Claudie, she started growling at me. I looked at her. She did intimidate me, she really did. I was actually very scared of her. So Claudie kept talking to me, and the woman kept growling at me. She had a few choice words for me. She didn't know me but she had a few choice words for me. I took about, I realized within a week after that, she couldn't intimidate me any more, and I got to sort of like her. As much as she tried growling at me and threatening me, I just sort of looked at her and said, "Yeah, OK." And within a month we were best of friends, and we were inseparable.

She passed away a couple of years ago. She was about a year younger than me. She and I spent a lot of years together on the streets, both homeless and doing various things. We were street sisters. We eventually became street sisters. And she passed away. When she finally passed away a couple of years ago, she was working at [one of Toronto's crisis shelters]. After Catherine and I started hanging around together and basically going from hostel to hostel.

Street sister? It's a family outside a family. It's the type of feeling that you have for somebody that goes beyond, I mean, it's the only family you have. When everybody else has disowned you, or you have disowned them, or lost things, there's one thing, there's one person who will be there regardless of what happens. They will protect you, as you would them. If you get charged they will jump in and say, "No, it was me who did it." And this is what this woman used to do, and I did the same for her. And it was, the word "street brother" and "street sister" are basically Native terms, for when the white man and the Native hung out together, then said, "You will be my brother, or you will be my sister". And in order to seal it, you mix the blood of the white man and the Native together saying, "Now you are my brother or sister". And that's what we did. So basically she is, she was a half-breed. She was Blackfoot Indian from Alberta, her mother is anyway, her father is completely Native.

We did it because that's how close we were. We were never

(seemingly callously) in government reports: poverty, substandard housing, domestic violence, sexual abuse, alcoholism, suicide, infant mortality, life expectancy, and work with women has been problem-focused (Beavis *et al.* 1997, Stout and Kipling 1998).

4.

Sarah speaks about experiences dating to 1970 when she turned 18 and left the care of Children's Aid. Thirty years later, I write in an article arising from research-in-progress on the development of Eva's Phoenix, a demonstration project designed to provide transitional housing as well as training and employment opportunities for homeless youth in Toronto:

"... complex relationships between youth, poverty and social assistance programs offers insights into reasons why more and more youth are becoming homeless. Economic restructuring and fiscal restraint (leading to an increase in the prevalence of part-time and temporary jobs available within the service and manufacturing sectors), as well as a growing lack of affordable housing particularly with the cancellation of government-subsidized housing programs across Canada have all resulted in increasing hardship for a number of people, including youth. . . ." (Bridgman n.d.[a]).

This system does not provide for adolescents over the

lovers, and it's not that I didn't particularly want to be, I always thought that one day we would, but never, but we were always so close that people literally thought we were real sisters. We were inseparable. We talked, we argued, we argued more than we talked, I tell you. And whenever we got into an argument, everybody stayed away. And then everyone would bring us back together again. But she argued with me more than I would argue with her, that was one thing. Then of course she would come back to me after how many weeks or months or even years later. The longest that we were ever apart was two years. After a couple of years or months she'd come back and say:

> *"Sarah, why was I angry with you?" "I don't know, Catherine."*
> *"What did you do?" "I don't know, Catherine."*
> *"Did I do something?" "I don't know, Catherine."*
> *"I was angry about you. Did you say something? What did you do?"*
> *"I don't know, Catherine. It could have been anything.*
> *I could have said something that you didn't like to hear.*
> *I could have done something that you didn't like to see.*
> *I don't know, but whatever it was, you would go off and*
> *I knew you'd eventually come back."*

And sure enough she would. And - well, we did. We spent, we would always end up sharing a room or finding a flop house or one of us would end up, because I ended up working a lot more, I would always end up paying for a room for however a length of time that we needed, until we got kicked out. But all those years we spent more time on the street and in hostels then we did in our own place. And the animals that we had would always be better fed than we would feed.

We'd end up, I got so sick of Kraft Dinner. I hated Kraft Dinner. I can't even take a mouthful of Kraft Dinner now without gagging. I can look at the package, but that's about as far. And I keep thinking that, well, I'll buy a package and just see if I can tolerate it now, and I make it up and I take a bite and I go "No thanks". So no, I can't take it any more. So that's just the way it goes - She told me the reason why she growled at me was she thought I was taking Claudie away from her. She was jealous of me. And I said, "Catherine, I'm the last person that you need to be jealous of. If anything, I'm envious of you because you've got a lot more than I ever had."

And she gave me the beginning of the encouragement. She encouraged me along. She gave me a sense of feeling needed, that I was somebody and not just a nobody. I think that's why we became close as really close friends. I mean as much as she put me up there, was the odd thing, she'd kind of lower me a notch too and let 'em know about it, too. But she was probably the best friend that I ever had at the time. But we sort of drifted apart as the years got older, as we ended up getting older, but even then, we always ended up finding each other and getting together and talking and spending a few hours. We'd always be in touch with one another, because we all had mutual friends and we still do have.

There were a lot of good times we had, and a lot of sad times we had together too. Catherine and I have faced an awful lot of deaths. People we knew, friends. I mean she had been shot, I've been stabbed. We've all had a lot of tragedies in our own life, even times, people killing themselves and stuff, lots of learning and survival skills. Lots of learning how to survive on the streets.

And it's not something I recommend anyone do, so they don't have to go through it. It's even tougher now than it was back then, because at least back then you could sleep anywhere and not worry about being robbed or raped or being bothered. You could sleep anywhere and feel comfortable and be OK. Too dangerous out there. Not something I recommend anybody to do now. Like as soon as I started realizing that things

age of 16 unless severe abuse is proven and they are in school (Fitzgerald 1993). From age 18 assistance is only available by working with a third party, exposing these youth to potential exploitation.

5.

In Bridgman (1999a: 157-158) Tom speaks of his "street brother" with the same intensity as Sarah speaks about her "street sister." The depth of the connection between the street and those who live on the street is understood from Tom's grief. When I asked him 'What does the word street mean to you?', he answered indirectly, slowly and haltingly. He told me about how his 'street brother' was hit by a streetcar in the middle of the night: "He was my street brother. We were very, very close. We were like this [Tom held up two crossed fingers], we were inseparable. We did everything together, except for having sex with the same woman, and shower together, stuff like that, but other than that . . . we did everything. And for two years, up until he died, we were inseparable. I never asked him why he was on the street, how he came to the street. I thought when it was time he would tell me. For the first time in my life I was trying to take care of myself. . . .[W]hen my brother needed me the most, I don't use the word brother loosely, when *were getting a lot worse out there on the streets, that's when I started getting off the street.*

Stanza VI. I Was the Guest Speaker

I started making a concentrated effort. It pretty much started after I had my first child. By that time I had been raped three times. I was knocked out the last time. It was done by a friend. It was done by a friend's boyfriend. The two other times - first time it happened when I first moved back to Toronto when I was 19, and I went downtown and it was my first allowance, and this guy had a bottle and we were just sitting there. I can't remember how it all started, and then he said he was going to walk me back to the subway, walked right by, then he knocked me over the head and dragged me into an alleyway and just raped me right off Yonge street, I think King and Yonge. And then the second time it wasn't an actual rape, it was an attempted rape, but it was close enough. And I, it was done by another friend's boyfriend who kept insisting I was asking for it when I knew I wasn't. And then the third time, I was also knocked out. And I had to get up the next day. I had to go to the university and do a sociology speech on homelessness. I was the guest speaker. I went there and I did it. Felt like a real pile of shit. But it wasn't until - I mean I got up, got dressed, looked at him, didn't say a word. I didn't know what to say. All I knew was that I had to concentrate. I was ready to call up this woman and tell her that I wouldn't be able to make it to the university to do the speech. Then I just got down to it and I said:

> *"No, I gotta do this.*
> *I gotta do it.*
> *I've got to get out of here.*
> *It's my only reason*
> *for getting out of here.*
> *So I went and*
> *did the speech and*
> *I just did not think about it*
> *until about a week later.*
> *And I started really*
> *thinking about it.*
> *I was a wreck.*
> *And I didn't even know*
> *what to do."*

I was 28, yeah, I was 28. 'Cause I was born in December, I had just turned 29 when my son was born. Wait a minute here - yeah, 29. So he was, there was only one person who knew that I was ever, that I was actually having a baby. I hid my pregnancy right though the entire time and then I didn't even have my son here. And there were only two people that knew. And the day that I arrived to have my son, I was not supposed to have him for another week, and I arrived there something like 2:00 in the afternoon. By 11:00 I was in the hospital giving birth. Actually it wasn't until I got there, that I actually felt comfortable for the first time. Well, I was with these two women that I stayed with, and actually the woman that I stayed with was also a good friend of mine, and she was actually in the delivery room with me. I had to argue with the doctor and the nurses to allow her to come in. It was a Catholic hospital. It had to be the man. "I don't have a man here. I want her." "Well, she can't come in." "Well, she'd better come in, or I'll do everything in my power to not have this kid. I'll lock myself somewhere, in a washroom. I don't care. That woman has to be in here." So they finally consented, and she had four kids herself, but it was the first time that she had ever seen a baby being born. So I was, she was very touched. I'm glad that she was there.

     Everyone asked me if I'd gone though prenatal care, and I

my brother needed me the most, I was too busy worrying about myself . . . and he died." The sense of brotherhood that Tom felt goes beyond blood ties. As Tom explains it: "I never asked him why he was on the street, how he came to the street. I thought when it was time he would tell me."

6.

We dream in narrative, day-dream in narrative, remember, anticipate, hope, despair, believe, doubt, plan, revise, criticize, construct, gossip, learn, hate, and love by narrative. . . we make up stories . . . about the personal as well as the social past and future. (Hardy 1968 in Finnegan 1998:1)

    Sarah's testimony belongs to life histories or personal narratives studied by many anthropologists, folklorists, psychologists, and narrative scholars. They offer important ways for understanding how the teller of the story makes meaning from their own experiences (Harman 1989, Ralston 1996, VanderStaay 1994) and how Aboriginal people have shaped their communities (Sanderson and Howard-Bobiwash 1997).

    Finnegan's (1998) elements of story-telling are: Sequential or temporal framework structures each story; stories are fashioned according to explanation, justification or coherence; a story said no. They said, "Well, how do you know what to do? And I said, "Don't you think it would be kind of natural for a woman to know exactly what they need to do in order to have a baby, without having to learn? Isn't it inherent? That all women know how to give birth? I think so." I've always looked at it - hell, if I believed every doctor that told me, I wouldn't be alive now, so -

Stanza VII. This Peace

I have 15 journals of my entire life. All ranging from 200 to 400 pages in each journal. I was seeing this other woman who turned into such a bad alcoholic that she was trying, I guess she was trying to slander me and ruin my reputation. Not that I had much of a reputation to ruin at the time, but she was trying her best to say that I was a beater, that I abused her and that I was a controller and every other thing. She was trying to convince everyone that this was the way that I really was. She was saying to them that they didn't really know me.

Now the funny thing is that the people that she was trying to convince were people that had known me for twenty years and had seen me in all states. So they knew that this was not possible. She was harassing me, and still trying to convince everyone that it was all my fault. Whereas I wasn't doing a damned thing. I was keeping away from her, I wasn't calling her. Yet she was calling to try to convince them that I was, when they knew full well that at that time she says I was suppose to have called I was sitting in the office with them, or I was in the kitchen cooking dinner or doing something that they knew where I was.

So when I moved, I thought it was great, this peace. I had just gotten accepted back into University, and I was so happy about going back to University I thought, thank God, my life is starting to turn around again. It didn't. I had to quit University because she harassed me, she was following me, she was calling, and she was making my life hell. And by that point I had quit drinking for nine years. I had stopped drinking all together. But the unfortunate thing is that because of all the harassment I was getting from her, it just made life real bad. So I eventually started drinking again.

And then she left. One day she just left. She was gone. Packed up and moved. No hide or hair of her has been seen since then. And by that point I had already moved again, because I just couldn't take it any more. The fact that after nine years of not drinking and all of a sudden picking up a six pack and having it last two days, that's still drinking.

Lots of people cheat on welfare. I guess you could say I cheated, and managed to be able to do it that way for, I would always, don't get me wrong, it's not like I cheated 100%. I always would say that I am working, I just wouldn't put the amount of hours. And when I wasn't working, I'd still put the hours down, so it made it look like, OK, she's working on something, but not enough that I'd have to worry about having taken anything off. There was just enough to say yes, I am working, I am making an effort and I am working on sporadic basis and this is how much I am making, and they never questioned. So I was fortunate. I've always been sort of lucky that way. I've never been questioned about anything I've ever been doing, even if it was illegal. But it was because I'd always been honest enough to go forward and say I am doing this. And the fact that, just to say that I am doing some of it, to be able to calm the waters.

I mean everything I started at this new place was the first time I had ever done anything. So it was a good learning experience for me. I was very nervous, even when I moved in, I was still very shy, still very withdrawn and was still learning about myself all that time. Those months were the biggest eye-openers for me, because it just gave me a sense, well, I finally knew what community was and what it was like to have people who liked me for what I am and not for what people thought I should

can potentially be generalizable. (universal in the particular.); and a story contains elements of recognized generic conventions, suitable to the audience, venue of performance/circulation and the protagonists.

Sarah begins with what she did not want to become: a "bag lady." "I felt something for them, and I needed to do something in order to make them feel like they were still wanted." is the moral lesson which sets the framework for the story. Sarah begins with "I was born. . . .", positions herself as a "fighter", a "survivor", and wills herself to overcome ill health, abuse, neglect, and homelessness with an unerring sense of "Sarah, you're here for a reason." Her story becomes an explanatory tale: "because" and "cause" feature prominently in her unabridged narrative. The story of her Native identity is broken. "I can't carry on a story if I don't know them." She carries still the memory of her son with her, and imagines that he too must create his own story, as she does.

The generations, past and present, lie behind the narratives, shadowy but deeply symbolic figures, setting personal activities in the wider cycle of time. (Finnegan 1998:99) *be, or what I'd been hearing all my life. And it was nice. Those were hard months but they were good months. I left because I couldn't handle the alcohol. It was cutting into my sobriety so badly that I couldn't keep my sobriety any more. You know, homeless people are the type of people who have been kicked out of their own homes, kicked out of their families, and they are homeless only because they don't have a home. But they continue to have a home, every - periodically. I was considered homeless, but I wasn't considered hardest-to-house. I've been homeless, and that's only because I'd been jumping from home to home to home for years. But the hardest-to-house person is someone that has been kicked out and can't get nothing.*

Stanza VIII. I Can Only Start Wtih My Own and Carry on with My Own.

My life, my stories began when I started living.
I don't know my family.
I don't know them.
I don't know them.
I go up there to Manitoulin Island but I don't know them.
I have no relatives at all.
But I can't carry on a story if I don't know them.
I don't know what's behind that story.
I can only start with my own and carry on with my own.
So I am the beginning of a generation
that'll carry on from me.
My son will carry on the generation with him.
Not from me.

Acknowledgments

I thank Sarah Easton (pseudonym), for sharing part of her life story. Gratefully acknowledged is the Social Sciences and Humanities Research Council of Canada for their support of my research through two Strategic Grants [Women and Change] (1995-1998 and 1998-2001).

References

Beavis, M., Klos, N., Carter, T. and Douchant, C. 1997. Literature Review: *Aboriginal Peoples and Homelessness*. Ottawa: CMHC.

Bridgman, R. (also known as Rae Anderson). n.d.(a) I helped build that: A demonstration housing and employment program for homeless. *American Anthropology.* In Press.

Bridgman, R. n.d.(b). Housing chronically homeless women *Housing Policy*

Debate. In Press.

Bridgman, R. n.d.(c). Despite a forsaken and sacred trust: Life in a safe haven for chronically homeless women. *Internat'l J. of Mental Health.* In Press.

Bridgman, R. 2000. My journey home: Homeless and Aboriginal and a woman. In J. Oakes, R. Riewe, S. Koolage, L. Simpson and N. Shuster (Eds.) *Aboriginal Health, Identity and Resources* pp. 93-104. Winnipeg:UofM

Bridgman, R. 1999a. The street gives and the street takes. In A. Williams (Ed.) *Therapeutic Landscapes* pp. 153-166. Lanham: Univ.Press of Am.

Bridgman, R. 1999b. "Oh, so you have a home to go to?": Designing a shelter for women street survivors. In R. Bridgman, S. Cole and H. Howard-Bobbiwash (Eds.) *Feminist Fields* pp. 103-116. Peterb., ON: Broadview.

Bridgman, R. 1999c. More than mere shelter: Incorporating art in housing for the homeless. In G. Hickey (Ed.) *Common Ground: Contemporary Crafts, Architecture and the Decorative Arts* pp. 104-111. Ottawa: Canadian Museum of Civilization.

Bridgman, R. 1998a. A "city" within the city. *Open House Intern'l 23*(1):12-21.

Bridgman, R.1998b. The architecture of homelessness. *Utopian St. 9*(1):50-67.

Fawcett, B. 1986. *A Book for People Who Find Television Too Slow.*Vancouver. BC: Talon Press.

Finnegan, R. 1998. *Tales of the City: A Study of Narrative and Urban Life.* NY: Cambridge Press.

Fitzgerald, M. 1995. Homeless youths and child welfare *Chld. Welf.4*(3):717-731.

Hardy, B. 1968. Towards a poetics of fiction. *Novel 2*:5-14.

Lionnet, F. 1995. Logiques métisses: Cultural appropriation and postcolonial representations. In *Postcolonial Representations* pp. 1-21.NY: CornellU.

Murray, L. and Rice, K. (Eds.). 1999. Introduction. *Talking on the Page: Editing Aboriginal Texts* pp. xi-xxii. Toronto: University of Toronto Press.

Novac, S., Brown, J., Guyton, A. and Quance, M. 1996a. *Borderlands of Home-lessness: Women's Views on Alternative Housing.* Toronto:WomServNet

Novac, S., Brown, J. and Bourbonnais, C. 1996b. No Room of Her Own: A Litera-ture Review on Women and Homelessness. (Report.) Ottawa: CMHC

Perreault, P. and S. Vance (Eds.). 1999. Preface or Here are our voices. In *Writing the Circle: Native Women of Western Canada* pp. xv-xxx AB: NeWest.

Ralston, M. 1996. *Nobody Wants to Hear Our Truth.* Westport: Greenwood Press.

Sandercock, L. 1995. Voices from the borderlands. *J. of Plan. Educ and R 14*:77-88.

Sanderson, F. and Howard-Bobbiwash, H. (Eds.). 1997. *The Meeting Place: Aboriginal Life in Toronto.* Toronto: Native Canadian Centre of Toronto.

Sarris, G. 1968. *Keeping Slug Woman Alive* Berkeley: University of California.

Stout, M. and Kipling, G. 1998. *Aboriginal Women in Canada: Strategic Research Directions for Policy Development.* Ottawa: Status of Women Canada.

VanderStaay, S. 1994. Stories of (social) distress: Applied narrative analysis and public policy for the homeless. *J of Soc.Distress & Homeless 3*:299-319.

---

[1]   Rae Bridgman (PhD) is an urban anthropologist, professor, and visual artist in the Department of City Planning, Faculty of Architecture at the University of Manitoba.

Arctic Climate Change:
A Case of Mounting Evidence

John Yackel and David Barber[1]

Abstract

Irrefutable evidence from atmospheric, cryo-spheric, oceanographic, and biological researchers indicate that the Arctic is experiencing a significant and rapid climate change. Northern and Indigenous peoples report retreating glaciers, increasingly shorter snow and sea ice seasons and recent incidences of sunburn among children. Climate models suggest an accelerated rate of Arctic warming over the next century, the processes creating this are briefly discussed.

Introduction

As we enter into the new millennium it is becoming increasingly apparent that the Earth system is experiencing profound and unprecedented change. Human population and technology have evolved to the point where we are no longer a passive part of the Earth system. Rather, we have begun to modify the other components of the system (e.g., cryosphere, atmosphere, lithosphere and biosphere) by our industrial and agricultural practices. In order to fully understand the complex issues of global environmental change that challenge society (e.g., greenhouse warming, climate variability, ozone depletion, deforestation, acid rain, desertification, biodiversity, etc), we must learn how to view the Earth as a system and identify the complex linkages and feedback processes that exist among its components. Decisions to implement mitigative measures are based upon both a scientific and pragmatic understanding of this interactive system. A more complete understanding will be achieved only through continued measurement, monitoring and modeling of system processes.

The Marine Cryosphere

Consideration of our polar climates, and in particular, the marine cryosphere, within global climate modeling efforts is paramount due to the enhanced sensitivity of these regions to environmental perturbations. Snow covered sea ice makes up the majority of the marine cryosphere. Sea ice forms when the ocean water reaches a temperature of approximately 1.8°C, and after doing so, provides a platform for the deposition and accumulation of meteoric snow. Several studies have noted that the addition of snow on sea ice can have a significant effect on the climate of the polar regions. This is because the physical, thermal and radiative properties of snow are so vastly different from both sea ice and ocean water.

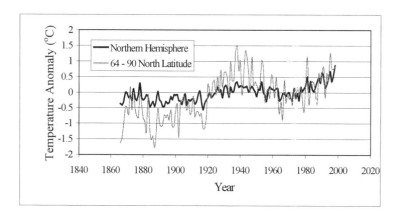

Figure 1. Average annual Northern Hemisphere and Arctic temperature anomalies (°C) from the 1950-80 mean. (Data acquired from NASA Goddard Institute for Space Studies.)

The sensitivity exists because the effect of snow covered sea ice is far out of proportion to its geographical area (Carmack 1986). The sensitivity arises due to a number of feedback processes operating between the cryosphere, hydrosphere and atmosphere, which may contribute to the amplification of any natural or anthropogenic perturbation (LeDrew 1986). The perturbation has been the introduction and increase in atmospheric 'greenhouse gases' since the industrial revolution. The climatic result of polar feedback processes is evident in the temperature record (Fig. 1). Annual average temperature anomalies from 1866 to 1999 are plotted for both the Northern Hemisphere as a whole and for the region between 64° and 90° north latitude. Trends are similar, yet the trend in temperature for the Arctic region is nearly three times hemispheric values.

The sea ice-albedo feedback mechanism is a complex system thought to be one of the dominant physical processes operating across the ocean-sea ice-atmosphere (OSA) interface (Ledley 1991). It is initiated with a perturbation to the snow/sea ice system, such as an increase in the surface temperature due to the advection of a warm air mass into the region. The resulting increase in the air to surface heat flux decreases the aerial extent of sea ice and snow cover, exposing a greater percentage of ocean water. The increase in open water, which has a much lower albedo (a measure of reflective ability) than snow covered sea ice, leads to a greater amount of absorbed solar radiation thereby increasing the total energy in the system; rising air temperature increases melting of snow and ice. If this was the only OSA feedback mechanism the polar regions would have experienced a runaway temperature increase long ago. There are several positive feedback processes operating within the system, with the destabilizing effects of these mitigated by only a few strong negative feedback's (Barry *et al.* 1984). Models suggest that when the system is perturbed, all feedback processes respond, but the relative importance of each feedback depends on the perturbation.

Our limited understanding of the physical processes is further demonstrated by differing projections of latitudinal temperature perturbations under a two times CO_2 atmosphere using results from six General Circulation Model (GCM) simulations (Fig. 2). These simulations provide contradictory evidence as to the response of the climate system at high latitudes, primarily because of uncertain roles of snow and clouds within the various feedback processes (Randall *et al.* 1994). The discrepancies highlight the importance and unresolved role of polar regions within our global climate system.

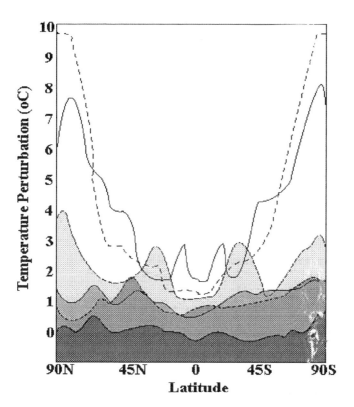

Figure 2. Latitudinally averaged temperature perturbations for six General Circulation Model simulations under a two times CO_2 atmosphere.

The first generation Canadian Global Coupled Model (CGCM1) (Flato *et al.* In Press) developed at the Canadian Centre for Climate Modelling and Analysis at the University of Victoria predicts that most of northern Canada, including nearly all of the Archipelago Islands, may experience a mean annual temperature increase of nearly 3°C by the year 2050 from 1980 levels, with much of Hudson Bay increasing by nearly 5°C. The feedback processes play a large role in the outcome of these computer-modeled projections.

Evidence for Arctic Climate Change

There have been numerous reports recently of a detectable change in the Arctic climate over the past three decades. For example, there has been a noticeable decrease in sea level pressure with anomalous atmospheric circulation in the Arctic (Walsh *et al.* 1996). This decrease in sea level pressure is consistent with a more variable and northward progression of the sub-arctic jet stream. The Arctic Atlantic ocean layer (200-500 meters) has warmed by approximately 1.5°C (Carmack *et al.* 1995).

Recently declassified Russian submarine data has been evaluated to show a reduction in the thermodynamic equilibrium thickness of Arctic pack ice from 3.1 m to 1.8 meters (Rothrock *et al.* 1999). Arctic sea ice data derived from satellite remote sensing for the 1953-1998 period indicate that 6 of the 10 minimum ice extent years have occurred since 1990, with increased regional variability in recent years. During summer 1998, record reductions in ice cover occurred in the Beaufort and Chukchi seas. Seven percent of the Arctic Basin that had been perennially ice covered was ice-free in 1998. Sea ice concentrations are currently reducing by approximately 34,000 km2 per year or 2.9% per decade over the past 18 years (Parkinson *et al.* 1999). The odds that this decreasing trend has occurred by chance are less than 0.1%. At this rate of ablation, we would experience an ice-free Arctic by the year 2050.

As a result, researchers at the Centre for Earth Observation Science, University of Manitoba have teamed up with the Canadian Ice Service in Ottawa to study the short and long-term effects of sea ice decay in the Arctic Archipelago. An earlier sea ice break-up has enormous political, environmental and economic implications for Canada, especially for regions within or adjacent to the Northwest Passage shipping routes (Barber *et al.* 1999).

At a more regional scale, the Geological Survey of Canada (GSC) has been studying the effects of climate change on permafrost in the Mackenzie Valley since large amounts of carbon are stored in Arctic ecosystems. Research suggests that much the Arctic tundra is in the process of switching from being a sink to being a source of CO_2. The change is coinciding with recent warming in the region and suggests that tundra ecosystems may exert a positive feedback on CO_2 concentrations and climate warming. The warming is believed to cause the soil to switch from sink to source by lowering the water table, thereby accelerating the rate of soil decomposition (CO_2 source) so that it dominates over photosynthesis (CO_2 sink) (Oechel *et al.*

1993). Another independent report indicates that from an 82-year data record, four out of the five earliest thaws on the Tanana River near Nenana, Alaska have occurred in the 1990's.

The biological community has also shown signs of climate change adaptation. The condition of western Hudson Bay polar bears has significantly deteriorated over the last 20 years due to a reduction in habitat (sea ice) as a function of increasing air temperature over the past 40 years (Stirling *et al.* 1999). In addition, Peary caribou in the Arctic have declined in population from 24,000 in 1961 to perhaps as few as 1,100 in 1997, mostly because of major die-offs that have occurred in recent years after heavy snowfalls and freezing rain covered the animals' food supply. A more variable climate including an increase in extreme weather events is consistent with a changing climate state.

The Greenpeace protest vessel Arctic Sunrise visited communities along the Bering Sea and Chukchi Sea coasts of Alaska, documenting observations by Native peoples which included: thinning sea ice, less precipitation, changes in migratory patterns of marine mammals and fishes (salmon in particular), retreat of the Bering Glacier and the advance of insect species into northern forests. Residents of Arviat, Nunavut, reported cases of sunburn in children (Winnipeg Free Press, 2000), until recently 'sunburn' has little meaning in Inuktitut.

Mitigating the Effects of Arctic Climate Change

Canada, as a signatory to the UNs' Framework Convention on Climate Change (FCCC) is part of an international effort to address climate change. At the recent Third Conference of the Parties (COP-3) to the FCCC, 1997 in Kyoto, Japan, over 10,000 participants, including representatives from governments, intergovernmental organizations, and NGOs discussed climate change. Following a week and a half of intense formal and informal negotiations, parties to the FCCC adopted the Kyoto Protocol on December 11, 1997. The Kyoto Protocol calls for Annex I countries of the FCCC to reduce their collective emissions of six greenhouse gases (GHGs) by an average of approximately 5 per cent below 1990 levels between 2008 and 2012. For Canada, this means reducing emissions by 6 per cent below 1990 levels by the period 2008-2012. The Protocol also establishes: emissions trading; joint implementation between developed countries; encourages developed and developing countries to work together on joint emissions reduction projects; continued investment in climate system science; identification of the impacts of climate change; and, update Annex I countries programs to facilitate adequate adaptation to climate change.

The efforts of Natural Resources Canada (NRCan) are part of a broad national response to climate change. In April 1995, Canada released its National Action Program on Climate Change (NAPCC). This program provides a strategy for all levels of government - federal, provincial and municipal and for decision-makers in all sectors of the Canadian economy to address climate change. In climate change adaptation, Canada has progressed in understanding the possible impacts of change through a series of Canada Country Study reports published by Environment Canada in 1997. NRCan research figures prominently in many of these reports. The reports combine scientific knowledge from a range of investigations and highlight the effects that could occur across Canada as the climate changes. NRCan also pursues memoranda of understanding and letters of cooperation with key national associations to encourage their members to take voluntary action on energy efficiency and greenhouse gas abatement, including: associations representing the oil, gas and coal; pipelines and electrical utilities; mining, retail and manufacturing; and homebuilders, municipalities and school boards.

Today, greenhouse gas emissions are rising since signing the 1997 Kyoto protocol. Canada must reduce emissions by approximately 26% to reach this target. This trend does not bode well for the sustainability of Inuit ecosystems in Arctic Canada. These recent developments leave numerous questions unanswered, with just as many likely to develop over the next several years. A salient list of broad ranging issues for the Inuit people and Canada as a whole include:

1. Will the rate of climate warming in the Arctic continue at current, lesser or greater rates? How will the International community respond to Canada and other Annex I countries that fail to meet their emission limits set out in the Kyoto Protocol?

2. How will a very different Arctic climate manifest itself within the various environmental, social and economic communities of Canada? Which of these sectors is likely to rise to the forefront of the political battlefield?

3. How will Inuit and Canada as a whole adapt to Arctic climate change? How will Arctic ecosystems adapt, diminish or perish in response to the expected continuation of rate of warming?

These questions will only be answered with continued measurement, monitoring and modeling of Arctic system processes. The salient analysis results must continue to be effectively presented to representatives from all levels of government so that policy decisions, such as those made at Kyoto, can be implemented.

References

Barber, D., Yackel, J. and Hanesiak, J. 1999. *Sea Ice Decay for Marine Navigation*

Barry, R., Henderson-Sellers, A. and Shine, K. 1984. Climate sensitivity and the marginal cryosphere, pp.221-237, In J. Hansen and T. Takahashi (Eds.), *Climate Processes . Geophys. Monog.* 29. 5:368.

Carmack, E. 1986. Circulation and mixing in ice-covered water. In N. Untersteiner (Ed.) *The Geophysics of Sea Ice* pp.641-712, NATO

Carmack, E., MacDonald, R. Perkin, R. McLaughlin, F. and Pearson, R. 1995. Evidence of warming of Atlantic water in the Southern Canadian Basin of the Arctic Ocean, *Geophys. Res. Lett.* 22:1061-1064.

Flato, G., Boer, G., Lee, W., McFarlane, N., Ramsden, D., Reader, M. and Weaver, A. In Press. Centre for Climate Modelling and Analysis Global Coupled Model and its Climate, *Climate Dynamics*.

Ledley, C. 1991. Snow on sea ice. *J. of Geophys. Res.* 96:(17):195-208.

LeDrew, R. 1986. Sensitivity of the Arctic Climate: A factor in developing planning strategies for Arctic Heritage. *Env Cons*13(3):215-228.

Oechel, W., Hastings, S., Jenkins, M., Riechers,G., Grulke, N. and Vourlitis, G.. 1993. Recent change of arctic tundra ecosystems from a net carbon sink to a source. *Nature.* 361: 520-526.

Parkinson, C., Cavalieri, D., Gloersen, P., Zwally, H. and Comiso, J. 1999. Arctic sea ice extents, areas, and trends, 1978-1996. *J. Geophys. Res. 104*(20):837-856.

Randall *et al.* 1994. Analysis of snow feedbacks in 14 general circulation models. *J. of Geophys. Res*. 99(20):757-771

Rothrock, D., Yu, Y. and Maykut, G. 1999. Thinning of the Arctic sea-ice cover. *Geophys. Res. Lett.*, 26:3469-3472.

Stirling, I., Lunn N. and Iacozza, J. 1999. Long-term trends in the population ecology of polar bears in Western Hudson Bay in relation to climatic change. *Arctic* 51(3):294-306.

Walsh, J., W. Chapman, W. and Shy, T. 1996. Recent decrease of sea level pressure in the central Arctic. *J Climate.* 9:480-486.

---

[1]   John Yackel is an Assistant Professor in Geography at the University of Calgary, Alberta. David Barber is a Professor of Geography and Director of the Centre for Earth Observation Science, University of Manitoba.

Inuvialuit Knowledge of Climate Change

Dyanna Riedlinger[1]

Abstract

This paper provides one example of how traditional knowledge can complement science-based Arctic climate change research. I discuss how cumulative knowledge of the environment held by local experts can contribute to the process of hypotheses formulation and the identification of research priorities in order to understand the potential impacts of climate change in northern ecosystems and the communities that depend on them. Assessments of change by the Inuvialuit community of Sachs Harbour are based on a rich knowledge of local trends and a historical connection to and reliance on the land.

Introduction

Many climate change forecasts, using general circulation models (GCMs), suggest that global warming associated with increased levels of atmospheric carbon dioxide will be felt earliest and strongest in high latitude regions (Cohen 1997, Maxwell 1997, Kattenberg *et al.* 1996). There remains uncertainty concerning the rate and extent of physical, biological and human impacts, particularly at local and regional scales. Understanding impacts and developing adaptive strategies will require approaches at appropriate spatial and temporal scales. Arctic climate change research is often hindered by inadequate observational data, seasonal limitations and a general lack of historical baseline data against which to compare change. For example, instrumental climatological data was not systematically collected until the 1950's in much of the Arctic (Maxwell 1980). Forecasts generated by climate models, while key to predicting change, simulate the climate at coarse spatial and temporal scales, and thus are not as useful for understanding local or regional impacts of change (Giorgi and Mearns 1991). Compared to other regions of the world, scientific knowledge of Arctic physical, biological and ecological processes is often inadequate for predicting impacts. Understanding climate-related change in the Canadian Arctic can enhanced by including local knowledge of the North, often termed traditional knowledge (TK), Indigenous knowledge or Inuit knowledge. TK is defined by Berkes (1999) as "a cumulative body of knowledge, practice and belief, evolving by adaptive processes and handed down through generations by cultural transmission, about the relationship of living things (including humans) with one another and their environment". It is "a way of life, based on the experience of the individual and the community, as well as the knowledge passed down from one's elders and incorporated in indigenous languages. The knowledge is constantly being adapted to the changing environment of each community and will remain current as long as people still use the land and the sea and their resources" (Fehr and Hurst 1996 1996). The extensive use and knowledge of the Arctic landscape found in northern communities is a rich source of ecological and environmental expertise that may in some instances be spatially and temporally more complete than other sources (e.g. Ferguson *et al.*1998).

Some work has been done to explore Inuit knowledge of climate and climate change (e.g. Fox 1998), specifically the role of oral history in providing a view of past climate (Spink 1969, Cruikshank 1984, Fast and Berkes 1998), and wildlife sensitivity to change (Ferguson 1997). Recent traditional knowledge projects associated with environmental change and cumulative impact assessments have demonstrated that accumulated knowledge of the land and environmental indicators allowed local experts to distinguish subtle patterns, cycles and changes in ecosystems (Bill *et al.* 1996), and to interpret and understand weather patterns and seasonal processes (MacDonald *et al.* 1997). Inuit perspectives of climate change have been documented (Riewe and Oakes 1994, Johnson 1999), and the need to include northern communities and traditional knowledge in global change research suggested (Kassi 1993, Kuptana 1996, Bielawski 1997, Cohen 1997). It is clear that TK of climate and community-based assessments of change can and should contribute to Arctic climate change research; it is less clear how this can be accomplished. Little work to date has explored the links between western science and TK in the context of Arctic climate change research.

In this paper, I explore how Inuvialuit TK and western science-based approaches can be used as complementary ways of knowing, understanding, explaining and measuring the potential impacts of climate change in northern ecosystems and the communities that depend on them. The process of formulating research questions and hypotheses is an example of a framework, or process, which facilitates the use of both traditional and scientific knowledge. The ideas expressed in this paper are based on findings from research in progress with a community-based, collaborative project in Sachs Harbour (*Ikaahuk*), an Inuvialuit community of 120 people in the Inuvialuit Settlement Region (ISA), Western Arctic. The project is organized and designed by the International Institute of Sustainable Development in partnership with the community of Sachs Harbour and involves filming a documentary on climate change from the perspective of the community, and exploring how TK can contribute to scientific research on climate change in the North.

Traditional Knowledge and Western Science

Cultures have unique ways of understanding, perceiving, experiencing and defining reality (Cashman 1991) based on cognitive understandings or views of the world embedded in distinctive historical, cultural and social experiences, or worldviews, that define and guide the relationship between humans and the environment. The cultural backdrop and worldview that shapes knowledge gained from western science is very different from the values, perspectives and processes that are associated with TK. Western science is a social construct; its development occurred largely within the internal dynamics of European thought and civilization (Goonatilake 1998). Inuit knowledge is based on cognitive understandings of the world embedded in Inuit culture, history and social organization, and is closely linked to the Arctic climate and environment (Kuptana 1996). Western traditions separate *knower* from *known*, whereas Inuit knowledge is obtained, held and applied by the resource users themselves as a part of daily life. Generally, but not exclusively, each way of knowing can be associated with unique contexts and scales.

The contribution of TK has been well documented in land use, environmental assessment, ecology, management, protected areas planning, co-management and contaminants research (Kuhn and Duerden 1996, Berkes 1999). The value of promoting collaboration between TK and western scientific knowledge is recognized, however, questions of how to link, integrate, bridge or *create a conversation between* (Kendrick, personal communication) TK and science recur in Arctic science and literature (e.g. Ferguson *et al.* 1998, Huntington 1998). Research that include TK may be outside conventional institutional funding structures and time lines, and are challenged by complex questions of intellectual property, data accuracy, consistency and cross-cultural awareness. The challenge of creating a bridge between two ways of knowing is compounded by the fact that science is seen to represent a universal, rational, objective approach to understanding the world; other ways of knowing are often marginalized as a result.

The differences and challenges associated with bridging the gap between western scientific approaches and TK, are key to finding common ground. Framing the discussion in terms of scale and context provides a useful starting point to highlight how two ways of knowing can complement each other more specifically, in understanding Arctic climate change. Linking TK and western science can enlarge, expand and enrich the extent and scope of climate change research, both conceptually (i.e. expanding the conceptual framework) and politically (i.e. involving communities in research).

Inuvialuit Observations and Arctic Climate Change

My research is based on accumulating evidence suggesting that climate change effects are already being observed at the community level in the Arctic. Changes in the seasonal extent of sea ice, fish and wildlife abundance and distribution, permafrost thaw and erosion are considered without precedent, and fundamentally different from natural change and variability in the weather (Riedlinger 1999). The community of Sachs Harbour maintains a direct reliance on and connection with the land through hunting, fishing, some trapping and small-scale tourism (sport hunting) (Inuvialuit Harvest Studies 1996, Sachs Harbour Community Conservation Plan 1992). Environmental change associated with changes in weather (known in Inuvialuktun as *sila*) such as breakup and freeze up times, animal abundance and distribution, and permafrost thaw have a significant and noticeable impact on seasonal activities. Brief examples of the kinds of climate-related change observed in Sachs Harbour are discussed below, as described from a series of interviews conducted in the summer and fall of 1999.

Sea Ice, Permafrost, Fish, Wildlife and Weather. Changes related to the seasonal extent of sea ice (*siku*), and the timing of its formation and breakup were consistent topics of discussion. Community members described how there is less or no multiyear ice floes (*otokrarpak*) in the summer, and that the permanent pack ice which once was visible to the community throughout the year is now further away. Spring break up is occurring earlier and faster, and freeze up, though perhaps not as noticeable as break up, is coming later. There is less landfast (shore) ice in the winter and hunters are unable to go as far out onto the ice. The annual ice is thinner now, and this has effects on ice movement, the formation and distribution of leads (*uiniq*), cracks (*aayuraq*), and pressure ridges (*quglungniq*). Increased permafrost thaw has had a visible impact on the landscape around the community, both inland and along coastal areas. The active layer is observed to be more extensive and develops earlier. Permafrost-related change was observed in the context of *the land going down in some places*, which may suggest increased thermakarst activity such as thaw slumps. Increased melting of the permafrost is resulting in the land getting *rougher*, the *water coming up as the land goes down*, more *mud and wet ground, holes in the ground, exposed ice on the hills and lake edges*, and *increased coastal and inland erosion and slumping*. This has an impact on the ability and ease of travel on the land, building stability and construction, erosion, roads, and other community activities, such as preparing gravesites.

There have been observations of southern warmer water fish species extending beyond their historical geographical ranges. In 1993, Bankslanders caught two species of pacific salmon (identified by the Department of Fisheries and Oceans as sockeye (*Oncorhynchus nerka*) and pink (*Oncorhynchus gorbuscha*) in their nets when traditionally such occurrences were unheard of. Least cisco (*Coregonus sardinella*), also known as herring or *qaaktaq* in the community, is more common now. It is clear that Inuvialuit hunters, elders and other community members have little uncertainty that weather-related change is occurring. Things are different now, and it is having a visible impact on traditional livelihoods and community life. Elders discussed change in the context of seasons rather than specific weather patterns; they described longer summers, shorter winters, and a faster melting season. For many, the years and the seasons are *getting crazy now*. Weather phenomena are more unpredictable, and there are more sudden changes that are increasingly more intense. Forecasting conditions and predicting weather are skills gained from generations of accumulated knowledge of weather patterns, storms and indicators of change. The weather determines when you can hunt, so hunters watch the weather. The ability to forecast conditions and predict change may be at risk. One elder described how *when there is going to be a big storm there is a sign and we prepare for it*. Now, he says, *I can't predict the weather like before* (Peter Esau, Sachs Harbour, NWT).

Linking Traditional Knowledge and Western Science

Environmental change associated with changes in the weather is already noticed in the North, and while scientists try to understand the impacts of change, communities are finding that changes in the weather are appearing permanent and are looking for answers as well. One process that may facilitate collaborative Arctic climate change research is the formulation of research questions and hypotheses. Collaboration between communities and scientists at the initial stage of research expands the scope of inquiry and also ensures meaningful participation and involvement of communities in research planning and design.

The method of empirical science is hypothetico-deductive; constructing hypotheses and testing them against observation and experience (Popper 1959, Peters 1991). Formulating research questions and hypotheses is seen as the most important (and subjective) part of the research process, and determines the research that follows. Researchers formulate hypotheses based on the possibilities of which they are aware; in other words, they choose their research questions from the set of concepts available to them (Keddy 1989). The kinds of questions asked are a product of the concepts and possibilities available; they originate within a culturally specific picture of the world and understanding of the relationship between humans and environment. In the western scientific tradition, this is often considered to be the correct picture of the world (Feyerabend 1987).

Limiting research to one 'correct' view of the world may limit our understanding of complex environmental phenomena such as global change. Inuvialuit knowledge can expand the range of concepts and possibilities upon which to base research questions and hypotheses by offering a different picture and understanding of the world. For example, TK can "nudge" the scientific imagination and give rise to new concepts (Goonatilake 1998). Observations of change are rooted in a rich knowledge of local trends, patterns and processes that is guided by generations of experience and embedded in a historical context. Even if we did know *how* to measure the impacts of climate change on the Arctic, we first need to know *what* to measure. In the Arctic, Inuit knowledge of the Arctic physical environment and ecological processes may exceed scientific knowledge in some instances. Community-based assessments of change are based on knowledge of expected change, or natural weather variability, as compared to unexpected change, or change that is outside of the historical experience of the community. For example, observations of increased land and coastal erosion from permafrost thaw were framed in the context of natural variability as distinguished from new change. Coastal and inland erosion and slumping are common occurrences, products of wind, rain, sun and waves.

> However, the slides [slumping] are all over now, not just in certain areas. People have seen them before, but there is more now. Before it was once in a while, mostly coastline. Now, more inland. Even a lake that dried up because an outflow developed.

Observations can provide a guide for climate change research in the North, adding temporal depth and spatial detail. TK of climate-related change may provide indicators or cues of change that may be missed, or rarely measured by western scientists. Detailed, cumulative knowledge of the weather, land and ice can expand the scope of inquiry through insight into questions about biophysical relationships, feedbacks between linkages, and driving factors. For example, how sensitive are muskox (*umingmak*) to changes in the weather? Where is permafrost thaw and soil erosion most obvious? How fast does it melt in the spring? What are the ice, wind, and temperature conditions during, before and after breakup? Answers to these kinds of questions can translate global processes such as climate change into regional and local scales and contexts, as well as providing a basis for predicting broader impacts of change.

In addition to broadening the conceptual scope of research, the political or social scope of research can also be expanded. Including communities in the initial phases of research results in the identification of research priorities as seen and from the perspective of communities. What changes are most noticeable? What kinds of changes are having the most impact on daily life and seasonal activities? The contribution of TK is about addressing the marginalization of northern communities from research and decision making as much as it is about the potential contribution to scientific knowledge. For example, the Sachs Harbour Community Conservation Plan (1995) identifies research priority for *ugyuk* (bearded seal) and *natchiq* (ringed seal), species identified as requiring research into the occurrence of "skinny" or deformed seals. Inuvialuit believe the increasing occurrence of skinny seal pups is an indicator of change related to earlier breakup and the lack of sea ice. Increasingly, communities are questioning conventional research methods and requesting more involvement in the design and implementation of research that affects both their communities and the resources they depend on. Northern communities are likely the first to confront climate-related change. Bridging the gap between community concerns and scientific research requires communities having an active role in determining research priorities. One scientist at a recent conference referred to this as a change in emphasis to "bottom-up science" (Carmack, 1999, special presentation to the Beaufort Sea Conference 2000).

Conclusion: Arctic Science as Two Ways of Knowing

Climate change research can provide a rich setting for linking TK and western science as two ways of knowing and understanding changes in the Arctic. This paper addresses the *how to* question of linking TK and western science, recognizing that this is only possible with both meaningful participation of northern communities in research and an acceptance of the knowledge of Inuit communities as knowledge and not merely information. The *how to* question is addressed here in the context of climate change research and the formulation of hypotheses and research questions. The process of hypothesis development provides a valuable framework to coordinate bringing together knowledge from both scientists and Arctic communities. TK can complement the process of hypotheses formulation through expanding the scope of inquiry and allowing for a broader frame of reference within which to ask questions. Collaboration between scientists and Inuvialuit can enrich an understanding of climate change in the North at a scale and in a context that is currently under-represented, and where changes are already being experienced. Arctic climate change research that reflects and is informed by two ways of knowing will be better suited to asking meaningful questions and involving northern communities.

Acknowledgments

I am indebted to members of Sachs Harbour who shared their time and experiences, especially Sarah Kuptana for taking me in and teaching me so much. This research would not have been possible without financial support from the Walter and Duncan Gordon Foundation, the Arctic Institute of North America Lorraine Allison Scholarship, and the University of Manitoba; as well as in kind support and the opportunity to participate in this project received from IISD and the community of Sachs Harbour. I am also grateful to Tim Papakyriakou and Duane Peltzer for improving earlier drafts of this paper.

354

References

Berkes, F. 1999. *Sacred ecology. TEK and Resource Management*. London and Philadelphia: Taylor and Francis.

Bielawski, E. 1997. Aboriginal participation in global change research in the Northwest Territories of Canada. In W. Oechel, T. Callaghan, T. Gilmanov, J. Holten, B. Maxwell, U. Molau, and B. Sveinbjornsson (Eds). *Global Change and Arctic Terrestrial Ecosystems*. pp. 475-483. New York: Springer-Verlag.

Bill, L., Crozier, J., Surrendi, D., Flett, L. and MacDonald, D. 1996. *A Report of Wisdom Synthesized from the TK Component Studies*. Edmonton: Northern River Basins Study.

Carmack, E. 1999. Special presentation to the Beaufort Sea Conference 2000. September 15-18, 1999. Inuvik, NWT.

Cashman, K. 1991. Systems of knowledge as systems of domination: The limitations of established meaning. *Agriculture and Human Values* 8 (1, 2):49-58.

Cohen, S. 1997. What if and so what in northwest Canada: Could climate change make a difference to the future of the Mackenzie Basin? *Arctic* 50(4): 293-307.

Cruikshank, J. 1984. Oral tradition and scientific research: Approaches to knowledge in the north. In: *Social Science in the North: Communicating Northern Values*. Ottawa: ACUNS (Occas. St. 9).

Fast, H. and Berkes, F. 1998. Climate change, northern subsistence and land-based economies. In: Mayer, N. and Avis, W. (Eds.). *The Cross-Canada Country Study: Climate Impacts and Adaptation*. pp.206-226. Ottawa: Env Canada.

Fehr, A. and Hurst, W. 1996. *Two Ways of Knowing: Indigenous and Scientific Knowledge*. Inuvik, NT: Aurora Res Inst.

Ferguson, M. 1997. Arctic tundra caribou and climate change:Questions of temporal and spatial scales. *Geo. Sc. Can.* 23(4):245-52.

Ferguson, M., Williamson, R. and Messier, F. 1998. Inuit knowledge of long term changes in a population of arctic tundra caribou. *Arctic* 51(3):201-19.

Feyerabend, P. 1987. *Farewell to Reason*. London: Verso.

Fox, S. 1998. *Inuit Knowledge of Climate and Climate Change*. Unpub. MES Thesis, Dept.Geography. ON: Univ. of Waterloo.

Giorgi, F., and Mearns, L. 1991. Approaches to simulation of regional climate change. *Rev. of Geophysics* 29:191-216.

Goonatilake, S. 1998. *Toward a Global Science: Mining Civilizational Knowledge*. Bloomington, IN: Indiana Univ. Press.

Huntington, H. 1998. Observations on the utility of the semi-directive interview for documenting TEK. *Arctic* 51(3): 237-42.

Inuvialuit Harvest Study Data Report. 1996. Inuvik, NT.

Johnson, T. 1999. World out of balance. *Native Americas: Hemispheric Journal of Indigenous Issues*, Fall/winter 1999.

Kassi, N. 1993. Native Perspectives on Climate Change. In G. Wall (Ed.). *Impacts of Climate Change on Resource Management of the North*. 16:43-49. Waterloo, ON: Dept of Geography, University of Waterloo.

Kattenberg, A., Giorgi, F., Grassl, H., Meehl, G., Mitchell, J., Stouffer, R.,

Tokioka, T., Weaver, A., and Wigley, T. 1996. Climate models projections of future climate. In J. Houghton, L. Meira Filho, B. Callander, N. Harris, A. Kattenberg and K. Maskell, (Eds). *Science of Climate Change.* pp.285-357. Cambridge: University. Press.

Keddy, P. 1989. *Competition.* Population and Community Biology Series. London: Chapman and Hall.

Kendrick, A. 1999. Pers. com. Ph.D. candidate, Natural Resources Institute, U.of Manitoba.

Kuhn, R. and Duerden F. 1996. A Review of TEK: An interdisciplinary Canadian perspective. *Culture* 14(1): 71-84.

Kuptana, R. 1996. *Inuit Perspectives on Climate Change.*UN framework convention on climate change. Geneva, 16-19 July.

Maxwell, B. 1980. *The Climate of the Canadian Arctic Islands and Adjacent Waters. Vol. 1.*Climatological St 30. Downsview, ON: Atmos. Environment Services.

Maxwell, B. 1997. *Responding to Global Climate Change in Canada's Arctic. Vol. II Canada Country Study: Climate Impacts an Adaptations.* Ottawa: Environment Canada.

McDonald, M. Arragutainaq L. and Novalinga Z. 1997. *Voices from the Bay: Traditional Ecological Knowledge of Inuit and Cree in the Hudson Bay Bioregion.* Ottawa: CARC and Sanikiluaq, NT.

Peters, R. 1991. *A Critique for Ecology.* Cambridge: Cambridge University Press.

Popper, K. 1959. *The Logic of Scientific Discovery.* New York: Basic Books.

Riedlinger, D. 1999. Climate change and the Inuvialuit of Banks Island, NWT: Using TEK to complement western science. *InfoNorth* 52(4):430-432.

Riewe, R. and Oakes, J. (Eds). 1994. *Biological Implications of Global Change: Northern Perspectives.* Environmental research series, Occas. pub. 33. Edmonton: CCI.

Sachs Harbour Community Conservation Plan. A Plan for the Conservation and Management of Renewable Resources and Lands in the Vicinity of Banksland, Northwest Territories. 1992. Inuvik, NT: Wildlife Mgt. Advisory Council.

Spink, J. 1969. Historic Eskimo awareness of past changes in sea level. *Musk-Ox* 5:37-40.

---

[1]   Dyanna Riedlinger is a graduate student at the Natural Resources Institute, University of Manitoba.

Chemical Contaminants in the Canadian Arctic

Lyle Lockhart and Gary Stern[1]

Abstract

In contrast to the intuitive expectation that the Canadian Arctic should be free of industrial contaminants because of its small population, limited industrial activity and geographic location, studies have consistently revealed the presence of a range of contaminants typical of human societies in temperate locations. These include the radioactive isotope, cesium-137, organohalogens like DDT and dieldrin, combustion by products like polycyclic aromatic hydrocarbons, and natural elements, especially mercury. In some instances levels of mercury and organochlorine compounds are high enough that restricted consumption of arctic animals should be implemented.

Introduction

The common perception of the Arctic as a pristine environment free from the influences of industrial man is giving way to a more troublesome perception of the North as a planetary sink for semi-volatile contaminants deposited by moving air currents. Evidence is now incontrovertible that chemical contaminants originating outside the Canadian Arctic have become dispersed widely there. One of the clearest examples of this phenomenon is the distribution of cesium-137, an artificial byproduct of the fission of uranium in nuclear bombs, released to the atmosphere during bomb tests (Hutchison-Benson *et al.* 1985). The detection of bomb fallout is so reliable that it has been used as an aid for dating arctic lake sediment layers (Lockhart *et al.* 1998). Fallout of cesium-137 and cesium-134 from the Chernobyl accident in 1986 was detected in the Canadian Arctic shortly after the event (Taylor *et al.* 1988).

Synthetic organic compounds like DDT, PCBs, toxaphene, HCH (hexachlorocyclohexane), chlordane and others have been identified consistently in samples from the Arctic. Several of these compounds were used extensively as insecticides in agriculture and public health following World War II. The uses of PCB were different since they were used in industrial applications, not as pesticides. These compounds are remarkable for their stability in the environment and for their ability to concentrate in successive steps of food chains. They are soluble in fat and so tend to concentrate in fatty organs of animals, notably those near the tops of food webs. As early as 1970, Reinke *et al.* (1972) identified low but measurable quantities of DDT, DDE and dieldrin in whitefish and lake trout from lakes in the Northwest Territories. Risebrough and Berger (1971) reported DDT and PCBs in fish from Minto Lake in northern Quebec. Subsequently, stable organochlorine compounds have been measured in fish and marine mammals from throughout the Canadian Arctic (Muir *et al.* 1990a,b). The atmosphere has been the inferred source of these synthetic organic contaminants (Risebrough and Berger 1971, Norstrom and Muir 1986) because no local sources exist to explain their distributions. Direct measurements of stable organochlorines in air samples have shown conclusively the ability of these compounds to disperse atmospherically (Hoff and Chan 1986).

Heavy metals provide a more complex problem since they are present naturally at all locations but their levels may also be enhanced by additions due to anthropogenic emissions from local or distant sources. Perhaps the clearest example is lead which was dispersed widely due to alkyl lead additives to gasolines. Different sources of lead have different isotopic compositions and so it has been possible in many cases to trace lead back to its sources using analytical techniques capable of discriminating among isotopes of slightly differing masses (Sturges and Barrie 1987). The isotope mixture has made it possible to show that lead deposits to the Greenland ice cap have declined as a result of lower contributions from North American sources after elimination of leaded gasoline fuels (Boutron *et al.* 1991). Similarly, the isotopic mixture has made it possible to detect imported lead in teeth of arctic marine mammals. Outridge and Stewart (1999) showed the contamination of teeth of walrus from northern Hudson Bay and Foxe Basin with industrial lead. Mercury is the most difficult heavy metal to deal with because it does not have a convenient difference in isotope ratios in different deposits. However, several lines of evidence suggest that levels of mercury have been increasing over the last century. For example, levels of mercury have been increasing in seals and whales (Wagemann *et al.* 1996), in sea

358

birds (Braune 1999), in lake sediments (Lockhart *et al.* 1998) and in archeological samples from humans and animals (Hart-Hansen *et al.* 1991, Wheatley and Wheatley 1988).

Intake of Contaminants by Arctic People

The driving force behind studies of contaminants in the Arctic is the high dietary intake of these compounds by indigenous arctic people which is calculated as the product of the amount of food eaten and the concentration of contaminant in that food. A detailed study of dietary intakes of contaminants by arctic people in the community of Broughton Island, Nunavut, (Kinloch *et al.* 1992) found that people in that community consumed considerably more wild foods than had been realized. Daily amounts consumed are shown in Fig. 1 (adapted from Kinloch *et al.* 1992). The overall average daily consumption reported by women and girls who normally consume wild foods was 460.5 g, while the figure was reduced to 276.4 g when averaged over all the people who responded, including both those who did and those who did not consume wild foods. The comparable figures for men and boys were 543.9 g for consumers and 326.7 g when non-consumers were included.

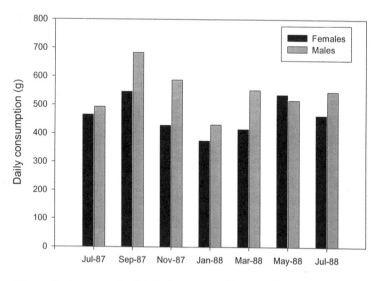

Figure 1. Amount of wild food consumed by people of Broughton Island, Nunavut, determined by surveys in 1987 and 1988.(Adapted from Fig. 1 and 2, Kinloch *et al.*, 1992)

Studies of PCBs in human milk have shown levels several times higher in women from the arctic coast than in those from southern Canada (Dewailly *et al.* 1989). Milk from Inuit women from northern Quebec had an average PCB concentration of 111 ug L^{-1} as compared with milk from Caucasian women in southern Quebec who had an average PCB content of only 28.4 ug L^{-1} (Table 1). PCBs are synthetic compounds with no natural sources and so there is no doubt that these PCBs are the result of human activities.

Table 1. PCBs in milk from women in northern and southern Quebec.					
	N	PCB in whole milk (ug L^{-1})		PCB in milk fat (mg kg^{-1})	
		Mean	Range	Mean	Range
Inuit women, northern Quebec	24	111.3	16 - 514	3.60	05 – 14.7
Caucasian women, southern Quebec	48	28.4	5 - 115	0.77	0.3 – 3.2
Data from Dewailly et al., 1989, Table 1.					

A similar trend has been found with mercury in people. Health and Welfare Canada (1979, 1984) surveyed the geographic distribution of mercury in blood of Aboriginal people from over 450 communities throughout Canada. They described blood mercury levels as follows: Under 20 parts per billion for normal range; From 20 to 100 parts per billion for increasing risk; and Over 100 parts per billion for at risk. Their results are represented graphically in Figure 2 showing the proportion of results exceeding the normal range (Wheatley and Paradis 1995). Northern people, especially those from coastal communities, tended to have higher proportions of results over the normal range than did people from southern aboriginal communities.

Unlike PCBs, mercury is a natural element present throughout the ecosystem. However, several lines of evidence indicate that inputs of mercury to the North have been increasing as a result of human activities outside the Arctic. The major source to the North appears to be the atmosphere and the major anthropogenic sources to the atmosphere are combustion of fuels and garbage and smelting of sulphide ores (Nriagu and Pacyna 1988). It is not yet clear how much of the exposure of northern people to mercury is natural and how much results from the recent increases in inputs of mercury from southern sources.

360

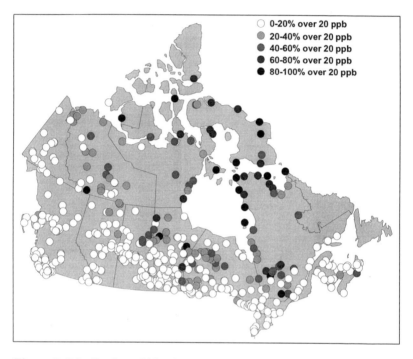

Figure 2. Distribution of blood mercury levels in people from Aboriginal communities in Canada. The symbols are shaded in accordance with the proportion of results in a given range for each community. (Data are plotted from tabulations by Health and Welfare Canada, 1979 and 1984.)

Contaminants in Food Animals

The major pathway supplying contaminants to arctic people are food animals which vary from community to community and seasonally but generally include herbivores like caribou, fish of several species and, in coastal communities, carnivores like seals and whales. The problematic contaminants are those that persist for long periods and accumulate through food chains. Aquatic food chains in the Arctic are several steps long whereas the steps to terrestrial herbivores are only two; aquatic animals are often more highly contaminated than terrestrial ones. Levels of most contaminants were reviewed by the Canadian Arctic Contaminants

Assessment Report (Jensen *et al.* 1997) and the Arctic Monitoring and Assessment Program (AMAP 1998). Contaminant levels in ringed seals is shown for PCBs (Fig.3). Marine mammals show higher concentrations of fat-soluble contaminants in males than females because females clear these compounds during lactation. The highest mean concentrations of PCBs in blubber were in males from Arviat (2066 ng g^{-1} [N=30]) but there was considerable variation. Similar data are available for fish and the geographic distribution of PCBs in lake trout is shown in Figure 4.

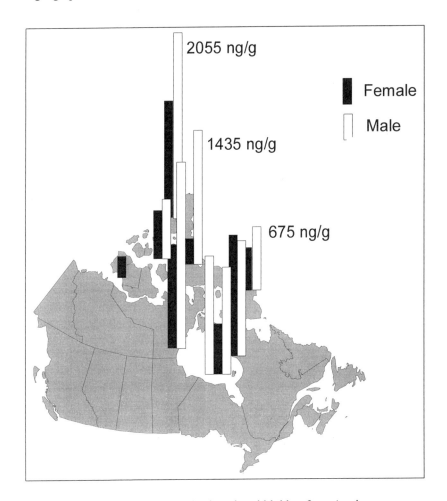

Figure 3. PCB concentrations in ringed seal blubber from Arctic communities, 1989 to 1994 (Data from Jansen *et al.* 1997).

362

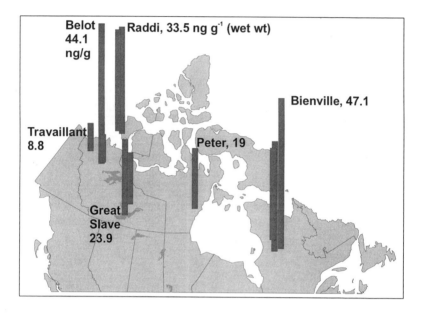

Figure 4. Mean concentrations of total PCBs in muscle of lake trout from several northern lakes (Data from Jensen *et al.* 1997).

In addition to the synthetic organic compounds, mercury is a problem in fish and marine mammals. The commercial marketing of fish in Canada limits sales to fish with mercury levels under 0.5 ug g^{-1}. The Medical Services Branch of Health Canada has recommended a lower limit of 0.2 ug g^{-1} for people who consume large quantities of fish (Health and Welfare Canada 1979). Different species of fish accumulate different quantities of mercury, depending on a number of biological factors, notably the feeding habits. Figure 5 shows the mean levels of mercury in lake trout from lakes in the Yukon, NWT and Nunavut. These mercury measurements have been accumulated over about 30 years partly from the Fisheries Inspection Laboratories and partly from research projects within the Department of Fisheries and Oceans. The numbers of samples vary from lake to lake and in some instances represent as few as two individuals. Nevertheless the data represent the best survey we have to describe levels over the broad geographic range of Northern Canada. Comparing the levels of mercury with those recommended for consumption, 16 % of arithmetic mean muscle mercury levels (11 samples) fell under the 0.2 ug g^{-1} level recommended for unrestricted consumption. 51 % (35 samples) exceeded 0.2 ug g^{-1} but did not exceed 0.5 ug g^{-1}. 32 % (22 samples) contained mercury over the limit of 0.5 ug g⁻¹ for commercial sale of fish in Canada. Recent evaluation by Health Canada of mercury concentrations in the edible muscle of catches of fish from several lakes in the southwestern NWT resulted in consumption advisories shown in Table 2. In addition to the recommendations listed Health Canada also advised that consumption by pregnant women and children be limited to half those shown in the table.

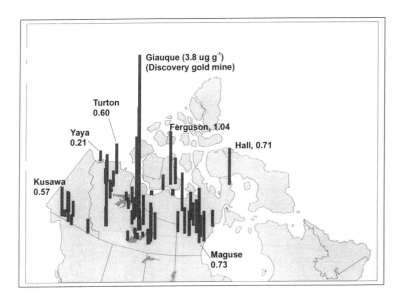

Figure 5. Relative mean mercury levels in muscle of lake trout from lakes in the Northwest Territories and Nunavut, 1971 to 1999. Arithmetic means were calculated with no allowance for fish size or gender. (Data from Food Inspection Service, Fisheries and Oceans, and Lockart, unpublished.)

Trends in Contaminant Levels

There are too few data to reach final conclusions about trends in levels of several contaminants. However, there are good indications that inputs of some have declined. For example, The Canadian Arctic Assessment Report gave evidence that air concentrations of HCH have declined by approximately 90% since 1980. This decline was anticipated based on changes in the global use of HCH outside the Arctic, notably in China and India (Jansen *et al.* 1997). Similarly, concentrations of lead have fallen in keeping with the declining use of leaded gasoline, especially in North America (Boutron *et al.* 1991). Trends in concentrations of several organochlorines in animals have been more ambiguous. This may be partly because of the shortage of data on early collections older than about 20 years and partly because analytical procedures have improved over the time since early collections were made. DDT in blubber of female ringed seals from the western Arctic was reported to have declined from over 500 ng g^{-1} in 1972 to about 300 ng g^{-1} in 1981 with a smaller decline to about 200 ng g^{-1} in 1991 (Jensen *et al.* 1997). There was a similar decline in blubber PCBs in the same seals from about 1200 ng g^{-1} in 1972 to about 300 ng g^{-1} in 1981 with little or no change between 1981 and 1991. However, DDT in narwhal from Pond Inlet increased from about 6500 ng g^{-1} in 1982 to about 9500 ng g^{-1} in 1994. During the period from 1972 to 1993/94, there was essentially no trend in DDT in male beluga from the Mackenzie Delta area (Jensen *et al.* 1997). Hence there is not a consistent trend of organochlorine compounds in marine mammals throughout the Arctic but rather a series of differing regional trends. Modern genetic analyses, and indeed the organochlorine residues themselves, have lead to the conclusion that some marine mammal species consist of several different stocks and so there is unlikely to be any single, consistent pattern for the whole Canadian Arctic.

Table 2. Consumption advisories recommend for several lakes in the Northwest Territories based on mean mercury content of muscle of the species listed.

Lake	Species	Consumption
Cli	Lake whitefish	no limit
	Lake trout	225 g/week
	Burbot	get more samples
Little Doctor	Lake whitefish	no limit
	Sucker	no limit
	Lake trout	no limit
	Pike and walleye	250 g/week
Turton	Lake whitefish	no limit
	Lake trout	330 g/week
Lac à Jacques	Lake whitefish	no limit
	Walleye	200 g/week
	Northern pike	390 g/week
	Walleye + pike	200 g/week
Manuel Lake	Burbot	no limit
	Lake whitefish	no limit
	Northern pike	430 g/week

Health Canada also advised that it would be prudent to limit fish muscle consumption by women of child-bearing age and by children to one half of the consumption levels recommended above.

Mercury poses the greatest potential problem for northerners who consume fish and marine mammals. An increase in mercury inputs to some parts of the North, relative to pre-industrial times, is anticipated because the major sources of mercury are associated with fossil energy sources and world use of these elements has grown even faster than population. Lake sediments integrate inputs of mercury over time, Figure 6 shows some northern lake sediment profiles. They show increases in mercury in the uppermost sediment layers that were deposited most recently implying increasing inputs relative to pre-20th century inputs. Exceptions appear to be in the northwestern NWT and Alaska where little or no indication of increased recent inputs in the sediments (Lockhart *et al.* 1998; Gubala *et al.* 1995). Levels of mercury in beluga whales and ringed seals have increased over the past 20 years (Wagemann *et al.* 1996) and a similar trend has been found recently in sea birds (Braune 1999).

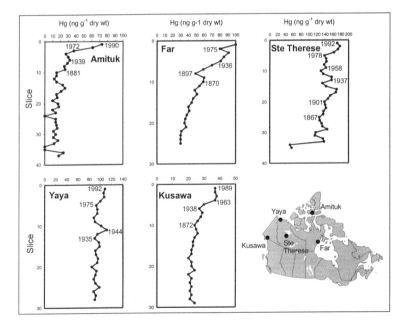

Figure 6. Down-core profiles of mercury in sediments from several Canadian northern lakes. Dates shown are estimates of the time of deposition of the mid-point of the corresponding slices and were derived from measurements of unsupported lead-210. Profiles of cesium-137 were used to judge the quality of the lead-210 dates.

The information on concentrations of mercury in fish shows no clear temporal trend. There were many analyses done on fish from the NWT in the 1970s but there were relatively few of a given species from a given lake and so the statistical power of comparisons between historic and current measures is limited. In some instances the same lake was sampled on more than one occasion. For example, five lake trout taken from Cli Lake in 1983 had an average mercury content of 0.390 ug g^{-1}. A larger collection of 49 lake trout taken in 1996 had a mean mercury content of 0.876 ug g^{-1}. (These latter values resulted in the consumption advisory for lake trout consumption listed in Table 2.) The fish were about the same size on each occasion, the average length being 477 mm in 1983 and 485 mm in 1996. Hence in this lake the levels of mercury appear to have increased somewhat over the interval between the two sampling periods. However, the sample of five fish in 1983 is too small to support a firm conclusion. Similarly, we have information on three lake trout from Rorey Lake in 1978 when the mean mercury level was found to be 0.487 ug g^{-1} for comparison with 48 samples in 1997 when the mean was 0.455 ug g^{-1}. In this instance, there is no indication of temporal change, but again the early sample is too small to support a firm conclusion.

Conclusions

A number of chemical contaminants have become dispersed throughout the Canadian Arctic. The strongest evidence for this derives from contaminants that are purely of synthetic origin and that were not used in the Arctic. For example, atmospheric testing of nuclear bombs resulted in fallout of cesium-137 throughout the Arctic. Equally clear evidence is given by the widespread presence of synthetic organic compounds (HCH, DDT, dieldrin, chlordane, PCB etc.) that have become dispersed throughout the Arctic by moving air masses. The Arctic appears to be a final planetary sink for these compounds since the area lacks the heat to efficiently revolatize them after they are deposited. The contaminants subject to most debate are the natural elements, especially mercury. Lead has several distinct isotopes which can often be used to discriminate between industrial lead dispersed via the atmosphere and lead present naturally in a given lake basin. Such studies have shown that the Arctic has been receiving inputs of industrial lead from non-arctic sources. Mercury does not have isotope mixtures convenient for making such a distinction and so the debate regarding sources is much more difficult. However, several independent lines of evidence suggest recent increases in inputs of mercury to the Arctic and this can be expected to drive national and international efforts to limit sources. The social consequences of contamination of basic foods used traditionally in northern communities are beyond the scope of this report. However, other studies indicate that these consequences are varied and significant (e.g. Usher 1992).

Acknowledgments

The studies upon which these comments are based have been supported by numerous agencies, communities and individuals. The principal financial support was supplied by the Northern Contaminants Program of the Department of Indian Affairs and Northern Development.

References

Arctic Monitoring and Assessment Program. 1998. *Assessment Report: Arctic Pollution Issues*. 859pp. Oslo: AMAP.

Boutron, C., Görlach, U., Candelone, J-P., Bolshov, M. and Delmas, R. 1991. Decrease in anthropogenic lead, cadmium and zinc in Greenland snows since the late 1960s. *Nature* 353. 153-156.

Braune, B. 1999. Contaminants in arctic seabird eggs. In S. Kalhok and L. Walker (Eds.) *Synopsis of Research Conducted Under the 1998/99 Northern Contaminants Program.* Indian Affairs and Northern Development Report QS-8599-000-EF-A1: 77-80.

Dewailly, E., Nantel, A., Weber, J.-P. and Meyer, F. 1989. High levels of PCBs in breast milk of Inuit women from arctic Canada. *Bull. Environ. Contam. Toxicol*. 43: 641-646.

Gubala, C., Landers, D., Monetti, M., Heit, M., Wade, T., Lasorsa, B. and Allen-Gil, S. 1995. The rates of accumulation and chronologies of atmospherically derived pollutants in arctic Alaska, USA. *Sci. Total Environ.* 160/161: 347-361.

Hart-Hansen, J., Meldgaard, J. and Nordqvist, J. 1991. *The Greenland Mummies*.192 pp. Washington, DC: Smithsonian Institution Press,

Health and Welfare Canada, 1979. *Methylmercury in Canada. Exposure of Indian and Inuit Residents to Methylmercury in the Canadian Environment*. 200 pp. Ottawa: Medical Services Branch.

Health and Welfare Canada, 1984. *Methylmercury in Canada. Exposure of Indian and Inuit Residents to Methylmercury in the Canadian Environment* 164pp. Ottawa: Medical Services Branch.

Hutchison-Benson, E., Svoboda, J., Taylor, H. 1985. The latitudinal inventory of 137Cs in vegetation and topsoil in northern Canada, 1980. *Can. J. Bot.* 63: 784-791.

Hoff, R. and Chan, K.-W. 1986. Atmospheric concentrations of chlordane at Mould Bay, N.W.T., Canada. Chemosphere 15: 449-452.

368

Jensen, J., Adare, K. and Shearer, R. (Eds.)1997. *Canadian Arctic Contaminants Assessment Report (CACAR)*. 459 pp. Ottawa: Department of Indian Affairs and Northern Development.

Kinloch, D., Kuhnlein, H. and Muir, D. 1992. Inuit foods and diet: A preliminary assessment of benefits and risks. *Sci. Total Environ. 122*: 247-278.

Lockhart, L., Wilkinson, P. Billeck, B. Danell, R., Hunt, R., Brunskill, G., Delaronde, J. and St. Louis, V. 1998. Fluxes of mercury to lake sediments in central and northern Canada inferred from dated sediment cores. *Biogeochem.* 40: 163-173.

Muir, D., Ford, C., Grift, N., Metner, D. and Lockhart, L. 1990a. Geographic variation of chlorinated hydrocarbons in burbot (*Lota lota*) from remote lakes and rivers in Canada. *Arch. Environ. Contam. Toxicol.* 19: 530-542.

Muir, D., Ford, C., Stewart, R., Smith, T., Addison, R., Zinck, M. and Beland, P. 1990b. Organochlorine contaminants in belugas, (*Delphinapterus leucas*), from Canadian waters. *Can. Bull. Fish. Aquat. Sci.* 224: 165-190.

Norstrom, R. and Muir, D. 1988. Long-range transport of organochlorines in the Arctic and sub-Arctic: evidence from the analysis of marine mammals and fish. In N. Schmidtke (Ed.) *Toxic Contaminants in the Great Lakes. Vol. 1. Chronic Effects of Toxic Contaminants in Large Lakes.* pp. 83-112. Chelsea, MI: .Lewis Publishers.

Nriagu, J. and Pacyna, J. 1988. Quantitative assessment of worldwide contamination of air, water and soils by trace metals. *Nature* 333:134-139.

Outridge, P. and Stewart, R. 1999. Stock discrimination of Atlantic walrus (*Odobenus rosmarus rosmarus*) in the eastern Canadian Arctic using lead isotope and element signatures in teeth. *Can. J. Fish. Aquat. Sci.* 56: 105-112.

Reinke, J., Uthe, J. and Jamieson, D. 1972. Organochlorine pesticide residues in commercially caught fish in Canada 1970. *Pestic. Monit. J.* 6: 43-49.

Risebrough, R. and Berger, D. 1971. *Evidence for Aerial Fallout of Polychlorinated Biphenyls (PCB) in the Eastern Canadian Arctic.* Contract Report CWS 7071-052. Ottawa: Canadian Wildlife Service.

Sturges, W. and Barrie, L. 1987. Lead 206/207 isotope retios in the atmosphere of North America as tracers of US and Canadian emissions. *Nature* 329: 144-146.

Taylor, H., Svoboda, J., Henry, G., and Wein, R. 1988. Post-Chernobyl 134Cs and 137Cs levels at some localities in northern Canada. *Arctic* 41: 293-296.

Usher, P. 1992. Socio-economic effects of elevated mercury levels in fish on sub-arctic native communities. In *Contaminants in the Marine Environment of Nunavik: Proceedings of the Conference, Montreal, September 12-14, 1990. pp. 45-50.* QC: Société Makivik and Centre d'études nordiques, Université Laval.

Wagemann, R., Innes, S. and Richard, P. 1996. Overview and regional and temporal differences of heavy metals in arctic whales and ringed seals in the Canadian Arctic. *Sci. Total Environ.* 186: 41-66.

Wheatley, B. and Paradis, S. 1995. Exposure of Canadian aboriginal peoples to methylmercury. *Water, Air, Soil Poll.* 80: 3-11.

Wheatley, B. and Wheatley, M. 1988. Methylmercury in the Canadian Arctic environmental past and present - natural or industrial? *Arctic Med. Res.* 47: 163-167.

---

[1]   Lyle Lockhart (PhD) is Head of the Arctic Contaminants Research Section, Fisheries and Oceans and Adjunct Professor in Zoology, University of Manitoba. Gary Stern (PhD) is a Research Scientist with Fisheries and Oceans, at the Fresh Water Institute, in Winnipeg.

The North Water Polynya:
Physical and Biological Aspects

CJ Mundy and David Barber[1]

Abstract

The North Water (NOW), located in northern Baffin Bay, transcends international borders and is of great interest to researchers from the physical, life and social sciences. The region contains a large recurring polynya while supporting coastal communities found along the shores of Canada and Greenland as well as a rich biological fauna. This paper introduces the North Water and provides an up to date review of the physical mechanisms and biological implications of its resident polynya.

Introduction

Throughout the winter months, the extensive Arctic sea ice cover is dotted with anomalous non-linear shaped openings referred to as polynyas (WMO 1970). They are present due to specific physical mechanisms that keep the local area devoid of sea ice. They can be restricted on one side by a coast, termed shore polynyas, or bounded by fast ice, termed flaw polynyas. Polynyas that occur in the same position every year are called recurring polynyas (WMO 1970). The latter type has also been sub-divided into: polynyas that remain open throughout winter and seasonal polynyas that close during the coldest months and open in early spring. Due to a polynya's dependence on atmospheric and oceanic processes affecting its sea ice cover, polynyas are thought to be sensitive to climatic variability and change (IAPP 1989). Further, specific types of polynyas have been hypothesized as acting as carbon sinks and may therefore help to mitigate rising CO_2 levels (Yager *et al.* 1995).

Critical to understanding the physical and biological aspects of polynyas, one must understand how they occur. Two generalized mechanisms, termed sensible and latent heat, act to form and maintain polynyas (Smith *et al.* 1990). A sensible heat mechanism involves an input of warm water from depth, which slows or even prevents the formation of ice in the area. A latent heat mechanism involves strong winds and/or currents that act to sweep ice away from an area faster than it can form. Ice flow is inhibited from entering the area by a coast, ice shelf, grounded iceberg or landfast ice structure. The mechanism's namesake comes from the latent heat of fusion released from continual ice formation, which contributes to maintaining the open water.

The North Water (NOW) refers to a region of anomalous sea ice conditions at the northern end of Baffin Bay (Fig. 1). It is shared equally between Canada and Greenland, which makes the region of international interest. Further, it is home to one of the largest recurring polynyas found in the Arctic. The NOW polynya has been acknowledged as perhaps the most biologically significant polynya in the Canadian Arctic due in part to its size and permanence (Stirling 1980, 1997). In the same respect, the NOW has drawn attention from a multitude of different academic fields including circumpolar specialists from the physical, life and social sciences. Of particular interest are the physical mechanisms that form and maintain the polynya and their relationship to climate variability and local biology. In this paper, we provide a brief overview of the NOW polynya including an up to date review of the physical and biological implications of the North Water.

A Physical Perspective

The formation and maintenance of the North Water polynya has been of interest off and on since its documented discovery by William Baffin in 1616 (Dunbar and Dunbar 1972). Many famous explorers frequented the area in an attempt to decipher how and why the open water occurred. A debate on the physical mechanisms acting to form and maintain the polynya evolved over the following centuries. Summaries of the history of knowledge on the formation and maintenance of the North Water are available in reviews by Nutt (1969) and Dunbar and Dunbar (1972).

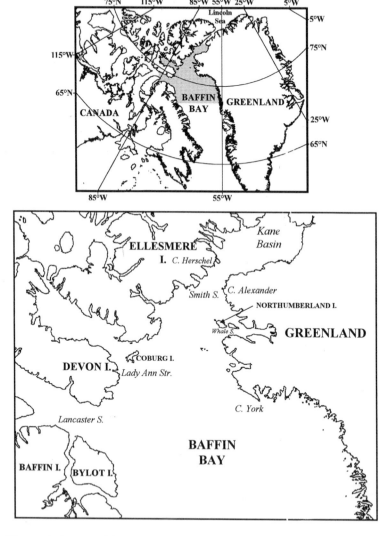

Figure 1. A map of the North Water of northern Baffin Bay.

The NOW polynya has all the requirements for a latent heat mechanism. Strong northerly winds and southward currents consistently push ice through Smith Sound (Nutt 1969, Muench and Sadler 1973, Ito and Müler 1982). The polynya forms in late winter, early spring when ice becomes congested at the head of Smith Sound and forms a landfast ice arch (Fig. 2). The structure (i.e., the Kane Basin ice bridge) blocks ice from entering the area while winds and currents sweep the newly formed ice to the south (Muench 1971, Pease 1987). Subsequently, there has never been any doubt of a contributing latent heat mechanism, however, bits and pieces of evidence have fueled debates on whether a sensible heat mechanism contributes or not.

Steffen (1985) documented the occurrence of warm water off the coast of Greenland and other locations within the North Water, concluding that sensible heat significantly contributed to the polynya's occurrence throughout winter and early spring. The possibility of a sensible heat mechanism had long been suspected (Nutt 1969, Dunbar and Dunbar 1972). The source was a well-documented warm water layer at depth moving northward along the west coast of Greenland called the West Greenland Current. Steffen (1985) was the first to provide convincing evidence of the current reaching the surface within the NOW. However, as Steffen's (1985) observations were only of the ocean's surface, Melling et al. (In Press) later noted that interpretation of the data in an oceanographic sense was ambiguous.

Bourke and Paquette (1991) examined the bottom and deep water of Baffin Bay. Contrasting to Steffen (1985), they concluded that there was not enough heat stored in the West Greenland Current to substantially contribute to the polynya's occurrence. Conversely, Lewis et al. (1996) later found the water temperature at depth to be substantially warmer than that observed by Bourke and Paquette (1991).

Modeling efforts have examined the possibility of a sensible heat mechanism. Mysak and Huang (1992) coupled a latent heat polynya model developed by Pease (1987) for the NOW polynya with a reduced-gravity, coastal upwelling model. They concluded that sensible heat via upwelling, which occurred on a slower time scale than the latent heat mechanism, played a role in determining the polynya width toward the Greenland coast. Darby et al. (1994) improved Mysak and Huang's (1992) model and came upon a similar conclusion, but noted that sensible heat only played a role during late spring, when heat loss to the atmosphere was reduced.

374

Figure 2. A RADARSAT ScanSAR image showing the ice bridge (formed in early March, 1998) composed of very thick multiyear ice floes (bright pixels). South of the bridge is the North Water polynya with various new ice type signatures visible. RADARSAT overpass dated April 11, 1998 at 21:18 UTC.

In 1998, during the International North Water Polynya Study, a data set that furthered the debate on the importance of sensible heat mechanism was collected. Initial results demonstrated that the amount of heat stored in the West Greenland Current play a minor role in the polynya's maintenance (Melling *et al.* In Press). No convincing evidence demonstrated the West Greenland Current reaching the surface. However, an analysis of the annual ice cover demonstrated that specific areas along the west Greenland coast can be explained by a contributing sensible heat mechanism (Mundy and Barber In Press) and warm air and surface waters from southern Baffin Bay(Barber *et al.* In Press, Mundy and Barber In Press). It was suggested that the timing of the Kane Basin ice bridge formation will become more variable with the present climate warming trend and may even cease to form in some years (Barber *et al.* In Press, Mundy and Barber In Press). This was supported by Barber *et al.* (In Press) who demonstrated the timing of formation to be substantially more variable throughout the 1990s as compared to the 1970s and 1980s.

A Biological Perspective

The predictability of recurring polynyas makes them important to all biological life (Stirling 1980, 1997, Massom 1988) including indigenous peoples (Schledermann 1980). The North Water is one of the most well known biological 'hot spots' in the Arctic. Since the 19th century, whalers have used the region to start an early whaling season (Nutt 1969). People of the Thüle culture, who largely depended on marine mammals for food, had settlements in the area for up to 3000 years, before which it was hypothesized that the polynya was not present (Schledermann 1980). Inuit hunters of Pond Inlet and Arctic Bay of northern Baffin Island also use the area to hunt narwhals (*Monodon monoceros*) and beluga (white) whales (*Delphinapterus leucas*) as they follow leads and cracks away from open water in early spring (Stirling 1980). These statements alone indicate a consistent highly productive region with a large marine mammal population in order to sustain the human needs.

The NOW is also very important to seabirds that forage solely in the marine environment and therefore need ice free water to gain access to their prey. Brown and Nettleship (1981) have demonstrated that most major colonies of cliff nesting birds in the Canadian Arctic were located in the vicinity of recurring polynyas.

Every year millions (*ca.*14 to 30 million pairs) of birds migrate to the North Water to feed and to breed along both the eastern Canada and western Greenland coasts, where there are widespread cliffs favourable for nesting (Nettleship and Evans 1985, Salmonsen 1981, Boertman and Mosbech 1998). During shipboard surveys made in the North Water, in 1998, Dovekies (*Alle alle*) were the most numerous birds sighted with densities at times of over 1000 birds per square kilometer of water. The polynya provides the seabirds with an extended period of time in which they can conduct their breeding activities, which include: post migration feeding, courtship, egg laying and incubation, chick rearing, molting and pre-migration feeding activities.

Much less information has been collected on the abundance/biomass of mammals, fishes, plankton and ice algae in the region (IAPP 1989). The NOW encompasses a vast area and it is hard to estimate numbers from very few observations. Finley and Renaud (1980) found very few marine mammals during aerial surveys made in mid March and mid May of 1978. They concluded that the North Water was not a major overwintering area for marine mammals. This work was re-visited during the International North Water Polynya Study and early spring sighting indicated that the North Water was most likely an overwintering area for bowhead whales (*Balaena mystiscetus*) (Holst and Stirling 1999), narwhals and walruses (*Odobenus rosmarus*). Other mammals that frequent the area throughout spring and summer include polar bears (*Ursus maritimus*), ringed seals (*Phoca hispida*), bearded seals (*Erignathus barbatus*) and beluga whales (Stirling 1980, 1997, Finley and Renaud 1980).To support these high numbers of birds and mammals, an enhanced and extended period of primary production is needed. The primary explanation for increased primary production in polynyas, at least in early spring, is related to light limitation. Solar insolation is the main limiting factor during the initiation of primary production in sea ice covered waters (Gosselin and Legendre 1990, Welch and Bergmann 1989). The attenuation of photosynthetically active radiation (PAR) through sea ice is substantial (Maykut and Grenfell 1975). Furthermore, a snow cover can significantly increase the surface albedo and PAR attenuation (Barry *et al.* 1993). With ice concentrations of 90% or less, the effects of snow and ice on PAR attenuation become negligible due to reflection of solar radiation through small leads and cracks. This results in an adequate supply of diffuse light for primary production to occur (Smith 1995). In a polynya, these conditions are available long before adjacent ice covered areas.

Collecting biological and oceanographic profiles during a 48 hr period, Lewis *et al.* (1996) observed that chlorophyll *a* (Chl*a*) concentrations, an estimate of phytoplankton biomass, were comparable with that of the well-documented phenomenon known as an ice edge bloom (e.g., Maynard and Clark 1987). The highest Chl*a* concentrations occurred along the western Greenland coast with a decreasing trend toward the eastern Canada coast. Chl*a* was also negatively correlated with water column nutrient concentrations, implying that the bloom had initiated along the Greenland coast and was progressively moving westward. Phytoplankton was found to occur in areas where evidence demonstrated the possibility of surface waters mixing with the West Greenland Current at depth. It was concluded that there was a connection between the possible sensible heat processes occurring in the polynya and the observed phytoplankton bloom (Lewis *et al.* 1996).

The International North Water Polynya Study proposed two hypotheses based on Lewis *et al.*'s (1996) conclusion: (1) a sensible heat mechanism would be associated with enhanced primary production due to early stratification, a subsequent warm surface mixed layer and replenishment of nutrients through upwelling; and (2) a latent heat polynya will be associated with a later primary production bloom due to late stratification (NOW proposal 1997). We note that initiation of primary production under a latent heat mechanism would still be earlier than adjacent ice covered areas. Preliminary evidence has demonstrated shallow water stratification (i.e. a shallow mixed layer depth), a condition required for the occurrence of a phytoplankton bloom, to occur first along the Greenland coast in the specific areas where a sensible heat mechanism was suspected (Mundy 2000). It was suggested that warmer temperatures and calm surface conditions, consistent with a sensible heat mechanism, along the west Greenland coast allowed the surface to stratify early, creating non-limiting conditions for an early primary production bloom to occur. Without upwelling the bloom would be short-lived due to nutrient depletion and no replenishment. International North Water Polynya Study (1997) suggested an early extended bloom would occur as a rectification for the rich wildlife found along the adjacent coasts of the NOW. No convincing evidence of upwelling was collected during the oceanographic portion of the North Water study (Melling *et al.* In Press). However, Mundy and Barber (In Press) highlighted areas that could be partly explained through the occurrence of a sensible heat mechanism via upwelling. Whether an extended bloom occurs in the NOW and its relationship to the physical polynya mechanisms is unconfirmed and currently being examined by the International North Water Polynya Study research network.

References

Barber, D., Hanesiak, J. and Piwowar, J. In Press. Sea ice atmosphere processes within the North Water polynya (NOW): Part 1

Barry, R., Serreze, M., Maslanik, J. and Preller, R. 1993. The Arctic Sea Ice-Climate System: Modeling. *Rev. Geophys.* 31:397-422.

Boertman, D. and Mosbech, A. 1998. Distribution of the little Auk (*Alle alle*) breeding colonies in Thule, Greenland. *Plr Bio.* 19:206-210.

Bourke, R. and Paquette, R. 1991. Formation of Baffin Bay bottom and deep waters. In P. Chu and J. Gascard (Eds). *Deep Convection and Deep Water Formation in the Oceans.* pp. 135-155. Amsterdam: Elsevier.

Brown, R. and Nettleship, D. 1981. The biological significance of polynya to Arctic colonial seabirds. In I. Stirling and H. Cleator (Eds). *Polynyas in the Canadian Arctic.* (OccPpr 45), pp. 59-65. ON:CWS.

Darby, M., Willmott, A. and Mysak, L. 1994. A nonlinear steady-state model of the North Water polynya. *J. Hys. Oceanogr.* 24:1011-1020.

Dunbar, M. and Dunbar, M.1972. The history of the North Water. *Proc. R.S.E. (B)* 72:231-241.

Finley, K. and Renaud, E. 1980. Marine mammals inhabiting the Baffin Bay North Water in winter. *Arctic* 33:724-738.

Gosselin, M. and Legendre, M. 1990. Light and nutrient limitation of sea-ice microalgae (Hudson Bay, Canadian Arctic). *J. Phycol.* 26:220-232.

Holst, M. and Stirling, I.. 1999. A note on sightings of bowhead whales in the North Water Polynya, 1998. *J. Cetacean Res. Manage.* 1:153-156.

IAPP. 1989. *International Arctic Polynya Program.* Arctic Ocean Sciences Board. Institute of Marine Sciences. Fairbanks: Univ. of Fairbanks.

Ito, H. and Müller, F. 1982. Ice Movement through Smith Sound in northern Baffin Bay, observed in satellite imagery. *J. Glaciol.* 28:129-143.

Lewis, E., Ponton, D., Legendre, L. and LeBlanc, B. 1996. Springtime sensible heat, nutrients and phytoplankton in the Northwater Polynya, Canadian Arctic. *Cont. Shelf Res.* 16:1775-1792.

Massom, R. 1988. The biological significance of open water within the sea ice covers of the polar regions. *Endeavour, New Series* 12:21-27.

Maykut, G. and Grenfell, T. 1975. The spectral distribution of light beneath first-year sea ice in the Arctic Ocean. *Limol.Oceanogr.* 20:554-563.

Maynard, N. and Clark, D. 1987. Satellite color observations of spring blooming in Bering Sea shelf waters during the ice edge retreat in 1980. *J. Geophys. Res.* 92:7127-7139.

Melling, H., Gratton, Y. and Ingram, G. In Press. Oceanic circulation within the North Water polynya in Baffin Bay.

Muench, R. 1971. The physical oceanography of the northern Baffin Bay region. In *The Baffin Bay-North Water Project.*Calgary: AINA.

Muench, R. and Sadler, H. 1973. Physical oceanographic observations in Baffin Bay and Davis Strait. *Arctic* 26:73-76.

Mundy, C. 2000. Sea ice physical processes and biological linkages within the North Water polynya during 1998. M.A. thesis. Wpg: U of M.

Mundy, C. and Barber, D. In Press. On the relationship between the temporal evolution of sea ice spatial patterns and the physical mechanisms creating and maintaining the North Water polynya.

Mysak, L. and Huang, F. 1992. A latent- and sensible-heat polynya model for the North Water. *J. Phys. Ocean.* 22:596-608.

Nettleship, D. and Evans, P. 1985. Distribution and status of the Atlantic Alcida. In D. Nettleship and T. Birkhead (Eds), *The Atlantic Alcidae*, pp. 53-154. London: Academic Press.

NOW Proposal. 1997. *International North Water Polynya Study.* GIROQ, QC: University of Laval.

Nutt, D. 1969. The North Water of Baffin Bay. *Polar Notes* 9:1-25.

Pease, C. 1987. The size of wind-driven coastal polynyas. *Geophys. Res.* 92:7049-7059.

Salmonsen, F. 1981. Birds. In F. Salmonsen (Ed.) *The fauna of Greenland*, pp. 161-360. Copenhagen: Glyldenal.

Schledermann, P. 1980.Polynyas and prehistoric settlement. *Arctic* 22:92-302.

Smith, S., Muench, R. and Pease, C. 1990. Polynyas and leads: Physical processes and environment. *J. Geophys. Res.* 95:9461-9479.

Smith, W. 1995. Primary and new productivity in the Northeast Water Polynya during summer 1992. *J. Geophys. Res.* 100:4357-4370.

Steffen, K. 1985. Warm water cells in the North Water, northern Baffin Bay during winter. *J. Geophys. Res.* 90:9129-9136.

Stirling, I. 1980. The biological importance of polynyas in the Canadian Arctic. *Arctic* 33:303-315.

Stirling, I. 1997. The importance of polynyas, ice edges, and leads to marine mammals and birds. *J. Mar. Sys.* 10:9-21.

Welch, H. and Bergmann, M. 1989. Seasonal development of ice algae and its prediction from environmental factors near Resolute, N.W.T., Canada. *Can. J. Fish. Aquat. Sci.* 46:1793-1804.

World Meteorological Organization. 1970. *WMO Sea Ice Nomenclature.* WMO Rep. 259, Geneva: WMO.

Yager, P., Wallace, D., Johnson, K., Smith Jr,W., Minett, P. and Deming, J. 1995. The Northeast Polynya as an atmospheric CO_2 sink: A seasonal rectification hypothesis. *J. Geophys. Res.* 100:4389-4398.

---

[1]   CJ Mundy (MA) is a Research Assistant with the Centre for Earth Observation Science. David Barber (PhD) is a Professor of Geography and Director of the Centre for Earth Observation Science at the University of Manitoba.

Monitoring the Harvest of
Vaccinium angustifolium

Shaunna Morgan and David Punter[1]

Abstract

Harvesting non-timber forest products (NTFP) may conserve and manage forest ecosystems while providing economic benefits to First Nations in the boreal forest. Therefore, protocols for establishing sustainable harvesting levels were designed and tested for the fruit of Vaccinium angustifolium (lowbush blueberry) in association with First Nation communities of Manitoba and Ontario. This was the first study to examine the effects of various harvesting intensities on V. angustifolium for two years. As harvesting intensity increased, berry mass and berry density decreased. Harvesting some (30%) or most (70%) of the berries may have had a stimulatory effect on berry density (increasing yield) compared with 100% harvesting intensity.

Introduction

Interest in the commercial potential and traditional uses of non-timber forest plants and plant products is increasing (Wickens 1991). Non-timber forest products (NTFP) are all biological materials, other than timber, which are removed from natural or managed forests for human use or consumption (Peters 1994, Broekhoven 1996). In recent decades, NTFP have been viewed as a means of providing economic benefits to local residents while conserving, managing and optimizing tropical forest ecosystems (Wickens 1991, Hall and Bawa 1993, Salick *et al.* 1995, Velásquez Runk 1998). In tropical areas, many indigenous and rural people continue to rely on NTFP for subsistence and have started to harvest additional NTFP to supplement their incomes (Peters 1994, Broekhoven 1996, Mahapatra and Mitchell 1997, Velásquez Runk 1998). In Canada and the United States, many people are harvesting NTFP in boreal forests and temperate rain forests for similar purposes (Foster 1992, De Geus 1995, Schlosser and Blatner 1995, Liegel *et al.* 1998, Pilz *et al.* 1998, Love *et al.* 1998).

Canada has an abundant 417.6 million hectares of forested land, which constitutes 45% of the total area of Canada (Shilts 1999) and about 80% of the Aboriginal (First Nation, Inuit and Métis) population (Shilts 1999). Owing to the lack of employment opportunities, the unemployment rate for Aboriginal peoples living on reserves is 28.7% (Statistics Canada 1999a), in contrast with Canadian national rate of 8.1% (Statistics Canada 1999b). The revenue generated from NTFP has been increasing over the past few decades in tropical areas (Burman 1990, Broekhoven 1996) and is also on the rise in North America (Molina *et al.* 1993). Therefore, NTFP may present a viable opportunity for economic development in the boreal forest regions where many Aboriginal experience high unemployment and low income levels. Central American communities currently harvesting NTFP are concerned with improving their quality of life by maximizing harvesting while minimizing harmful ecological effects, retaining control over their lands and resources, minimizing costs related to harvesting and sustaining their traditional culture (Velásquez Runk 1998). Canadian First Nation populations have similar concerns and harvesting of NTFP is believed to be an excellent way to provide employment in forested regions while still conserving forests. This was the impetus for the creation of monitoring protocols for the sustainable harvest of NTFP in the boreal forest region of Canada.

Objectives and Methods

The first objective of this study was to establish monitoring protocols for a boreal NTFP plant species using various harvesting intensities. Monitoring protocols were designed to monitor plant productivity and detect changes due to harvesting intensity. Plant productivity in this instance is loosely used to mean the sustained production of vegetative and reproductive units from one year to the next. The second objective was to include First Nations leaders and elders in a community-based study to guide us in a direction consistent with their values regarding NTFP. Finally, the principal objective was to collect data from the monitoring protocols for two growing seasons, analyze the data to test the effects of the various harvesting intensities on the NTFP, and make recommendations for the refinement of the monitoring protocols.

Sagkeeng First Nation (on the Winnipeg River, Manitoba) and Ojibways of Onegaming (Lake of the Woods, Ontario) were chosen as partners because of the positive and enthusiastic attitudes of the Chiefs, environmental officers and Elders to the proposed study. During a meeting with the Sagkeeng Elders, many plant species were discussed as possible candidates for study. The criteria for species selection were: i) plant with high frequency and abundance; ii) plant traditionally used by the community; iii) plant with potential market value. *V. angustifolium* (blueberry) was agreed upon as an appropriate study species. The Chief, environmental officer and Elders at the Ojibways of Onegaming also agreed that *V. angustifolium* was appropriate. Elders of each community guided investigators to traditionally harvested *Vaccinium* sites. Three *V. angustifolium* sites were established in Ontario and four sites in Manitoba.

The monitoring protocols followed a hierarchical design. Four harvesting intensities were decided upon: 0% harvesting (control), 30%, 70% and 100% harvesting. Within each site, three groups (blocks) of four similar 1m² plots were established. Within each block, plots were spaced a minimum of 1m apart and were systematically selected based on the abundance and percent cover of *V. angustifolium* within the plot. Within each block, treatments were randomly assigned to the plots.

In 1997, members of Sagkeeng First Nation worked alongside the primary researchers gathering the data in Manitoba. Once Sagkeeng members could identify common plant species they actively participated in the data collection. Furthermore, Sagkeeng members were instructed in plant collecting, plant identification, and plant mounting. These skills were taught with the hope that Sagkeeng members would be able to continue the monitoring in the future. The densities of *V. angustifolium* shoots and berries were counted before (1996-Y1) and after (1997-Y2) harvesting in four 0.0625m² subplots in each plot. Percent cover values for all species within the 1m² plots were also estimated and recorded. Plots were then harvested. The 100% plots of each site were harvested first to calculate the fresh mass of berries to be harvested from the 30 and 70% plots. Fresh masses of the berries were measured to the nearest gram using HOMS Model 2 (1 kg X 10 g) and Model 100g (100 g X 1 g) instrument and laboratory spring scales.

Analyses were based on productivity values collected before (1996-Y1) and after (1997-Y2) harvesting. A logarithmic transformation was performed on the original data [$X' = \log_{10}(X + 1)$]. These values indicated that sites in Manitoba and Ontario were floristically different. Therefore, means for percent cover, berry mass, shoot density, and berry density of all species were calculated and presented separately for each province. Student's Paired t-Tests were performed using Microsoft Excel 5.0a for Power Macintosh™ to test statistical significance of differences between Y1 and Y2 for each treatment. Analysis of variance (ANOVA) was performed using Data Desk® 4.1 Exploratory Data Analysis. Least significant difference (LSD) post hoc tests were also performed with Data Desk.

Results and Discussion

Monitoring protocols designed for *Vaccinium angustifolium* detected effects of harvesting at differing intensities. Percent cover and berry mass proved to be efficient measures of relative productivity between years. Of particular importance, this study showed different harvesting intensities affected berry production.

In Manitoba, all treatments showed some decrease in Y2 for percent cover and berry mass. Interestingly, as harvesting intensity increased, the decrease in the percent cover was relatively smaller (Fig. 1-A). The only significant reduction in mean percent cover was observed within the control (T-test, $p = 0.04$, $df = 10$). Decreases in percent cover following 30% and 70% harvesting were similar and intermediate to decreases observed in the control and 100% harvesting. However, no significant differences in percent cover were found between treatments (ANOVA, $p = 0.5784$, $n = 11$). An inverse trend was observed in the mean mass of fresh berries; as harvesting intensity increased the negative effect became greater (Fig. 1-B). The 30% harvesting intensity caused no significant change in the mean berry mass. The 70% treatment had a relatively moderate negative effect and within the 100% harvesting intensity a significant decrease was observed (T-test, $p = 0.022$, $df = 10$). No significant differences were found between treatments for berry mass (ANOVA, $p = 0.352$, $n = 11$).

In Ontario, unlike Manitoba, no trends or significant changes between years were observed in the mean percent cover of *V. angustifolium* (Fig. 2-A). Although changes in berry mass were insignificant (ANOVA, $p = 0.1450$, $n = 9$), trends similar to those in Manitoba were observed (Fig. 2-B). As harvesting intensity increased, berry mass decreased from year to year. This trend is strengthened by the fact that it was evident in Manitoba and Ontario (Figs. 1-B and 2-B). However, changes between

384

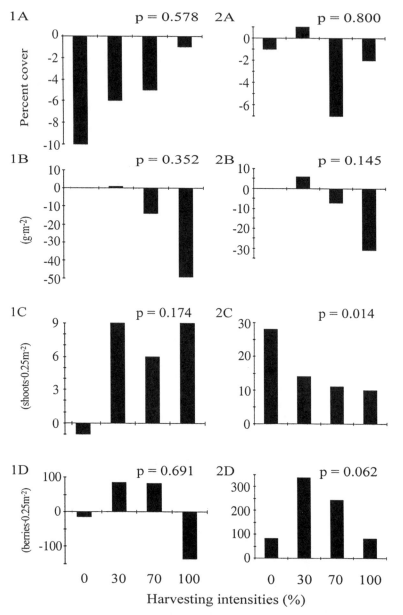

Figures 1 & 2. Changes in *Vaccinium angustifolium* from 1996-97.
1-Manitoba 2-Ontario.   A) Percent cover   B) Fresh berry mass
C) Shoot density   D) Berry density. P values are from ANOVAs.

treatments were not significant. This may have been due to variability of berry production within treatments.

Many studies (Black 1963, Jordan and Eaton 1995, Penney *et al.* 1997) have looked at second year cropping after rotational burning and showed that second crop blueberry yields are consistently smaller than first crop yields. In these studies, 100% of the berries were harvested, so the 100% harvesting intensity results of this study are comparable with these. Jordan and Eaton (1995) found a decrease in berry production to be attributed to increased resource allocation to vegetative growth after the first crop is harvested, whereas, the first year after burning relatively more resources are allocated to bud, flower and berry production. This may explain the general decreases observed in the 100% harvesting intensity.

The suggestion that resources are allocated to vegetative production after 100% harvesting (Jordan and Eaton 1995) was supported by the change in percent cover of *V. angustifolium* in Manitoba (Fig. 1-A), whereby a significant decrease between years for percent cover was seen within the control and no appreciable decrease was seen within the 100% harvesting treatment. This suggests that 100% plots actually increased in percent cover relative to that seen in the control. However, when tested, no significant differences were found between treatments for percent cover (ANOVA, $p=0.578$, $n=11$). Interestingly, this trend of increasing percent cover with increasing harvesting intensity was not observed in Ontario where there were no significant changes in the percent cover of *V. angustifolium* between years or between treatments. The difference observed between provinces may be attributable to differences in nutrient resources at the two locations, however this was not tested. If resources permit, other environmental factors should be considered in future studies. Soil samples may show differences in mineral, nutrient and water availability which could explain some of the differences observed from year to year and between treatments. Insufficient quantities of minerals, nutrients or water may limit blueberry growth. Additionally, light readings may also show differences from plot to plot and could explain some of the observed differences in berry productivity (Aalders *et al.* 1969, Hoefs and Shay 1981). We attempted to control for such environmental variables by using a nested experimental design. However, monitoring of these environmental factors would allow for a more critical assessment of the monitoring protocol.

Curiously, harvesting 30% or 70% of the berries resulted in little or no change in the next year's berry production. Comparison of the change in berry mass resulting from the harvesting of 30%, 70% or 100%

of berries over a specific area was not entirely unbiased. Of course, if 100% of the berries are harvested the mass will be greater than if 30% of the berries are harvested. A relatively large mass allows a greater range for change from one year to the next, just as a relatively small mass leaves a small margin for change. Indeed, this may explain differences between treatments illustrated in Figs. 1-B and 2-B and may be a plausible explanation of these results. Further study is required to determine if the trends found resulted from harvesting intensities or sampling design. Counting berries on a per stem basis is recommended as this method may decrease the variability within treatments and allow for more accurate results. Furthermore, if berries were harvested at various harvesting intensities on a per stem basis it may help to reduce variability, thereby mitigating the bias of harvesting over a large area.

The three harvesting treatments appeared to promote more shoot growth than the control yet, no significant differences were found between treatments in Manitoba (Fig. 1-C, ANOVA, $p = 0.174$, $n = 11$). Significant increases of shoot density were observed within treatments following 30% harvesting between years (T-test, $p = 0.042$, $df = 11$) and 100% harvesting (T-test, $p = 0.014$, $df = 10$).

In Ontario, all treatments showed significant increases in shoot density between years. As harvesting intensity increased, the mean change in shoot density decreased (Fig. 2-C). The greatest mean increase was observed within the control (T-test, $p = 0.001$, $df = 8$). Within the 30% harvesting and 70% harvesting intensities intermediate increases were observed (T-test, $p = 0.009$; $p = 0.003$, respectively, $df = 8$), and the 100% treatment increased the least (T-test, $p = 0.005$, $df = 8$). Significant differences were also found between treatments (ANOVA, $p = 0.0136$, $n = 9$). A post hoc test found significant differences between the control and the other treatments (LSD, 30% - 0, $p = 0.006$; 70% - 0, $p = 0.005$; 100% - 0, $p = 0.015$; $n = 9$).

Harvesting intensities had opposite effects on shoot densities between years in Manitoba and Ontario (Figs. 1-C and 2-C). The shoot density increased with harvesting intensity in Manitoba and decreased with harvesting intensity in Ontario. That no significant differences were found between treatments in Manitoba may be attributed to the amount of variation for shoot densities within treatments. However, significant increases were found in the 30% and 100% harvesting intensities between years. In Ontario, significant changes between years were also found. It is well documented that *V. angustifolium* naturally increases in cover by producing more stems to replace older, less productive stems as the plant matures (Hall *et al.* 1979, Hepler and Yarborough 1991, Nams

1994). Therefore, these increases may have been a result of natural aging in the population.

Some of the variation for the shoot density may be attributed to the size of the area sub-sampled, 0.25m² (four 0.0625m² subplots). Nams (1994) found 0.025 m² is the most efficient and precise quadrat size for measuring blueberry stem density. Furthermore, Nams (1994) found that smaller quadrats were better for worker morale, since the larger the quadrat, the more difficulty there is in counting numerous stems. Refined techniques for sub-sampling of the plots may reduce variability that was seen not only in shoot density and but also in berry density.

Furthermore, the measurements of numbers of stems per unit area rather than shoots per unit area should be considered since this appears to be the standard method for evaluating above ground vegetative productivity in the blueberry industry (Yarborough et al. 1986, Eaton 1994, Nams 1994, Jordan and Eaton 1995, Penney et al. 1997). A shoot, as defined for this study, consisted of one to many stems all originating from the same place in the ground or more precisely, a ramet. Many researchers first clip the blueberry plots and then count the number of stems clipped (Ismail et al. 1981, Jensen 1986). Stem densities were likely overlooked because non-destructive sampling methods were practised. Nams (1994) compared the accuracy of counting stems in 0.025m² quadrats in the field and clipping stems and counting them in the lab and found no significant difference in accuracy between the two methods. Stem densities may be a more accurate method of assessing the effects of harvesting intensity on vegetative reproduction. Accordingly, stems should be counted rather than shoots for future blueberry monitoring protocols and a smaller area should be sub-sampled.

Additionally, shoot densities collected in the summer of Y2 in Manitoba are much lower than shoot densities collected in the fall, which may make changes in shoot density (Fig. 1-C) appear as though harvesting intensity did have an effect. The differences between summer (Y2-S) and fall (Y2-F) shoot densities may be partly attributed to variability between data collectors.

During the summer months of 1997 (Y2) employees from the Sagkeeng First Nation assisted in data collection. Nams (1994) identified differences between observers as a large source of variation in data. One initial training session provided to those untrained in botany was most likely inadequate for teaching the abstruse task of identifying what we defined as a shoot. For future reference, Nams (1994) recommends a brief demonstration at the beginning of every data collection day to reduce variability between researchers. In comparison, the shoot densities for Y2-S and Y2-F in Ontario were collected only by primary researchers and there is very little variation between the summer and fall densities.

In Manitoba, no significant change was observed in the control for berry densities between years. Similar mean increases were observed following 30% and 70% harvesting (Fig. 1-D). A mean decrease was observed following 100% harvesting although this was not significant. No significant differences were found between treatments (ANOVA, p = 0.6911, n = 11) likely due to extreme variability in berry densities that occurred in all treatments.

In Ontario, all treatments showed an increase in berry density from Y1 to Y2. The increase in berry density in the control and 100% harvesting were not significant changes (Fig. 2-D). In the harvested treatments, as the harvesting intensity increased, the effect on berry density decreased. The greatest increase in berry density was observed in the 30% harvesting intensity (T- test, p = 0.0001, df = 8) and significant increase was also observed in the 70% treatment (T- test, p = 0.024, df = 8). The differences between treatments narrowly missed significance (ANOVA, p = 0.0624, n = 9).

Despite the insignificance between treatments similar trends were observed in Manitoba and Ontario for berry density (Figs. 1-D and 2-D). The controls and 100% harvesting intensities did not produce as many berries in Y2 as plots where 30% or 70% of the berries were harvested. These results were unexpected. Since this was the first study to investigate harvesting blueberries at various intensities no literature exists to compare with these peculiar results. One may speculate that harvesting some or most of the berries stimulates berry production in the following year. However, although more berries were produced, no appreciable gains in berry mass were observed. This indicated that the berries may have been of a reduced size. Interestingly, the increase in berry density following 30% and 70% harvesting supports trends observed for berry mass, and seems to indicate that it may indeed be the harvesting producing the effects and not a poorly designed sampling method. Again, further study is needed to test how harvesting intensity affects berry density. As previously mentioned, in the future berry densities and harvesting should occur on a per stem basis.

Conclusions

Monitoring protocols were tested in Manitoba and Ontario to assess the impact of harvesting *Vaccinium angustifolium*, the lowbush blueberry.

First Nations communities were successfully included in the study. Good working relationships were established with the environmental officers of both communities through the initial contact with the Chiefs. The cooperation of experienced and knowledgeable community Elders was achieved through the environmental officers. Furthermore, these Elders guided researchers to traditional harvesting locations. Once the protocols were established Sagkeeng First Nation provided additional human resources to help in data collection and to train community members in monitoring protocols. Sagkeeng is actively seeking the means to continue the monitoring.

Monitoring different harvesting levels of *Vaccinium angustifolium* for two years produced unexpected results. This project is the first to examine effects of different harvesting (other than 100%) levels on blueberry production. As harvesting intensity increased, mass and berry density tended to decrease. Interestingly, harvesting some (30%) or most (70%) of the berries appears to have had a stimulatory effect on berry density, resulting in an increased yield compared with the control or the 100% harvesting intensity. As this is the first study of its kind, one can only speculate as to the biological reasons behind this phenomenon. It is hoped that the recommendations made here will be implemented to elucidate the effects of harvesting *Vaccinium angustifolium* and form the basis for an opportunity for people living in economically depressed areas in boreal forest regions to supplement their incomes.

References

Aalders, L., Hall, I. and Forsyth, F. 1969. Effects of partial defoliation and light intensity on fruit-set and berry development in the lowbush blueberry. *Horticulture Research* 9:124 - 129.

Black, W. 1963. The effect of frequency on rotational burning on blueberry production. *Canadian Journal of Plant Science* 43:161 - 165.

Broekhoven, G. 1996. *Non-timber Forest Products: Ecological and Economic Aspects of Exploitation in Colombia, Ecuador and Bolivia.* Gland, Switzerland: IUCN .

Burman, J. 1990. A need for reappraisal of minor forest produce policies. *The Indian Journal of Social Work 51*(4): 649 - 658.

De Geus, P. 1995. *Botanical Forest Products in British Colombia: An Overview.* Victoria, BC: Queen's Printer.

Eaton, L. 1994. Long-term effects of herbicide and fertilizers on lowbush blueberry growth and production. *Canadian Journal of Plant Science 74*:341 - 345.

Foster, S. 1992. Harvesting medicinals in the wild: The need for scientific data on sustainable yields. *Wildflower 8*(3):18 - 22.

Hall, I., Aalders, L., Nickerson, N. and Vander Kloet, S. 1979. The biological flora of Canada 1. *Vaccinium angustifolium* Ait., Sweet Lowbush Blueberry. *Canadian Field-Naturalist 93*(4): 415 - 430.

Hall, P. and Bawa, K.1993. Methods to assess the impact of extraction of non-timber tropical forest products on plant populations. *Economic Botany 47*: 234 - 247.

Hepler, P. and Yarborough, D. 1991. Natural Variability in Yield of Lowbush Blueberries. *Horticulture Science 26*(3): 245 - 246.

Hoefs, M. and Shay, J. 1981. The effects of shade on shoot growth of *Vaccinium angustifolium* Ait. after fire pruning in southeastern Manitoba. *Canadian Journal of Botany 59*:166 - 174.

Ismail, A., Smagula, J. and Yarborough, D. 1981. Influence of pruning method, fertilizer and terbacil on the growth and yield of the lowbush blueberry. *Canadian Journal of Plant Science 61*: 61 - 71.

Jensen, K. 1986. Response of lowbush blueberry to weed control with atrazine and hexazinon. *Horticulture Science 21*: 1143 - 1144.

Jordan, W. and Eaton, L. 1995. A Comparison of first and second cropping years of Nova Scotia lowbush blueberries (*Vaccinium angustifolium*) Ait. *Canadian Journal of Plant Science 75*: 703-707.

Liegel, L., Pilz, D. and Love, T. 1998. *The MAB Mushroom Study: Background and Concerns*. AMBIO. Special Report No. 9: 3 - 7.

Love, T., Jones, E. and Liegel, L. 1998. *Valuing the Temperate Rainforest: Wild Mushrooming on the Olympic Peninsula Biosphere Reserve*. AMBIO. Special Report No. 9: 16 - 25.

Mahapatra, A. and Mitchell, C. 1997. Sustainable development of non-timber forest products: implication for forest management in India. *Forest and Ecology Management 94*:15 - 29.

Molina, R., O'Dell, T., Luoma, D., Amaranthus, M., Castellano, M. and Russell, K. 1993. *Biology, Ecology and Social Aspects of Wild Edible Mushrooms in the forests of the Pacific Northwest: A Preface to Managing Commercial Harvest*. U.S. Department of Agriculture Forest Service. General Technical Report PNW-GTR-309. Portland, OR.

Nams, V. 1994. Increasing sampling efficiency of lowbush blueberries. *Can.adian Journal of Plant Science 74*: 573 - 576.

Penney, B., McRae, K. and Rayment, A. 1997. Long-term effects of burn-pruning on lowbush blueberry (*Vaccinium angustifolium* Ait.) production. *Canadian Journal of Plant Science 77*: 421 - 425.

Peters, C. 1994. *Sustainable Harvest of Non-timber Plant Resources in Tropical Moist Forest: An Ecological Primer*. Landover, MD: Corporate Press.

Pilz, D., Molina, R. and Liegel, L. 1998. *Biological Productivity of Chanterelle Mushrooms in and near the Olympic Peninsula Biosphere Reserve*. AMBIO. Special Report No. 9: 8 - 13.

Salick, J., Mejia, A. and Anderson, T. 1995. Non-timber forest products integrated with natural forest management, Rio San Juan, Nicaragua. *Ecological*

Applications 5(4): 878 - 895.

Schlosser, W. and Blatner, K. 1995. The wild edible mushroom industry of Washington, Oregon and Idaho: A 1992 survey. *Journal of Forestry* 93(3): 31 - 36.

Shilts, E. 1999. Forest fortunes. *Canadian Geographic 119*(4): 34.

Statistics Canada. 1999a. Selected Demographic, Cultural, Educational, Labor Force and Income Characteristics of the total population by On/Off Reserve (3), Age Groups (6) and Sex (3) Showing Aboriginal Groups (8A) for Canada, Provinces and Territories, 1996 Census (20% sample). Dimension Series: Portrait of Aboriginal Population in Canada (94F00X11XCB). Statistics Canada, Ottawa.

Statistics Canada. 1999b. Canada Labour Force Characteristics, Monthly from January 1976, Seasonally Adjusted Includes LF Characteristics by Age & Sex; Labour Force, Unemployment & Unemployment Rate by Industry, Occupation & Class of Worker; Hours of Work by Industry, 1996 Census (20% sample). (SDDS 3701 STC (71-001)). Statistics Canada, Ottawa.

Velásquez Runk, J. 1998. Productivity and sustainability of a vegetable ivory palm (*Phytelephas aequatorialis*, Arecaceae) under three management regimes in Northwestern Ecuador. *Economic Botany 52*(2): 168 - 182.

Wickens, G. 1991. *Non-wood Forest Products: The Way Ahead*. Rome, Italy:FAO-UN.

Yarborough, D., Hanchar, J., Skinner, S., Ismail, S. 1986. Weed response, yield, and economics of Hexazinone and nitrogen use in lowbush blueberry production. *Weed Science 34*: 723 - 729.

[1]   Shaunna Morgan (MSc) is an Aboriginal Research Associate and instructor at the Centre for Indigenous Environmental Resources (CIER). Dave Punter (PhD) is a Professor in Botany at the University of Manitoba.

Overpopulation, Poverty, and Wildlife Extinction

Robert Wrigley[1]

Abstract

Incessant human population growth is viewed as the leading cause of most of humanity's scourges, such as poverty, war and starvation. While the wildlife-conservation movement is valiantly attempting to save the world's remaining diversity of life, this effort is overwhelmed by mounting numbers of people. The obvious solution of birth control and family planning remains largely unknown or ignored -- a heritage of our ancient customs and religious beliefs.

Introduction

Under the onslaught of an ever-increasing human population, it has become clear that humanity and the world's environments and ecosystems are now under serious threat. In their landmark books, Ehrlich and Ehrlich (1970) and Wilson (1992) demonstrated with overwhelming evidence that reducing the human population, and hence lessening demands on natural ecosystems, is the over-riding factor in the struggle to conserve the natural world. The current frenzy for exploiting natural resources and escalating environmental degradation by the world community are in stark contrast to traditional beliefs of Aboriginal Peoples about Mother Earth. The spiritual inter-relatedness of earth, water, plants, animals and people demanded that great respect be shown to each part of this unity of life. They appreciated (as few people do today) that their very survival depended on caring for the natural world.

However, in past times and present, when people are in desperate need, they have little choice but to exploit Nature to the fullest of their abilities and technologies. Witness the rapid extinction of hundreds of species of large animals in North America, Europe, Madagascar, Australia and New Zealand, shortly after early people arrived and populated these land masses. The American Great Plains region formerly supported a fauna of large animals as rich as that found today in Africa. In the last 18,000 years, rapid climatic changes, ecosystem dislocations, and particularly over-harvesting by people, have left a decimated assemblage of large animals. Over 73% of large mammals and large birds in North America were wiped out (Martin and Klein 1984).

Overpopulation and Conservation

Dedicated wildlife conservationists valiantly try to manage ecosystems and wildlife populations by conducting research projects, establishing large natural preserves, maintaining genetically diverse captive-breeding programs, developing education programs, and many other activities. But increasingly they are being overwhelmed by the demands of an ever-growing human population. As a biologist and educator, I find it disheartening how infrequently the critical topic of birth control and family planning are stressed in society. We feel justified and safe in discussing human overpopulation and the resulting habitat loss and environmental degradation, but fear to tread further to the logical conclusion. True, family planning is a taboo subject fraught with public-relations risks, and it may challenge dearly held concepts about individual rights and family, however, it is ultimately the most important message our leaders and educational institutions can champion in saving the Earth's ecosystems, for us and for their treasury of wondrous plant and animal life.

Perceiving the Problem

It is a daunting task to be heard and understood by people who do not wish to be confronted with lifestyle restrictions, or depressing facts about human poverty and the demise of wildlife and the environment. Pre-election platforms of political leaders often include promises to eliminate or alleviate the serious problem of child poverty and related tragedies of society. While no one questions the desperate need to find solutions, discussions and programs centre on treating symptoms and seldom on the over-riding cause of the dilemma -- lack of family planning.

As long ago as 1798, a young British clegyman and economist Thomas Robert Malthus pointed out, in his "Essay on the Principle of Population", that in favourable times food production increases in an arithmetic progression (2,3,4,5) while the human population (like all life forms) increases geometrically (2,4,8,16). Unfortunately, this compounding of humanity means that the population will always outstrip food supply and social services, leaving an ever-increasing segment of people without adequate resources on which to survive or to lead a decent quality of life.

Unknown to most people, species are tuned by natural processes, over immense periods of time, for parents to produce (on average) only a sufficient number of *surviving* offspring to replace themselves -- meaning two. Ancestral females of our species evolved the ability to have over a dozen children in their short lives -- a necessity under high levels of mortality. Around 20,000 years ago, there was an estimated world population of three million people, which likely had a negligible effect on their surroundings. To ensure tribal survival and integrity, customs and spiritual beliefs of our ancestors became ingrained with the concepts of large families and dominion over all other life.

The Population Explosion

The discovery of agriculture around 9,000 years ago changed everything, generating a giant leap in human birthrate and survival. Starvation lessened as an ever-looming factor in limiting population numbers, as it had likely operated effectively over millions of years of human evolution. During the period of the Egyptian Pharaohs, the world's population passed 100 million, 250 million at the time of Christ, 500 million by 1650, and 1 billion by 1850 (Ehrlich and Ehrlich 1970). With improving technology for food production and distribution, medical care, and social programs, numbers climbed to 2.5 billion in 1950 and 6 billion in 1999.

By the year 2050 (within our children's lifetime), it is anticipated that the burgeoning human population will level off between 11 and 15 billion, driving over 25% of the Earth's wildlife (or biodiversity) into extinction (Wilson 1992). The World Wildlife Fund believes one-third of all plant and animal species could be gone in 20 years. We are now losing wildlife at the rate of 75-100 species per day (Wilson 1992), squandering through ignorance and greed a 3.6-billion-year heritage of life on the planet. Humans now consume almost half the entire world's photosynthetic capacity (Girardet 1999). In terms of biomass, there is an estimated 250 million tonnes of humanity and over one-half billion tonnes of our livestock (Cincotta and Engelman 2000). There are simply not enough room and resources for all us and wildlife to survive. We surpassed a sustainable level, in balance with Nature, many centuries ago. A study of global human numbers revealed that the existing population is already three times the planet's carrying capacity to provide a reasonable lifestyle (Pimental 1994).

The Human Tragedy

Countless millions of children die of starvation and neglect each year, and over half the world's population is seriously malnourished and drinks contaminated water, in spite of massive humanitarian efforts by generous countries and agencies. Some organizations (including certain religious and political groups) and leaders continue to encourage large families, in an outdated effort to maintain their institutional power and influence; but at what cost? Few people appear to realize that all this human suffering, loss of wildlife, and environmental damage are needless, preventable through education and the practise of family planning in which couples produce no more than two children. Ancient customs and religious beliefs die hard.

To maintain the present course is madness and irresponsible. Nature's ecosystems progressively curb plague species like ours through drastically increased rates of mortality -- escalating famine, terrible wars over contested lands and beliefs, clashes over disappearing resources, devastating outbreaks of old and new diseases, massive loss of life from each major natural event of weather and earth movement, debilitating stress, and poisoning from thousands of toxic and waste products (all negative-feedback loops in the jargon of biologists).

A Matter of Education

When will parents, educators, politicians, and clergy gain the knowledge, courage and dedication to speak out and support family planning? When will leaders and the public recognize that overpopulation is the root of so many community problems, and stifles our most earnest efforts to solve them. While the birthrate in Canada and a few other countries has finally dropped below two young per couple, there are still many parents exceeding this essential limit, and often without the resources to care for them. Even if parents can afford to raise many children, each individual in a first-world country consumes and pollutes over 18 times that of a poor person in an under-developed country, thereby compounding the negative effects of overpopulation, and postponing the obvious solution.

As Malthus pointed out so long ago in harsh economic terms, 'the surplus' is destined for a life of poverty and misery. Society's caring social programs, technology, and natural resources can never keep pace with the incessant demands arising from exponential human population growth. The survival of life-support systems and wildlife, our civilization, and social justice depend ultimately on an ethic of family planning, communicated through the teaching of life skills at home, school and church, and supported by governments, concerned groups, industry and the media. With a right to reproduction must come knowledge and responsibility.

Conserving Biodiversity

Wildlife species cannot be "saved" in the long term by protecting them solely in a cocoon of captivity in zoos. Without the existence of sustainable wild populations -- free-ranging, interacting with their environment, and evolving -- each species will end up hopelessly inbred, a mere genetic shell of its ancestral stock, and eventually doomed to extinction. Humans and all other species were created within magnificently complex ecosystems, and without these nurturing wombs they will surely pass away before their time. Maintaining natural ecosystems is absolutely dependant on a massive reduction in the current human population, which cannot occur without family planning, which in turn relies on a strong educational message backed by resources.

What Can We Do?

We may stagger under a feeling of hopelessness as we become conscious to what is happening to our only home -- the Earth -- and to the terrible plight of so many people and wildlife. One often hears the question, "What can one individual do to help?" Many of us respond by attempting to live in moderation, purchasing wisely, donating to worthy causes, recycling materials, and by supporting conservation legislation. While these actions are positive steps, by far our most significant individual contribution is to have two or fewer children. In the long term, this is the only factor that really counts.

References

Cincotta, R. and Engelman, R.. 2000. *Nature's Place; Human Population and the Future of Biological Diversity*. Washington DC: Population Action International.

Ehrlich, P. and Ehrlich, A. 1970. *Population, Resources, Environment -- Issues in Human Ecology*. W. Freeman and Company.

Girardet, H. 1999. Greening Urban Society. *World Conservation 1*:10.

Martin, P. and Klein, R. (Eds.) 1984. Quaternary Extinctions -- A Prehistoric Revolution. University of Arizona Press.

Pimentel, D. 1994. Quoted in; Mobilizing to combat global warming, by D. Hayes, *2000. World Watch*, March/April 2000.

Wilson, E. 1992. *The Diversity of Life*. New York: W.W. Norton and Company.

[1]   Robert Wrigley (PhD) is a biologist who has worked as a curator, educator and director of the Manitoba Museum of Man and Nature and Oak Hammock Marsh Interpretive Centre, and as curator at the Assiniboine Zoo.

Saulteaux Land Use:
Manitoba Interlake Region, 1842-71

Yale Belanger[1]

Abstract

> The Fairford Saulteaux of Manitoba's Interlake area utilized a vast region for fishing, hunting, trade, ceremonies, gardening, and sugar production. Utilizing archive source material, this paper determines Saulteaux land use from 1842-1871 and their corresponding territorial claims made prior to Treaty 2 negotiations in 1871.

Introduction

The Fairford Saulteaux submitted a petition to the Canadian government in 1871 calling for treaty negotiations clearly establishing territorial boundaries (Archibald 1871,Tough 1994). This area was the land base the Fairford Saulteaux considered theirs and territory that was to be formally recognized as such by treaty, thereby ensuring a resource base for future generations while prohibiting settler encroachment into the region. Unfortunately, a clear distinction of why these boundaries were chosen was excluded. Traditional fisheries, frequently utilized hunting territories, or even customary campsites were not specified. A review of archive source material indicates that between 1842-71 Fairford Saulteaux material and cultural needs could be met using land within these boundaries. This boundary mapped fishing, camping, moose, elk, and deer hunting sites. Provisions were also made for gardening, trading, religious ceremonies, sugar production, and travel routes required for ease of access to sites within Fairford Saulteaux territory.

Missionary Contact

Archive source material dating back to 1842 and secondary sources were utilized to determine Fairford Saulteaux land use. For 12 years following his arrival in 1842, Reverend Abraham Cowley kept comprehensive notes in daily journals and wrote detailed correspondence which recorded Saulteaux seasonal rounds and campsite locations (Church Missionary Society[CMS]). Reverend William Stagg replaced Cowley in 1854 and carried on this tradition. Finally, the Saulteaux reserve request was unearthed in the Archibald (1871) papers, including a detailed map outlining precisely where territorial boundaries lay. Interestingly, when all the sites were positioned on mylar overlay maps of the region and then superimposed upon one another, what became instantly clear was that these boundaries, which were so carefully outlined in 1871, had always existed in the form of mental maps according to the site placements extracted from Cowley and Stagg's journals.

Water Claims

Included within the original demarcation are the Dauphin, Warpath, and Two Rivers, as well as the Lake St. Martin water bodies. Various other water bodies are also included within these boundaries, specifically, all territorial waters extending from McBeth Point to Dancing Point on Lake Winnipeg and a portion of Lake Manitoba. The water claim is logical as the Saulteaux utilized various water bodies within the region for community subsistence, as fisheries were critical to their survival. The best fishing was at Lake St. Martin but other sites located along the shores of Lakes Winnipeg and Manitoba and the Dauphin River were also utilized when Lake St. Martin fish stocks dwindled. The fall fishery enabled the Saulteaux to survive the winter when game populations were low, providing a constant source of high protein food stuffs prior to the maturation of potato and turnip crops and the return of game animals.

Examining the Saulteaux request, it is apparent that the Saulteaux were concerned with transportation throughout the region. Almost every point within the demarcated territory was accessible by water, making it possible to travel from the Mantagao River to Dancing Point down to Garden Island unimpeded. Garden Island is located within the 1871 boundary request and is mentioned prominently in various works about the Ojibwa and Saulteaux of the central Manitoba region (e.g. Brown 1985, Peers 1994, 1987, Tough 1994). For those sites that were not easily accessible by water travelling within close proximity was possible, as Brown (1985: 4) states, "To the Saulteaux and their trading associates... waterways, even if large and sometimes rough, were opportunities, not impediments". In addition, Nelson, Fidler, and a number of nineteenth century explorers and traders clearly indicated that "people goods, and information readily crossed the lake by boat and canoe in summer, and over the ice in winter" (Brown 1985: 4). Transportation routes were also needed for frequent renewal of familial ties extending to Berens River across Lake Winnipeg. Transportation access to hunting territories was important and provisions for this were made in the 1871 request. Fairford was also a Midewiwin site where Saulteaux from the region would meet each June and again in October for religious ceremonies (CMS A-86 Cowley papers 1842-54). Garden Island (located off the northwest coast of Peonan Point) was a popular gathering spot for inter-tribal trading in which the Fairford Saulteaux frequently participated (CMS A-86 Cowley papers 1842-54, Peers 1994, 1987).

Contact with Hind and Saulteaux Metaphysics

Further evaluation of archival source material and secondary sources provided more precise information on how the Saulteaux defined their territory. During the Hind Expedition of 1858, Saulteaux Chief Papernas informed all of the expedition's members that Garden Island belonged to him but expressed no objection to expedition members exploring the region (Hind 1969: 30). Chief Papernas further stated, "that as chief of the band he claimed the whole country from Fisher River, on Lake Winnipeg to the mouth of Partridge Crop River" (Hind 1969: 30). This region parallels the amount of land later requested in 1871, although the 1858 boundaries differ significantly (Figure 1). Land use derived from the 1871 request is more focused to the region north of Fairford whereas Chief Papernas claimed the region south and to the east of the community. It is plausible to conclude that this territory was used at one point and that by the time the seventy Saulteaux outlined their territorial boundaries in 1871, the seasonal rounds had been altered due to shifts in game animal migration patterns and increased resource exploitation due to greater numbers of settlers. These boundaries as expressed by Hind (1969) may be his misinterpretation of Chief Papernas's explanation. The record is limited and beyond his territorial claim, Chief Papernas provided little more detail, resulting in a statement of ownership and no explanation for how those boundaries were defined.

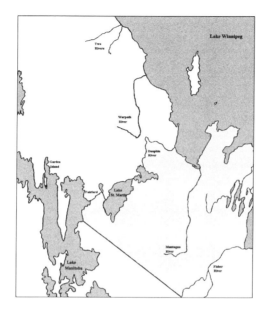

Figure 1. Homelands of the Fairford Saulteaux with the controversial 1858 boundary identified.

Equally important are the stories Hind collected from the Saulteaux during his brief stay at Fairford, stories about Manitous and the little men who lived off of Steep Rock Point just south west of Fairford (Figure 2). The little men were feared according to Hind (1969: 39), who stated "the Indians who hunt in this part of the country do not visit, being persuaded that 'little men' live in the caves and holes into which the rock has been worn by the action of the waves". Known to lurk in the water's depths, little men were lost souls who lived in cliff faces of lakes and rivers that the Saulteaux would have actively avoided (Asikinak 1995:97). The Saulteaux went on to detail many stories indicating where the little men dwelled to which Hind (1969:133) commented that "there is scarcely a cave or headland which had not some legend attached to it, familiar to all the wanderers (Saulteaux) on these coasts".

Interestingly, Hind (1969) displayed the same attitude when told of the Manitou that inhabited Manitobah Island, located beyond the 1871 boundaries. Hind (1969) did also state that the Saulteaux "could not be persuaded to land" upon the island due to the presence of a Manitou, indicating knowledge of the region and a fear of reprisal should any Saulteaux set foot upon the island, explaining also why it was left out of the 1871 claim. Manitobah Island was an area of avoidance and land use within this region was limited due to a respect of the Manitou; Steep Rock point was an area that was also avoided due to the little people living there. Although these regions were avoided, the Saulteaux were aware of many similar sites within the region the stories told to Hind. These stories indicated that this was familiar territory that was mapped mentally, and passed on through oral tradition. The Saulteaux did not explain their apprehension for entering these sites and regions; Hind (1969) indicated the Saulteaux did not elaborate on their beliefs. In each story the little men and Manitou were unfriendly supernatural spirits to be avoided (Jenness 1977). Hind (1969) also mentioned that Manitous lived in the west side of Lake Winnipeg; minimal detail is provided making it impossible to locate these sites.

Inter-tribal Trading and Hunting Territories

In 1858, Saulteaux told Hind that Dancing Point, which makes up the northeast corner of the 1871 boundaries, was a ceremonial spot, but beyond this brief description no other information was provided (Figure 2). Located along Lake Winnipeg coast are a number of Saulteaux and Cree communities that are relatively close to Dancing Point, where summer trading, ceremonial events, or other inter-tribal gatherings likely took place. For example, to travel from Norway House to Dancing Point is approximately 170 kilometers and if Cree from the Pas travelled to Garden Island (Tough 1994), then it is reasonable to consider Dancing Point an accessible site to many Aboriginal groups located throughout the region. The continued importance of Dancing Point is indicated by its inclusion in the 1871 reserve request.

Chief Papernas explained that a war road once followed the area located between the Warpath River and the Little Saskatchewan River just south of Dancing Point. This was the "war-road of the Ojibways and Swampys of Lake Winnipeg when they proceed on their periodical excursions against the Sioux" (Hind 1969: 28). The river 'road' was also used by the Assiniboine and Sioux when they occupied the region (29). In addition, the land located along the Warpath River was also utilized. The Warpath River was included in the 1871 request as Going to War River, indicating its historical importance and that it was recognized as part of the overall Saulteaux land base (Hind 1969).

Except for Manitobah Island, every spot catalogued by Cowley and Stagg (1842-1871) fall within the 1871 requested boundaries, including Garden Island, Dancing Point and Steep Rock Point. Garden

Island was where Hind first came into contact with Chief Papernas who claimed ownership of the island (Figure 2). Historically, Garden Island, which is also known as Big Tent Island, Potato Island, or Sugar Island had been a Midewiwin site. It was also an annual gathering place for summer trade (Peers 1994, HBCA B.122/3/1 fos. 9-10), gathering maple syrup (Kohl 1985), and camping in the area (CMS A-86 19 May, 1842). Maple sugar was used as a preservative and could be sprinkled over meat, boiled fish, or wild fruit for added sweetness. It was mixed with wild plums and then buried until winter when the plums were divided and boiled with dry meat for added nourishment in lean times (Kohl 1985: 319).

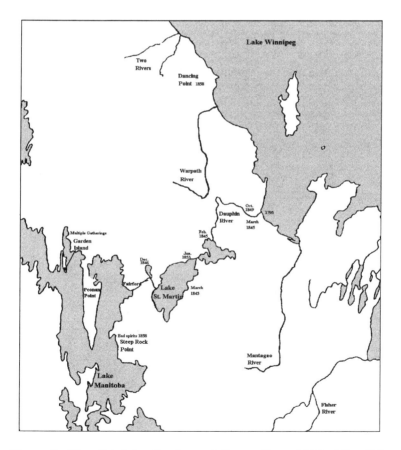

Figure 2. Sites listed by Cowley and Stagg (Peers 1994) fall within the 1871 requested boundaries.

Fairford was a site "of great resort among the Indians of this part of the country, and hence the probable reason why a selection of this site was made for the establishment of a mission" (Hind 1969: 34-35, CMS A-86 23 March 1842). The remainder of the sites listed by Cowley and Stagg (Peers 1994) (Figure 2) came as a result of the two missionaries looking for Native people to convert and frequently encountering Saulteaux campsites. Many of these sites were located along waterways such as the Dauphin River or located on the shore of Lake St. Martin providing easy access to fish and primary water routes critical to summer transportation. The dates when the missionaries reached these sites indicates that most were fishing sites, as spring and fall fisheries were usually held beginning in March and October respectively. Interestingly, there is one site located a short distance north of Fairford that Cowley visited in December 1846 which does not fit into the overall pattern. This could be due to the fact that during this period dysentery followed a measles outbreak and that many of the Saulteaux sought respite from the diseases' effects (CMS, A-86, October 1846). Also, Cowley states that since "the arrival of the rum (from bootleggers) the Indians have almost entirely deserted us. They seldom or never come to hear indeed their great desire for rum has driven them all into the woods to hunt the means of obtaining it", including selling their household possessions to purchase alcohol (CMS A-86 17 December, 1846). It is also possible that the site was either a family winter hunting camp or a site found because Cowley ventured further into the bush than he normally explored.

Hunting also played an integral role in the Saulteaux lifestyle. Moose, deer, and elk meat was used for food and skins were used for clothing and shelter. The major summer deer hunting regions were located across Portage Bay on Peonan Point as well as on the landmass north of Garden Island. Falling within the 1871 boundary request is a minor overlap of hunting territories also utilized by the Anishinaabe from Waterhen, located northwest of Fairford at Waterhen Lake (Stock 1994). Deer were attracted to waterways in the morning and evening to drink while seeking relief from the heat (Boulanger 1972). They stood in shallow water for hours during the day, seeking relief from insects where they were descended upon by Saulteaux in canoes or ambushed by Saulteaux stationed in trees and bush located alongside the waterway. Dead animals were then transported back to Fairford in birch bark canoes, which could effectively transport "heavy loads of poultry, provisions, flour, salted meat, and other heavy goods" (Kohl 1985: 169).

Elk meat supplemented the fall fishery as annual preparations were made for winter. The main elk hunting regions were located at

Peonan Point (also the site of the summer deer hunt) and a small region to the northeast (Stock 1994). Elk were hunted by "running down the game", until it was trapped or stumbled, at which time it was killed (Kohl 1985: 122-123).

Two main regions within the 1871 boundaries were for moose hunting in winter, spring, and fall (Stock 1994)(Figure 3). In addition, the spring and fall moose-hunting region makes up the northwest corner of the Saulteaux's 1871 boundary request and the winter hunting site also falls within this boundary.

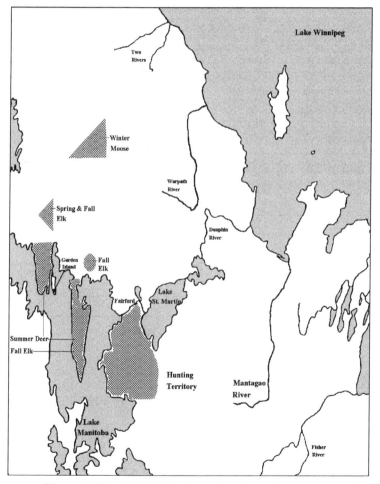

Figure 3. The Fairford Saulteaux hunting territory was contained within the 1871 boundaries.

The spring and fall hunting site was also shared with the Waterhen Anishinaabe (Stock 1996), although the Saulteaux recognized this region as part of their territory according to the reserve request of 1871. In the fall, moose were tracked and hunted along the shoreline of a regional water body by boat (Boulanger 1972). In the winter moose were run into deep drifts, which required great skill to keep the moose from escaping (Boulanger 1972). Once a thick ice crust had formed, it was easier to hunt moose as they were chased over the crusted snow tiring quickly by constantly breaking through the crust (Fidler 1820, Maclean 1896).

A Fairford Saulteaux hunting territory was contained within the 1871 boundaries that followed the length of Steep Rock Point and doubled back to the south tip of Lake St. Martin (Hind 1969). Although within Chief Papernas's 1858 territorial claims, the Fairford Saulteaux hunting territory extending from Fairford all the way to the Fisher River. By 1871, the Fairford Saulteaux were more concerned with claiming the territory north of Fairford and Lake St. Martin.

The only continuous-use site located within the 1871 demarcation is the fishing site at the Kisaskatchewan River, located at the Narrows of Lake St. Martin about 25 kilometers east of Fairford. Cowley first catalogued this site in January 1853, when the fish stocks at Fairford had disappeared and a new site was required for the fall fishery in order to acquire the fish needed for their winter subsistence (CMS, A-97, 6 September, 1854). The Kisaskatchewan River was the primary fall fishing site where the Saulteaux prepared great quantities of pounded and dried fish, as well as fish oil. This transition from Fairford to the Kisaskatchewan River fishing site occurred with relative ease, even though both Cowley and Stagg experienced difficulty procuring the quantity of fish numbers they required for their winter survival. In contrast, the Saulteaux were fully aware the fishery could easily be relocated to the Kisaskatchewan River indicating a far-reaching knowledge of the region.

Conclusion

The Fairford Saulteaux were cognizant of what constituted their territory but they were also aware of regions that extended beyond their 1871 boundaries and there is little conclusive evidence indicating that the Fairford Saulteaux utilized land outside the 1871 reserve request boundaries. Everything the Saulteaux required for survival was found in this territory. Within this territory, the resource base was used extensively as exemplified by multiple fishing, hunting, and camping sites. From 1842 to 1871, land use patterns indicated minor alterations to seasonal rounds rather than complete usurpation of existing ways. Also, it appears that the reserve request was a well-thought out representation of Fairford Saulteaux territory whose designers took into account what would be required of the land and of the government to ensure future generations success and happiness.

References

Archibald, A. 1871. Archibald Papers. *Provincial Archives of Manitoba (PAM),* Winnipeg, MB. MG 12, A1.

Asikinak, W. 1995. Anishinabe (Ojibway) legends through Anishinaabe eyes. In O. Dickason (Ed.), *The Native Imprint: The Contribution of First Peoples to Canada's Character, 1(1815)* pp. 93-102. Alberta: Athabasca University.

Brown, J. 1985. Central Manitoba Saulteaux in the 19th Century. In W. Cowan (E.) *Papers of the Sixteenth Algonkian Conference* pp. 1-8. Ottawa: Carleton University.

Boulanger, T. 1972. *An Indian Remembers - My Life as a Trapper in Northern Manitoba.* Winnipeg: Peguis Publishers.

Church Missionary Society Papers (CMS) n.d.*Provincial Archives of Manitoba (PAM),* Winnipeg, MB. Microfilm copy: A-86 & 97.

Fidler, P. 1820. General Report of the Manitoba District for 1820. Hudson's Bay Company Archives. *Provincial Archives of Manitoba (PAM),* Winnipeg: HBCA B.51/e/1.

HBCA (Hudson's Bay Company Archives) B.122/3/1, fos. 9-10.

Hind, H. 1969. *Narrative of the Red River Exploring Expedition of 1857-58.* New York: Greenwood Press Publishers.

Jenness, D. 1977. *The Indians of Canada.* Toronto: University of Toronto Press.

Kohl, J. 1985. *Kitchi-gami: Life Among the Lake Superior Ojibway.* St. Paul: Minnesota Historical Society Press. [First published 1860]

Maclean, J. 1896. *Native Tribes of Canada.* Originally published in 1896, re-Published in 1980, Toronto.

Peers, L. 1994. *The Ojibwa of Western Canada: 1780-1870.* Manitoba: University of Manitoba Press.

Peers, L. 1987. *An Ethnohistory of the Western Ojibwa, 1780-1830.* Unpublished Master's Thesis. Department of History, University of Manitoba.

Stock, K. 1996. *The Traditional Land Use of the Waterhen First Nation Vis-à-Vis a Forest Management Plan.* Unpublished Master's Thesis. Department of Geography, University of Manitoba.

Tough, F. 1994. *As Their Natural Resources Fail: Native Peoples and the Economic History of Northern Manitoba, 1870-1930.* Vancouver: UBC

[1]   Yale Belanger (MA in Native Studies, University of Manitoba) is a doctoral student in the Department of Native Studies at Trent University in Peterborough.

Integrated Management in Canada's Arctic and Sub-Arctic.

Sara Melnyk, Helen Fast and Thomas Henley[1]

Abstract

> Canada's Oceans Act (1997) directs that integrated management be undertaken to ensure the sustainable use and health of coastal ecosystems. One aspect of this broad objective is the development of an effective integrated management planning process. Such a process will identify social, cultural, environmental and economic values, and so provide a solid basis for future management plans. The application of methods used to apply this concept is described in terms of Manitoba's marine coastline.

Oceans Management in Canada

Canada's *Oceans Act* (1997) gives the responsibility for leading and facilitating oceans management to the Department of Fisheries and Oceans. Further, it charges the Minister of Fisheries and Oceans with developing a national strategy for oceans management (DFO 1998a). One aspect of this responsibility is the integrated management of coastal zones, which are characterized as the transition between terrestrial and marine or aquatic environments. The purpose of integrated management is to manage activities that occur in, or affect, Canada's estuarine, coastal and marine waters, while fostering sustainable development and maintaining or enhancing the health of these ecosystems. Integrated management is an ongoing and collaborative approach, which brings together interested parties to incorporate social, cultural, environmental and economic values in the development and implementation of comprehensive plans and management processes (DFO IMWG 1999). In the context of integrated coastal zone management, this document will review methodologies commonly applied. This discussion provides background for the development of an integrated management planning process unique to Canada's arctic and sub-arctic coastlines, using Manitoba's marine coastline as a case study.

Setting Coastal Zone Boundaries

The coastal zone constitutes the area of transition between the land and sea interfaces. The boundaries of such areas are often uncertain, however, making the specification of management boundaries a key component of any integrated coastal zone management plan. There is a great deal of debate in the integrated coastal zone management literature as to the appropriate definition of the coastal zone, and it has been noted that putting boundaries on such areas is inherently prone to difficulty (Hegarty 1997, Cicin-Sain and Knecht 1998). As a result, there is no universally accepted definition of the coastal zone, with some researchers claiming that the coastal zone defies definition (DFO 1998b, Hegarty 1997, Vallega 1993). Technically, the coastal zone is a spectrum considered to include the area stretching from the highest terrestrial tidal level to the edge of the continental shelf, including rivers, estuaries and drainage catchments along with the bottoms and shorelines of such water bodies (Cayer and Biagi 1994, Wildish and Strain 1994). Within the coastal zone, five categories can be identified within the interface spectrum, including inland areas that have the potential to affect the marine environment; coastal lands, such as wetlands; coastal waters, such as estuaries; offshore waters, which are considered to extend to the outer edge of the 200 nautical mile national jurisdiction; and high seas, which are beyond the jurisdictional limit (Cicin-Sain 1993). In practice, what the inland coastal zone boundary often encompasses can range from entire watersheds to only the immediate strip of shoreline adjacent to the coast (OECD 1993). The offshore boundary can range as far as the 200 nautical mile exclusive economic zone of a country (OECD 1993), a limit over which Canada has claimed jurisdiction as a signatory to the Law of the Sea Convention. While ideally management boundaries should be defined by determining the extent of the relevant interactions of biophysical, economic and social factors, delimiting such a boundary often proves to be constrained by the impracticality of using such large scales (Scura *et al*. 1992).

On- and offshore boundaries must be selected carefully for coastal zone management, based on a number of factors. If the terrestrial boundary is excessively large, covering an entire watershed for example, the focus of the management plan on the land-sea interface may be diverted. Similarly, the seaward boundary must be of a manageable size and scale in order to provide meaningful management objectives and results, taking into account factors such as the continental shelf and marine processes. The inland boundary should be large enough to encompass all activities that could affect the resources and waters of the coastal zone. However, this area may be too large to manage, and it is recommended (Cicin-Sain and Knecht 1998) that a narrower inland boundary be accepted that embraces the majority of such activities. Regarding the seaward boundary, most marine activities affecting the coastal zone are within the 12 nautical mile jurisdiction, however with new technology allowing for oil and gas development to take place in deeper waters a larger boundary may be necessary (Cicin-Sain 1993, Cicin-Sain and Knecht 1998).

In spite of the importance of having a clearly defined coastal zone, a 1996 worldwide study of nations practicing integrated coastal zone management (Cicin-Sain and Knecht 1998) showed that more than half of the 48 respondents reported that the landward boundary either varied according to use or was not clearly determined (Table 1). 38 percent of reported the same true of seaward boundaries. Nations in a similar developmental state as Canada, determined terrestrial boundaries according to use and marine boundaries located at the 12 nautical mile territorial sea boundary (Cicin-Sain and Knecht 1998). There is no universally accepted definition of the coastal zone; diversity exists between and within nations.

Variation between jurisdictions likely occurs because the coastal zone management boundaries are often determined based on what is being managed in order to include the targeted resources or activities (DFO 1998b, Cicin-Sain and Knecht 1998, OECD 1993). Boundaries should also be designated according to what can be agreed upon by the community in which the plan is to be implemented (DFO 1998b). Therefore, the coastal zone boundary should extend as far inland and seaward as will be necessary to meet management objectives (DFO 1998b). For example, coastal zone managers in Oregon have extended the seaward boundary to the continental shelf (35-80 miles offshore) arguing that the resources and activities within this zone vitally affect the state's citizens (Cicin-Sain 1993). In the context of Canada, the designated boundary must embrace environmental, sociocultural, political and economic conditions, as well as present and future demands. It is necessary to note that narrow boundaries may be beneficial in terms of heightening public awareness of the coastal zone, while broader boundaries will enable management to embrace a wider scope of activities at the possible expense of inhibiting public understanding (Cicin-Sain and Knecht 1998).

Table 1: Nature of Integrated Coastal Management (Cicin-Sain and Knecht 1998, pp. 51-52).

	All (%) N=48	Developed (%) N=14	Mid-Developing (%) N=14	Developing (%) N=20
Landward Boundary				
0-100m	4	0	14	0
100-500m	8	7	0	10
500m-1km	4	0	0	10
1-10km	10	0	7	15
Extent of local government jurisdiction	4	7	0	5
Watershed	6	0	14	10
Varies according to use	38	50	36	30
Not yet determined	19	21	29	15
Uncertain	6	14	0	5
Seaward Boundary				
Mean low or mean high tide	2	7	0	0
Arbitrary offshore distance from tidal mark	17	0	14	30
3 nautical mile territorial sea	6	7	7	5
12 nautical mile territorial sea	21	36	14	15
Edge of continental shelf	2	0	0	5
Limit of national jurisdiction/200 nautical mile	8	7	21	0
Varies according to use	23	21	21	25
Not yet determined	15	14	14	15
Uncertain	6	7	7	5

When scale puts a practical limit on the extent of management boundaries, proxy boundaries can be used, including physical criteria, political boundaries, arbitrary distances or selected environmental units (OECD 1993, Scura *et al*. 1992). Physical criteria generally refer to the continental shelf for the seaward boundary, while administrative boundaries refer to those that are politically determined, such as national territorial waters, which have the advantage of being easily representative and legislatively viable (OECD 1993, Scura *et al*. 1992). Arbitrary distances may be used to determine inland and seaward boundaries, and while they may be easily definable they have little significance to interactions occurring within the coastal zone (Scura *et al*. 1992). It has been argued that employing an ecosystem approach to management through the selection of environmental units is the most desirable method based on its holistic nature (OECD 1993). However it may be difficult to delineate such areas accurately and scale may be too great for efficient management (Scura *et al*. 1992). In most ongoing integrated coastal zone management plans, politically determined jurisdictional boundaries appear to be the most commonly used approach for delimitation of the coastal zone (Vallega 1993), although boundaries should extend as far inland and seaward as necessary to achieve management objectives (OECD 1993).

Apportioning and Mapping the Coastal Zone

According to Knecht and Archer (1993), the second key component of an integrated coastal zone management plan, following the identification of coastal boundaries, is the establishment of an inventory and the designation of areas of concern. This information serves as an indication of the current rate and nature of resource use, and future development potential (DFO 1998c). It is based on site specific literature and input of interest groups, as described in this paper. However, the difficulty inherent in classifying a long coastal region, such as that of Canada's arctic, necessitates the subdivision of the overall area into management units. Typical examples of management units are features based on environmental, geographic, administrative and use characteristics (Lalumiere and Morisset 1998), which can be further divided into specific resource components (Cayer and Biagi 1994). Apportioning down the coast into such units enables the planning process more flexibility in addressing issues because they will be defined at an appropriate and manageable scale (Institute for Research on Environment and Economy 1996).

By dividing information in such a manner, the use of computer tools such as databases and mapping programs can be used to analyze the data and create a baseline for the development of thematic maps (Cayer and Biagi 1994). Many studies have used geographic information systems (GIS) to develop thematic maps and convey information (DFO 1998c, Peyton 1994, Pheng *et al.* 1992) with the reasoning that such tools efficiently provide information regarding the coastal zone. One advantage of this approach is that the use of GIS maps can assist in increasing the understanding of interest groups with regard to linkages in the coastal zone. A second advantage is that in turn participating groups are able to more effectively use such information in decision-making and planning processes (DFO 1998c). Further, thematic maps can be developed using GIS and can be enhanced using software packages such as Adobe Illustrator. By using GIS and drawing software together, better maps may be achieved in terms of effectively communicating information to the community than are seen using only GIS, since thematic maps tend to be less complicated, more accessible and more visually attractive. Such maps can transmit information in terms of community values (through the prioritization of issues) and in doing so can provide a more comprehensive view of the region and the interests therein (Lalumiere and Morisset 1998). Thematic maps can greatly aid in the depiction, and thus consideration, of multiple-resources uses and values (Beatley *et al.* 1994).

Assessing the information is commonly accomplished using matrices (Cayer and Biagi 1994) in which the importance of certain aspects of the coastal zone, such as activities and concerns, can be ranked according to establishing priority (Lalumiere and Morisset 1998). These criteria and the outcome of the analysis will be a reflection of the values of the community (Cayer and Biagi 1994).

Community Involvement Techniques

Consensus-Based Decision-Making Processes. Traditional public consultation methods involved telling the public of decisions after the fact. These methods are no longer adequate for decision-making processes (Hildebrand 1997, Hanson 1998). The need for community involvement in management plans is becoming increasingly apparent, as the role that their interests and views play in management success is realized (Jacoby *et al.* 1997, Luttinger 1997). Community groups tend to have a greater awareness of the coastal environment (Wernick 1994), as well as a dependence on its resources.

The first step toward involving the community in a consensus-based decision-making process such as integrated coastal zone management is to determine who the interested parties in the community are, recognizing that "community" does not necessarily refer to a geographical or political definition (Cayer and Biagi 1994, Ellsworth *et al.* 1997). Interested parties include those individuals or organizations that have a direct or indirect interest in the community, and those who will be affected by the implementation of a coastal management plan (Cayer and Biagi 1994, Clark 1995, Ellsworth *et al.* 1997). Interest groups typically include coastal residents and organizations, representatives of the various economic sectors, conservationists and government agencies (Jorge 1997). Since it would not be feasible to include every individual in the planning process, representatives from key interest groups must be identified in such a way as to closely represent the diverse interests of the community members (Cayer and Biagi 1994). In addition, interests that are not found in the mandate of any group must be considered by including individuals with such interests. Representatives from interest groups must be identified and contacted to promote awareness of the project (Cayer and Biagi 1994). Concurrently, the proposed project must be thoroughly explained to the group or group representative prior to inviting participation (Cayer and Biagi 1994), in order to ensure that a transparent, trusting, committed relationship and process are initiated. What is meant by participation must be clarified at this point (Dahl 1997), as well as anticipated time commitments required. While participation can be construed to mean consultation, true participation in the management process can only occur if resource users have influence over how the resulting plan will be structured (Dahl 1997).

Participatory Techniques. Successful integrated coastal zone management is dependent on community participation, since interest groups can provide valuable information pertaining to management issues and perceptions of the environment. They can also identify information gaps (Chua 1992). Many approaches can be used to engage community participation. Based on the integrated management literature those that tend to have the greatest success are the use of topic groups, surveys, seminars and interview schedules. Topic groups can be used as a forum for identifying which resource issues will be addressed by the formation of a group of representatives.

This technique may be advantageous in that it allows for rapid data compilation. However, there may be disadvantages in that the participants must make a formal commitment, and as a result true representation of the community may not be realized due to the demands of the process. The most commonly used method for including the community in integrated coastal zone management projects is mailed questionnaires or surveys. This method is advantageous since a larger population base can be included. However, response rates may be low, thus leading to poor community participation and representation. Seminars may be used to provide a relatively informal forum for participation, but should be used intermittently throughout the process, rather than as the primary method since relevant information is difficult to ascertain (Edwards *et al.* 1997). Interview schedules are an informal technique used to target representative groups in which certain questions are asked of the respondent, with new questions or lines of questioning arising during the interview (Pido and Chua 1992). This method may facilitate the compilation of greater amounts of information, however data collection can be particularly time consuming compared to other methods.

Whether utilizing survey or interview techniques, it is necessary to recognize that human behaviour is not based on simple judgements, but rather on graded opinions. For this reason it may be necessary to present the subject with a series of options or criteria from which to choose. This method also allows for faster administration of the questions. Valuable insights can be garnered by asking subjects open-ended questions, which will provide the opportunity to further explain perceptions and values. Responses from community members may be influenced by a number of factors which should be recognized at the outset. These can include level of income, access to resources, and the ability to participate and influence community affairs (Pomeroy *et al.* 1997). The same survey or interview instrument may not be appropriate for different target groups within the community, based on their different characteristics and objectives (Knecht *et al.* 1996). However, there should be a degree of similarity between such instruments with each group being asked a set of common questions followed by a set of more specialized questions more specifically focussed on the group in question (Hegarty 1997, Knecht *et al.* 1996).

Application to Manitoba's Marine Coastline

A step wise model process for integrated management planning was inferred from the literature: define coastal zone boundaries which include major activities and processes; form management units based on political, ecological, geographical and human use characteristics; catalogue and map activities and values in a format that is easily understood by a wide audience (this step occurs before, during and after stakeholder consultation); and consult with all interested parties, using whatever method is most efficient for the specific situation, as to the activities, values and concerns associated with the coastal zone. These steps were applied to develop, implement and evaluate a model process for integrated management planning for Manitoba's 1,400km sub-arctic marine coastline (Figure 1) (Melnyk 2000).

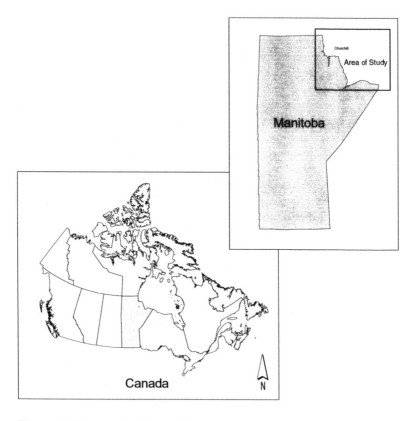

Figure 1. Site map showing study area.

Manitoba's marine coastal interests had not been examined in the context of integrated management, despite the range of divergent activities. The coastal zone plays an important role in local economies and possesses important social values, ranging from recreational activities to archeological sites, with the environment linked to these activities. Shipping and tourism, and possible oil drilling or mining, are of economic and social value. Manitoba's coastal zone is ecologically significant with two wildlife management areas, several areas of ecological interest, Wapusk National Park and designation of heritage river status to the Seal River. Social and cultural values are recognized in the designations of York Factory and Fort Prince of Wales as national historic sites. Nunavut Territory has rights to manage and harvest resources from Hudson Bay, and future interest in developing infrastructures, such as roads or transmission lines, connecting the territory to Manitoba.

The application of the steps are: the coastal zone boundaries were defined as 3km inland and 10km offshore, measured from the low water mark, and capture most human and ecological resource uses. In situations where these boundaries were not sufficient, they were increased as required. Manitoba's coastline was apportioned into five management units, based on existing political boundaries, ecological significance and human use characteristics (Figure 2, Table 2) existing maps, literature and interviews conducted in Churchill.

Table 2: Management Units: Boundaries and Justifications

Unit	Area Represented	Justification for Division	Boundaries
A	Cape Tatnum	Existing boundaries of Cape Tatnum Wildlife Management Area	*West* = Province of Ontario *East* = Hayes River
B	Hayes and Nelson Rivers estuaries, York Factory, Marsh Point	Ecological importance & intensive human activities (hydroelectric development, tourism)	*West* = Hayes River *East* = Nelson River
C	Wapusk National Park	Existing boundaries of Wapusk National Park	*South* = Park boundary *North* = Cape Churchill
D	Button Bay to Cape Churchill	Region encompassing most intensive human and ecological resource use activities on the coast	*West* = Button Bay *East* = Cape Churchill
E	North of Button Bay, including North and Seal rivers	Existing ecological boundaries (Arctic tundra and Mageuse Uplands)	*South* = Button Bay *North* = Territory of Nunavut

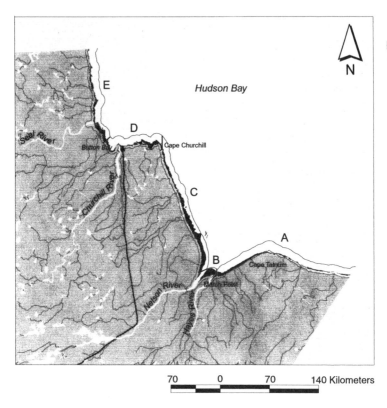

Figure 2. Management units for Manitoba's marine coastline.

Summary maps were produced using ArcView GIS and Adobe Illustrator software packages. They illustrate political and ecological boundaries, and resource use activities. The combination of graphics and text produced easily read and interpreted maps more likely to be useful during integrated management planning exercises. Interviews focussed on participants in Churchill, the only coastal community in Manitoba using the snowball sampling method to select interested parties. Individual interviews were scheduled at the participant's leisure and anonymous. Qualitative interviews, or open-ended questions, are easily adaptable in terms of time required and content, so that each individual was able to provide as much information as s/he wishes. Unlike a quantitative interview, a qualitative interview includes a general question guide, not a specific set of questions (Babbie 1998). Information collected during these interviews was displayed on the summary maps.

Conclusions

In a technical sense, no comprehensive method by which to inventory resource use activities and concerns exists to relate terrestrial and marine environments in the integrated coastal zone management literature. This study has developed a process on which to base integrated coastal zone management planning activities for Canada's arctic and sub-arctic coastline, using summary maps depicting ecological and political boundaries, and resource use activities.

Ultimately, the success of this model can only be determined in its usefulness as a foundation for integrated management during planning exercises. It does however present a foundation on which to base such planning initiatives (Lalumiere and Morisset 1997). It appears that this is a good model, and can easily and efficiently be applied to coastal zones. In particular, this model may be appropriate for coastal zones with similarities to Manitoba's coast in terms of the number of communities and the awareness of the stakeholders of coastal resource use issues, such as those of the Canadian arctic and sub-arctic. Community involvement is necessary and desirable for management planning, and through application of this model advancements can be made toward community-based decision making, as is the goal of Canada's *Oceans Act*.

References

Babbie, E. 1998. *The Practice of Social Research*. Belmont, CA: Wadsworth.

Beatley, T., Brower, D. and Schwab, A. 1994. *An Introduction to Coastal Zone Management*. Wash:Island Press.

Canada. 1997. *Oceans Act*.

Cayer, A. and Biagi, M. 1994. Community based ocean management strategies. In P. Wells and P. Ricketts (Eds.), *Coastal Zone Canada '94, 'Cooperation in the Coastal Zone': Conference Proceedings*. 2:497-513. Dartmouth, NS:Coastal Zone Canada Assoc., Bedford Institute of Oceanography.

Chua, T. 1992. The ASEAN/US coastal resources management project: initiation, implementation and management. In T. Chua and L. Scura (Eds.) *Integrated Framework and Methods for Coastal Area Mgt*.

pp. 71-92. Manila, Philippines: Int. Center for Living Aquatic Resources Management.

Cicin-Sain, B. 1993. Sustainable development and integrated coastal management. *Ocean and Coastal Management* 21: 11-43.

Cicin-Sain, B. and Knecht, R. 1998. *Integrated Coastal and Ocean Management: Concepts and Practices.* Washington: Island.

Clark, J. 1995. *Coastal Zone Management Handbook.* FL: Lewis.

Dahl, C. 1997. Integrated coastal resources management and community participation in a small island setting. *Ocean & Coast. Mgt* 36: 23-45.

Department of Fisheries and Oceans. 1998a. *Marine Protected Areas.*

Department of Fisheries and Oceans. 1998b. *Backgrounder: Integrated Management of Activities in Canada's Coastal and Ocean Waters.*

Department of Fisheries and Oceans Advisory Committee on Integrated Coastal Zone Management. 1998c. *Toward a Canadian Framework for Integrated Coastal Zone Mgt.*

Department of Fisheries and Oceans Integrated Management Working Group. Meeting, December 15, 1999. Ottawa.

Edwards, S., Jones, P. and Nowell, D. 1997. Participation in coastal zone management initiatives. *Ocean and Coastal Mgt* 36: 143-165.

Ellsworth, J., Hildebrand, L. and Glover, E. 1997. Canada's Atlantic coastal program: a community-based approach to collective governance. *Ocean and Coastal Management* 36: 121-142.

Hanson, A. 1998. Sustainable development and the oceans. *Ocean and Coastal Management* 39: 167-177.

Hegarty, A. 1997. Start with what the people know: a community based approach. *Ocean and Coastal Management* 36: 167-203.

Hildebrand, L. 1997. Introduction to the special issue on community-based coastal management. *Ocean and Coastal Management* 36: 1-9.

Institute for Research on Environment and Economy. 1996. *Community Empowerment in Ecosystem Management.* Ottawa: IREE.

Jacoby, C., Manning, C., Fritz, S. and Rose, L. 1997. Three recent initiatives for monitoring of Australian coasts by the community. *Ocean and Coastal Management* 36: 205-226.

Jorge, M. 1997. Developing capacity for coastal management in the absence of government: a case study in the Dominican Republic. *Ocean and Coastal Management* 36: 47-72.

Knecht, R. and Archer, J. 1993. 'Integration' in the US coastal zone management program. *Ocean and Coastal Management* 21: 183-199.

Knecht, R., Cicin-Sain, B. and Fisk, G. 1996. Perceptions of the performance of state coastal zone management programs in the United States. *Coastal Management* 21: 141-163.

Lalumiere, R. and Morisset, J. 1998. Pilot project (stage II). *Reference Framework for the Integrated Management of the Les Escoumins Riviere Betsiamites Coastal Zone.* Unpublished joint report. Sept-

Iles.: Group-conseil Geniva, Quebec and Habitat Management and Environmental Sciences Branch, Fisheries and Oceans Canada.

Luttinger, N. 1997. Community-based coral reef conservation in the Bay Islands of Honduras. *Ocean and Coastal Management* 36: 11-22.

Melnyk, S. 2000. *Integrated Management Planning in Canada's Arctic and Sub-Arctic: A Case Study of Manitoba's Marine Coastline.* MNRM Thesis. University of Manitoba, Winnipeg.

Organisation for Economic Cooperation and Development. 1993. *Coastal Zone Management: Integrated Policies* Paris: OECD.

Peyton, D. 1994. Geographic information systems as a coastal zone management tool. In P. Wells and P. Ricketts (Eds.) *Coastal Zone Canada '94, 'Cooperation in the Coastal Zone': Conference Proceedings.* Dartmouth, NS: Coastal Zone Can Assoc, Bedford Inst of Oceanog.

Pheng, K., Paw and , J and Loo, M. 1992. The use of remote sensing and geographic information systems in coastal zone management. In T. Chua and L. Scura (Eds.) *Integrated Framework and Methods for Coastal Area Management.* pp. 107-131. Philippines: ICLARM

Pido, M. and Chua, T. 1992. A framework for rapid appraisal of coastal environments. In T. Chua and L. Scura (Eds.) *Integrated Framework and Methods for Coastal Area Management.* pp. 133-148. Manila, Philippines:International Center for Living Aquatic Resources Mgt

Pomeroy, R., Pollnac, R., Katon, B. and Predo, C. 1997. Evaluating factors contributing to the success of community-based coastal resource management. *Ocean and Coastal Management* 36: 97-120.

Scura, L., Chua, T., Pido, M. and Paw, J. 1992. Lessons for integrated coastal zone management: the ASEAN experience. In T. Chua and L. Scura (Eds.) *Integrative Framework and Methods for Coastal Area Management.* pp. 1-70. Manila, Philippines:ICLARM.

Vallega, A. 1993. A conceptual approach to integrated coastal management. *Ocean and Coastal Management* 21: 149-162.

Wernick, B. 1994. Community-based planning of marine protected areas: the role of environmental non-governmental organizations. In P.Wells and P. Ricketts (Eds.) *Coastal Zone Canada '94, 'Cooperation in the Coastal Zone* 2: 529-535. NS: CZCA,Bedford Inst of Ocean

Wildish, D. and Strain, P. 1994. Science and coastal zone management. In P. Wells and P. Ricketts (Eds.) *Coastal Zone Canada '94, 'Cooperation in the Coastal Zone'* 5: 2139-2148.Dartmouth, NS: Coastal Zone Canada Association, Bedford Institute of Oceanography.

[1]   Sara Melnyk is a graduate student at the Natural Resources Institute, University of Manitoba; Helen Fast (PhD) is the Integrated Management Advisor, Oceans Sector, Central and Arctic Region, Department of Fisheries and Oceans; Thomas Henley (MA) is an Associate Professor at the Natural Resources Institute.